"Lauren Gregg's detailed explanation of what it takes to reach the top in *The Champion Within* shows why she is so admired by American girls playing soccer."

— ROGER ROGERS
Editor, Women's Soccer World Magazine

"Long before it was fashionable to be an advocate for the women's game, Lauren Gregg was promoting the development of youth players — our future. She is **truly a visionary**."

— CHARLOTTE MORAN
**Eastern Pennsylvania Youth Soccer Association
Former National Chair, Girls Olympic Development Program**

"Lauren Gregg's book, *The Champion Within*, offers **incredible insights into what separates the best from the rest**. It is also full of special lessons for the athlete and coach. The champions reveal their secrets, how they organized their training and the challenges they overcame along the way. "If you are a serious athlete with high aspirations or if you coach serious players, then indeed, you must own and use *The Champion Within*. Special thanks to Lauren Gregg for this important work."

— TONY DiCICCO
Head Coach, U.S. Women's National Team

"Lauren Gregg has dedicated her professional life to developing soccer in America. The insights that she shares in *The Champion Within* serve to further her cause. Lauren's work is **a must read for anybody who loves soccer and wishes to succeed**."

— HANK STEINBRECHER
General Secretary, U.S. Soccer

"**The definitive book on the women's game**, written by one of the most influential coaches in the world of soccer. *The Champion Within* is a must read for any player or coach serious about gaining the competitive edge of proven champions."

— DR. COLLEEN M. HACKER
U.S. Women's National Team Sport Psychologist

The
Champion
Within

Training for Excellence

By Lauren Gregg

With Tim Nash

The Champion Within
Training for Excellence

was published in the United States by

PO Box 3293, Burlington, NC 27215-0293
800-551-9721

Design and Production by Jan Cheves, AGA Publishing
Cover Photo by Frank W. Ockenfels
Back Cover Photo by Kathleen Gregg
Additional Photos by J. Brett Whitesell, Mike Stahlschmidt, Phil Stephens, Tony Quinn, Michael Allen, PAM/ISI, Perry McIntyre, Colleen Hacker and Frank Hogan.

First Printing: October 1999

ISBN: 1-887791-07-8

Printed in the United States of America

Contents

DEDICATION

Discover the champion within you.

Acknowledgments

By Lauren Gregg

"To whom much is given, much is also required."

Soccer has always been and always will be a player's game. That's what I love about it. As a player, I was absolutely engrossed with every aspect of the game. Plain and simple, I loved to play. I was, and am, passionate about the game. Growing up, like many of our early heroes in the sport, I played with boys and participated in many other sports. My brother John and I would play soccer in the front yard. He would teach me little moves, and I would spend hours on them. It wasn't until I was fourteen that there was an organized soccer team to play on. Yet, I never felt deprived, because I went forward with an optimism that there would be soccer at the highest level one day.

This book was written for all of you who have dared to ask "how?" Over the years there have been so many players that have come to me wanting to know what steps they need to take to reach their dreams. All of these questions led me in many ways to write this book. My hope is that it will reach more of you than I can by myself. I hope to help each of you realize that everything you need is within you. So, thanks for asking all the questions. I hope they will be answered here.

There are so many people who I am grateful to know, to have worked with and to have in my life. It's because of all that I have been given through soccer that this book was written. I want to share with you all I have learned through the road that I am traveling. Many people made these opportunities possible for all of us.

First, I must thank my family. Having them all there when we won the first-ever Olympic Gold Medal in 1996 meant the world to me. My parents, my brothers, John, Jim and David, my sister, Kathy, and nephew Ben, all traveled to Athens. I am grateful to my parents who always allowed me to choose my direction. They instilled in us a desire to learn, work hard and be good people. They always allowed me to follow my heart and dreams. For this, I am thankful.

While pursuing my Master's in Education from Harvard, in Counseling and Consulting Psychology, I served as an assistant soccer coach. Toward the end of my academic program at Harvard, Bruce Arena called from the University of Virginia. He asked if I would be interested in beginning their women's soccer program. I knew this was a calling I had to answer. To build this program was an incredible experience. The more I gave, the more I was given in return through the sport and the people I have had the fortune of working with. Bruce Arena, his family, and the university community made it a wonderful experience over the ten years. Bruce's leadership and early guidance helped me to embark on this journey.

During my tenure, from 1986-1995 at the University of Virginia, I had the opportunity to work with and still remain friends with one of the most inspirational champions I have ever known — Linda Bunker, Dean of the Education School, who lives her life each day as I hope to lead you to discover, your success road, enjoying each moment along the way. Dean Canevari's support of me and our young program will always be remembered.

At the same time, I have had the opportunity since 1989 to serve as the assistant coach for the United States Women's National Team. From 1986 to 1988 I trained and competed for our national team. That next year, I accepted the offer to serve as the first women to work with any national team in soccer in the United States. I have seen the program grow from a handful of events to having an opportunity to coach World Champions in 1991, Olympic Champions in 1996. I am thankful for these incredible opportunities and to all of the players with whom I have worked.

Certainly, having the opportunity to play for and coach with former U.S. National Team Coach Anson Dorrance has been an integral part of my development. He has also influenced me through his continual reminder of how important it is to give back to the sport.

I am also appreciative of the time and care with which many players provided interviews to Tim Nash for this book. They have always been ambassadors for the game and their significant contributions here are a small reflection of all they have done for the sport and young people. In addition, special thanks must go to all of the members of the team behind the team — Dr. Mark Adams, Dr. Doug Brown, Dr. Colleen Hacker, April Heinrichs, Dr. Don Kirkendall, Steve Slain — that have contributed to the tradition of soccer excellence and to this book.

In 1995, after ten years, I resigned from the University of Virginia to devote all of my attention to our quest to win the first-ever Olympic Games for women's soccer. It was one of the most difficult decisions of my life, but necessary if I was to be able to look back and know I had done everything I could to make our dream come true. Tony DiCicco and I have made a great team, and I have appreciated having the opportunity to work together with him since 1991. After the Olympic Games, I was also given the responsibility of our U-20 Women's National Team (now, U-21). I take this responsibility seriously and with pride. It is a wonderful opportunity to pass on the tradition and the process of becoming a champion. I would like to thank Hank Steinbrecher for supporting my tenure with the United States Soccer Federation, as well as the women's national team program. His vision has been vital to our success.

Throughout my career as a player and a coach, there have been many other people that have paved the way for all of us that need acknowledgment. Without the efforts of Marty Mankamyer women's soccer would be nothing like it is. Jim Cromwell, spearheaded a ground swell of support, without which it is unlikely women's soccer would have been included in the 1996 Olympic Games. He, with Marilyn Childress, along with others, headed a grassroots campaign that resulted in a Congressional Resolution to introduce women's soccer to the Olympics. Charlotte Moran and Louise Waxler, have selflessly given of themselves to the sport. I am grateful for their personal and professional support. To all of my coaches and friends who have supported my passion, and to all that have made women's soccer what it is today and all it will become, thank you.

This book has been a great way for me to share what I have been given. More than anything, I want to empower young people to reach their goals and dreams. Know that all you need is within you. It has been a way to pay homage to some of the greatest players and people in women's soccer, ever. Tim Nash believed in the story and the necessity of telling it. I am thankful for his tireless enthusiasm in the process which began several years ago. He has been a mainstay toward the realization of this book. His genuine love of the game and desire to make a positive contribution made our partnership a valuable one. A special thanks to Jan Cheves for her thorough and patient work in the publication of this book. We hope you enjoy the stories, their messages and grow excited about all that you can become.

Thanks to all of the players I have coached, who have been part of every page in this book.

Preface

By Lauren Gregg

In writing this book, I hope to provide a resource for young players that I believe will influence participation of girls in athletics, as well as enhance the experiences and development of young girls in soccer. During my involvement with youth players, I am constantly asked similar questions: "How do I become a great player?" ... "What else can I do to improve this or that?" ... "How did Mia become the best?" ... "Will you teach me how to train?" While I happily fill their ears and hearts with facts and pertinent stories, I can only touch handfuls at a time. I know there is a yearning out there that I hope this book can begin to satisfy.

My belief, and the premise behind successful teams, is that players have a responsibility for their own development. The willingness to train "when no one else is watching" is a consistent theme of player development and maximizes the team's effectiveness. Readers of this book will get a glimpse of what champions do. This concept is a crucial part of training for excellence.

The early lessons we faced with the national team have served us well. It was then that the foundation of self-training was born. The vignettes of players' experiences and the information from professionals in the sport is presented in a way that makes young players say, "That could be me." I want the book to answer them in return, "Yes, that is you."

In my career as a player and as a coach, I have had the privilege of being at the forefront of the growth of the women's game. I would like to share the knowledge I have gained from being on the cutting edge of the game on many levels. I understand player development. Now, with a keen sense of responsibility and passion for the game, I have sought to share the elements that empower a player to discover the champion within.

This book is about the process of becoming a champion. It's a comprehensive and innovative soccer training book, designed specifically for the athlete. The theme is about taking responsibility for personal development, that the ability and responsibility for greatness rests with the individual player.

My hope is to empower players to organize their environments, make appropriate choices, and understand the scope of what is involved in training for excellence. The integration of anecdotes and messages from players and professionals in women's soccer give a special genuineness and appeal that will not only guide player development, but inspire and influence their lives.

Lauren Gregg

Introduction

By Tim Nash

In the summer of 1996, I was in Orlando, Fla., covering the Olympics. More accurately, I was covering the United States Women's National Soccer Team in the Olympics. On July 24, I ventured to the University of Central Florida soccer complex to watch the U.S. Women's National Team train. A day earlier, the team had defeated Sweden in their second Olympic match. They had one day to prepare for China in Miami, and training this day was light and loose. I stood by the fence with swat teams, FBI agents, bomb-sniffing dogs and other media members, just sort of killing time. After the practice had ended, Lauren Gregg came up to me and said, "I want to write a book."

Lauren and I knew each other, but not well. In fact, I was a bit surprised when she approached me. At the time, I was working on a book with Michelle Akers, and a year earlier, I had written one with Anson Dorrance. Lauren asked me if I would be interested in working on a book with her. I told her, "I want to fill the bookshelves with quality women's soccer books."

That was all she needed to hear.

The first interview for this book was conducted in the Radisson Hotel during a national team training camp in Greensboro, N.C., in April of 1997. I sat in the lobby and spoke individually with Kristine Lilly, Julie Foudy, Tiffeny Milbrett, Brandi Chastain and Shannon MacMillan. Lilly was the first interview, and as we spoke, Danielle Fotopoulos entered the lobby on crutches. Danielle, getting her first real shot at cracking the national team roster, blew out her ACL that morning at practice.

The last interview for this book was done by phone in February of 1999. I called the national team training facility in Orlando, Fla., and interviewed six players who had been invited into residency training in preparation for the 1999 Women's World Cup. The last of the six I spoke with that day was Danielle Fotopoulos. Danielle had come full-circle from a dejected player on crutches to a budding international star. There was no miracle of modern medicine involved, no secret rehab techniques. Danielle, plain and simple, worked her way back to a form that was better than before. She eliminated every excuse available to someone facing months of excruciating pain and hard work. She just went about the business of becoming the best player she could be.

And that is what this book is all about — the process of becoming a champion. It's interesting to hear champions describe champions. Rarely does their definition involve trophies, medals, titles or honors. They all speak of the process. They are proudest of the accomplishments they have made when no one was looking, the little everyday things that are difficult to achieve, but need to be done.

This book was also a process. It took me to Greensboro, N.C., Hartford, Conn., (twice) Minneapolis, Minn., Orlando, Fla., (three times) Washington, D.C., (twice), and Chapel Hill, N.C., countless times. I conducted interviews in corners of hotel lobbies, on sidelines after training sessions, by phone, in one Starbucks (Michelle Akers' favorite hangout), two college campuses, and one player's living room. I interviewed twenty-nine current or former players, one current head coach, one former head coach, one sport psychologist, one exercise physiologist, and two strength and conditioning experts.

All the while, Lauren busily pounded out the meat of the book, and we added stories and advice from players, coaches, and doctors as we went along. The original plan for the book did not pretend to be as extensive as it turned out. Lauren decided to get information from the very best in women's soccer, which led us to include more and more experts as we progressed. In the meantime, the book grew and grew.

All three books I've helped write have been about champions. It's fascinating to work with champions. They have a work ethic and a sense of responsibility that leaves little doubt why they are accomplished, successful people. Priorities are in proper order, their lives are very well-balanced, and they all speak fondly of the process. Their most satisfying memories are not of being crowned, but rather what they learned about themselves while they were chasing the crown.

I would like to personally thank all the players and coaches I interviewed. Each one — from the rookies to the veterans, the now famous to the soon-to-be-famous — was very gracious in providing their time and thoughts while I picked their brains for the smallest details about their personal training and their largest hopes and dreams. They were very helpful in providing extremely thorough answers and offering personal experiences which every young soccer player can use as a model for their own development.

Without the incredible patience and understanding of my wife, Cheri, and our two children, Allison and Ian, I would never have been able to dedicate the time and energy to this book project.

I would also like to thank Lauren, the hardest-working person I have met. Before I started working with her, I had no idea the depth of her involvement in American soccer. She gives her time, energy and expertise constantly. And she does it simply for the love of the game and out of a sense of responsibility to the sport that has provided her with so much over the years. I'd like to thank her for allowing me to be a part of such an interesting and rewarding process. After all, it's the process that matters.

Foreword

By Mia Hamm

I remember playing all kinds of sports growing up, but it seemed like I was always playing soccer. I played with my friends, with my family in the yard, at recess, whenever I could.

When we played soccer with our friends, we played little games like "How many kids can you dribble past, how many kids can you nutmeg?" And I was always very competitive in those games. When I was in youth soccer, I loved to have the ball. When you are that little, every time you touch the ball, it's exciting, so you want to make the most of it.

I've gone through so many stages of development, but I still love to play little games. I do little dribbling things around cones, just like eight year olds do. And I do simple shooting drills. When I dribble through cones, I try to do it as fast as I can with as few mistakes as possible. It's amazing what you think of when you are by yourself.

It's funny, when we do clinics, I'll say, "Hey, have you ever done this?" The girls get really excited and say, "Yeah." It's important that they know we do the same things in practice that they do. We just do it at a higher level. I always tell them that there is a difference between training and practicing. Training is what we do. It's when you are totally focused and the intensity level is high. Practicing is when you are trying to get something down, trying to perfect something. But if you want to make it game-like, training is what it is all about.

When I first started out in college, there was a lot of frustration and disappointment for me. I remember my coach, Anson Dorrance, talking about it so much. Strikers fail the majority of the time, and it can get very discouraging. I had to learn not to get frustrated with all my failures and to turn that negative energy into something positive, like winning the ball back.

Everybody on the field fails. With strikers, it's just easier to see. At the higher levels, the opportunities to score are few and far between. I had this conversation with Bill Palladino, our assistant coach at UNC. He would say, "Mia, when you lose the ball, your head goes down right away. You've got to figure something out." Anson and I worked on it, too. He gave me examples, and one was Carla. When she gets mad at herself, she uses that energy to win the ball back. Other players just blow it off. They told me I had to figure out the best way for me. I tried to channel the negative energy into working hard to win the ball back.

I learned a lot from my mistakes. And there were so many of them. I became more of a student of the game. Anson, Dino and Tony DiCicco helped me with that. Just being smarter helped. I learned that the more competitive the level, the less chances you get. The important question is how do you make the most out of those opportunities?

I remember I used to take the dumbest shots. I would get to the endline and still try to shoot, and, of course, there was no angle from which to shoot. I must have missed ten goals like that my freshman year, and I must have assisted on twenty goals like that in the sophomore year. Being that kind of student of the game really helped.

I learned a lot from April Heinrichs and Michelle Akers. I can't play the kind of physical game that Michelle plays, and I can't play the mind games that other strikers play. There are some international strikers who really get into the defender's head. You are always wondering what she is going to do. I had to learn what was best for me.

I remember I played one national team tour on defense. Anson had this crazy scheme before he retired, "Let's see if Mia can play in the defense?" Well, I didn't do very well. I did okay, but I gained a lot of respect for what forwards can do defensively. I learned this because I noticed it was a lot harder to play defense when there wasn't pressure on the ball, and it was a lot easier when there was. Why wouldn't I want to make it harder for the defender to play? Why wouldn't I want to do that for my teammates? When there is no pressure on the girl with the ball, you have no idea where she is going to serve it. If she is under pressure, her options are cut severely. For me, as someone who had never really played back there, it became clear what I should be doing.

The most important thing I learned was I couldn't depend on my offense. I just couldn't! Some days it just wasn't there. The thing I could count on was my defensive effort every single game.

If you talk to anyone on this team, they will all tell you they need to improve. And it's not just one thing, it's every single aspect of the game.

First of all, I made a decision to be fitter. I don't think I really understood what being fit was until my junior year in college. I think Anson would agree. It was not until my junior year that I wasn't afraid of fitness. Once I made a distinct effort to be a better defensive player, I was more comfortable and more confident. I was thinking, "I can't score like Michelle" ... "I don't have the leadership that April has" ... "I don't have the dribbling skills that Carin has" ... "What could I bring?" I learned I could bring a defensive work rate. I soon learned that when I was winning balls and putting defenders under pressure, it gave me offensive confidence. I wasn't thinking about every little thing. I just wanted to make sure my touch was good.

I would win a ball, and we would almost score. That felt good, so that's what I really started working on. In 1992, I started putting more effort into it, and that's when my offensive game started picking up. It was because I had a lot more confidence. It felt so good to hear the comments from my teammates like, "You really worked hard today," or "You made all the difference."

Once I realized that being consistent meant I had a good performance, it was like all the pressure was taken off. I used to think that every time I stepped on the field I had to score, and that was all I thought about. People rate your game by how many goals you scored, but that's not how I rate it. I know I had a good day if I was a consistent presence on the field — offensively and defensively.

I wasn't the best athlete in my family. My brother Garrett was. And I have three sisters who can do things that I could never dream of doing. With this team and in college, I know what I bring to every game. There are times when I walk off the field, and I say to myself, "That was pretty good." But most of the time, I feel it wasn't consistent. There are stretches where I might lose concentration. Whether it was two minutes or five minutes or thirty minutes, I know. And I'm the one I have to answer to.

I can count on one hand, the games I walked off the field saying, "I didn't make that many mistakes, and the mistakes I made I can live with." The perfect example is I just recently watched the 1991 NCAA Final against Duke on tape, and you know what? The one image in my mind is there are ten seconds left and we are winning 9-1. And who is still running? Kristine Lilly. That's why I know I'm not there yet. That's reality for me.

"One is not only capable of excellence, but one is responsible for excellence, an awareness that it exists and you can lean toward it, aspire to it. We have it in us to be splendid."
— Maya Angelou

Qualities of Champions

What makes the United States one of the best teams in the World? Winning at this level is rather elusive. There are so many variables that need to fall into the right place for a team to succeed. And yet, the United States women's national team has developed consistently successful individuals and teams in women's soccer. This team and these players have transformed over the past decade, and yet there remain common threads of success. During the weeks and months before the Olympics, we would relish any insights former Olympians had about their successes and their failures. We hoped to learn something that would give us an edge. I want to try to give you a window into the story of how it all came true for us.

Photo by Michael Allen

"A champion is someone who trains when no one is watching."

— *Carin Jennings Gabarra*
1991 World Champion
1996 Olympic Gold Medalist

Photo by Perry McIntyre

"At this level, almost everyone has the physical tools to be the best. It comes down to a few things: how bad you want it, what you do when things get hard, and whether you are able to stay focused amid turmoil, challenge, chaos and demands. It's all in your head and in your heart."

— *Michelle Akers*
1991 World Champion
1996 Olympic Gold Medalist

Photo by J. Brett Whitesell

"A champion is someone who does not settle for that day's practice, that day's competition, that day's performance. They are always striving to be better. They don't live in the past. For example, winning the gold medal August 1, 1996, was the best thing ever. August 3rd, 1997, you've got to go on to something else. You can't step out onto the field and expect anyone to roll over because of what you did a year before. Champions think about that everyday. You need to stay on the edge of your game. You need to get better every year. You need to leave them in the dust and leave no question of who is the best. That's what a champion is — that person who perseveres and doesn't ever get satisfied with what they have done in the past."

— *Briana Scurry*
1996 Olympic Gold Medalist

"A champion is all they can be in every facet of their lives. They prioritize what they need to get done. But for me, it's someone who works every single day on being a better person."

— *Shannon Higgins Cirovski*
1991 World Champion

"When you see a championship team, you see that everybody has the full dedication and commitment to the same goal and wants to do everything they can. What it comes down to is commitment and dedication to your goal. On a team, each player has to have that commitment, because you could have some players who are just riding the coat tails of the others and not doing the full 100 percent.

"A champion is also someone who proves themselves in every environment. No matter what level you are playing, you still play to be your best. It's all about hard work. That's where a champion comes in. You can either stick to your goals, or you can just go through the motions and rest on your status. But it's all about work."

— *Kristine Lilly*
1991 World Champion
1996 Olympic Gold Medalist

"You champion yourself in every way. You get through the practice 150 percent. You finish the fitness faster than you did the last time. I think the best way to describe this team is it's not just when the game whistle blows. You are training and working harder than you did yesterday, and you are going to work harder the next day than you did today. It's knowing you are going to hurt. And in that hurt, you are going to be better. When it's all over, you've done it right. And you feel good about yourself. Being satisfied is almost like doing just enough. It has to be more than enough."

> *— Brandi Chastain*
> *1991 World Champion*
> *1996 Olympic Gold Medalist*

Photo by Michael Allen

"Everyone on our team has a fighter's mentality, everyone wants to win. Everyone on the team has huge hearts. It's like they'd die for you on the field, and that's very comforting. If you are having a bad game, or something's going wrong, you know they are going to pick up the slack because it's happened to them before. That's why I love those guys."

> *— Carla Overbeck*
> *1991 World Champion*
> *1996 Olympic Gold Medalist*

"A champion is passionate, loves what they do and always wants to bring that passion out in everything they do. If you are passionate about something, that will enable you to be the best you can be. I am a champion because I love to play soccer. I'm actually amazed that I'm a Gold Medalist. I just played soccer because I loved to play soccer. That's why. I was passionate about what I did, and I loved to do it. I did my best and it took me to a gold medal."

> *— Tiffeny Milbrett*
> *1996 Olympic Gold Medalist*

"Every journey starts with a first step."

Chinese Proverb

Psychological Section

"Mentality — you know it when you see it."

The psychological pillar may be one of the most important and the least attended to of all the aspects of a soccer player. Most athletes cite their emotions and their mental state as the key variable in their performance. Working on your mental skills is critical to your success as an athlete. It is at least as important, and perhaps more important, as technique, understanding tactical nuances of the game, or physically conditioning yourself for the demands of the game. Unlike how fast you run, or whether or not the coach plays you, you can work on the following psychological dimensions:

▲ **Confidence:** Performance and confidence are very much related. We will explore avenues and resources to improve your confidence. Hard work, fitness, knowing your strengths, overcoming challenges, and preparation can be important sources of confidence. You will come to appreciate that what works for one person may not be what works for another.

In this section, I'll share with you many players' stories about what they do to help their confidence. Sometimes it may have little to do with soccer. Whatever your sources of confidence may be, it's important for you to learn that about yourself.

▲ **Training Mentality:** Developing a competitive training mentality is crucial. The psychological dimension necessary to be a competitor and how to foster that quality will be expanded upon. Being competitive is a necessary element of getting to the next level.

Do you enter every training session intending to be the best and to help your teammates be their best? It's important to understand that you can be competitive on the field and still maintain your friendships off the field. While not everyone may be like you, this will be an important distinction between your goals and those of your teammates. Being competitive doesn't mean playing dirty. It means playing to be your best, playing to win. Whether it's a one-v-one duel, or a four-v-four small-sided game, train for excellence and play to win.

We always begin every national team training camp with a "mentality session." This allows us to revisit a fundamental core to our success — our mentality. In conjunction with the individual and small-sided competitions we play, we usually do fitness as well. The fitness test is as important psychologically as it is to give us information about our players' conditioning.

As we will discuss in the Physical Section, fitness is a tremendous psychological challenge. Mastering it can be a tremendous source of confidence. While mentality is rather an elusive term, I hope this section will illuminate and define it; how to seek it and embody it. This acquired permission to be your best will not only help you, but it will help your team set new training standards. You will learn to train like you play in a match. All aspects of playing — technical, tactical and physical are influenced by how you train.

▲ **USA Mentality:** This is a collective result of all that this book addresses. It's about resolve. It's a dynamic that engrosses our audience. It's seen in the smallest of moments and the grandest of feats. It's sometimes captured and leaves the audience awestruck. And yet, often it occurs with no one to bear witness. You know it when you see it. It beats in each player's conviction and is embodied through the collective spirit of one of the finest teams this sport may ever know.

▲ **Psychological Skills:** What are they and how can you improve them? This chapter will address specific psychological skills techniques you can learn to enhance performance, including goal-setting, imagery, visualization, self talk and more.

In soccer, psychological skills have only recently been given necessary attention. But I'm sure each of you will acknowledge the role your thoughts and emotions can play in your performance. How many of you have been in the "zone," where everything went right? From your first touch of the ball, you just knew it was going to be a great day. Yet, when asked to explain what you did or how this brilliant performance came about, you are unable to explain it. Psychological skills training works to implement a methodology to your performance state. Then you can replicate behaviors and feelings to help ensure success.

How many of you have also had the opposite experience? You just know from your first touch that it just isn't going to be your day. Or you couldn't find your lucky socks or the bus is late or the game is delayed and it is hard to recover. I ask this question anytime I work with players and always receive a nod yes.

One goal of this section is to help you realize that you are in control of your response to circumstances, and you can do things to write your script for the game, despite whatever unexpected occurrence arises. And just because you missed your first shot or your first touch went off your kneecap, you can still overcome it and have your dream performance. Like scoring goals, psychological skills are aspects of your game that need training as well — if, that is, you want to gain an edge. Many of these skills were used by our women's national team and are considered core elements in performance.

Joy Fawcett thrives in one-v-one duels.

Photo by J. Brett Whitesell

*"The greater the artist the greater the doubt;
perfect confidence is granted to the
less-talented as a consolation prize."*
— Robert Hughes

CHAPTER I
CONFIDENCE

It all starts with preparation. If you come to appreciate one thing from this book, I hope it's that preparation and all of the hard work that goes along with it is the foundation for excellence. Confidence and self-esteem can be enhanced through your preparation. Some of the confidence will come from the fact that you have become a better player, but also from the fact that you have worked so hard at becoming all that you can be. You know you have prepared for the moments you are going to face — just like studying for an exam. You know that there is a good chance the player you are going against hasn't prepared the way you have, and you'll just feel good about it.

"The dedication and commitment we have is a major reason why we have been successful," says Kristine Lilly. "But it goes a lot deeper than just on the field and in training camps. When we are on our own, we don't have someone pushing us or helping us. We take the attitude that we have to do this for ourselves and for the team.

"Our work ethic is amazing," adds Kristine. "When you see us working on the field, you can see the difference between the veterans and the younger players because the veterans never stop. That's what we try to get across to the younger players. When you are doing fitness, for example, you're dead, but you are going to make it. Against Norway in the Olympics, at halftime we were losing, but we all knew we were going to score and win. We just knew it. We weren't scared, we were excited."

Know what makes you special. Being aware of your strengths is absolutely one of the most important things you need, not only to get to the next level, but to develop a confidence base in your game. Everyone has qualities that are unique. Identify them and develop them. They are what will set you apart, and they're something you can fall back on when things get rough. So spend time on your strengths, not just your weaknesses.

"If you need to work on confidence, you go back and work on the things you are really good at," says Jen Grubb, U-20 women's national team 1997 Nordic Cup Champion. "That's always a good starting point. You can always rely on your strengths, and you can always go back to them. For me, it is my long-ball service. I know that will always be there, and I can go back to it and feel more confident."

Too often, young players are told to work on their left foot, which is "terrible," or work on heading because "you really can't head, you know." And that's fine. But to ignore your

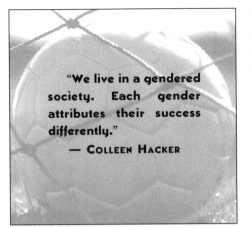

"We live in a gendered society. Each gender attributes their success differently."
— COLLEEN HACKER

strengths is to ignore why you are special. You are certainly not going to make a team because your left foot isn't as bad as it used to be, but you may make a team because your shot is the best in the state or your first touch is nearly perfect. By training your stronger skills as well as your weaker areas, you will begin to gain confidence and feel good about your game and about yourself.

"One of the pillars must be outstanding. There has to be something about you that gets you to the next level. There are a lot of good players that are pretty well rounded, but they have to have that one special thing. You have to make your strengths *your* strengths," advises Shannon Higgins Cirovski.

The next step in developing or improving confidence is accepting your strengths and being willing to attribute success to yourself. Can you say, "I am good at that," or "It's what makes me special." This is an interesting paradox for girls and women in general. There is a tendency for women to defer their success to someone else or to the team, and then take responsibility for loss or failure themselves. This becomes important in discussions about confidence, because if we are unable or unwilling to acknowledge facts about ourselves, we potentially lose a significant source of confidence through self-affirmation.

"We live in a gendered society," says Colleen Hacker, the national team's sport psychologist. "Each gender attributes their success differently. For instance, males attribute success to internal factors — 'I won because I'm good. I got the job because I am talented.' Ask a female why she got the job, and she'll say, 'I don't know, there were all these good people. I kind of lucked out.' Women will also credit success to luck — 'I was at the right place at the right time, I feel fortunate' — words like that.

"When you ask men why they failed, you'll hear, 'It was a stupid test.' Why didn't you get picked? 'He already had his mind made up.' It's okay to attribute your success to your ability. You'll feel better, you'll feel proud, and it affects your confidence."

While giving credit to yourself when credit is due is a valuable part of developing confidence, make sure you are making an honest assessment of your ability and talent. After every mistake or poor performance, a variety of excuses will be available for your use. Just remember, false praise can lead to a false sense of confidence.

One way to work on confidence is to reduce the ways you lose confidence. By that, I mean throughout games or in training, soccer players make mistakes. It's a fact. But all of us react differently to those mistakes. How you react will greatly influence your performance and, in turn, your confidence. "Each mistake is a learning experience," says Brandi Chastain. "Moping around just compounds it. It's what you do after the mistake that's important. You can recover from them. You have to make a positive out of a negative. I believe that personally because I make mistakes all the time."

Certainly, it's a lot harder to be confident when you are not playing well. But ask yourself this question: Are you not playing well because you are putting so much pressure on yourself that you are afraid to make a mistake? Or maybe your coach gets on you for messing up. The vicious cycle begins: 'I need confidence to play well' ... 'I play well when I am confident.' Sounds familiar doesn't it? We've all been there.

Earning Confidence

Kate Sobrero wasn't always a starter for the U.S. Women's National Team. As a youth player, she was considered too small to play. She was under five feet tall and very thin. But a consistent part of her story is how hard she was willing to work. "Being small, I had to work my tail off to be on the team," she says. "I've never been the best player on any team I've been on. I always just worked hard." Kate was moved from position to position until finally she played in the back and found her passion. "I loved it," she says. After winning a national championship at Notre Dame in her sophomore year, she attended a national team training camp. She passed out during fitness. Now, she had a choice — to give in to that moment, or not to internalize where she was, but rather to control where she went from there. She knew what happened from that point on would be up to her.

Kate went to work. She came in as an over-aged player with the U-21 Women's National team. Every camp, I remember doing a double take at times. She was much better every time she came in. "I knew I was an athlete who plays soccer, not a soccer player who is a great athlete. I realized I needed to spend a lot of time on my skills. I spent a lot of time in the racquetball court hitting balls off the wall, working on my touch, and I did every kind of Coerver imaginable." Kate recalls. Her confidence came from how hard she worked. She stepped back and looked at what she could do, what she could control, and she got it done. Many players would have gone in the opposite direction. Instead, Kate made a choice to do everything she could. As a result, she became more and more confident and re-entered the national team program a new player. Her fitness became the cornerstone of her mental toughness. Despite breaking her jaw in her first camp back, Kate persevered yet again. She came back and won a spot in the starting lineup for the 1999 Women's World Cup. Overcoming challenges, controlling what she could control, and a lot of hard work all contributed to her becoming the player she is. And even now, either before or after training, Kate can be seen working on some aspect of her game.

When Christie Pearce joined the national team, it was pretty overwhelming for her. She had never played at that level before, and she was being asked to switch from the striker position where she enjoyed so much success in college, to defender. There was so much to learn. The pace of everything was brutally faster and input from the coaches seemed constant. She recalled an important moment for her when she realized she could decide how she would react to this process. "You have to learn from your mistakes, which is hard," Christie remembers. "I watched everything possible and tried to take it all in. You feel like you are always getting corrected or the drill stops with you. I found it hard, but you just have to take it. You can't get frustrated. You have to keep telling yourself, 'I'm playing a new position. I'm learning.'

"If you don't give 100 percent and you approach it lackadaisically, it's not going to work," Christie continues. "I tried to stay focused and show the coaches that I was trying to do my best, not getting frustrated and not putting my head down. That's not what they want to see, and that's not what I wanted to do either. I made a lot of mistakes, but I just kept my head up and didn't let it bother me."

That's easier to say than do, isn't it? But the message is clear. You can choose how to respond to yourself and others. And in difficult circumstances, you need to be your own best friend. In Christie's case, she was coming into the national team for the first time. On top of that, she had to learn a new position. Not easy. You may find yourself in a position with which you are unfamiliar and need to find a way to thrive.

You should also try to avoid tying your confidence to things over which you have no power. Confidence needs to be associated with things you can control. You cannot control what the coach does. You can control how well you play, and consequently one would hope, you'll get more playing time. But can you see that playing time is not ultimately in your control? So it's dangerous to say "I am confident because the coach is playing me," or "I have lost confidence because the coach isn't playing me."

Not making the team is a way many people lose confidence. If you don't make a team, it's hard to not take it all to heart. You feel as though you are not good and then lose confidence. Ironically, you need to work to have a more productive response to being cut, or else you won't make it the next time either. You need to be the one who judges your preparation, your ability, and you need to be the one who massages your confidence. It would be easy to blame the coach again, or let what happened be an excuse to stop working. Or worse still, affect how you feel about yourself.

Jen Grubb had tried out for the Under-14 state team one year. In the end, she didn't make it, and of course she was disappointed. But she was able to move past it and realize that moping about it wouldn't help her reach her goal, which was to make the regional team.

"Believe in yourself," Jen says. "Things come full circle. It's hard when you don't achieve a small goal. But when you stay motivated and keep working, it will come back and pay off. Start with believing in yourself. Otherwise it's going to be tough to realize your goals."

Danielle Fotopoulos and Aly Wagner both overcame serious knee injuries to make the national team residency program in early 1999. Confidence played a major role in their recoveries. Says Aly, "I've actually gained confidence from being injured. Just knowing what I accomplished and what I came back from is a source of confidence for me. It's made me a stronger player and person."

Overcoming obstacles can be a wonderful source of confidence and self-esteem. All of you, as all of the players you will hear from in this book, will encounter challenges in your career and life. Your perseverance and optimism in overcoming difficult times are essential. This will be true individually, and in accomplishing goals as a team. No climb is without struggle. It is at the very heart of adversity that you can find your greatest strength. Even in injury, being cut, and after losses, we can grow — if that is what we choose.

Confidence isn't tied to soccer per se. Certainly, soccer affects life, and life affects soccer. You've all probably experienced times when soccer isn't going well, so you have trouble with school, or relationships, or another facet of life. Or conversely, if you are having trouble in school or had a fight with a friend or family member, sometimes it's hard to concentrate on soccer. So, as much as it's important to prepare to be a soccer player, it is vital to have your house in order. Take care of business outside of soccer. That means being a good student. Stay on top of your work and apply the same lessons about discipline and striving for excellence to your overall life. There are many things in your life which need addressing. If you don't take control of these aspects of your life, any one of them may come back to haunt you. You can control good eating habits, good sleeping habits, the quality of person you are, and many other areas. All of these can contribute to your overall confidence and sense of well being.

"Confidence is an overall thing," says Jen Grubb. "It doesn't have to be sport-related to affect your confidence."

Lastly, there are times when you simply have to "act as if" or "fake it" until you make it. Colleen Hacker often reminds us that there are times when you must act as if you are confident or happy or whatever. What you'll come to realize if you walk with your head up high or put a smile on your face, you'll start feeling that way. Soon the attempt to "act as if" will become both who you are and how you feel.

THE CHICKEN AND THE EGG

By Anson Dorrance

Confidence is a really difficult thing. It's a chicken and egg thing. I ask my athletes, "Are you confident and then you play well? Or do you play well and that makes you confident?" Then I watch them sort through the question. It's an impossible question for most people to answer.

Most people lack confidence because they don't play well. You have to play well to become confident, but you have to be confident to play well. So how do you break the cycle? Sometimes, you have to help the player build confidence, and they have to help themselves as well. Sometimes, you have to construct confidence when nothing is there. Some players break through by becoming confident first. Some players do something that causes them to play well, and then they become confident.

You have to have the kind of mindset that is powerful and forgiving. The people who are supremely confident forgive themselves for poor performances. They don't dwell on it and feel sorry for themselves, subsequently spiraling down into even poorer performances.

You don't want to have a temperament that when any kind of adversity hits, you end up going into a "woe is me mentality," hanging your head and feeling sorry for yourself. This is what I've always admired about Kristine Lilly. The more frustrated she got, the harder she ran. The more complicated her life was, the more intensity she played with. It was interesting watching her sublimate her frustrations. She'd just run harder and harder and harder. She has the ability to take adversity and turn it into energy.

The old saying is "If you have lemons, make lemonade." Kristine would take frustration and find a way to turn it into additional adrenaline. I think all the great athletes have the strength to take adversity and convert it into something positive.

Part of the construction of yourself as a champion is to welcome these things, and to understand that you are going to have adversity. You also have to understand that the extraordinary players are fraught with huge challenges.

The quote from Robert Hughes — *"The greater the artist the greater the doubt; perfect confidence is granted to the less-talented as a consolation prize"* — is telling us that great champions don't go through life feeling on top of the world and incredibly confident every minute of every day. They have doubts, too. They fight through it, and use the doubt as a motivator to do more.

If someone out there doubts themselves in a lot of different areas, they're not alone. We all have doubts. Champions have the capacity to deal with it. They can take adversity and grind it into some powerful life force.

CHAPTER II
TRAINING MENTALITY

There's only one way to go about training — with all that you have. We call it "training on your edge." And it starts with how you focus and concentrate, even during warmup. We want to teach players to train past what is comfortable. Take the Coerver ball skill series, for example. Do you do them so you are stretching your muscles to go quicker, almost to the point of making a mistake? Or do you go through the motions? If you only train what is comfortable and familiar, that's the type of player you will be — comfortable and familiar. That won't help you be your best.

Developing the right training mentality begins with you. When you are training away from your team, you should be working with the same intensity that you bring to the team. When you are with your team, you want to train in a way that inspires your teammates to work harder. For us, it's an expectation that begins with our leaders, the veteran players that have been in the trenches. They know anything less is not acceptable, nor enough to be the best.

A big mistake players make is to train one way, and then expect to play at another level when game time comes. The way you train in practice is the way you will play in the game. Training intensity is about developing habits, and anyone can create these habits or traits. Carla Overbeck is a tremendous leader and competitor. She demands a great deal of herself every day because she knows the training standard of the world champions begins with her.

In our training camps, we keep score in every drill, and our veterans take each exercise or game very seriously. They know they are being evaluated every time they come into camp on whether or not they are going to help us win. They know that what they do matters. We want to create a game-like atmosphere in training. If you are keeping score for a game involving our veterans, you had better get it right, because the first time you call out a wrong score, you'll hear about it. They know every point and will dispute anything questionable because winning is on the line. It matters. Train for excellence.

"The great thing about our team is that it gets nasty at times, but we all understand that's what is making us better," says Tisha Venturini. "Let's say I am going against Mia in one-v-ones. The harder we go, the more we are helping each other. If I am going fifty percent on defense, that doesn't make her any better. Sure, you can get angry. I get angry, but once the practice is over that's it. It's healthy. It gets bad at times, but the personalities on the team won't let it carry off the field. Everyone understands that to be the best in the world, this is how we have to train."

Competition is a crucial ingredient in elite player development. As I mentioned, the goal for training is to prepare you for a game. Games are about competition, so training should be as well. Games are about performing at a quicker, more intense pace. They are about execution. So train those things. If the games are more demanding physically and are played faster and harder than what you do in training, then you need to create that pace in training day-in and day-out. Even on lighter training days before a match, game focus and sharpness should be there.

"Competing, to me, is just a mentality that says you can never let down," says Shannon Higgins Cirovski. "It's trained in practice by the fact that we put ourselves in situations where we have to compete to survive. It makes you tougher when every single day you are out there trying to survive. It's an attitude that says, 'I'm not going to lose. I'm never going to give up.'"

We do a lot of one-v-one work in training. In one-v-one, there can be only one winner, and we record wins and losses. It's going to be you or me. We compete in small-sided games, we compete in heading duels, we compete against ourselves on fitness. We're always looking for the players who factor into the margin of victory. You can become better at training by playing to win. Recall Mia's opening thoughts when she said there's a difference between training and practice. You can learn to train with a consistent winner's mentality. But first you must understand that how you train makes a difference in how you'll play. You can't turn mentality on and off. You must work to foster an environment that makes it permissible to be a winner and to work hard. You must believe that competition can be part of development.

The best player in the world in the 1991 Women's World Cup was Carin Jennings (now Carin Gabarra). She had not grown up in an environment that asked a lot of her. It was almost foreign to her, as it will be to many of you. Some of you will be more instinctually aggressive and competitive, but you will still need to learn, to some degree, just what your limits are. Odds are, you are not training nearly as intensely as you could.

"I think you have to experience it," says Carin. "Some players are more naturally intense in every practice. You have to have a good work ethic. Lilly can do it, April could do it. For me, I had to learn how to practice with intensity. I didn't train that way in college, but as soon as I saw it, I could do it. Still, you have to want to do it."

One of Carin's strengths as a player was her incredible dribbling ability. She was one of the best in the world at going one-v-one and quickly finding an opening for a pass or a shot. She developed that skill, in part, by playing with boys and men. Many national team players grew up playing with boys. In fact, a good portion of the elite players trained with, or against, brothers and boyfriends, and some of you actually are training with boys now. This is a very good way to develop training intensity. Boys love to compete and challenge each other in anything. So, if being tested and stretched is what you are after, this can be a great environment if used properly. By properly, I mean you must find the appropriate-aged young man and situation. If you find someone who is more interested in beating you at all costs, it won't do you any good. But good old fashioned arm wrestling, per se, is healthy.

Kristine Lilly trains every second of every practice as if the clock is winding down in an Olympic final. Not a second is wasted; not a morsel of energy is saved. It's all left out on the field. It isn't a one-time deal. Day-in and day-out, year after year, she invests more than any other player into her training. Her consistency is extraordinary. And despite having played in more international matches than any other woman or man in the world, her standard remains as our standard.

"I played on boys' teams growing up, from second grade to eighth grade," says Kristine. "Since I was different, I had to prove myself. I had no special treatment. I could compete with them, so I had the confidence of being able to hang with boys. A big thing was that they treated me as a player, so growing up I realized that girls can do whatever boys can do. I think that has helped my game tremendously, because I think I have the attitude that I can accomplish anything, and I am going to keep working at it until I do.

"When I was a freshman in high school, they told me I had to go play with the girls," Kristine adds. "I think that helped me a lot because I was better than the majority of the girls, and that was new to me. Then, I had to learn to push myself even more."

What's important about what Kristine says is not just that playing with boys helped her develop confidence and forced her to prove herself. It's important that she also played with girls. The balance between always being stretched — whether you're playing up an age group or are with players faster and stronger, as with boys, for example — and finding a niche and a place to succeed and dominate is crucial. If you have too much of one or the other, the balance will be off. If you only play with boys, you might be always playing one- or two-touch to get rid of the ball. You will lose the opportunity to become creative. On the other hand, if you always play with lesser players, you may not be asked to play quickly enough or develop any tactical agility, because you can get away with not playing quickly or cleanly, or can merely out-work your opponent.

Not all of you will be comfortable being competitive. A good way to begin is by training the one-v-one dimension of your game. We call it the "dueler's mentality." Find a friend that's willing to train with you. You can create small goals with your extra shoes. Play

> ## ON COMMITMENT
>
> *"I approached practices the same way I approached games. You can't turn it on and off like a faucet. I couldn't dog it during practice and then, when I needed that extra push late in the game, expect it to be there. But that's how a lot of people approach things. And that's why a lot of people fail. They sound like they're committed to being the best they can be. But when it comes right down to it, they're looking for reasons instead of answers. If you're trying to achieve, there will be roadblocks. I've had them; everybody has had them.*
>
> *But obstacles don't have to stop you. If you run into a wall, don't turn around and give up. Figure out how to climb it, go through it, or work around it."*
>
> — *MICHAEL JORDAN*

in two directions or simply to a single goal, or shoe, like half court basketball. But keep score! Developing the confidence and desire to be a dueler is important, no matter where you play on the field. As a front-runner you must be willing to take on defenders. Mia Hamm, April Heinrichs, Tiffeny Milbrett, Carin Gabarra, Kristine Lilly and Shannon MacMillan are one-v-one artists. Yet, for as many times as you see them succeed and get a shot or a goal, there are probably ten other times we don't remember. It's that relentless pursuit of the breaking point between you and your defender that's vital. One-v-one artists need to know it's okay to take risks, because it's all part of wearing down the defender.

In the midfield, your job is to seek and win duels — challenge for a head ball, win a tackle, come up with a loose ball. That's your bread and butter. In the defense, your job is to win the one-v-one duel. Can you outlast your attacker? Do you take pride in your defense? Do you refuse to let them get by you or get a shot? Dueling can even exist between two goalkeepers. In the book *Training Soccer Champions*, Anson Dorrance discusses how important he felt having competition between goalkeepers is to their development. Tony DiCicco has a series of games our goalkeepers enjoy playing called "Keeper Wars." Tracy Ducar, one of our national team goalkeepers, describes this duel in the Goalkeeper Section. Our field players love to watch the keepers go at it, because it gets so intense, and they have a blast. They can watch the keepers strategize in a second and work to "break" their opponent. It's great to watch, and fun to play. Bring this to your team and find the energy your goalkeepers have for this game and the benefit they get from it as well.

The Take-on Mentality

Being a one-v-one artist is not always the most popular job you can have. We asked April Heinrichs what advice she would give a young take-on artist who is constantly criticized by parents or teammates, coaches or opponents. "Get some earplugs," April said. "Be prepared to take criticism."

When you're young, taking players on goes against what coaches and parents often believe to be necessary for you to be a "team player." April's ability to deal with criticism, her confidence and sheer love for what she was doing allowed her to keep on doing it. "We play the game because we love the game," April says. "If you love the game, you want the ball and the last thing you want to do with it is give it away!"

The world has so few great take-on artists because they have to survive the onslaught of criticism and repetitive failure. If the attacker wasn't repeatedly thwarted by the defense, there would be more goals. The attacker holds on to their wonderful commitment to take-on, because maybe the twelfth time will be the one that makes the difference in the match. One of Tiffeny Milbrett's and Mia Hamm's exceptional qualities is their willingness to take risks. They play to make a difference and put themselves on the line over and over. All you remember is the one where they break through to score, or that dazzles the crowd. But there were earlier moments that set the stage. They are rare in that way.

Cindy Parlow came out of Tennessee to be one of the top young one-v-one artists in the world. Cindy remembers those challenges growing up and how her team supported her because her dribbling talent resulted in goals — not always goals for herself but for her team.

"Very early when I was starting into club ball, I had people trying to get me to stop dribbling," says Cindy. "Everybody was calling me a ball hog, and I was trying to adjust to it. I was passing when I should be dribbling and dribbling when I should be passing. I had it all mixed up. But my club team was very receptive to my dribbling. I don't think they saw me as a ball hog because I didn't score that much. It was hard to call somebody selfish when they were not the one scoring. I never look at statistics. I'm not really interested. I figure as long as I'm doing the best I can, and go to every practice and play as hard as I can, that's good enough for me."

Finding the balance between selfish play and being overly cooperative isn't always easy. Some players err being too selfish and need to recognize when they need to pass. Others need to be more selfish and take responsibility on the ball. If you are faced with a one-v-one situation, you must have — or work to develop — an instinct to take on.

The Ultimate Duel

The Olympic Showdown: Hege Riise vs. Tiffany Roberts

An often-overlooked, but crucial ingredient in the USA's gold medal performance in the 1996 Olympics was the play of Tiffany Roberts against Norway in the semifinals.

Norway's Hege Riise, the most valuable player in the 1995 World Cup and the 1996 European Player of the Year, was a major threat to the American pursuit of the gold medal. The U.S. coaching staff decided to assign Tiffany Roberts to mark Riise. It would be the only time during the five Olympic matches that the USA would sacrifice one of its players in order to eliminate an opponent.

Known for her tenacity and aggressive defending, Tiff rose to the challenge in front of 64,196 fans, severely limiting Riise's effectiveness.

"I felt honored when Tony said, 'I have a special assignment for you,'" says Tiffany. "She is considered one of the best players in the world, someone who could hurt us. Here's this great player, and he's asking *me* to mark her out

Photo by J. Brett Whitesell

of the game. Some people might say, 'Oh, that's the last thing I want to do, run around shadowing this girl.' But I'll play goalkeeper if they want me to.

"I remember when I was in high school, watching tapes of the '91 World Cup. I would look at the girls on the bench and say, 'I'd do anything just to be a substitute on that team.' So it was an honor that Tony put me on her."

Tiffany fully understood the importance of her job and the personal risks involved if Riise were to rip apart the USA. However, she stayed focused on the task and ignored the pressure. In fact, she flourished.

"It would have been huge against me if she even got an assist," Tiff says. "I remember thinking, 'Don't even let her get the ball.' I loved it. I felt like I could do it, and I wasn't really worried about it. At halftime, everyone was so supportive, encouraging me to keep it up."

Tiffany's performance had a huge impact on the game. Not only was Riise not a major factor, but because Tiff was able to render Riise less effective, Kristine Lilly never had to bother helping Tiff out. Lilly was free to concentrate on attacking the Norwegian penalty area, and she was an extremely dangerous player on the field.

CHAPTER III
A DRIBBLER'S CONFIDENCE

By Mia Hamm

There are so many different things involved with one-v-one. Everybody has to find their own strengths and their own style. For example, Carin Gabarra was one of the greatest dribblers in the game. She had a very acute dribbling style. Carin's style had a lot of severe cuts, radical to the point where you couldn't stay with her. My style is more direct. It's based more on change of pace. One of my strengths is acceleration — my first three steps. So I try to use those strengths.

When I got to college and started playing with the national team, I was introduced to the Coerver series. For me that was great, because there was a structure. So when I wasn't in an organized setting or with my team, I could always do this series of dribbling drills. That helped me a lot because to this day, I don't feel I'm one of the most technical players, but it gave me confidence.

Some of the really good dribblers in the women's game are very creative. And that's something we don't see with girls as much as I think we should. We are so good at following directions, I think sometimes we lose that ability to go outside the lines, be a little creative and say, "You know, I think I'll try it this way."

When I do a clinic, I'll set up a drill and tell girls how to do it. But sometimes they

Mia Hamm's willingness to take-on is what makes her one of the most dangerous front-runners in the world.

Photo by J. Brett Whitesell

can't do it the way I've just explained. If I say, "Okay, I want you to receive the ball with a defender on your back and cut it to your right." They will do it that way even if the defender is at their right shoulder. Then I'll tell them to base their decision on what they see. On the reverse side, that's such a positive quality because we listen so well.

Coaches play a very important part in developing dribblers. There are good ways to teach someone and not-so-good ways. There are times in practices when you need to be told, "Hey, it's not okay to do that." But there are other times when it's much better to be shown other ways to do it. We don't always have to be told we're wrong. Sometimes we just need to be shown other ways to do it, and to be shown the benefits. For me, it was like, "Yeah, you're right. That makes perfect sense." That's really all it took.

Granted, it probably takes ten or fifteen times, because when you are so used to doing it one way, it's hard to change. But I was never told, "Stop!" I was told, "Okay, when you get around the corner, here are your options — shoot, pass the ball here, or pass the ball there." Your percentage of success goes up when you make decisions that way, and that's what it's all about. It isn't about how many goals I score. It's about our team winning, and can I increase my team's chance of winning.

CHAPTER IV
THE CONSTRUCTION OF CHARACTER

By Anson Dorrance

I have always admired players who are psychologically strong. The players who impress me are the ones who are constantly raising the bar on themselves. As they achieve one level, they fight to get to the next level. It's the art of never being satisfied. For most players, as soon as life gets uncomfortable or training gets uncomfortable, they shut down. The challenge is to fight through every level of discomfort to get the next level.

The reason most players don't achieve their potential is that the process takes them into an unpleasant area. They don't like the discipline of getting up early and training, and they don't like the pain of pushing to go beyond one level to get to the next. This process is not comfortable. The end result is, but the process is not. It takes a remarkable kind of discipline and hardness to fight this human tendency.

It's almost a leap of faith. In a way, when you are doing your training, you don't know if it is going to take you to your goals. You hope it does, but you can't be sure. You have all these people telling you, "This is what I did to improve." But you don't know if it's actually going to work. You have doubts. There is no formula. There's nothing that says, "If you do this, you will be on the team." There are so many variables. It's not an easy process to fight through because there are so many different issues that you can't control.

IN THE SMALLEST OF MOMENTS

It's amazing how much you can get done in an hour-and-a-half training session. Certainly we as coaches must be prepared, so the players can go after it for ninety minutes. I love what our captain volunteered about a small but significant way for you to show mentality and respect for your coaches and teammates. "When a coach calls you over, they want your attention. It shows them respect to jog over," says Carla Overbeck. "You're not chatting and wasting time. If you finish a five-v-five game, you jog off for water. That's mentality."

Carla points out a very simple yet telling aspect of training that everyone can do, something anyone can bring to their team. It can start in the smallest of moments. Get your team in the habit of jogging on and off the field for everything. You'll be amazed at how much more you can get done. Also, in a ninety-minute game you don't get to take a five minute water break in the middle of the half. So, again, train the habits you'll need for a ninety-minute focus.

There is a great quote about the Olympics. "It's not the triumph, it's the struggle." The thing people remember about athletics is not necessarily scoring the goal. What I remember about athletics is being at the gymnasium wall in Greenwich, Conn., thumping the ball against the side of the wall. That made me a better soccer player. Those are my most positive memories, even though at the time, it was painful.

All great athletes will tell you that winning championships and scoring the winning basket or goal or touchdown gives you an exhilarating feeling. But that alone is not enough. The fight and the struggle are very satisfying. The fight and the struggle itself produces a very wonderful hardening, strengthening, great-to-be-alive feeling that you can feel even if you don't make it. What you are experiencing is the pulse of your own character during that struggle.

An integral part of the psychological dimension is confidence. One great way to gain confidence in yourself is by working hard. Hard work gives you confidence to play well. Working harder than anyone else will give you extraordinary confidence. All these things feed off each other. Since you can't guarantee that you will play well, you can guarantee that you work hard.

One of my favorite quotes is from Theodore Roosevelt: *"It is not the critic who counts, not the man who points out how the strong man stumbled, or where the doer of deeds could have done them better. The credit belongs to the man who is actually in the arena, whose face is marred by dust and sweat and blood, who strives valiantly, who errs and comes short again and again; who knows the great enthusiasms, the great devotions, and spends himself in a worthy cause, who at the best, knows in the end the triumph of great achievement; and who, at the worst, if he fails, at least fails while daring greatly, so that his place shall never be with those cold and timid souls who know neither victory nor defeat."*

I think you can contribute to the construction of your own character. I think you can do that through an understanding of what it is you really want to be, or what qualities you genuinely want to possess. I have always been stimulated and inspired by great men and women and what they felt was vital or important. You need to construct yourself with the pieces of the processes of the amazing people you know. Or you should be regularly looking for great books in order to do a search of the powerful qualities of the human spirit and learn from the people who can explain it, or be motivated by the extraordinary people who have lived it. These mentors don't need to be in your sport, but they should have a discipline that carries over into your sport. You need to construct yourself, and you can do that through a never-ending process of renewal.

Most of my reading is not about athletics. I read about greatness, and I share as many of these stories as I can. I give all my seniors Victor Frankl's *Man's Search for Meaning*. There is not a better book I've read about adversity. It talks about how you can't control all the events in your life, but you can control your reaction to them. Having the capacity to control how you react to every situation is the measure of your strength. There are many remarkable books like that out there. I genuinely feel that part of your construction of character and strength is the way you make these stories a part of your own fabric. You should constantly seek out these kinds of things. I also feel you should not develop just one dimension. You should develop all your dimensions, and a part of your strength is going to be your balance.

To prevent the nihilism that seems to be the dark side of athletic success, your spirituality has to be nurtured. Regardless of any kind of success and construction of confidence and mentality, I try to make sure even our greatest athletes keep a humility about themselves. I feel it all ties in.

CHAPTER V
BEING COMPETITIVE

By Tim Nash

Which is more important to you, making friends or becoming the best player you possibly can? That's a dilemma many girls face as they attempt to advance to the next level. However, it doesn't have to be an either/or choice. You can do both.

"I remember growing up, I wanted to win, but not at all costs," says Carla Overbeck. "You had friends on the team, and you wanted everyone to like you. It was hard. It's part mentality and part process — just knowing that it's okay if you beat this person because you are trying to make her better. When I got to college, I certainly *wanted* to win, but I didn't win a one-v-one my entire freshman year. I had to learn, and I learned from the other players around me. When you see someone going after it in practice, it's contagious. When you see someone busting their hump, you want to do it too."

You can put a hard, clean tackle on your best friend and remain buddies. You can beat your teammate in a one-v-one drill and laugh about it later, and you can be beaten in a team-wide competition without ending up disliking your fellow players. This situation is a daily occurrence on the U.S. National Team, but at other levels, being popular often replaces being good.

One of the best examples of friendly, yet fierce, competition is the Tisha Venturini vs. Angela Kelly wars at University of North Carolina practices. Angela Kelly, a four-year team-mate and roommate of Tisha at Carolina, played for the Canadian National Team in the 1995 World Cup. For UNC, Tisha played attacking midfielder; Angie played defensive midfielder. In practices, they were frequently matched up against each other, often to the horror of their coach, Anson Dorrance. They would hammer each other to the point where Dorrance would cringe at every thunderous tackle or violent mid-air collision. He just knew a season-ending injury could occur at any moment.

"Lots of girls are afraid if they make a hard tackle they are going to make the other girl mad," says Tisha Venturini. "Or they're afraid if they score a goal, their teammates will get mad. But Ange and I are great friends. We went at each other hard, very hard. But with us, it was more about respect than anything else. We were going to work each other hard and not give the other one an easy way out. A lot of kids are ashamed of working their hardest, or afraid of winning. But we go out and try to make the other player work hard, and to do that, you have to give it your best. When we go against each other, we are like, 'I'm going to give you my best shot to help you out.'"

There is no substitute for intensity. The most effective training environment is the one where players are going game-speed, tackling hard and trying to win every single competition with which they are faced. April Heinrichs, the former captain of the U.S. National Team and an All-American at the University of North Carolina, was the ultimate practice player. Whenever she stepped on the field, she was there to win. Even in what some would call meaningless situations, April was competing like a world championship was riding on it, because in her mind, it was.

Along the way, she angered some of her teammates with her aggressiveness in practice. "Why is she playing so hard?" they thought. "It's just a practice." But April's play soon became the standard upon which the U.S. National Team was founded. "April refused to sacrifice her own level of excellence just to be popular and wonderfully mediocre," says her former coach, Anson Dorrance. "I admired her tremendously for that. She became the standard that we tried to live by."

You probably all know players like April, players who seem to give it their all and play all-out in seemingly meaningless situations. When you talk to your friends about these players, you usually say, "... but off the field, she's really nice." It boils down to setting standards for yourself and living by them.

"I think players have to be mature enough to understand that on the field it's okay to be a different person," says Cindy Parlow, who went to college as a 17-year-old. "It's okay to go in hard for a tackle, knock someone down and not help them back up. They have to realize that it's nothing personal. But off the field, you have to come back together again, be friends and forget about that tackle ... and maybe even joke about it. That's just the level of maturity that you have to have."

It is not an easy process to begin, but once you establish your standards, it becomes easier, and eventually second-nature. "I found it hard, especially when I came to Carolina," says Cindy. "I didn't know many of the players, so my first thought was to prove myself on the field, then people would respect me. I was very, very shy. I still am, and I didn't talk much. When I came to school, I think people might have taken my shyness as stand-offish or arrogant."

Laurie Schwoy had to prove herself almost immediately when she arrived at UNC. Much in the same way April Heinrichs did, Laurie established herself as someone who would not back down. "I was having a heading duel with a senior, and she said she won, but she really didn't," says Laurie. "So we had some controversy."

The easy thing for Laurie to do would have been to bow to the senior's popularity and sink back into the group of intimidated freshmen. She chose another way. "Anson asked me if she won, and I said 'No,'" remembers Laurie. "So we had another duel, and the whole team was chanting her name because she was the senior and I was the newcomer. It was scary, and I was nervous because they all wanted me to lose. They weren't pulling for me. But you just have to go for it, be bold and show your personality."

Laurie won the duel.

Photo by J. Brett Whitesell

USA Mentality

CHAPTER VI
USA MENTALITY

By Tony DiCicco

The USA mentality has many prongs to it. Certainly, the top criteria in establishing this mindset is for our players to understand we are going to out-work our opponent. We out-work our opponent because the work ethic tends to be a catalyst to release the special athletic and technical gifts our players have.

Part of the mentality is that we are going to make the game uncomfortable for the opponent by working hard on both sides of the ball. We get them in a game that's difficult for them to play. There have been games where our opponent has played very well against us, but at the end of the game, they have nothing left. We really try to take everything out of them. We try to play the game at a pace which they can't continually play for ninety minutes.

"Our work ethic — when we are together and when we are on our own — is amazing," says Kristine Lilly. "I think we have a bigger mental game than a lot of other teams. We have the mentality that we want something and we are going to work very hard to get it. We have a never-die mentality. It's kind of a stubbornness."

Photo by Colleen Hacker

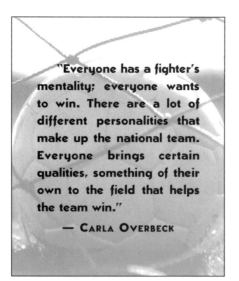

"Everyone has a fighter's mentality; everyone wants to win. There are a lot of different personalities that make up the national team. Everyone brings certain qualities, something of their own to the field that helps the team win."

— CARLA OVERBECK

Part of the USA mentality is that you're going to be matched up with one particular player, or different players in your zone. You have to establish your presence — or your dominance — in that zone. And our mentality is "How big is your zone?" Maybe you can be pretty dominant in a small area of the field. But our mentality is to keep stretching your zone, making it bigger and bigger, so that your zone and your teammate's zone start to overlap. Now we are dominating more of the field.

The mentality has to be something thick with resolve. It can't be an act or a facade. Sometimes your opponent is going to be every bit as good as you are. In that case, it becomes about which one of you is going to be able to survive ninety minutes of warfare. You have to be prepared to give more than just a display of power at the beginning with hopes that your opponent will cower to you. You have to be prepared to show your best and expect the opponent to fight back because they are strong as well.

So it's not just an initial veneer. It's more than that. It's a resolve to play hard for ninety minutes. It's about being beaten during the game and not giving in to your opponent's ability, but raising your level another notch. It's about telling yourself, "Good job, but let's see if I can play at this next level now." It's about being beaten on an individual play and not becoming a spectator. It's about sprinting back and maybe getting another chance to win the ball back. And it's about running with a teammate if somebody breaks in behind the defense. You can become a spectator and hope the ball doesn't go in the net, or you can make the run to get into that play. That's all part of the mentality. It's a conscientious effort that covers every aspect of the game.

Take a player like Kristine Lilly in the Olympic final against China. I don't know how many times we were beaten in the midfield, but at the top of the eighteen, she was still winning that ball back. She was always getting back and giving herself and the team another chance to win the ball back. That's why we won the Olympic gold. And Kristine's effort wasn't just because it was a big game. It's much deeper than that. It's a thick team commitment and resolve.

Every player wants to showcase themselves. That's why they are here at this level. They know they have something special, and they want to display it. Whether it's to family and friends or big crowds or just a few people. But the mentality goes beyond that. It goes to a team pride.

"Everybody on our team wants to be the best and to make the team the best," says Michelle Akers. "We are all committed to making those around us the best. I think that's a big part of it. Watching some teams play, it's clear that they are out there for themselves as individuals. Our team plays for their teammates, and that makes an incredible difference."

Our players are going to fight for their teammates. Not everybody is going to be on top of their game. Some players are going to be injured or struggling, or maybe they have a heck of a matchup with a very, very good player, and they are struggling to contain her. With team pride, her teammates can pick up a bit of that role by working a little harder, with the knowledge that someday the favor will be returned.

"There are a lot of different personalities that make up the national team," says Carla Overbeck. "Everyone brings certain qualities, something of their own to the field that helps the team win. Everyone on this team has a huge heart. It's like they'd die for you on the field and that's comforting. If you are having a bad game, you know they are going to pick up the slack because it has happened to them before. That is why I love those guys."

The USA Mentality is about playing lousy and still winning. There have been games where we struggled, and we knew we were struggling. We knew the game was below our standard. And we didn't just say, "We know that was a bad game. We'll be better next time." No, we fight through that game and win it. It's not fun to play in games like that, but we have to play as a team and figure out how to win. The mentality is being prepared to take physical risks ... and taking them. It's going in hard for every tackle, or sliding just to get a piece of the ball because maybe that touch will allow a teammate to do something productive with it.

You have to have self-confidence. You have to have a level of self-esteem that's going to be the foundation of the pride you are going to develop as a player. You also have to have pride in your fitness. We don't train fitness at the national team level. We test it. We want to see your fitness evolving. When you are away from this team, you have to be working on your fitness. And that doesn't mean just doing one exercise. It's aerobic fitness, anaerobic fitness. It's weight training. It's nutrition. You have to have pride in that, so when you come into this environment, you have self-confidence based on all the things you've done to be a better player physically.

As you go higher and higher up the pyramid, the talent pool is getting better and better. The margins between players are getting smaller and smaller. The best way to go into a try-out situation is to play as well as you can the first day. But you know the next day you are going to take it up another level, and the next day you take it to yet another level, and so on. And then, eventually, you are standing by yourselves. Everyone else has fallen off. Because they are so pleased with the way they played the first day, they thought, "If I keep playing this way, I'm going to make the team." No, it's the players who keep finding another level at which to play that will make the team. That's part of the mentality — always testing your limits and adding on to your game and simply becoming a better player.

"Players have to evaluate their strengths," says Carin Gabarra. "They all have one solid reason why they will make a team. You have to work on that one area because that's what makes you special. It may be that you tackle hard, or your work ethic, or finishing, heading or defending. It may be your attitude, or something else not directly related to soccer. If you are pretty good at everything, you might not stand out as much as someone else who is great at one or two things."

There are times when we play a game, travel, play another game, travel and play another game. We still have to win that third game. We can't be satisfied with the way we played the first day. You have to handle tryout situations the same way. You play the first day and hope you play well. If you don't play well, you have the mentality to turn it around the next day and get it going in the right direction. That's all part of your psychological training to get the most out of your game.

What is *not* the mentality? Well, it's not knowing how to motivate yourself, and I'm not talking about

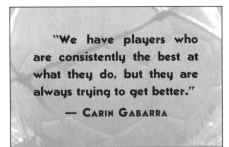

"We have players who are consistently the best at what they do, but they are always trying to get better."
— CARIN GABARRA

Photo by J. Brett Whitesell

motivating yourself to go out and train. The wrong mentality is taking an opponent lightly, and I've never respected that in athletes. In our situation, most of the teams we play are inferior to us, and that's not a knock on them. They are just in different stages of their development than we are. For us to take a team lightly is such a mistake. And that's not a mentality we can use. If one player has that mentality, ten other players have to work harder to make up for it. And they have to work twice as hard to eliminate it. If two players have that mentality, it's almost impossible to counteract it. If you take an opponent, yourself or your training too lightly, it's dangerous. If you do that too often and make excuses for it, it will just grow and grow and grow. It's just not something we can allow. Anyone who wants to play at elite levels can't have that kind of mentality. Look at Michael Jordan. He may be struggling at the beginning of the game, but you know at the end, if the game is on the line, he's going to be there. That's the mentality you want. You are not going to be perfect all the time. But can you say to yourself, "Hang in there. I know I'm having a tough day, but my team is going to need me in the eightieth or ninetieth minute." And you find a way.

Another very important part of the mentality is team chemistry — being part of the team, traveling together, living together, working together, training together, consideration for each other. Whether it's helping with baggage, or being a solid roommate for a person, being on time, or just being able to smile when you are tired and have traveled all night. If you are cranky and moaning, you are going to bring the whole team down. If you don't have the right mentality, you'd better be a pretty special player for the coach to stay with you.

I think one of the most important things for the United States is our leadership, and that's another component of the mentality. Some may lead in one aspect of their play. Maybe they have a long throw-in, that's a leadership role. Maybe they are vocal from the bench, or they take a leadership role with the reserves in practice. Maybe they are organizers on the field. Perhaps they are leaders by example. Everyone has to be on that continuum. If they are not, they have to find some way to take a leadership role.

If you look at our veteran players, they are honed and hard athletes. It's something that all our athletes need to embrace. And the message from our leadership is that if you want to play on this team, you have to be like this, too. And I see our young players getting that message. Some of the new players are already exhausted just being in this environment. On the first day, we do fitness, and I call it mentality training. It's really not fitness training. We show them right away that this is the mentality we have. We are going to out-work our opponent. We are always challenging our players. We challenge them in practice, we challenge them in games, in meetings, everywhere. That's how you develop that mentality. And it's what gives us an edge.

CHAPTER VII
COLLEEN HACKER
ONE OF A KIND SPORT PSYCHOLOGIST

We were fortunate to have a sport psychologist with us during our preparation and consistently through the Olympics, and Colleen Hacker was invaluable to us in winning the Gold Medal. Plain and simple, she's an absolute gem. For us, she was important for so many reasons. Certainly, she gave the players an objective, informed person to use as a sounding board. Her conversations with the players were entirely confidential, and that allowed the players to have freedom in expressing themselves.

Photo by Colleen Hacker

"You can choose to begin to work at any point," says Colleen Hacker, shown here with Carla Overbeck after the gold medal game.

> "She had a phenomenal sense of how to use her role to help us. The beauty of what Colleen did was that none of it was pre-fabricated. It's hard to step back and really give an unbiased opinion or compliment. We were all immersed in being a team-mate, being a part of U.S. Soccer, but she had a perspective none of us had."
>
> — TIFFANY ROBERTS

There are a lot of misconceptions about the role of a sport psychologist. People assume that a sport psychologist comes in to "fix" things, and that the players go through therapy sessions. That's certainly not the case with Colleen.

"Would someone say to Tony DiCicco, 'If the players don't know how to play soccer, then you help them, right?'" Colleen says. "These players aren't head cases. They are already mentally tough people. They are already disciplined. Some sport psychologists don't do very well because they come in and talk to them like they are kindergartners."

There is a stigma around the word "psychologist." There's an assumption that if there is a psychologist involved there must be something wrong. Colleen wasn't there to solve personal problems so much as to enhance performance. "Even now there is still this awkwardness mostly because of well-meaning people hanging around the team," says Colleen. "They say, 'Oh you're the team shrink?' Or one of the support staff persons calls you a "psychiatrist." I get all of those kinds of things. Another is 'So if they're having problems, you help them out?' Or, 'So, like if they start freaking out or choking, you help them?'"

Most elite athletes always believe they can improve. They believe they can learn new strategies and enhance their mental skills just like you would spend time on your technical skills or physical conditioning. Our philosophy toward our preparation is that if doing certain activities could help even one percent here and one percent there, it could be the margin of victory. It all matters.

"At first, some of the players were skeptical," says Michelle Akers. "I know I was. Because my dad is a shrink, I'm familiar with 'shrink tactics.' I was wary of her at first. I thought, 'How can this lady help our team?' Boy, was I surprised."

One of the first things Colleen did was erase all doubts and ease any apprehensions about having a psychologist as part of the staff. She earned our trust. It began during her first meeting with the team. We were in San Diego, at the ARCO Olympic Training Center. Colleen presented a wide range of options, a smorgasbord of psychological skills. Then she did a critical thing. She asked the players what they wanted and needed. "It was very, very important to me that athletes were in charge, in control," Colleen says. "My whole focus is to create a smorgasbord to put the things out there that I know to be helpful. No one knows better than the players what will help."

Colleen used the coaches and the players as her guides. She never imposed her own solution, but rather through constructing environments, through dialogue, or even the simplest of mediums, allowed us to arrive at the decisions or solutions we needed. "I literally made a commitment that the players were in charge, and I am proud and excited about that," says Colleen. "They controlled whether or not I was used, or how I would be used and when I would be used. With some sport psychologists, athletes have this feeling that they are being watched, being invaded — 'How are you doing today? — Quit asking me how I am doing!'"

The responsibility again rested with the athlete to utilize her services. The great thing about Colleen is that there is never a time limit. If you don't use her right away and then a year later think maybe you might try talking with her, that's fine.

Understanding and accepting your role on a team is important. Embracing it is even more important. It's vital for players to know what's expected of them. We wanted the Olympic team players to do what only they could do and do it to the best of their ability. Colleen helped the coaches define roles for the players and the staff. We came to appreciate every day what we had in each other and in ourselves.

"Colleen was a major factor in our winning the gold medal," says Kristine Lilly. "Everybody had a defined role, whether it was Shannon coming in for two minutes and scoring a goal, or if it was somebody sitting on the bench saying, 'I'm going to sit here and be supportive until it is my time to go in.' It helped everybody to be comfortable with everyone else on the team.

"The best thing she did for us, was all the team-building," adds Kristine. "It made us all equal. In the team-bonding exercises, we were all vulnerable. We were doing things for the first time, so nobody was good at any of them. Then when we get out on the field, everybody has their different strengths. For instance, Mia is a quicker dribbler than I am, and I would think, 'Gosh, why can't I do that?' But the team-bonding stuff we did showed us that we are all vulnerable in different ways, we all have our weaknesses. You just have to say, 'Okay, help them.' It was all about helping each other."

Many players and coaches feel team chemistry is an illusive quality, a stroke of luck. As if some teams have it, and some teams don't. That's true to some degree, but what players and coaches often don't realize is that they can contribute to the environment of the team. That they can affect positive or negative team chemistry. We believe it's an active process we invest in every day.

Most of you will not have access to a sport psychologist. Each skill discussed teaches you ways to improve on these aspects yourself. Find what works for you. It's important to recognize that psychological skills and your psychological state are tied into everything you do — how you train, your psychological hardness, your ability to correct a bad situation and your ability to play with confidence.

A DEFINING MOMENT

Colleen was at the Olympic team's residency camp three weeks before the Olympics. She had "*Colleen's Corner,*" where she posted thoughts, mental skills work and the time of a meeting on psychological skills for anyone who wanted to come. This one would be on imagery.

"These poor players have eight million things on their minds," Colleen says. "I mean, they are training five million hours a day, and they're exhausted. Imagine the environment! All they need is one more meeting. I don't care if it's a meeting on how to die rich, it's just one more thing being asked of them.

"Eleven people came! This was a wildly critical evolutionary marker for me. Eleven people came — nine of them starters. That was a defining moment. Who's asking for it? It's the people who have the world championship trophy from 1991, the most gifted — nine of eleven starters. Look at what that says. It ties into the philosophy about preparation — they were going to leave no stone unturned."

*"Mental skills, like physical skills,
can be learned and improved with
practice and systematic training."*
— *Colleen Hacker*

CHAPTER VIII
PSYCHOLOGICAL SKILLS TRAINING

By Colleen Hacker

Competitive athletes spend a great deal of time and energy training, honing and developing their bodies for competition. Every facet of conditioning, of technical refinement and of tactical sophistication is addressed through coaching, self-training and competitive experience. The four pillars of soccer — technical, tactical, physical and psychological — are well-known to any player or coach in this country. Our training sessions, however, seem to focus almost exclusively on the three pillars that comprise the physical dimension, those below the neck. Just as you train to perfect tactical and technical speed and ability, your mental abilities and attitudes require systematic training as well. The fact of the matter is that many of the greatest barriers to excellence on the soccer field aren't created by deficiencies in skill or knowledge. The greatest stumbling blocks are often the psychological barriers athletes impose on themselves. Mental skills, like physical skills, can be learned, developed and improved with practice and systematic training.

The ultimate goal of Psychological Skills Training (PST) is to help each athlete reach an optimal level of performance based on what is possible for that particular athlete. When members of our 1996 Olympic delegation were interviewed regarding what abilities and qualities they believed were most important for Olympic success, mental attributes were listed in the first five spots. In a distant sixth place came physical abilities. Heading the list was "mental toughness." No matter who is interviewed, men, women, world champions, or Olympic heroes, one idea consistently emerges, mental attitude separates champions from near-champions. Yogi Berra's famous quote reminds us that, "sport is ninety percent mental and fifty percent physical." You can fault his math but not his logic.

Increasingly, coaches and athletes at all competitive levels are using sport psychology to help them gain a competitive advantage in the sporting arena. Athletes want to know how to manage stress, control anxiety, build or maintain confidence, overcome adversity, deal with the challenges of injury and utilize imagery, goal-setting and productive thinking patterns. (1)

What is the Role of a Sport Psychologist?

How you personally respond to the sport psychologist working with your team or with you as an individual is a significant factor. It will influence the potential outcome of that working relationship. Do you feel comfortable talking with that person? Do you trust and respect their

WHO NEEDS IT AND WHEN?

Sport psychology is not just for "problem athletes" or "head cases" anymore. It's an essential part of training for every athlete, regardless of their age, sex or ability. Psychological Skills Training should be woven into every aspect of your soccer life including practices, conditioning, match analysis and competition.

Certainly, mental skills and mental toughness will not overcome the pitfalls of an ill-conceived game plan or poor technical skill or speed. Without question, however, what you think and how you feel affects how well you perform, how long and hard you train and ultimately, how successful you will be in your sport. Elite athletes realize that the challenges and demands of competition can sometimes have an adverse effect on their motivation, enjoyment and performance. See if any of these examples seem familiar to you:

1. Do you consistently perform better in one environment than another (better in practice, for example, than in games or vice-versa)?
2. Has nervousness or anxiety ever negatively affected your performance?
3. Has the discouragement following a poor performance in one game lingered so that you soon found yourself in an emotional or playing slump?
4. Do certain opponents, teams or venues psych you out?
5. Do you ever find yourself mechanically going through the motions at practice with little care or motivation?
6. Do you spend a great deal of time thinking and worrying about what has or might go wrong?
7. Do you compete to win and for the sheer love of competition, or simply not to lose or feel embarrassed?

If you can answer yes to any of these questions — and many more that could be listed regarding the psychology of competition — then you realize what a powerful tool the mind can be. Athletes must learn how to relax at appropriate times before, during and after competition. Otherwise, valuable energy is drained from the body and emotional energy is wasted on unproductive worry or fear. (2)

Athletes need the power of concentration and the ability to stay focused on what they are doing in practices and in games. Just like being at your physical peak for competition, athletes need to learn how to be at their peak mentally. They must learn to get psyched up but not psyched out. Athletes must also learn how to deal with failure, injury and adversity.

When PST is used along with technical, tactical and physical training, then the full capacities of the athlete are being developed. When all four pillars of soccer are consistently addressed, remarkable breakthroughs in performance will not be far behind.

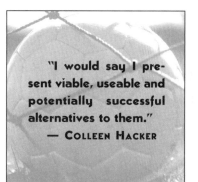

"I would say I present viable, useable and potentially successful alternatives to them."
— COLLEEN HACKER

knowledge of you, of your sport and of the competitive process? Can you be honest, relaxed and open with this person? Does the sport psychologist mirror the values and work ethic of you as a player and of your team? Does the sport psychologist understand your sport and the unique demands that it places on performers? Also critical is an on-going relationship and trust developed over time. Without question, the single best piece of homework you can do is to check credentials and follow up with personal references from team, sport governing bodies or individual athletes.

Here is a partial list of some of the more common functions of sport psychologists:

1. Development of performance enhancement programs

2. Utilization of psychological assessment techniques

3. Problem intervention services and consulting services for athletes, coaches, trainers and others who work directly with athletes

In the following sections of this chapter, several of the most commonly used psychological strategies for peak performance will be discussed. A brief definition of each technique will be followed by a practical application section listing specific and simple exercises you can do on your own or with your team.

Imagery

In order to understand the powerful effect that imagery has on performance, you need to understand two important principles. First, when you are relaxed and vividly imaging — even for a short period of time — your mind and body cannot tell the difference between what is real and what is being vividly imagined. When you clearly picture yourself performing a soccer skill, your brain sends out signals to your muscles. And without any apparent movement, your body is actually being trained, and your brain is storing that information as if it actually happened. The second principle essential for understanding imagery is that our attitudes and habits of thinking develop from the thoughts we have most frequently. In essence, we become what we think about most often.

Research tells us that approximately ninety-two to ninety-nine percent of Olympic athletes report using imagery for competitive preparation. Imagery can be used to learn and practice new skills and strategies, to rehabilitate from injury, to prepare for competition and to help analyze performance afterwards. It can be used with other psychological skills and to improve communication and other interpersonal skills. Imagery doesn't take much time. In fact, there is good evidence that the beneficial effects of imagery can be experienced with as little as ten minutes of rehearsal per day. We know that imaging a skill, or a tactical game plan often facilitates performance. In some cases, it can be almost as effective as physical practice. (3)

1. Athletes can image before performing and during competition. In fact, using imagery in competition may help keep athletes focused on their event, feel more confident about their performance and experience a greater sense of control of their emotions and level of arousal. (4)

2. Athletes who use imagery are more likely to set winning as a goal and see themselves achieving this goal. This belief may help them to practice longer and harder and give them that extra bit of energy during competition. Confident athletes use more mastery (coping successfully with challenging situations, handling the stress and excitement of competitions, remaining calm), performance imagery (giving 100 percent effort) and have better kinesthetic imagery ability than less confident athletes.(5) (6)

3. Athletes who use imagery experience a greater sense of confidence, a feeling of control and a greater ability to focus. Coaches and athletes must understand, however, that imagery is most beneficial as an adjunct to training not a replacement for skill or actual physical practice. Imagery also exerts a powerful motivational effect in that athletes see themselves winning rather than losing and successfully performing as they would prefer to perform. Elite athletes are as likely to image externally (seeing themselves as a camera would, in the third person) as internally (imaging through ones' own eyes).

Application

1. Start out simple. Gradually increase the complexity of the imagery training. For example: start out imaging a circle, then a square and then a triangle. Learn to hold that image without distracting thoughts or losing concentration for one full minute. After you are able to successfully control that image, then change the color of each object. Perhaps a red triangle followed by a blue square, etc.

   Images should be vivid and under your control. Next, picture yourself executing a simple and familiar skill, like dribbling. Again, control the image so that you can now "see" yourself faking an opponent, shielding the ball with hard physical contact and kicking the ball to a teammate or past the keeper into the back of the net.

2. Imagery is enhanced if preceded by some form of relaxation. Initially, you may need to lay quietly in a dark room and systematically relax each major muscle group prior to imagery. Later, with practice, you will be able to effectively image with just a full, single belly breath.

3. Practice imagery outside the competitive environment before you use it in a game or at practice. Image in the morning when you wake up or at night before you go to sleep. Then, practice imagery before practice and eventually within a training session. Before long, you will be able to image effectively before a contest and even within a critical game. After all, that's the environment when we most need to utilize our psychological skills.

4. Images should be positive, realistic and done in moving pictures.

5. Imagery is enhanced if you can utilize all of your senses. For example, see the crowd, teammates and your opponents. Feel the touch of the ball on your cleats, chest, foot, or wherever. Try to hear the noise in the stadium or field and the sounds of coaches, spectators and other players. Taste the salty sweat on your lips and recall the familiar smell of a freshly cut pitch. It is important that you feel the skill, movement and/or emotion that accompanies the focus of the particular imagery session. Skilled athletes have tremendous kinesthetic ability in their sport. They know the feel of a good first touch without looking or without someone else having to tell them how they performed.

6. Use "trigger words" to match your images and emotions. For example, "slice and dice" for eluding defenders off a dribble, or "like a rocket" for a description of a powerful shot on goal.

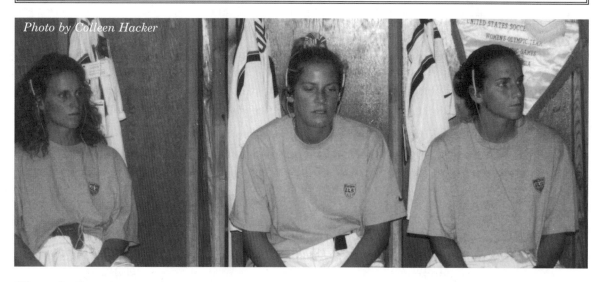

Photo by Colleen Hacker

Olympic Imagery

One of Colleen Hacker's most appreciated contributions to the Olympic team was making audio and video tapes for the players. "She made an audio tape for me," says Kristine Lilly. "It was how I wanted to picture myself on the field. It was music that I liked and she spoke on it about confidence and wanting the ball. I would listen to it before every game, and if I was lacking confidence it built me right back up. That played a huge role in my game. Sometimes at my position, I go stretches where I don't get the ball. Then I'd start thinking, 'When I get the ball I can't mess up because it's my only chance.' So I had to balance that."

The video portion of Colleen's tape production also served to make the players more confident. "The tape she made for me was cool," says Carla Overbeck. "She picked songs we liked and added clips of things that we did well. She said, 'Now watch this on your own.' But we'd have a party at our house — Foudy would watch hers, then Carin, then Lil, then me. It was fun."

Goal-Setting

Goal-setting is one of the most consistently utilized psychological and behavioral training tools in any Psychological Skills Training program. We frequently refer to goal-setting as the "Staircase to Success." The top of the stairs is our ultimate destination and the goals we set along the way are the step-by-step path we follow to get there. Goals create a focus of attention toward which we direct our energies and effort. A tremendous amount of research supports the value of goal-setting in enhancing athletic performance. (7)

Goals can increase our persistence at a task in the face of adversity. They can increase our focus and motivation. Goals can also lead to more effective and efficient practice sessions, to greater feelings of pride in accomplishment, greater feelings of self-confidence and heightened intrinsic motivation. Goals help alleviate boredom and increase our likelihood of both achieving and enjoying the activity.

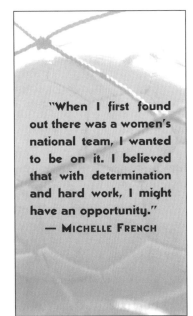

"When I first found out there was a women's national team, I wanted to be on it. I believed that with determination and hard work, I might have an opportunity."
— MICHELLE FRENCH

Studies with athletes consistently reveal that specific, challenging and realistic goals lead to higher levels of performance than "do your best" goals or no goals at all. Goals need to be difficult but optimally challenging and realistic. Unrealistic goals should be avoided. If goals are too difficult and continued failure occurs, motivation can be expected to drop and performance deteriorate. Generally, goals can be classified as either outcome or process goals. Outcome goals are product measures of success based on the scoreboard or other external measures of success.

The problem with outcome goals is that the athlete only has partial (or no) control over these. In other words, I could set an outcome goal to score ten goals this season but because of stellar goalkeeper saves, I might only score eight. Performance goals are based on process measures of success, and they are goals over which the athlete has virtually complete control.

DREAM BIG

"A lot of young kids are afraid they have a dream that's too big. Scoring five goals in a season is an easy dream to realize, and it's easy to admit to yourself that five goals is your goal. But the dream of being an Olympic athlete ... a lot of kids are afraid to admit that, because most won't get there. That's what really helped me. I actually admitted to myself that I had that dream. That was a big part. When you're young, you say, 'Yeah I'll be there,' because you don't really understand the risks involved. It was, and still is, worthwhile.

"What keeps me going year after year? You have to take little steps to get there. It is like a swimmer who wants to shave five seconds off their time. They cannot just jump in the pool and get there. They have to realize how many laps they are going to have to swim to get those five seconds off. Over the course of years, you can break it down into steps. It's not the million laps it would take, it's the little steps that help you make it."

— JEN GRUBB

So, if I want to improve my scoring chances, I might set a performance goal to take an additional 100 shots with my right and left foot every week of practice for the entire season. Performance goals also have the benefit of increasing the likelihood of outcome goals being met even though that is not the primary focus. In other words, by taking 200 more shots per week, I am more likely to score goals than I would have without that practice. Players should aim to set at least three or four performance goals for every related outcome goal that is set. Players can set goals to improve technical ability through increased practice time or repetitions. Their goal could be to improve conditioning through specific days of lifting weights or decreasing times in fitness tests, or their goal could be to improve psychological skills by committing to specific PST principles on certain days of the week, times at practice or minutes each day.

The following goal-setting guidelines are aimed at providing athletes and coaches the necessary steps required to reap maximum benefits in team or individual performance:

1. Goals must be objective, measurable and visually identifiable. That is, athletes should be able to measure distance, score, time, accuracy and observable behaviors performed.

2. Athletes should set their own, individual goals, and these must be important and meaningful to them rather than done to please parents, coaches, trainers, etc.

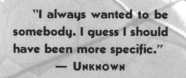

"I always wanted to be somebody. I guess I should have been more specific."
— UNKNOWN

GOAL-SETTING PROBLEMS

The most common problems in goal-setting are:

1. Setting too many goals in too short a time
2. Setting general rather than specific goals
3. Setting outcome rather than performance goals
4. Failing to write the goals down and to elicit social support for their accomplishment
5. Failure to monitor and update goals based on individual level of performance and potential for improvement

3. Goals should focus on what the athlete can control performance goals rather than outcome.

4. Goals should focus primarily on individual rather than team performance. Again, the athletes have more control over themselves than over their teammates or coaches.

5. Goals must specify a particular standard of proficiency to be accomplished in a specified time.

6. Players should set proximal (this day or this week) and distal goals (this year, my career).

7. Goals should be difficult, but realistic and attainable, with effort and persistence.

8. Goals should be stated positively in terms of behavior or accomplishments that the athlete wants to achieve rather than behaviors to avoid or stop.

9. Athletes should write their goals down (not just think or say them) and they should solicit social support from at least one other person who knows and supports their specific goals.

10. Goals need to be evaluated and adjusted. Accountability should be taken to maximize their effectiveness.

Self Talk

Players can't perform their best when they're berating themselves or dwelling on past mistakes. Also, an athlete must be fully engaged in the moment and not worrying about what may happen down the road. Attention is strange. You can't perform optimally while you're concentrating on concentrating. Ideal performance occurs when attention is effortless.

Many players simply do not realize that they are likely to be in constant dialogue with themselves as they play, especially when they're performing poorly or have recently made a mistake. Often our attention shifts from the task at hand to self-defeating statements about our errors or ineptness. If you aren't already aware of your own internal dialogue, monitor your own self-talk patterns at practice or in games. Is it helpful, positive and conducive to good performance? Would you talk the same way to a teammate under those same circumstances?

And, what would the effect be if you did? Here are some guidelines to follow:

1. Focus on positive self-statements, not negative.

2. Focus your thoughts on the present, not the past or future.

3. Instead of focusing on results or outcomes, focus on relaxing and letting your body take over.

4. Focus on statements that are aimed at improving your self-confidence and increasing your expectations for ideal performance.

5. Focus only on the details and parameters over which you have control, not on external people or things over which you have partial or no control. Exercise your most powerful choice: The power to control your own thoughts! Make a concerted effort to carry yourself — your external appearance — the way you want to feel even though it may not reflect how you are actually feeling at the moment. Productive emotional responses are learned behaviors and they take time and

STAYING READY

Shannon MacMillan can look back and smile now, but it wasn't all that easy on July 28, 1996 in Athens, Ga.

Shannon was on the bench, watching a nail-biting Olympic semifinal between Norway and the United States. She was itching to get in the game.

"Like ten times, someone would go down or would be limping, and Tony would say, 'MacMillan warm up.'" Shannon recalls. "And then he'd say, 'Okay sit down.' First of all, it was frustrating watching my team gut it out when I wasn't out there doing my part. I was just saying to myself 'Just give me a chance.' The game was so intense, and I would get up and get psyched up and then sit down ... up, down, up, down, up, down."

With the game tied 1-1 in sudden-death overtime, Shannon finally entered the game.

"The hardest part about coming off the bench is finding the game and getting your touch," she says. "I still remember my first touch was down in the corner and the ball just bounced off my knee. After my first touch, I said, 'That's just not going to do it.'"

Shannon didn't bury herself because of her bad first touch. Her brief dialogue served to re-focus her. And that was all the self-talking she needed to do. Her next touch on the ball ended the game. She drilled a shot past the Norwegian keeper and sent the USA into the gold medal match.

Making Dreams Come True

By Tim Nash

When Tiffany Roberts was in the third grade, her teacher gave the class an assignment — draw a picture about your "best dream." Tiffany gave it some thought and decided she wanted to be an Olympic gold medalist. Actually, she decided she wanted to win three gold medals. So she drew a picture of herself standing on the medal platform with three gold medals hanging round her neck.

"I think setting goals is huge." Tiffany says. "I set my goals at a very young age. That's where it started — knowing what I wanted and doing everything in my power to get it."

Active in a variety of sports at the time, Tiffany became enthralled with the Olympics on TV. "My dad was a great athlete and my older brothers played sports all the time," says Tiffany. "My dad got me playing soccer when I was five or six. Plus, all the kids in our neighborhood were guys, so I was always playing football in the street and stuff like that. I was involved in gymnastics as well. I didn't see soccer on TV, but I played it, so I wanted to be in the Olympics in track, gymnastics and soccer. I just thought it was so cool that Mary-Lou Retton played a sport, and because she was so good at it, she got to be on TV."

Tiffany made a rapid rise through the Olympic Development Program and suddenly found herself as a member of the U.S. Women's National Team. "It all happened so fast," she says. "A month before I was brought into the national team when I was 16, I was reviewing tapes of the 1991 World Cup with my high school coach. He was showing me what kind of player I could be. Then a month later, I was being pulled up to play with that same team. I always believed that with a lot of hard work and determination, I could someday be on the national team, but I didn't think it would happen so fast. The national team and the Olympics were consistently on my mind.

"My first camp with the national team was a complete shock," Tiff adds. "It was the end of the inter-regional tournament in Florida. They were picking the U-20 national team to stay over another week, and Clive Charles, the U-20 coach then, said, 'Tiffany, you've been asked to stay over another week, but you're going with the women's team.' I thought he made a mistake. I thought he meant the U-20 team. I had to go back to him and say, 'Wait ... can you repeat what you said?' And he brought me to Anson and totally embarrassed me. He said, 'She just wants to make sure that she really is going to camp with you guys.' Anson just looked at me and said, 'You're with the big girls now.' And I just said, 'Okay ... thanks.'

"I drove with Lauren from Boca Raton to Ft. Lauderdale. She was just trying to make me feel comfortable, telling me what camp was going to be like, because I had no clue. I was thinking, 'Do I have enough clothes for another week?' So when they started handing out gear to me, I was like 'Wow! This is pretty cool!'"

Tiffany played for the USA in the 1995 Women's World Cup and earned a spot on the 1996 Olympic team. As the Olympics grew closer, Tiff began to realize she was going to get her chance at a gold medal. For three weeks leading up to the gold medal game, Tiff watched on TV as Olympians in other sports received gold medals. Without fail, tears filled her eyes as athlete after athlete received their medals. As she watched, she told anyone who would listen, "In three weeks that could be me!" When the moment finally came, the tears did not.

"I couldn't believe that!" she says. "Not a tear came out. It was just an unbelievable experience, especially at my age. Now what am I gonna do? I guess I'm gonna have to set more goals for my life. Maybe I should get started on the track and gymnastics medals."

practice to perfect. Mental toughness will help you avoid panicking when things get difficult or crazy. It will keep you calm and focused in adverse situations and in big game moments. It will allow you to persevere with confidence and resolve when the battle appears to be lost. You will keep fighting when others are ready to quit. The tougher your opponent, the more you will love the challenge.

You will exude confidence and strength and a passionate belief that the tougher the competition, the more you love the opportunity to compete. You will radiate confidence, poise and persistence.

Controlling "The Jitters"

Almost all athletes experience pre-game nervousness to some extent. The heart beats a bit faster and your mind is aware that something special is about to take place. A certain amount of anxiety and a feeling of readiness is critical for optimal performance. These feelings should be expected and welcomed.

Athletes should and must learn to control their anxiety and emotions, rather than allowing the body and mind to control them. An individual in control of their anxiety is more likely to be performing in the zone of optimal performance. The benefits include greater sensitivity and control of the body and mind. They experience less localized muscular tension, improved recovery rate, more conducive conditions for the onset of sleep, appropriate muscular tension to delay the onset of fatigue and a training supplement to other psychological attributes such as imagery and self-confidence.

> ## GAINING A MENTAL EDGE
>
> Colleen showed us that thinking is critical. Critical thinking is even more critical. Brandi Chastain explains it well when she says the psychological skills the team learned from Colleen Hacker weren't used because something was wrong, but because something could be even better.
>
> "Prior to Colleen coming in, I don't think we understood how important having someone like her was," says Brandi. "Then, when we got her, we thought why haven't we had her the whole time. It's not a case where we didn't understand the psychological dimension, it's that we didn't get everything out of it that we could. She helped us be better critical thinkers, be better self-evaluators. Being in the right frame of mind really can make or break your performance for that day."

Application

1. Find a safe and quiet place where you will not be distracted for fifteen to twenty minutes and assume a comfortable position sitting or lying down with your eyes closed.

2. Focus on your breathing by placing one hand (with the palm open) on your belly and the other (palm open) on your upper chest. Feel the rise and fall of your chest and stomach.

3. Consciously inhale slowly and exhale even more slowly. As you inhale, begin to concentrate on making the breath originate and end with your belly. Your belly should expand when you inhale and retract when you exhale.

4. Relaxed and controlled breathing occurs from the stomach while anxious and stressful breathing occurs from the chest (the chest would rise and fall with each inhalation and exhalation). When athletes become stressed, their breathing becomes more rapid, shallow and from the chest. Efficient breathing is deep, slow, quiet and regular.

5. Practice controlling your breathing (belly breathing for relaxation) quietly and alone at first. Then, try to calm your breathing in other stressful situations, for example when driving on the highway or in a difficult interpersonal situation that causes you anxiety. Gradually, and with practice and time, you will be able to control your anxiety in pressure-filled situations by controlling your breathing.

6. Practice rhythmic breathing in which the inhales last half as long as the exhales, meaning if you inhale on a count of four, you should exhale to a count of eight. Find the proper one-to-two ratio for yourself.

7. Practice "count to five" breathing in which you say the number "five" to yourself on the inhalation and then on the exhalation say "I am more relaxed now than I was before" and continue that process with four, three, two, and then one.

Performance Preparation

One of the most important and often overlooked elements of psychological skills training is the development of an effective pre-game preparation strategy. Athletes train for every situation they might face in soccer but neglect the unique time and opportunity that pre-game preparation affords.

Often it is the importance of the game, the crowd or some other external event that most influences an athlete's pre-game mood and focus rather than the athlete themselves. Confident athletes know they have trained hard and well for competition and they enter contests in control of their own thoughts and feelings. Before events, they are free from negative thoughts and worries and are not distracted by outside variables. They are activated but not anxiety-ridden. They are focused and ready.

Your pre-game routine will take time to develop and should reflect your personality, needs and unique characteristics. Although highly individualized, an effective pre-game routine should have several important elements:

1. You should clearly have identified the common characteristics of your previous best performances. What were you thinking, feeling and doing? Not doing? What words, images and descriptions would you use to describe your ideal pre-game state? Have you considered your food intake, and timing? The travel to and from the field? Have you thought about your general physical warmup time and your sport-specific training? What are the psychological characteristics that coincide with these behaviors? What will you be doing, thinking, saying and feeling in the last few minutes before the start of the match and what about the first few minutes of the game?

2. All of these situations should be described and defined in detail. You want to be in control. You want to be able to make the necessary adjustments if you are not at the exact physical, emotional or psychological state most conducive to optimal performance. Remember, self-responsibility and self-control are the goals and the essential skills needed for optimal performance.

3. Develop realistic, positive and meaningful self statements that describe how you feel or want to feel for today's performance. These statements should be based on real strengths that you have identified. Be extremely specific.

4. You need to develop a thought-stopping strategy when negative or worrisome thoughts enter your mind and replace those with constructive, powerful, performance-enhancing ones. Your self statements should generally be in the present tense, and should reflect preparedness, commitment, ability, adaptability and resolve.

5. You should engage in a brief mental rehearsal of your game plan both individually and team-wise. The key is to develop a feeling of greatness, preparation and ability to successfully execute the skills necessary for victory.

6. You must implement this procedure constantly and faithfully and not just employ it prior to the "big game" or critical matches. Your pre-game preparation is as integral to the game as is your touch of the ball or runs in support of teammates.

7. Combine previous best performance characteristics with specific phrases, behavior, focus cues and mental images of success. This routine should be written down at first including times, actual phrases and images.

8. Engage in "best friend" communication by talking to yourself with the same language and the same energy and support that you would use with your best friend or teammate under the same circumstances.

9. View failures or temporary setbacks as learning experiences and motivational incentives. Failure is necessary for ultimate triumph and is certainly not fatal. Note the error, extract the lesson, make corrections and move on. Move on physically, emotionally and mentally.

What Can You Do on Your Own?

Unfortunately, many athletes approach the practice and game environments with very different attitudes. Practices are often something to "get through," to endure and to finish as quickly and as painlessly as possible, rather than critical performance opportunities to create, develop and perfect. Games, on the other hand, are the reward, "show time" and filled with emotion, anticipation and excitement.

The familiar adage "practice makes permanent" rings as true for psychological skills training as it does for technical and tactical skills training. If you want to be a big game performer, consistently replicate that performance standard over and over and over throughout the practice environment. If the only real pressure an athlete faces is on competition day, then dealing with competitive pressure, anxiety and do or die feelings will not be well-practiced. If you give yourself multiple attempts to get an important skill right in practice, day after day and week after week, then you will not be training properly (psychological training) for the demands of competition.

Periodically, athletes should create pressure situations in practice that exactly replicate both the demands and the consequences of competition. You don't get to take three penalty kicks in a row and record how many you scored out of three. In a game you only get one (an all-important *one*) chance. Re-create that pressure in practice. You don't get to dribble from the mid-stripe line and take ten shots on goal to see how many you can make in a game. In fact, you may get only one or two chances the entire match. Coping successfully with adversity and failure is also a critical skill for top level soccer players.

Create and re-create that kind of pressure in practice. Learn to cope with that kind of pressure and those types of demands. For example, simulate game conditions occasionally in order to practice and refine effective pre-game and in-game strategies. In this way, you can practice under more game-like conditions and monitor how well you respond under those conditions. An additional advantage of this simulation training is that you can develop specific and personalized competition plans for enhancing performance.

Olympic Performers

No matter how talented or experienced you are, almost all athletes experience self doubts and, at times, lose confidence, feel the beginnings of burn out, a loss of motivation or experience the effects of having their emotions hurt rather than facilitate performance. Olympic athletes are no different. As a sport psychologist for the U.S. Women's Olympic Team, it was imperative that I knew the athletes as players and as people. I talked to athletes individually about what they thought, felt and did when they were playing well and performing as they liked and expected to perform.

Because these athletes are constantly striving for ways to refine and to perfect their game in all areas, they are the first to know when they are not performing at optimal levels. Unlike many recreational athletes, these players approach their sport with professional commitment and resolve. They want to "get it right" and they are willing to do the work necessary to make it happen.

A few of the specific psychological skills that we utilized with the Olympians in 1996 included imagery, distraction control, energizing techniques, sleep inducement strategies, goal setting, attention and concentration control, thought stoppage, interpersonal communication techniques, anxiety control strategies, self-confidence enhancement, mental preparation for tactical demands and requirements and team building exercises.

> "A situation like playing in the Olympics is very intense. There is a lot of pressure from within and outside. With Colleen, we had someone we could go to and talk to personally. That was very important. She was there to help, and that was nice to know. Our team really benefited from her being there. She was not the type of sport psychologist who is going to try to analyze you. She is very positive."
> — CARLA OVERBECK

Photo by Colleen Hacker

COLLEEN HACKER'S OPTIMAL PERSONAL PERFORMANCE TIPS

There are other simple techniques that you can use to help you achieve a more consistent degree of optimal personal performance. Some of these include:

1. Listen to music that stimulates your feelings of competing well, strong and successfully. Ideally, you should combine listening to your own personal music tape while imaging yourself performing in an actual game or on the practice field. Listening to your tape three to four times per week will help you form a strong and powerful association between the music and your desired ideal performance state.

2. Create your own imagery video tape by filming your last several matches and editing important clips that capture how you want to look, feel and perform on the soccer field. It is not a performance evaluation tape. The goal is not to critique, analyze or alter your performance.

   Rather, the video should elicit feelings of control, confidence and success. As you watch the video, you should try to re-create all the sensations and emotions that you would be feeling on the soccer field as if you were actually engaged in the activity. Some players prefer to have music during the video while others prefer it to be quiet with only the visual pictures available.

3. Practice the power of positive thinking. It is the one area of your life where you can exercise complete control. Positive thinking does not necessarily result in competitive success, but negative thinking almost always results in poorer performance and more negative expectations.

   Mentally tough athletes have learned to gain control over their thoughts so that when they experience negative thoughts or emotions they are able to both stop and replace those images with more positive, success-oriented thinking. Instead of trying to change negative thinking behavior, try replacing it. Use positive, present tense affirmations that convey, with great conviction, your belief in yourself, in your abilities and in your chances of successfully executing the action at hand.

Frequently, after talking with players and hearing the issues they faced, we worked together to create a script that was eventually recorded onto an audio-tape. The script lasted anywhere from five to eight minutes and was individually designed with each athlete's personal style, needs issues and language in mind. Some tapes included music in the background, some were interspersed with quotes or belief statements from the athletes themselves, and others recorded thoughts or phrases associated with a peak or previous best performance. Athletes were guided to picture things exactly as they would like to see them happen. They were realistic and detailed. Sometimes athletes would see and hear their thoughts about a great play, handling a referee's bad call or a teammate's error. In each instance, they would mentally, visually and emotionally rehearse what they want to have happen.

Additionally, we (Lauren, April and myself) created imagery tapes of each athlete aimed at reinforcing the myriad of skills, tactical demands and performance expectations for that player. These tapes also lasted approximately five to seven minutes and utilized the musical preference of each athlete. Again, each tape was specially geared to the unique characteristics of that particular player. Athletes were asked to view the tapes alone at least five days each week. Some were created to enhance self-confidence, some to imprint a particular game focus, some to concentrate on energy, and belief in teammates and still others dealt with coping with physical play or positive expectations.

Finally, we developed trigger words, phrases or actions for different athletes to focus their attention and reinforce their commitment to a particular psychological skill that an athlete was working on. Some of these techniques were developed from an athlete's own idiosyncrasies, such as pulling their socks up when they need to pull up more energy in the game, picking up a piece of turf and tossing it away to symbolize letting go of a negative thought or belief, or looking for a particular color on the field to trigger a refocusing on the mental game plan. The point is, each technique was developed in consultation with a specific athlete and individually tailored to her particular personality, needs and temperament. There was no one technique applied to every member of the team. Rather, the focus was on individuality and specificity.

Throughout this chapter, I have outlined the framework and rationale for implementing a Psychological Skills Training Program. See Appendix D for further summary and additional references. (8) There is no question that the program will work. The only question now is, are you willing to work the program? The time to start is now.

Photo by Colleen Hacker

A golden moment for Julie Foudy

Physical Section

"Mentally, it makes you tougher and stronger knowing you can run past or run more than any team you face."
— ***Carla Overbeck***

CHAPTER I
FITNESS IS YOUR RESPONSIBILITY

The most important aspect of fitness is to accept responsibility for it. Once you realize that you're responsible for your own fitness, you need to begin by understanding the process of getting fit. The great thing about conditioning is that you can determine how fit you are. It's very empowering to master your body and mind, and the knowledge and the habits you create will serve you for a lifetime. Fitness is a foundation from which anything becomes possible.

"The first time I came into camp I was a freshman in college, and I failed the fitness test," remembers Sara Whalen. "I had no idea what to expect. I thought I was fit, but it was not this level of fitness. I wasted a lot of time that week. From day one, I had no confidence. There are so many points of the game that you should be working on, you shouldn't be wasting your time in camp trying to get fit. I came in fit next time and did great. I passed everything, and I felt great. I was confident, and I could concentrate on playing."

It's critical to have a consistent and committed approach to your conditioning. You're in it for the long haul, and it isn't always easy or fun. We term this year-round, year-after-year approach to your conditioning "fitness-basing." Fitness-basing is a process that does not occur overnight or in a few weeks. Short-term fitness gains are shallow and can lead to injury. The rewards of being fit are tremendous. Everything becomes easier with a good fitness-base, and confidence is perhaps the most significant gain. Being fit can give you a huge psychological advantage. You can look at your opponents and know you have out-worked them in your preparation. "Fitness certainly is an aspect of your game that you need very much," says Carla Overbeck. "We are always determined to be the fittest team at any tournament."

It's a phenomenal source of confidence for an individual player as well as a team. "Mentally, it makes you tougher and stronger, knowing you can run past or run more than any team you face," says Carla. "Or maybe in the last few minutes when you are losing, your fitness is going to carry you and provide confidence, give you that extra edge or the winning goal."

The leadership of the national team has created an expectation — almost a culture — regarding our fitness standards. National team players train out of respect for their teammates. They would never want to let each other down. You need to work to set the standards for your team.

"When I think of our leadership, I think of Overbeck, Foudy, Lilly, Hamm, Chastain, Akers, Fawcett, Venturini," Tony DiCicco says. "All of them are very, very concerned with their fitness. When we do fitness, guess what? All the top players are at the top of the fitness ladder. If you are a young player coming on to our team, you won't see Mia Hamm down at the bottom of the fitness ladder. Players you have read about and looked up to are among the fittest. And fitness isn't getting fit for the season. Fitness is a life-long endeavor. That's why triathletes are not people who are just out of college. There is a layering process that has taken place."

Fitness isn't fun for most people. Becoming fit can be a very demanding process and presents us with huge challenges. The easy part is that you are in control. You are capable of becoming fit and staying fit. The hard part is when your mind comes into play. When you are training on your own, it's you versus yourself. Or in a match, it's you versus your opponent. This is part of what we term the psychological dimension of a player.

"A huge part of fitness is mental," says Laurie Schwoy. "In college, we know we are going to do fitness every Tuesday, and all day in class we look like zombies because we are dreading it. It's all psychological, and that's where a lot of girls fold."

Psychological hardness comes into play on two different levels. The first is your willingness and commitment to endure the physical pain of conditioning. Second, a measure of your mentality shows when your fitness is tested. Some players pass fitness tests because they are fit. Some players will pass because they are reasonably fit and psychologically hard and can rise above the pain and push themselves to pass. Some players fail because they are not fit, and a fourth group fails because they give in to the test itself even though they are fit enough to pass. It just hurts too much.

This section of the book will provide you with a basic understanding of the main components of the physical side of the game. First, let's list the main aspects of physical conditioning: both aerobic and anaerobic conditioning; strength and flexibility; speed and explosiveness; agility and balance. We will provide in-depth discussion on each of these aspects, as well as provide you with training tips in each area. The Physical Section also provides you with sample foundation conditioning programs we have used with clubs, regional teams, collegiate programs and our youth and full national teams. It will also include sample physical tests you can do, as well as standards from all levels to measure the soccer-related physical dimensions of your game.

First, we need to cover the different types of conditioning programs. We will bring you through a basic running program that addresses both types of physical demands — aerobic and anaerobic. Aerobic training is a steady-state, low-intensity, longer-duration type of activity. Anaerobic training is shorter in duration and more intense. The type of running players do in a soccer game is not entirely one or the other, but rather some aerobic, some anaerobic and some combination of each. Fartlek training, a variation on interval training, is a term used to describe a conditioning method that involves periods of short, more intense work around periods of longer, less intense work.

The chapter on strength training provides you with an understanding of the basic muscle groups utilized as a soccer player. Steve Slain, our strength and conditioning coach for the 1996 Olympic team and co-founder of Sport Specific Training Group in Orlando, Fla., will discuss the tenets of weight training and provide a foundation strength program that can be utilized with adequate supervision and at the appropriate ages. For many of you, there is not an opportunity to get into a weight room for a myriad of reasons. We understand that, so we have outlined creative ways to improve your strength and overall muscle conditioning that can be equally as effective.

The chapter, The Recovery Process, offers a broad spectrum of ways to both replenish your energy stores as well as regenerate your physical and psychological well-being. We've identified four potential areas you can address to enhance your body's ability to recover from training and maximize your performance state: stretching and massage, cross-training, periodization (the role of balancing your training within a season, as well as, a year-round schedule), and nutrition.

In the nutrition chapter, Dr. Doug Brown, our national team physician, talks about nutrition as a training tool. It could be one of the most important chapters in the whole book. Good nutrition may have life-long health benefits. So why not start the habit now? You can control how well you eat through what you eat. Do not underestimate the value of good nutritional habits. I know many of you feel invincible, and you think it doesn't matter what you eat. It does. We felt Doc Brown's attention to this aspect of our training gave us an edge in reaching our goals of becoming not only the best women's soccer players, but the best team in the world.

The sports medicine chapter will be familiar to everyone. All of us who have played the game have incurred injury. Dr. Mark Adams, our Olympic team physician, played an important role in our winning the gold medal. He provides you with insights into injury prevention, management and rehabilitation. Injuries should not be time off or a period of down time. Through stories from the doctors, as well as athletes, you will see that you can stay fit and become a better soccer player, even without running or touching a ball, while recovering from injury.

While we hope to provide you with a better understanding of your body and knowledge of the most common injury treatments and rehabilitation, please realize this is in no way a substitute for being evaluated by your own sports medicine physician and rehabilitating with a sports physical therapist.

We want you to embrace the notion that fitness is within your control. We want to show you how to take responsibility for your physical development, as you do in all aspects of becoming a soccer champion. It's our goal to educate you on the main physical components of a soccer player and how to train and develop in each area. Setting markers and being able to test and evaluate your progress becomes important in realizing your goal. For your comparison, we've included many testing options for each of the main physical components, as well as standards from all levels. Further information is provided in Appendix C — Supplemental Conditioning Options. Training guides, self-tests and training logs are provided in Appendix B.

I hope this information will empower you to take responsibility and become the best athlete you can be. The guides will help you take steps toward this end. Work hard. Start now and stay with it.

Listen to your body — *Exercise at an appropriate level. Training examples in this book are based upon the standards of elite athletes, and they are intended for fit people in reasonably good health. Be sure to have a pre-participation medical evaluation by your physician before beginning any physical conditioning program. If you experience any unusual discomfort or symptoms while training, stop immediately, and consult with your coach, parents and physician — even if you have already had a pre-participation medical evaluation. The symptoms may be a sign of an underlying medical condition that warrants attention.*

Carla Overbeck, a world-class soccer player and athlete, created a culture of fitness excellence.

Photo by Mike Stahlschmidt

CHAPTER II
CONDITIONING

The two basic types of conditioning you need to address in your fitness program are called aerobic and anaerobic. These are conditioning methods that differ in how they utilize oxygen. Anaerobic occurs with insufficient oxygen in the muscles. Aerobic training utilizes oxygen to produce energy.

Aerobic training is the endurance component. It's your conditioning base. It involves longer, more steady-state activities. For example, a twenty-minute run will help you "cruise" up and down the field. Anaerobic refers to shorter, more explosive activity like a twenty-yard burst to get by a defender. A simple way of evaluating your anaerobic conditioning is to judge your ability to sprint at or near your maximum as often as you need throughout the match with as little recovery time as possible. If you make a sprint and then need to walk or rest for significant periods of time, you might not be there yet.

It's important to lay down a good foundation. Remember the deeper the foundation, the greater structure you can build on it. So you want to have a good endurance base first. Remember, the endurance aspect is the aerobic training, and it involves more distance running. But you can't start out running four miles if you

Photo by J. Brett Whitesell

haven't done anything in a few months. It's a process. Performing too much work before you are ready will result in an injury. Do not expect to get fit overnight. If you move through the program too quickly you will not go as far. We recommend any physical program you undertake be overseen by a coach or a trainer. Prior to beginning any program or a season you should have a "pre-participation" physical. Dr. Mark Adams discusses the importance of this exam in Chapter X — Sports Medicine for the Elite Female Soccer Athlete.

Since there are different types of running needed as a soccer player, you must train them all. The game becomes a balance between sprinting, cruising, jogging, walking and recovering. It doesn't do you any good to only be able to go for a twenty- or thirty-minute run. Soccer fitness is about your ability to recovery quickly from performing an activity, and then be able to do it again. And you can train recovery. You need to be able to perform work — either a sprint, or a cruise — and go again. That's the key to being a fit soccer player.

> "Being the fittest people out there is something in which our whole team takes pride. And it's something you don't need anybody to help you with. You can do it all by yourself."
> — CARLA OVERBECK

> "The important moments are not necessarily when we are on the field with the coach, but what we are doing when we are not with the team."
> — SHANNON MACMILLAN

Fartlek training has some higher intensity segments mixed into the run. It's both aerobic and anaerobic. It contains duration, intensity, and recovery. You determine how much work and how much rest you get. For example, start your regular run. When you feel comfortable, increase your running pace for some distance, maybe to the second telephone pole or mailbox. When you reach the pole, slow back down to the speed at which you think you were running before you picked up the pace. When you have recovered from the first harder run, do it again. Pick out a landmark, increase your pace, then slow down to the pace at which you think you were running before the harder pace. As your fitness improves, those slower-paced portions of the run will actually be getting faster and faster and the number of faster runs during your workout will become more frequent and more intense.

Photo by MiniPros Sports

Fitness testing is both a physical and psychological challenge.

Can you sprint as often as you need with as little recovery as possible? In games, if you find yourself avoiding a run or hiding on the field because you are too tired, chances are you are not fit enough and need to train your ability to recover.

Foundation Aerobic Conditioning Program

There is a quick checklist you should go over before you get started: Always adequately warmup by stretching and easing into any activity; make sure you have good shoes; make sure you are hydrated (drink some water before you go). Once you break a sweat from your warmup, you are ready to begin the more intense portion of the workout.

Sample Aerobic Program

1. To get started, jog for twenty to thirty minutes, ideally on a soft surface. For ages fourteen to sixteen, jog for twenty minutes; thirty minutes for high school and college ages.
   Repeat this a few days a week.
2. If you are too sore the day after you run, wait until the next day to go again.
3. Continue this jogging at a comfortable pace for a number of weeks. A comfortable pace is one where you can carry on a conversation without getting breathless.
4. Your goal should be to jog four to five days per week.
5. After a few weeks, you can add Fartlek training. For example, on a twenty-minute run, at every five-minute mark increase your pace for thirty to forty-five seconds.
6. As you develop a base, start timing yourself or measuring your distance.
7. To ensure you are training hard, try to beat your time for two or three miles each time you run. Or if you are running for twenty minutes, see if you can go a little bit farther each time.
8. As your base is established over this first month, you can add in more Fartlek training. If you were running three days a week, one run could remain a distance run and make the other two Fartlek runs.
9. When you are doing a Fartlek run, go from a continuous jog to a run which is some where in between a jog and a sprint. It's a marvelously effective but under-used method of training.

Foundation Anaerobic/Aerobic Training Program

This program can be started after a minimum of three weeks and a maximum of six weeks depending on your base when you started working on the aerobic program. The anaerobic and aerobic phase is a combination of both activities.

In this phase, you will do shorter distance work and more sprint work. It can be done two ways. You may run a shorter distance, say two miles at a certain pace, and then run a series of more intense runs. For example two times around a quarter-mile track at a good pace. Now you need a watch to track your pace with two to three minutes rest in between each. Or you may incorporate the distance and the intervals into one activity.

Sample Anaerobic/Aerobic Program

1. Review checklist before beginning.
2. Adequately warmup before beginning any activity. Stretch, have water available and wear good shoes.
3. Based on your fitness, you will select a number of days a week to work on a mix of aerobic and anaerobic activity. If you have followed the foundation program, you should be running four or five days per week.
4. Start when the second hand of your watch reaches the top, then run as far as you can in fifteen seconds. (Probably 80-100 yards is likely; a grass football field is a good place to do these next two programs because of the yard markers.)
5. Take forty-five seconds to walk to the other side of the football field.
6. When the second hand comes to the top again, you start ready or not.
7. Run for fifteen seconds to the other end of the field.
8. When fifteen seconds is up, you have forty-five seconds to get back to where you started. So you are working for fifteen seconds and resting for forty-five, or a one-to-three ratio.
9. Start by doing six to eight of these. Rest for five minutes, then repeat.
10. Once you can do two sets of six to eight, three or four days a week, go to one set of fifteen.
11. It's easy to lose track, so remember to look at your watch when you start. Ten minutes of clock time means you have done ten runs.

> "The first time I came in with the national team, in 1987, I did pretty well. Then we didn't have another camp for five months, and I was just awful. It seemed like I couldn't do anything. It was all related to my fitness. On the college and club teams I played for at that time, I really didn't have to worry about fitness. I was just told, 'Stand up here, get the ball and score.' But with the national team, the majority of what I needed to do required being fit. I started working on my anaerobic fitness, because that's the kind of player I am — sprint, jog, sprint, jog."
>
> — CARIN GABARRA

It may look like this:

Week One:	2 sets x 8 runs
Week Two:	1 set x 15 runs
Week Three:	2 x 10; decrease rest in between
Week Four:	1 x 20 runs

If you want to do more, add another 10 runs the next week.

Second Example: Here is an interval program which I introduced several years ago to each level I coach. It involves a similar philosophy, but has a greater emphasis on training the recovery process.

▲ Run from one end of the field to the other as fast as you can (our standard for 120-yard field is a 17-19 second range).

▲ Give yourself thirty seconds to jog back to where you started. This requires that you are recovering at a higher intensity than if there was not a standard to meet. The idea behind this is to work early in the game to get into position so you are rested when you are required to work intensely again.

▲ Then, take thirty more seconds at the starting line before you repeat.

▲ Repeat the above six to eight times; rest and repeat.

▲ After a few weeks go to one set of ten to twelve.

▲ Add extra rest on number three, six and eight. Extra rest is fifteen seconds.

I like to use this method when training players for a lot of reasons. First, it trains the primary running state — the cruise. Second, it trains your ability to recover. Say you are playing flank midfielder in a match, and you just made a sprint to get at the end of a cross. The goalkeeper comes out and catches the cross. Guess what? You have to get in gear and get back into position.

For this very reason, we set a maximum time to return to the origin of your run. Then we allow a rest period. This means you will be more rested and ready when you must perform work again. It's what I call work early, then rest.

FIVE SPEEDS OF SOCCER

Don Kirkendall, a sports exercise physiologist formerly at Duke University and now at the University of North Carolina at Chapel Hill, works with our national teams. He has studied the demands of the game for the female soccer player.

Understanding the demands is important to help you train what the game requires of you. Dr. Kirkendall points out that the game is generally divided into five speeds:

1. **Walking:** Two-thirds of the game is spent walking or jogging.

2. **Jogging:** Two-thirds of the game is spent walking or jogging.

3. **Sprinting:** 800 to 1000 meters out of six miles, or a half-mile out of six miles is spent sprinting in multiple sprints of ten to forty or so yards.

4. **Cruise:** One-and-a-half miles is spent cruising.

5. **Backwards:** Small amount

The important thing to understand about these training concepts is that you train your ability to run at a particular speed and lower. In other words, if you train at a jog you get proficient at a jog and at walking. If you train at a cruise, you get good at a cruise and walking and jogging. So you say, I'll train at a cruise to improve my ability to cruise and jog and walk.

---

*"I have to be position-specific with my training.
Now that I'm in midfield, I do less of my
sprint program and more shuttle runs."
— Michelle Akers*

CHAPTER III
POSITION-SPECIFIC FITNESS TRAINING

As you mature as a player, you will be asked to play certain positions. You will accept that assignment and do everything you can to be as good as you can be in that position. What we have come to realize is that players in different positions have specific physical demands. Forwards, for example, need to have speed, quickness and the ability to accelerate. Understanding the physical requirements of the position you play can give you information about how you need to train.

Midfielders need tremendous stamina and endurance, as well as the ability to change direction. Julie Foudy, for example, can cruise all day. Michelle Akers, a forward in the 1991 World Cup, played in the midfield on the Olympic team. She recalls how her physical training changed as a result of playing a new position. "I learned I have to be position-specific with my training now," Michelle says. "Now that I'm in midfield, I do less of my sprint program and more shuttle runs."

Goalkeepers, obviously, have different demands than field players. Their movements are often very powerful and explosive. So, in addition to having base endurance, they need to train for their position as well. Some goalkeepers use this as an excuse not to have an overall fitness level equivalent to that of field players, saying they don't need to do the running. Be careful. Goalkeepers need tremendous local muscle endurance and power. While the chapter on goalkeepers addresses more specifically the types of training keepers need to do, I love that our goalkeepers pride themselves in being fit, period. Tracy Ducar is a very fit and dedicated athlete, soccer player and goalkeeper. She talks about the responsibility she feels towards this aspect of her game.

"I look at my fitness a little differently than a lot of goalkeepers do," Tracy says. "I would prefer myself to be as fit as the field players. Part of that reasoning is a confidence factor. It helps me feel ready — more than ready — for anything that comes up. I get tired of hearing field players say, 'Oh you don't have to do the fitness we have to do.' So I try to get myself to their fitness level. Close at least. I'm not going to be as fit as Carla, but I want to be close. So that means I'm going to do 120s on my own, and cones on my own, usually once a week. I will also do my plyometrics — jumping over the ball or jumping over boxes in the weight room. I think it's important that the field players see the goalkeepers working hard.

"We do need to do a lot of goalkeeper-specific fitness, but there is no reason why keepers can't be as fit as the field players," Tracy Ducar adds. "We do a lot of pressure training (see Goalkeeping Section), which is a lot of up and down stuff we need to make a save or get to a rebound. We also do a lot of leg work. Then we get the field players saying, 'I wouldn't want to do that.' It's just a different type of fitness."

Briana Scurry also notes that a goalkeeper must find the balance in her training that will maximize her ability to do her job — keep balls out of the back of the net. "A lot of it is speed work and agility," Bri says. "For our position, being able to jump quickly and get up off the ground quickly is key. The longest distance run you should do is about two miles. When you run long distance, you are training a muscle fiber that you don't really want to train for the goalkeeper position. You are training the wrong (slow twitch) fibers, and this may hinder you."

This is the same message Carla Overbeck offers when discussing her efforts to improve her overall speed. Spending too much time on distance will develop the muscle fibers that are called "slow twitch." The shorter, more explosive movements or runs are facilitated by "fast twitch" muscle fibers. The type of training you do will develop one or the other or both to varying degrees. Does that mean you shouldn't go out for a long run if you feel like it? Of course not. But be sensitive to what season you are in, what the demands of your position are, and what you are hoping to accomplish. It's the appropriate balance in your training that's important.

Photo by Phil Stephens

Kate Sobrero secured a starting spot on the 1999 World Cup team and is emerging as one of the best defenders in the world.

CHANGE OF DIRECTION

The ability to change direction is critical in soccer. Consequently, in your physical training be careful not to do only straight ahead conditioning.

As a collegiate coach, I would always know who had done enough playing and soccer-specific training over the summer. The players that had done pure "running" as a primary means of preparing for pre-season were very sore because they hadn't used the muscles needed to play soccer. They hadn't trained the ability to change direction, to accelerate and decelerate. Ideally, playing in competitive games has to be a consistent part of your preparation. Otherwise, you must perform the sport-specific movements to train the muscles required to play soccer.

"I feel my strengths are my acceleration and changing directions," says Mia Hamm. "A lot of the Coerver moves combine both of those things — high-speed change of direction and quick acceleration after one or two touches.

When changing directions, you need to be able to have your body in a position to either control the ball, or receive the ball to burst past an opponent.

"When you change directions quickly, it's important to be in control of your body, and that's something I have just recently learned," says Michelle Akers. "I've learned that I'm a flailer. I flail everywhere. When I stop, I'm off-balance and my arms are flying all over the place. I should be together, staying compact in one unit. That way, I can effectively go in another direction and move efficiently.

"Being a flailer has probably been why I got injured so much," adds Michelle. "When you are off-balance and in contact with another player, bad things are going to happen. So I'm learning to not flail. If you watch Kristine Lilly, she's not a flailer. She is always in balance and ready to move. She's never flailing around. Joy's the same way."

Tiffeny Milbrett changes direction with great balance and low center of gravity.

Photo by J. Brett Whitesell

*"After weight training for a few weeks, I felt I could
get to the ball or to a tackle quicker because
I was a little stronger and a little faster."*
— *Tiffeny Milbrett*

CHAPTER IV
STRENGTH TRAINING

The benefits of strength training, as you will discover throughout this section, are enormous. It should be considered a supplemental conditioning tool. Our players weight train to tone, strengthen and improve explosive power. And strength training serves a very important role in injury prevention. In some instances, it may factor into less severe injuries. Strength training also can play a critical role in the recovery process and your confidence on the field.

"You feel strong, and you feel confident," says Carla Overbeck of weight training. "You know if you are going up for a header, or if someone is running at you in the eighty-ninth minute, you are going to be able to win the header or track that run. Mentality and confidence are certainly what soccer is all about."

While an immediate benefit of weight training is improved strength, a very important by-product of it is that you feel stronger, as well. "Strength training has helped me a great deal ... absolutely," says Lorrie Fair, who, at five-foot-three, is one of the smaller players on the national team. "It also has given me confidence to know I can go up against bigger people, because I know I might be stronger. A lot of it is your momentum, because momentum is all about body mass and your speed together. One helps the other in your overall performance."

Photo by Colleen Hacker

Push-ups are an easy way to work on your upper-body strength.

Some young players are still skeptical of weight training. Maybe some of you have been told that soccer players don't need to lift weights, or that you will get too bulky. "There is no need to be scared or worried," says Tiffeny Milbrett. "After weight training for a few weeks, I felt I could get to the ball or to a tackle quicker because I was a little stronger and a little faster. And even if I am not, I feel better because I've worked my body in ways that it wouldn't have been worked if I hadn't weight trained."

Where you are in terms of your season — in-season versus your off-season —determines what types of weight training you should do. For example, in-season you should be doing less strength training and more of a maintenance program. Conversely, in the off-season, when you have more time for your muscles to regenerate, you can afford to do more strength work. When you weight train hard, you actually break down your muscles, and they need time to rebuild. Rest is important to building strength, power and endurance.

"A mistake I made when I first started weight training was I wasn't cycling my workouts," says Michelle Akers. "I was doing the same workout throughout the year. I was doing high reps and low weights. In the off-season, I needed to build bulk with low reps, and during my busy time (in-season), I should lift lighter just to maintain. I was busting with low weight and a lot of reps the entire time."

The essence of any weight-training program is overloading your muscles in a controlled manner to cause them to break down. It is in their repair and rebuilding that gains are made. "Another mistake I made was that I didn't understand that your rest days are when you build your muscles back," says Michelle. "When you lift, you are tearing your muscles down, and when you rest you are building them back up. I was constantly tearing them down, and not giving them time to build back up. That's why I still schedule in my rest days."

Remember, any strength-training program should always be designed and overseen by a strength and conditioning coach.

THE MAJOR MUSCLE GROUPS TO TRAIN:

Upper Body Muscles

1. **Chest:** These muscles allow you to push.

2. **Biceps:** These are located on the front side of your upper arm. They allow you to pull up your lower arm. They contribute to your ability to use your arms in running and holding players off the ball.

3. **Triceps:** Triceps are on the opposite side of your arm from the biceps. They work in the opposite fashion to your biceps. These muscles allow you to extend your elbow and are very helpful in holding off players.

4. **Lats:** These are found underneath your arms along the sides of your body. They give your upper-body strength and contribute to your trunk strength.

Upper-body strength is an important tool for a soccer player. Have you ever been out for a period of time, or not played a game for a while, and when you came back you noticed how sore your upper arms were? This is from getting hit by your opponent's arms as they try to hold you off, or from your trying to hold them off the ball. Goalkeepers must have the strength to go up to catch and hold a cross in a crowd. All players can use upper-body strength to their advantage.

Muscles of the Lower Body

1. **Hamstrings:** These are the large muscles behind the back of your upper leg. They help you sprint. In sprinters, these muscles are very strong. They pull your heel to your butt.

2. **Quadriceps:** These are also called thigh muscles. They are very important in kicking. There are four muscles that make up the quadriceps, hence the name.

3. **Hip adductors/hip abductors:** These muscles pull your legs together or apart. The adductors are the muscles that pull together (my trick to remembering that is you "add" numbers together). The abductors allow you to bring your leg away from your body.

4. **Hip Extensors/Hip Flexors:** These muscles allow you to swing your leg forward and back. The extensors allow you to extend your leg back, as when preparing to kick a ball, you cock your leg back. Hip flexors are the muscles that bring the leg through when you kick the ball and follow through.

5. **Gluteals:** These are your butt muscles. They are power muscles. Gluts help you make the connection between your back and hamstrings and are vital for jumping, balance and overall stability.

6. **Calves:** These are the large muscles in the back of your lower leg. These are important in going up and down on your toes. They also help point your toe down when shooting.

Lower-body strength training is important in injury prevention and layering in your endurance base. If trained properly, lower-body muscles can improve explosive movements. In soccer, the ability to explode and your ability to accelerate — your first step — are critical to beating players.

Core Muscle Group

Your core muscles, abdominals (front and side) and lower back, are very important to balance and agility. This is sometimes referred to as trunk stability. Sometimes as a result of an injury, you have to re-learn or re-train your muscles. Certainly, balance and your trunk strength often are lost due to injury and being off the field. Michelle Akers, who has overcome many injuries and has had to miss a great deal of time with a chronic illness, epitomizes what it means to train your body to be a soccer player. She has learned to pay close attention to her core muscles.

"I think every soccer player forgets about their abdominals," says Michelle. "For me, being sick for so long, I realized that my skeletal muscles would weaken if I didn't play. Getting injured affords you the opportunity to step back and look at why you might be getting injured, in what areas you are weak. And then you can strengthen those areas."

Equally important to gaining strength through weight training is understanding how to use your strength. I have seen some very strong players not use their body well and some players with less strength dominate physically. Translating your strength into effective play becomes important. Forwards and defenders are often fighting each other off to either hold possession or regain possession of the ball. Cindy Parlow, Mia Hamm, Tiffeny Milbrett, and Danielle Fotopoulos, all front-runners, invested in their weight-training programs. They felt it significantly improved their game and helped them deal with the demands of their position at the highest level. Mia is the best one-v-one player in the world and opponents will stop at nothing to slow her down. She has players constantly hanging on her, pulling her, pushing her.

Danielle, who suffered an ACL injury in 1997, is a strong front-runner who our defenders struggle to knock off the ball during training. She brings a new dimension to our front line and challenges our defense much like playing against the Norwegian attack.

"Weight training has been huge for me," says Danielle. "My size and strength are my strong suits, so I have to be sure to do weight training. It's helped in a lot of areas. One is injuries. Other than my knee injury, I don't really get big injuries that would keep me out for a long time. I think weight training is responsible for that. It keeps your body toned, and it makes you feel good, knowing you've done everything you can."

In addition to having definite practical applications, strength training, like fitness, can give you confidence. Tiffeny Milbrett who had not traditionally been a player who did much weight training, discovered many different benefits when she began to train the physical dimension of her game. Not only did she feel stronger but she gained confidence from this investment in her body. "I had been one of those who hadn't lifted weights," says Tifffeny. "I did it for about two weeks, and I felt it helped a great deal. For me, it wasn't so much that it helped my confidence, but it nourished my body in ways that it hadn't been nourished. At my base, I was solid. I was strong."

Speed and explosiveness can also be maximized through some types of strength training. There are strength-training programs that utilize upper- and lower-body muscles groups, as well as back and trunk muscles. Two great success stories are Carla Overbeck and Cindy Parlow. Carla did an extensive off-season program, including a series of free weight techniques which are beyond the scope of this book. By itself, the free-weight program Carla uses would not be enough. But she combined it with her sprint-series workouts and a modification in the amount of distance running she did. The result was her position on our national team speed ladder improved eight places, meaning she out-raced eight players she previously could not beat when speed was tested at national team training camps. Carla will describe this process in Chapter VI — Speed Training, later in this section.

It's mandatory for a player at any level, including the highest level, to have a person whose expertise is in strength and conditioning design the actual program. If you have access to a weight room at your school or at a health club, make use of their personnel. Many of you will not have access to full-fledged facilities, and we will address how you can be on a strength program using your body weight and innovative exercises to accomplish many of the same goals.

I remember growing up as we headed off to weight train, my mom and dad would say, "You know, if you did some yard work, you would be just as well off." Actually, there is some truth to that, and we will share tips on how to accomplish similar physical gains after we have explained the foundation strength program.

CHAPTER V

WEIGHT TRAINING AND FLEXIBILITY IN THE YOUNG ATHLETE

By Steve Slain

Steve Slain was our strength and conditioning coach, as well as our massage therapist, for several years, including 1996 when we won the Olympic Gold Medal. His role was tremendously important in ensuring that we maximized our conditioning. He tailored programs to fit individual needs, helped players recover through attention to flexibility and stretching, which is an important adjunct to strength training. One additional role was to help us coordinate all aspects of our preparation from a conditioning end. We would talk about the intensity levels of practices, when to taper, when to rest, and how to balance everything so we minimized injury and maximized our development. He was a factor in our gold medal, for sure.

Two of the most overlooked and misused components of training are weight-resistance training and flexibility. When I was working with the women's national team, I noticed a deficiency in proper and consistent weight training. If I could see it with that group, I know it's also the case for some of you. I'm sure not all of you are getting the proper information.

At whatever level you are competing, it's important to have an understanding of the demands of the sport on your body. That's why a consistent weight-resistance training program is important. Unfortunately, a lot of you do not begin a weight program until you are rehabilitating from an injury. Weight training won't stop you from getting injured. But with a good foundation in weights, your injury might not be as serious. And, most importantly, you will recover faster.

You may have been told that you shouldn't weight train because it won't help you, or it will slow you down. Well, ask Michelle Akers, Mia Hamm, Carla Overbeck or Julie Foudy how important a consistent and proper weight-training program has been in their careers.

What are the benefits of a properly prescribed and supervised weight-resistance program?
1. Increased muscular strength
2. Increased muscular endurance
3. Increased flexibility
4. Increased confidence on the field
5. Decreased risk of serious injury and faster recovery from injury

You may ask how old you should be before beginning a weight-resistance program? It has been documented by scientific and medical authorities that children should be encouraged to participate in weight-resistance training. However, my biggest concern is that you may be getting the wrong information. For example, you may be getting your information from muscle magazines or from the guy at the local gym. You cannot just go to a club or gym and begin to lift.

The young athlete should focus on body weight exercises, like push-ups, sit-ups, lunges and pull-ups. They should develop their cardiovascular fitness using calisthenics and games. Resistance training for these athletes should place a high emphasis on technique. Fitness fun and exercise should be the young athlete's primary goal.

Once you as an athlete have a clear understanding of technique using body weight only, and when you have a good foundation of flexibility training, then proper progression and continued supervision are critical to adjust to your improving needs. I can't stress enough the importance of supervision. We supervise our Olympic athletes, so you, too, should be under qualified supervision. In addition, before starting any physical training, you should be checked by your physician, or a certified sports physician.

Tisha Venturini balances her strength and conditioning program with flexibility training.

Photo by Frank Hogan

Factors that should be considered before starting a weight-training program are:

1. Am I ready to participate in a weight-training program? Have I had a physical?
2. What is the right program for me?
3. Do I have someone that can supervise me in lifting techniques and design the program suited for me?
4. Do I have access to equipment that fits me and is appropriate for my needs?
5. Is my program designed to address in a balanced fashion my cardiovascular, strength and flexibility needs?
6. Do I have a good understanding of safety and the proper usage for each piece of equipment in my program?

Once you have a good foundation of technique in all lifts, and once you have been on a consistent basic exercise program using body weight only, then you can progress to the number of exercises and start adding some resistance to the exercises, like stretch cords. Make sure you build in the appropriate recovery time and concentrate on good technique.

It's vital to have a good foundation before going into the weight room. You must have a foundation in body weight exercises, be confident in your form and techniques. In high school and some college-level environments, the weight rooms are not user-friendly for female athletes. I have encountered players at all levels who have been mistreated, and at times, intimidated in these environments. Do not jeopardize yourself.

Weight training, if done properly, can extend your career as an athlete. We want you to feel confident walking into a weight room, not intimidated. As with the other aspects of your training program, consistency and commitment are very crucial.

Foundation Strength Program

This program is designed for the younger, or beginner athlete. It works mainly on upper-body weight-resistance training exercises in order to develop muscular strength and endurance.

Many of these basic exercises can be done without weights or machines, or when you are traveling and do not have access to a facility. You should do this program three times per week — Monday-Wednesday-Friday, or Tuesday-Thursday-Saturday — or two times per week — Monday-Thursday, or Tuesday-Friday. You may do one-to-three sets of exercises, starting with one set and progressing to three sets as your fitness level improves.

A "repetition" is the number of times a weight is lifted. A "set" is the completion of a designated number of repetitions. Be sure to breathe, always breathe! Breathe out during the most difficult part of the exercise. Breathe in during the easiest part of the exercise. Make breathing as natural as possible. Don't force it.

Basic Body Weight Exercises

1. **Push-ups**   1-3 sets of maximum repetitions
2. **Pull-ups***   1-3 sets (4-6 reps)
3. **Squats**   1-3 sets (10-15 reps) can use body weight or a broom stick
4. **Step-ups**   1-3 sets (10-15 reps) with each leg to start
5. **Abdominal crunches**   1-3 sets of maximum (50 max)
6. **Rotary crunches**   2-3 sets (15 reps)

* In the beginning, if you are having trouble getting up to the bar or doing many repetitions, begin with what are called "negatives." A negative is when you do the exercise with gravity instead of against it, making it easier. For example, when doing a pull-up, start in the up position and lower yourself down.

Once you have mastered the basic Foundation Fitness Program, you can move to the more advanced program. This basic circuit was one that was utilized by the women's national team, while they were in camp. The basic circuit incorporates an overall body workout and should be performed two-to-three times per week.

When using machines or free weights, always start with a weight that you can perform for twelve repetitions with perfect form. Once you have performed two sets of twelve repetitions in perfect form, you can increase the weight. The increase should be conservative weight as to not compromise your form and technique.

Some points to remember:

▲ Never lift alone. Always have a partner.

▲ Never try any one rep maximum weight.

▲ Take your time, don't rush and sacrifice quality.

▲ Don't compete with your partner, be encouraging.

▲ Be patient; be consistent.

Advanced Program

1.	Front lunges	2 x 12
2.	Side lunges	2 x 12
3.	Step-ups	2 x 12
4.	Standing heel raises	2 x 12
5.	Hamstring curls	2 x 12
6.	Lat pull downs	2 x 12
7.	Chest press	2 x 12
8.	Shoulder press	2 x 12
9.	Lateral shoulder raises	2 x 12
10.	Biceps curl	2 x 12
11.	Triceps pushdown or kickbacks	2 x 12
12.	Abdominals	5 x 25

* Pull-ups	2-3 sets of max
* Dips	2-3 sets of max

* Start with negative movement until you feel strong enough to do the whole range.

As you build your foundation in weight training, you can progress to more advanced exercises. Building a base is very important, so it's important not to move too quickly, especially at younger ages when your bones are still growing. Then, move up from there. Remember to utilize people who are certified in the strength and conditioning areas — certified athletic trainers or physical therapists — to get answers to any questions or specific needs you may have.

Being on a properly designed functional weight-training program for soccer increases performance and reduces the chances of injury. The performance increases will be in strength, speed, power and flexibility. In addition, the confidence you will gain from these improvements in your play may help take your game to the next level.

Photo by Colleen Hacker

Katey Fawcett (top) helps Kristine Lilly (left) and Julie Foudy (right) do their push-up routine.

INNOVATIVE STRENGTHENING IDEAS

Some of you might say, "I don't have access to weight-training facilities." If that's the case, you may have to be more innovative to secure a similar benefit to what you felt you needed or wanted from weight training.

The following are a few ways you can strength-train away from your team without any devices.

Photo by Colleen Hacker

You can always do **sit-ups** and **push-ups**. Do as many as you can of each. Rest and repeat. Sit-ups and trunk exercises are important to develop your core and you do not need a weight room.

For explosive leg training, you can do a series of **jumps**: Jump over a box or some other barrier. Do sets front to back, and side to side. Another great exercise is where you start in a squat with the ball, then jump up and reach the ball as high as you can while you jump as high as you can. Go back down and repeat.

Other "**jumps**" can also improve your leg strength such as V-jumps, tuck jumps, and split leap jumps. Sets of **one-legged hops, or double leg jumps.** Excellent for your calf muscles and quadriceps.

Biking on a hilly course or **running a hilly course** can develop leg strength. **Jumping rope** is a good cardiovascular as well as local muscle endurance and quickness workout. Step-ups, lunges and other body weight-resistance activities can be done to create a strength work-out. Coervers done for explosiveness can also help serve as an alternative for lower-body weight training, change of direction and agility.

Running stadium stairs is good for leg power. You can run on each step or every other step. You can use **rubber tubing** to do all kinds of upper and lower body strength work.

As Steve mentioned, you can do many different body weight exercises. **Wall sits**, for example, are great for your quadriceps. This is where you sit with your back against the wall and your legs out at a ninety-degree angle. Do it for as long as you can hold it, maybe starting out at thirty seconds. With time and practice, you will feel your legs get stronger and be able to hold the sitting position for longer and longer periods. Then, try resting and repeating it.

BE CREATIVE!

CHAPTER VI
SPEED TRAINING

Carla Overbeck is a tremendous example of how you can improve and maximize your speed. As we discussed in the strength chapter, there were several aspects of her training that contributed to her speed gains. Certainly, her strength and explosive power was a factor. She also explains that changing the types of fitness conditioning she did was vital. And lastly, the addition of speed work and incorporating form-running into her program contributed greatly to her increased speed.

"I think a mistake I made in college and even a little bit after college was that I was running long distances," says Carla. "I like to run, so I would run four or five miles a day every day. What I didn't know was running the same pace all the time was making me slower. I wasn't that fast to begin with, and I'm still not that fast. I didn't realize that same-pace running was making me slower because it was working different muscle fibers. After I learned that, I changed my routine a little bit and actually got faster. When I run now, I don't stay at the same pace. I might sprint hills or do some kind of Fartlek training.

"They say you can increase your speed ten percent," adds Carla. "I think it's true. I was at the bottom of the speed ladder, but now I'm at the middle. It's funny, my fitness base is pretty deep, and when we do a lot of sprinting stuff after practice, I'll go above people on the speed ladder just because they are tired. If we were fresh, they would beat me every time."

A common question I'm asked is, "How can I improve or maximize my speed?" Although you can only improve your inherited speed by around ten percent, most people are not maximizing what speed they have. Speed is technique-based. By improving your arm and leg motion, increasing your strength, and training your speed, you can make even greater strides.

There are a few basic elements to the technique of running that can influence and improve your speed. Dr. Don Kirkendall gives us some examples.

1. To improve your initial take off, do not take a big first step, actually take a small one. The way Vern Gambetta teaches it, someone stands in front of you and has a hand out. You start to fall and touch the hand, and your first step is when you touch the hand. It can't be too big or you'll fall. (1)
2. Use your arms. Arm action is important, and most people neglect it.
3. Drive your legs. Push hard through your legs.

"One-hundred percent sprint speed is probably not something most soccer players use," says Dr. Kirkendall. "It takes time to get up to full speed. You are probably sprinting around

Photo by J. Brett Whitesell

ninety to ninety-five percent in a game. Any track coach will tell you when you train sprinting ability, you don't train at a hundred percent. If you train at a hundred percent, you tire too quickly, and your technique falls off. After all, your technique is what you are trying to train. Most people train at ninety to ninety-five percent because they can get to that speed in about thirty meters or so.

"If you break it down, most sprints are ten to forty meters, so not a lot of players ever get to top speed," adds Don. "If a person is at top speed, they're probably not going to be able to receive the ball. The only thing they are going to be able to do is one-time it ... and probably not very accurately."

It's also important to note that if you train at a high speed, or a full sprint, you can increase risk of injury. In a way, it's self-limiting because you cannot sprint at a hundred percent over and over. We call it "speed endurance," which is the ability to repeatedly perform the various types of runs required of you in a game. However, because we do many different kinds of runs in a soccer game, we are clearly not at a full sprint every time, nor are all the runs the same distance.

When we do speed-endurance training with the national team, we allow maximal rest time between runs to try to ensure as high a quality of run as possible for as many as we do (see Appendix C). We build up over the course of the year the number of sprints or close-to-maximum-speed short runs. In the beginning, we do longer sprints and fewer of them. As the year goes on, we usually add more sprints but decrease the distance of each sprint at the same time. For example, we may do 100s, 80s, 60s and 40s early in the season or pre-season. But when we get closer to competition we will do more sixty-, forty- and twenty-yard sprints. The reason we do so many is, again, to train our ability to recover and go again at an intense pace as often as the game demands of us.

"Soccer isn't really about those 120-yard sprints," says Lorrie Fair. "That might help, but how many times are you going to see that kind of sprint in a game. Maybe a few times a game. It's mostly five-yard bursts. Soccer is all about changing speed, and that's basically all strength and conditioning."

Don Kirkendall discussed the necessity of proper technique, and there are many form-running exercises that can improve your speed. Form-running exercises are running patterns that isolate aspects of the mechanics of running. For example, high-knee running is a form-running exercise, as are butt kicks. Each serve to train your muscles in the basic elements of the technique of running efficiently and correctly, and each can be performed first without and then with arm movement. Through repetition and practice of form-running techniques, a habit called "muscle memory" is formed. Your muscles are learning ways of moving efficiently.

Form-running exercises are useful only if your form is good. Running requires technique of leg movement as well as arm movements. And as is the case with weight training, it's important to have someone teach you the appropriate mechanics and techniques. A great resource is to utilize a track coach or conditioning coach. They can help you refine your technique.

There are also what are termed "sport specific movements." Steve Slain, Dave Oliver and Jeff Turner have founded, "Sport Specific Training Group," a training center in Orlando, Fla. They teach young athletes movements which serve as a warmup, conditioning and speed/agility movements relative to their sport. As a soccer player, for example, you are required to cut and change direction. Therefore, you should perform various cutting and change-of-direction exercises. A soccer player needs quick feet, so you need to train for foot quickness. An example of this would be rapid foot fire. Another vital dimension you can work on as a soccer player is your explosiveness. You can work on more power movements and acceleration.

"Don't ever think you can't improve your speed," says Dave Oliver. "You can. Improving your running technique is the most immediate way to improve speed. Running efficiently will not only make you faster, but will help you conserve energy over the course of a game."

Dave works with hundreds of high school, college and elite athletes and sees very similar mistakes being made at all levels. Here are a few simple tips from Dave:

If you want to increase straight-ahead speed and acceleration:

▲ Work your arms aggressively — beat the drum.
▲ Drive your knees in coordination with your arms.
▲ Remember that the force you put into the ground is the force the ground will give back to you.

If you want to increase lateral speed:

▲ Use your arms for balance.
▲ The movement of your hips will control the quickness of your turn.

As a rule, stride length times stride frequency equals speed. Your stride length is the distance between each stride, and stride frequency is the number of strides in a given distance. With this formula, we know that increasing speed is dependent on increasing stride length and stride frequency.

A good way to work on both your stride frequency and stride length is a drill called *Barrier Strides*. Here's how you do it:

> Set a series of six to eight barriers in a row at a distance of five feet apart (a barrier should be six inches high). Run the length of the row of barriers so that both feet contact the ground between each barrier. This trains your stride frequency. On your second time through, run the same row of barriers placing one foot between each barrier. This trains your stride length. Increase the distance between barriers by one foot (6, 7, 8 feet, etc.) for three successive sets.

"I think a big misconception is that if you jog three miles a day you'll be fine," says Julie Foudy. "You do need the cardiovascular stuff you get from running, but you still need to do some power, strength and speed work. I'll usually run two or three miles a few times a week. I'll do sprint work at least once a week — 20s, 40s, 60s. I'll do 20 x 20s, 15 x 40s, and 10 by 60s. I give myself adequate rest in between because it's more about speed than endurance. I will also do ten-yarders because in the center of midfield you need explosive burst. I try to mix up sprint and power as much as possible."

Chapter VII
THE RECOVERY PROCESS

So far, we have discussed the term "recovery" as the time period (seconds and minutes) between runs or exercises. This chapter extends the concept of recovery to include the hours and days between workouts and games.

Recovery is allowing — either actively or passively — your body to heal, rejuvenate and build. Muscle building is a constant process of breaking down and rebuilding, and taking time to recover is very important. Without recovery time, your work will be wasted. Learning ways to help you recover from workouts should be viewed with equal importance as the training itself. Maximizing the recovery process can be done through the use of days off, periodization, nutrition, massage, stretching and cross-training.

Lactic Acid is an end-product of very high intensity exercise. It's what causes the heaviness that you feel in your thighs after you run up a couple flights of stairs or after that endline-to-endline run. The soreness that often comes two days after a hard workout is called "delayed onset muscle soreness." This is due to actual damage to the muscles that will be repaired over the next few days One way to enhance your recovery is to consistently and properly warm up and warm down.

Days off are vital to any good training program. Your body rebuilds during this time, and if you don't give yourself enough time to regenerate, you may get injured and/or lose some of your enthusiasm because of fatigue. Fatigue can be either, or both, physical and psychological.

Nutrition and good eating habits can help you regenerate. The two-hour window is one additional way to recover from one day to the next after a match or very demanding training session. The two-hour window entails taking in carbohydrates within two hours after a hard practice or a match. The two-hour time period refers to when it's most beneficial for your body to absorb glycogen. The carbohydrates break down and are stored in your muscle as glycogen, and the two-hour window is when the muscles will take in the most glycogen, and therefore, are best prepared to perform the next day. The nutrition chapter will go into more detail about the two-hour window.

Massage is a valuable resource for recovery. We don't always have massage therapists with us. For example, in 1997 when my U-20 Women's National Team won the Nordic Cup, we played a grueling schedule of four international games in five days. Massage was crucial to our ability to recover, and it was a daily team activity. We partnered up and massaged each other's legs and stretched every night. Without question, it helped us recover a bit

The Recovery Process

Light Jog
Stretching
Massage
Rest

better for each match. Many of you will also be playing more than the ideal number of games in youth tournaments. Remember the philosophy that every little component may be the difference. Leave no stone unturned.

Periodization addresses the different seasons within the year of a soccer player — pre-season, in-season and post-season, and off-season training blocks. As I mentioned in the running program you need to find the right balance of training and the "seasons" of the year help with that. That's why it is vital for you to take care of your fitness before your season begins. You can — and should — do that on your own. It allows your team to focus on development, to prepare to compete and not just get fit.

"My training is dependent on what season it is," says Tracy Ducar. "In the off-season, my top priority might be lifting and fitness. The physical aspects of my game are going to be more important than the technical aspects when I am not getting many games. During the season, fitness, lifting and plyometrics have a different role and have to fall to the bottom. The tactical aspects become the most important because I just can't get enough of that in the off-season. In-season, I have a team to play with, we have video equipment, more games and coaching."

In-season, you are playing games, and the demands on your body are high. If you enter your primary season without being fit and try to accomplish fitness all at once, you'll wind up injured, or at a minimum, sore. Off-season is a time we use to develop strength, speed and power, which are demanding on your muscles. Days off are required to re-build muscle. The off-season sometimes can afford you the luxury of more days of recovery than in-season when you may have several games in a week. The recovery days allow us to push the muscles harder because we can ensure adequate rest for rebuilding.

In addition to paying attention to what type of activities you perform in each season, it's important to balance the types of conditioning you are doing within that season. If you spend all your time on one aspect and ignore others, you may wind up with an injury and out of sync as a soccer player because of the spectrum of physical demands on you. Michelle Akers has had to come back from many injuries in her career, in addition to having Chronic Fatigue Immune Dysfunction Syndrome, which at times causes paralyzing fatigue. It's almost baffling how she does it. Yet, because of her incredible discipline and comprehensive approach to her conditioning, she remains an icon in the women's game. She appreciates and attends to the delicate balance.

"One of my problems was that I was doing a speed program when I ran, but I was ignoring quickness and agility — the cutting stuff," says Michelle. "I had to figure that into my fitness workout, so I would have a total workout. I came into a camp one time after doing this speed program, and I thought I was fit. But I couldn't cut without falling over. After that, I had to adjust."

The key is developing a balanced and comprehensive workout ideal for you. What do you need to work on to get to the top of your game physically? If there is a college or high school track coach near you, perhaps seek their advice for getting started and for specific feedback.

"There are so many different things you can do. You don't have to just run or just kick a soccer ball," says Kristine Lilly. "Joy is a perfect example. When she was pregnant, she couldn't run, so she did aerobics every day until she couldn't do them anymore."

At one time or another, all of our national team players have had to find ways to stay fit without playing soccer. They may have been injured, need a break from soccer or, as in the case of Joy Fawcett and Carla Overbeck, pregnant. Don Kirkendall remembers a

SELF-MASSAGE THERAPY

By Steve Slain

Massage therapy joins weight training, fitness, nutrition and stretching as vital components of your training routine. It improves circulation and helps rid the body of waste products. Most importantly, it prepares muscles for healing and accelerates recovery so the soccer athlete can consistently train at an optimum level.

FOUR TYPES OF SPORTS MASSAGE:

1. PREVENTATIVE and RESTORATIVE Massage is administered during training periods and after competition.
2. CURATIVE Massage helps heal damaged muscular and connective tissue.
3. PRE-EVENT Massage warms muscles for competition by stimulating blood flow. It also calms the athlete with anxiety and pre-competition nerves.
4. POST-EVENT Massage can reduce muscle tension, minimize swelling and soreness and encourage relaxation. Should be short, light, relaxing and absolutely pain free!

Take note of possible strains, sprains and blisters. Ice areas for inflammation and consult with your athletic trainer or physician on any areas of trauma, like swelling, discoloration and excessive pain. The type of self-massage discussed here is simple and basic. I do suggest going to a professional sports massage therapist once in a while to receive a full massage and learn some new techniques.

WHEN NOT TO MASSAGE AN AREA:

Inflammation
Sprains/Strains
Rashes and changes in the skin
Infection (local or general)
Skin irritation

Severe pain
Fractures
Blood clots
Bleeding and bruising tissue
Varicose veins

Please Note: As with any new training procedure, check with your medical staff if you have questions regarding your condition.

The main areas of massage for the soccer player are the lower back, gluteus area, hamstrings, gastrocnemius/soleus (lower back leg), quadriceps, shins and feet. This varies with goalkeepers who need more upper body work because of their constant stretching and diving. Our main concentration is on the lower body, since that is the area used the majority of the time.

LET'S TALK ABOUT BASIC TECHNIQUES:

▲ **Direct Pressure:** pressing straight down on the muscle with fingertips or thumb for fifteen to thirty seconds.

▲ **Compression:** with the heel of the hand, use a pumping action to compress the muscle against the bone. This is similar to direct pressure in that a straight push is applied.

▲ **Friction:** the main focus when using friction is moving tissue under the skin. Friction manipulation prevents and breaks up local adhesions in connective tissue, especially over tendons, ligaments and scars. No lubricant is used with this technique. Friction massage is performed by either a circular motion around the muscle fibers of the affected area or by rubbing back and forth across the muscle fibers with fingertips, thumb or heel of the hand.

▲ **Petrissage/Kneading:** requires that the soft tissue be lifted, rolled and squeezed. Once the tissue is lifted, the full hand is used to squeeze the tissue as it rolls out of the hand, while the other hand prepares to lift additional tissue and repeat the process. This is a very good technique for softening the superficial fascia. Make sure you lift enough tissue so as not to pinch yourself!

Try incorporating this into your cool down after practice. The women's national team would partner up and work on each other when we traveled. It can be a lot of fun, and it created a camaraderie between players.

day when he was working at Duke University, where Carla serves as an assistant women's soccer coach. His office overlooked the football stadium, and one day he looked out his window and saw a woman running up the rows and rows of stadium stairs early in the morning. A closer look revealed it was Carla, pregnant with her first child. That is a champion.

Cross-training is the use of non-sports specific activities for pleasure or exercise. It's a great way to enhance your conditioning, and it can also serve to help you recover. You can choose to exercise muscle groups other than those that were used, leaving time for your "soccer muscles" to recover. At times, you have to find other ways to exercise while letting your "soccer muscles" recover. Cross-training, I believe, is a great way to balance your overall training. There can be a significant carry-over from other sports or activities that can help you as a soccer player. I believe you should feel free to play another sport while you are young if you enjoy it. I played three sports through my second year of college.

If you are injured, cross-training is an important part of staying fit while rehabili-tating. If you're hurt or your body is just worn down from one type of activity, you can make cardiovascular progress by exercising another part of your body that isn't fatigued. For example, Mary Harvey (above) spent many months rehabilitating from knee and back surgery. She used the stationary bike as an alternate means of conditioning to stay fit as she recovered. Dr. Mark Adams took Brandi Chastain and Mia Hamm to the pool periodically throughout the Olympics. The pool exercises served to rehabilitate their injuries, exercise their heart and muscles, while allowing the injuries to heal. Lastly, and perhaps as important as any reason, it can give you a break from the grind of training. It can be fun. Our players sometimes roller blade, bike, play basket-ball or swim. While these cross-training activities may not be the primary source of fitness, they can supplement and serve to make the process more enjoyable, especially if you are one of those players who struggles to work on fitness on your own. There is more than one way to get it done.

"For me, track really complemented soccer," says Tiffany Roberts. "I think the reason I'm able to stay so fit is that I started developing my fitness-base when I was really young. I don't lose my base as easily as some girls because I have built it up from a young age, and I've been able to add on to it. I was running track before I was playing soccer. My parents had me running in Tiny Tot races starting when I was four years old. It has especially helped me when I've been injured. I don't lose my fitness."

Photo by Leonardo Morales

FAVORITE WAYS TO CROSS-TRAIN

"In our off-season at school, we play a lot of roller hockey. I love it. I go out there every night. You need something different, and the tactics of it are very similar to soccer."

— *LORRIE FAIR*

"I ride my horse. Actually, it's great for my core, especially with my horse because you have to hang on our else he's gonna lose you. I also like to play tennis, water ski, do a lot of hiking and swimming. Swimming is great because, first of all, it's relaxing. But it gives my legs a break."

— *MICHELLE AKERS*

"I enjoy biking or running on the beach. Basketball helps me a lot, too. Defensively, it's almost the same stance, and the angles are similar. It's almost exactly the same except you get more width on a soccer field."

— *CHRISTIE PEARCE*

"Racquetball. With racquetball, you have to time the ball and the ball is moving a lot faster, so it can be good for your reflexes."

— *MARY HARVEY*

"I enjoy shooting hoops or going on a bike ride with a bunch of people. Or racquetball. Strength training is another a way of cross-training."

— *TIFFENY MILBRETT*

"I love to roller blade. I go for hours."
— *KRISTINE LILLY*

"I did swimming, gymnastics, basketball and volleyball."
— *ALY WAGNER*

CHAPTER VIII
TIPS ON GETTING AND STAYING FIT

1. Think *Fit for Life*

Know you are in it for the long haul. Understand that getting fit takes time and doesn't happen overnight. The earlier you develop habits of good health and regular exercise, the healthier you will feel, and it's more likely these habits will stay with you. Choose to be fit for life.

2. Schedule It

One way to increase your chances of getting fit is to structure it into your day. Whether you work on a job or are in school, you have demands on your time. Family and friends want your time. I recommend putting it down on your schedule, like you would a class, or a test, or a job commitment. This is something that Joy Fawcett, one of our fittest players has incorporated into her training habits.

"Staying fit is something I know I have to do, so I schedule it and make it part of my day," she says. "Even if it's as little as a half an hour, or as long as an hour-and-a-half, knowing it's part of your day makes it easier."

3. Look for solutions, not excuses

Kristine Lilly, who grew up in Connecticut, remembers being on the national team with Debbie Belkin, a native of New England and someone who was always fit. "Anson would always use her as an example," says Kristine. "Debbie said she would always run in the snow. You have to make your own environment. So I would run outside as much as I could because I think that made me tougher. I would also find some place inside to work with the ball as much as I could."

4. Obstacles or Challenges

When Joy Fawcett and Carla Overbeck were pregnant, they had to find ways to modify their training regimen to accommodate their pregnancies. For many women, this is time off. For Joy and Carla, it meant being even more disciplined to stay as fit as possible while pregnant. Whatever your challenge is, or whatever obstacles seem to be preventing you from working on fitness, recognize that there's a way to overcome them. It's in your control, so create your own environment. Be the type of player that can always find a way.

5. Be Intelligent; find a balance

"The person who fills the physical dimension is the one who has an intelligent and consistent work ethic to improve all the physical qualities," says Anson Dorrance. "The reason I say intelligent is that you have to have an understanding of how these things can work against each other. If you are developing a cardiovascular base, it can retard your speed. If you are running twenty or thirty miles a week, it may detract from your ability to sprint. Developing speed alone can retard agility. You need to develop a balance of these things."

6. Keep a Journal

"When I first realized that I needed to do more than just play soccer, I wrote everything down — strength training, what I was lifting, the date I needed to be prepared, etc.," says Michelle Akers. "I had each week mapped out, including my days off."

7. Find Something You Enjoy

Although this is not always possible, there are times when you can choose how you go about fitness training.

"There are so many things you can do to stay fit that you should be able to find something you like to do," says Joy Fawcett. "Unless you are training for something very specific, there are a lot of things you can do, and you should be able to do what you want."

8. Find a Partner

Another suggestion is to find a training partner, so you can hold each other accountable. You have to show up so you don't let your partner(s) down. It can also be very helpful simply to have someone to keep you company or assist you. Even if it means your mom or dad, sister or brother, they can help by timing you and giving you support.

"I worked out with my boyfriend a lot through high school because that was when I needed extra strength, extra power, extra everything," says Cindy Parlow. "We played one-v-one all the time."

Playing yourself into shape is very efficient. For example, one-v-one is a tremendous fitness option, as well as demanding psychological, tactical and technical challenge.

9. Know when to take a break

"It is hard when you are tired," says Tiffeny Milbrett. "It doesn't mean your passion for the game is leaving you. It just means you are tired and need a rest. And I think it's good to understand the difference. It's scary when you think, 'I'm not enjoying this ... is my passion gone?' No way. Come on, if you are tired, what else do you think is going to happen? You are going to shut down."

10. Trust the process

"It is hard to start, but the rewards will be huge," says Laurie Schwoy. "The hardest thing is just getting out there and getting started. And it is the best feeling when you are done."

CHAPTER IX

ESTABLISHING GOOD NUTRITION HABITS

By Douglas W. Brown, M.D.
Team Physician, U.S. Women's National Team

Nutrition is certainly an area you can influence and one that can directly impact your performance. We have been lucky to have Dr. Doug Brown, orthopedist, oversee our sports medicine program. His keen attention to detail and wonderful appreciation of the margin of victory has helped us maximize our success. Doc Brown along with Kris Clark spent time educating our players on the specifics of nutrition, but perhaps more importantly, on how all of it tied into our performance state. The chapter he has provided will offer you great insight into gaining the edge through nutrition.

In addition, you will see how we applied this information into our training programs. In the 1996 Olympic year we developed the "water brigade" a catchy name for our hydration program. This was put in place to ensure that we were adequately hydrated during the tremendous heat and humidity of the Games. Also, daily menu options and a day-of-game meal schedule are provided.

In preparation for the 1995 World Cup, we established a goal of trying to assist the players in achieving optimal nutrition and hydration. Our strategy was to tap into the same no-nonsense, professional mentality that these players used to approach the other aspects of their training. As has been described elsewhere in this book, these players individually, and as a group, already had a tradition of excellence which governed the way they traveled and lived together, the way they trained, and the way they performed on the field.

The first thing we needed to take into account was that these athletes already have more than enough to occupy their attention. What they did not need was a confusing and complicated, semester-length course in nutrition. They did need a practical and scientifically valid understanding of key nutritional principles. As disciplined and dedicated as these players are in many aspects of their lives, they are also products of their homes, their previous experiences, and their culture. Virtually all of them already had ideas about nutrition, some valid and some questionable. In American culture today, especially among young women, there is no shortage of ideas about nutrition, and this team was no exception. More than a few players could recite the number of calories, grams of fat, and a host of other facts for dozens and dozens of food products, and all of them, it's fair to say, paid considerable attention to what they weighed and how they looked.

At the same time, we knew from being around the players on long road trips that they generally had a good attitude about food. As part of a team mentality of "no whining", even when meals were unappealing, you'd rarely hear complaints, and most players learned to eat what they needed and to supplement on their own when necessary. My impression was that as a team they all subscribed to the notion that you had to eat properly to perform optimally, and they tried to do it, but there were some wide differences in defining what "optimal" was.

Knowing all that, we first tried to reduce the concepts of nutrition for soccer players to a simple core of knowledge which would also be persuasive because of a foundation in good science. Wherever possible, we wanted to show them examples of how these concepts had been tested and proven in athletic situations, and to have them recognize the special nutritional requirements of elite athletes. We understood some element of persuasion and "winning over" would be needed. Kristine L. Clark, Ph.D., R.D. of Penn State University, was by far our most

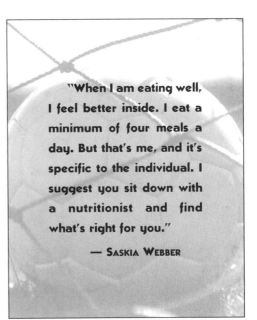

"When I am eating well, I feel better inside. I eat a minimum of four meals a day. But that's me, and it's specific to the individual. I suggest you sit down with a nutritionist and find what's right for you."

— SASKIA WEBBER

valuable resource, and we used her many writings and lectures as sources of accurate and appropriate information — like *"Nutritional Guidance to Soccer Players for Training and Competition."* (2) We then set out to teach the core of knowledge to the players, and then to set up systems and situations within the team framework which would reinforce them and make it easier to be successful.

Throughout this process, we banked on the idea that these players, once educated and persuaded, would be as professional about this aspect of their preparation as they were about everything else — and they were.

As we began more intense preparations for the 1999 World Cup, and in an effort to re-commit to the program, we sent the following letter to all the players:

It's been about three years since we first initiated a campaign to help all of you achieve the "edge" that optimal nutrition and hydration can give you. What we're outlining below is nothing new to most of you. We want these guidelines to become second nature, if they're not already. Our goal is to make optimal hydration and nutritional replenishment as routine a part of your life as brushing your teeth — something you do without thought. You have many other important issues that need your attention and concentration.

For the benefit of those of you who weren't around for the original "indoctrination" during the run-up to the '95 World Cup and the '96 Olympics, and as a reminder to those of you who were, I want to outline the key principles behind our thinking.

1. Depending on your position and the type of match you're involved in, your average heart rate for 90 minutes can be as high as 80-90 percent of maximum.

2. The average distance you cover can be about 10 km (6.2 miles), with an all-out sprint every 90 seconds. The average calories burned will usually be in the 1600-1800 range, and virtually all of those calories will come from stored glycogen. Your body makes that glycogen primarily from the carbohydrates that you eat.

3. The glycogen that you use during a match is stored mainly in muscle, and some in the liver. Typically, you will use up all of your stored glycogen by the end of a match.

4. If you train properly and take in carbohydrates optimally, you can influence your muscles to store more glycogen, and thus push out the limits of when you'll run low or run out (i.e., hit the wall).

5. Muscle biopsy studies in soccer players have shown conclusively that less well-trained athletes run out of muscle glycogen well before a typical match is over. Well-trained athletes, on the other hand, will either run out very close to the end or not at all.

Not only are you better off by training and eating in ways that induce your muscles to store more glycogen, but, if you take in readily usable carbohydrate (like that contained in sports drinks) just before a match and during halftime, your body will burn that material right away, thus putting off until later the burning of your muscle glycogen.

6. If you want the edge over your competition of having more glycogen on board and running out after they do, you need to be a little bit of a fanatic about "feeding" your muscles in an optimal way — and obviously doing the requisite training. You need to be both "well-fed" and "well-trained."

7. The other major issue which governs on-field performance is hydration. Actually, more athletes "run out of gas" more frequently due to dehydration than due to low muscle glycogen. In other words, dehydration is the leading cause of deteriorating on-field performance.

8. Under typical game conditions, you can easily lose two liters of fluid — even more if it's hot. Dry, desert heat is especially treacherous because you don't realize how much you're losing — it evaporates away so quickly. You lose water not only by sweating (which is a cooling mechanism), but also, unnoticed as water vapor, with each breath. (Airplanes have very low humidity, and you lose lots of water during flights without realizing it. You should assume that after a multi-hour air flight you're dehydrated and make special efforts to re-hydrate. Many of you already try to drink lots of fluids during flights.)

9. If you want to accurately monitor how much water you actually lose in a practice or a match, simply weigh yourself before and after. There's an old saying, "A pint is a pound the world around", so you're down a quart for every two pounds you lose.

10. Physiologists have calculated that as little as a two percent weight loss will impair performance. For example, two percent of 120 pounds = 2.4 pounds = almost 1.5 quarts. Translation: If you're down about 1.5 quarts (roughly a liter), your performance will be affected.

11. Because all of you are tough and competitive and have had lots of previous experience, you're used to coping with fatigue. I would bet that all of you have played many times — maybe even played well — with levels of dehydration greater than what physiologists recommend. In fact, the way soccer is played — with limited opportunities for re-hydrating during a match — dictates that many times you'll have to play somewhat de-hydrated. My point is simply this: Why not do whatever you can, whenever you can, to minimize the problem?

FOOD SOURCES

Carbohydrates are important in providing energy when exercising. They provide fuel. Simple carbohydrates have little to no food value. Simple sugars provide a quick fix. Complex carbohydrates are longer lasting and have more nutritional value. They are great sources of energy. They are an excellent food for the recovery process.

Examples of Complex Carbohydrates:

Grains: Bread, cereal, rice, pasta; *Fruits:* Fruits are all carbohydrates; *Vegetables:* Up to eighty percent carbohydrates; *Milk:* Fifty percent carbohydrates, fifty percent protein (Milk also contains an important mineral, calcium. Calcium is responsible for muscle contraction and relaxation; also, fast twitch muscle productivity.).

Examples of Simple Carbohydrates:

Fructose, lactose, sucrose and glucose — some fruits, juices, soft drinks and candy.

Protein is the primary source from which muscle is made. It plays a role in cell growth and, therefore, is a factor in developing muscle. Protein should be somewhere between fifteen to twenty percent of your daily calories. Sources of protein are: meats, fish, poultry, cheese, eggs, milk (dairy), nuts, legumes and whole grains.

Fat is an important part of your diet. Fats are known as oils or lipids. Insufficient amounts of fat in your diet can affect how well you burn carbohydrates. Fat and carbohydrates work together to provide energy. There are certain vitamins that require fat to help them be absorbed into your body. They are referred to as fat-soluble vitamins (A, D, E and K). In addition, fat is important in insulating and protecting your body. You need fat in your diet.

Vitamins and **minerals** have very specific functions in the body. Your body cannot make vitamins, and therefore, they need to be in your diet. Vitamins, although necessary, are not sources of energy (A, C, E, D and B-complex). Minerals regulate many processes in the body. Some of them play a part in the ability of your muscles to work for periods of time. Examples of minerals are, calcium, potassium, iron, chloride and sodium.

THOSE ARE THE BASIC PRINCIPLES. THE SOLUTIONS ARE AS SIMPLE.

1. Off the field and well before any match, you need to be sure you're eating a good, balanced diet with enough carbohydrates to replenish the glycogen that you repeatedly burn when you train and play matches.

2. One way to think of it is, in general, two-thirds of what's on your plate should be carbohydrates. Of those carbohydrates on your plate, eighty percent should be "complex" (i.e., grains, veggies, and fruits) and only twenty percent should be "simple" (i.e., sugars). If you want a number, approximately five-hundred grams of carbohydrates per day would be a good target. But, remember, this is a lot of carbohydrate and it assumes you're training hard and burning up roughly that amount. Don't ever forget that nutritional guidelines for elite athletes are different than for normal people!

3. There is a window of time during which your body is especially efficient at replenishing the glycogen that you burn — within two hours of the exercise. If you ingest usable carbohydrates during that time, they get converted quickly to glycogen and then go straight to your muscles. You can still replenish muscle glycogen hours later, but not as efficiently. Feeding your muscles during this two-hour window becomes especially important when you're training hard, day in and day out, and when you're in the midst of tournaments with matches every two to three days. What should you eat and/or drink during the two-hour window? Glucose containing drinks (like Gatorade, etc.) and complex carbohydrates (like bagels, cereal, crackers, PowerBars, etc.). How much? Basically, reasonable amounts and whatever you can tolerate. Something is better than nothing. A final word: You can't take advantage of this two-hour window, if you don't have the material to eat or drink! So take it upon yourself to be sure to have your own stash of appropriate food.

4. The whole science behind the glucose drinks (like Gatorade, etc.) is that the carbohydrates that they contain are absorbed very quickly and become usable virtually immediately as energy sources. There is no longer any debate about it. If you drink these drinks before a match and during halftime, you give your body's energy sources a measurable boost. The more you take in, the more the boost.

5. There is actually nothing magic about Gatorade and the other similar drinks. They are basically six to eight percent glucose solutions. For comparison, most sodas are about eleven percent glucose solutions, and typical orange juice is about twelve percent. The sports drinks do have some added electrolytes — aimed at replacing small amounts of them. But the real important stuff, especially from a soccer player's standpoint, is the simple carbohydrates (glucose, fructose, or sucrose) that they contain.

6. The higher concentration carbohydrate drinks (like GatorLODE) are simply an attempt to push the envelope a little more. They contain more carbohydrate material, but the concentration makes them less palatable to some people and less easy to digest. Even the six to eight percent drinks like Gatorade are too much for some people to take in comfortably. Nevertheless, even if you have to dilute these drinks, any carbohydrate that you get makes you better off. If you just drink water, you're working on the dehydration issue (and that's good), but you do nothing to boost your energy stores. You really need both water and glucose.

7. Obviously you have to balance how much you can drink with how it makes you feel. It's counter-productive to take in so much Gatorade (and/or water) that you feel

terrible. On the other hand, these materials are absorbed very quickly, and a full feeling for a few minutes should be gone rather quickly.

8. It so happens that the body absorbs water a little more efficiently if there's a little glucose to go along with it; so the water that Gatorade contains (the major ingredient is water, not glucose) actually gets in a little better.

9. If you're really intent on getting the maximum edge that carbohydrate drinks and water replenishment can give you, you should use every practice and every match to assess your own experience with how much water and how much carbohydrate drink you can tolerate and still feel okay. You need to develop a very clear understanding about how your body reacts to various "doses" and under different conditions. The more you experiment on your own and learn what you can and cannot tolerate, the more confidently you can manage your replenishment under crucial game conditions. An international match is not the right time to experiment with taking in more than you're accustomed to.

10. Our goal — as coaches, trainers, and physicians — is to try to have all the materials readily available for you at training, at matches, and afterwards so you can get what you need, but you have a role to play, also. You can help by doing whatever you can to ensure that you always have adequate supplies of (a) water, (b) carbohydrate drinks, and (c) complex carbohydrate snacks — at training, at matches, and in hotels afterwards. Better still, you can take responsibility for having your own stash of carbohydrate snacks and/or carbohydrate drinks for after training or after matches.

One of the exceptional things about the Women's National Team is the values and standards you've established over the years and that you continue to maintain — for working hard, for minimizing complaints, for pitching-in on the road with whatever needs to be done. It would be ideal if you would all agree to add optimizing fluid and nutritional replenishment to the list of things that you wholeheartedly support and help each other to maintain.

PRE-GAME MEALS

We have taken Dr. Brown's input very seriously. Our pre-game meal incorporates his advice. The pre-game meal is the last big meal you eat before competition. The meal is designed to prevent you from experiencing hunger while playing, and it should maximize your performance by providing the optimal amounts of energy stores in your body. Remember, you have blood glucose and stores of glycogen in your muscles to replenish. Carbohydrates are important to give you fuel to burn. They are ideal in the pre-game meal because they are digested quicker and absorbed faster into the blood stream.

It's okay to have small amounts of protein. Small portions of broiled chicken, for example, are fine. Large quantities of protein or foods high in fat may take longer to digest and therefore remain in the stomach during your competition. If you eat too much fat or protein — or if you eat it too close to the event — you may divert blood flow to your stomach and not to your muscles, possibly influencing your performance. Not to mention the uncomfortable feeling of running on a full stomach. Make sure you drink plenty of water throughout the day of your game.

Based upon the time of the game your meal choices will vary. If you have an early morning game, your meal the night before is most important. With time, your body will let you know what works best for you.

"THE WATER BRIGADE"

Water is one of the most critical elements in performance. Your body is largely composed of water, up to seventy percent. Dr. Brown explained that if you are dehydrated or under-hydrated then you may not perform as well as you could or should. The key is to not wait until you're thirsty. We actually had a water program for the Olympics, nicknamed "The Water Brigade." We would joke about it. But believe me, it was taken with the utmost seriousness. During the first game of the Olympics, we played Denmark. It was over a hundred degrees in Orlando, Fla. In July. Hot. Humid. Our players kept getting water at any and every opportunity. We left bottles around the field or if there was a stop in play, they came running over to the bench. Yet, Denmark wasn't drinking at all.

We had conditioned ourselves to want water. We began the process months before the first game, introducing more frequent water breaks and making our bench players more alert and ready to provide water for the players on the field at any available moment. As a result, we became accustomed to wanting and having water more often.

Ideally, it's good to have small amounts of water every fifteen minutes when performing intense work. Denmark, on the other hand, had trained in cold temperatures and had required less water during their preparation. In the second half, all of a sudden you could see Denmark hit a wall. We cruised to a 3-0 win.

Water is important in regulating your body temperature, and therefore, in helping you cool down during workouts. Water also serves to move nutrients through the body. The standard recommendation is to drink between six and eight glasses of water a day. As mentioned earlier, every fifteen minutes or so during a workout can help your performance. One way to monitor your fluid intake and fluid loss is to measure your weight every morning at the same time. Then, weigh yourself after practice. Keep track of the amount of fluid you are losing from sweating. If the next day you are down from your baseline weight, odds are you haven't replenished what you have lost. We kept a log like this during our preparation for the Olympics. If you are dehydrated, it can take up to forty-eight hours to replace lost fluids.

Sample Day-of-Game Meal Routine

Game Time: 4:00 PM

8:30-9:00   **Breakfast Options:** Cereals, milk, juices, fruit, bagels, toast, water

12:00   **Pre-game Meal Options:** Pasta with sauce on the side, chicken, fruit, peanut butter and jelly, maybe plain rice, rolls, a vegetable, milk, juices, water

4:00   **Game:** All Sport, Gatorade, water, Power Bars, dry cereal in locker

6:00   Two-hour window begins. Snacks should be available after the game en route home — bagels, cereal, fruit, Gatorade, water

7:00   **Post-game Meal** varies but always includes carbohydrate choices, some protein option (chicken is very popular with our team), a vegetable, plenty to drink: water, juices, electrolyte drinks (All Sport, Gatorade)

Favorite pre-game meal: Kristine Lilly: "My favorite pre-game meal is pasta — without the sauce ... "it makes me burp" — or peanut butter and jelly, fruit, salad, oatmeal."

Snacks of national team: Bagels, dry cereal, Power Bars (Akers), pretzels, Bold and Zesty Chex Mix (Scurry), pizza, Slushies; and I must admit they have a sweet tooth: Sprees, Skittles, Smarties, gum, and Julie Foudy's favorite, Snickers.

Sample Menu Ideas

The following are sample menu ideas we provide our hotels when we travel:

Breakfast: Selection of dry cereals, fresh fruit, hard boiled eggs, breads (bagels, toast, english muffins), peanut butter and jelly, orange juice, assorted juices, coffee, tea, water, skim and two-percent milk

Choose one daily: Pancakes, french toast, waffles

Lunch and Dinner: Have daily: Bread, rolls, peanut butter and jelly, fresh fruit, juice, ice tea, soda, water, coffee, plain rice or plain pasta. Main dish choices: Rice, potatoes (baked or fried) salad, vegetables, cold cuts (turkey, ham, cheese), pasta with marinara sauce on side, chicken dishes, fish, soups, pizza, mexican night, lasagna, meat (a few times a week)

Dessert: Cookies, yogurt, fruit, pie or cake occasionally

TRUST THE PROCESS

Athletes tend to put a lot of pressure on themselves. The toned bodies you see on our team or on top collegiate teams, take time. Their bodies become leaner and more toned through years of training and proper nutrition. Take the advice Dr. Brown provides and learn about what your body needs and how to take care of it.

You cannot get there by dieting. If you eat well and exercise regularly, your body will take care of itself. If you are having trouble knowing what to eat, or how much to eat, or what your body needs given your athletic goals, see a nutritionist, preferably one who works with athletes so they appreciate how many calories you burn every day.

Our nutritionist, Kris Clark, would speak with us a few times a year. She gently re-visited all the basics, but tried to make it more interesting, and she related it to our needs as athletes.

"Kristine Clark was awesome," says Kristine Lilly. "She didn't give you the same old boring 'eat your four food groups' talk. What I got out of it was that we need to eat everything. There is a fat-free kick these days, but women need to eat fat. We need to eat protein. She made us feel that we could eat anything. She also made us realize that as athletes we were different from the normal Joe on the road. We can eat more because we burn more. The amount of calories we need is different. The diets you see in magazines are not for us. If we stuck to those diets, we would be sticks. She taught us to eat whenever we are hungry and not to stuff ourselves at one meal. She taught us to eat what we wanted and not to worry."

When you are young, you believe you are invincible, and you think eating right really doesn't matter. It does. Remember, this book is about learning habits that will benefit you for a lifetime. Taking care of your body and giving it what it needs is a habit worth starting right now.

Performance is directly tied to nutrition. Remember the *"no stone unturned"* philosophy. If you can gain even a percent or two from good nutrition, that may be the difference between achieving your goals or helping your team. Nutrition is one more aspect you can control in your preparation. It is an essential element in training for excellence.

CHAPTER X

SPORTS MEDICINE AND THE ELITE FEMALE SOCCER ATHLETE

By Mark Adams, M.D.
Team Physician, U.S. Women's National Team

Most athletes, at some point in their careers, will experience an injury. Dr. Mark Adams, our team physician from the 1996 Olympic Games, has provided a chapter on common terms, soccer related injury, and the role of rehabilitation. It does not serve in any way as a substitute for seeing your own doctor, preferably one who works with athletes. Dr. Adams discusses the necessity of a pre-participation medical evaluation prior to any sport activity.

In addition to the factual information you will gather, I want you to realize being injured can be an active process. Too often, injured athletes become out of shape, distant from their teams and feel far from the sport they love. I want you to come away from this chapter realizing that you can find ways to stay fit, contribute to your team and become a better soccer player. All of this requires being a little creative and keeping a positive attitude. Dr. Adams played a vital role in our team's success in 1996.

Sports Medicine and the medical care of the female athlete changed drastically with the passage of Title IX in 1975. Prior to this, female participation in organized sports was much less than that of males, and females comprised a low percentage of the total of the athletic team population. Passage of this national law has had the effect of extending sporting and recreational opportunities to the female athlete more equal to that of men. More women are, as a result, playing soccer at all levels. It has been estimated that more than six million females participate in soccer in the United States. This includes recreational leagues, interscholastic teams, and college level participation.

Soccer has also introduced women to a contact sport. The unfortunate side of increased participation in contact activities, however, is the parallel increase in athletic injuries to females. The National Collegiate Athletic Association (NCAA) injury surveillance programs reveal high injury rates for women participating in soccer. The incidence may be higher at more elite levels.

When we think of sports medicine injuries, usually major joint problems come to mind. Historically, knee injuries are feared as they have the potential to shorten promising careers.

Recent developments in recognition, treatment, and rehabilitation have made it possible for many female athletes to enjoy recovery from injury. Since injury is a constant feature of athletic participation, all persons involved with athletics at any level, be they athlete, coach, trainer, or physician, will find themselves involved in the recognition and treatment of injuries.

This chapter will focus on common soccer injuries. It is not intended to be an all-inclusive guide to self-care. Rather, it will lay groundwork for early injury recognition, and provide you with basic understanding of the injury process.

Common Injury Terms

A common terminology extends across the spectrum of injury. An understanding of the basic medical terms associated with sports medicine may make understanding your injury easier. The following are common injury terms.

Fracture: A fracture is a break in the continuity of a bone. Athletes and trainers should consider the diagnosis of fracture after any significant musculoskeletal trauma. This is especially important when you have local deformity, swelling, bruising or significant pain. Possible fractures should be splinted in the field and the patient transported to an appropriate medical facility for x-rays and physician evaluation.

Dislocation: A dislocation is displacement of bone from its normal position in a joint. With a dislocation, there is loss of limb function and you are usually suddenly unable to move the joint in question. Deformity is generally visible, and swelling and point-tenderness are immediately present. An x-ray examination may be the only way to distinguish a dislocation from a fracture. On occasion, a dislocation may be reduced (put back in place) on the field.

Subluxation: Subluxation is a partial or incomplete dislocation. It's not common to have deformity since the joint has not moved completely out of position. Symptoms include joint pain and transient loss of function.

Sprain: A sprain is an injury to a joint that damages the ligaments connecting the bones together to form the joint. The force creating a sprain is usually an excessive stretch or shear. Any ligament can be affected in this way, but the ankle and knee ligamentous structures are especially prone to injury. Pain, local swelling, and discoloration may be evident, and the patient may exhibit apprehension whenever the joint is examined. Looseness, or joint laxity, may result when sprains occur.

Strain: A strain is an injury to the muscle or musculotendinous unit which usually results from contraction or excessive forcible stretch. Acute muscle strain can occur within any major muscle group, yet the most commonly involved in the lower extremity is the quadriceps, abductors, hamstrings, and the Achilles complex. You may be immediately aware that the muscle has been damaged. Occasionally, it feels as if something has "popped" in the affected muscle area. The Olympic sprinter putting up with a hamstring injury is a good example of acute muscle strain. Symptoms are local pain and muscle spasm with hematoma (bruise) formation and loss of muscle function. A defect in the muscle may at times be palpable.

Contusion: A contusion is a compression injury or direct blow to the soft tissues of the body. Usually, this occurs to a muscle or musculotendinous unit but may also involve a bursa, or even bone. This is especially common in contact-type sports. A contusion creates local pain and stiffness which is increased twelve to twenty-four hours following injury. There may be localized tenderness and bruise formation at the site of injury.

Acute Injury: An acute injury is one that results from sudden injury with rapid onset. Most of the above injuries occur in an acute setting.

Overuse Syndrome: This is an injury that occurs from repetitive micro-trauma over a longer period of time. Constant repetitive stressing of the body day after day can lead to microscopic changes involving soft tissues or bones. This may in turn lead to constant pain during and after activity.

These common terms apply to an injury regardless of its anatomical location. A fracture in the lower extremity may be treated much the same as a fracture in the upper extremity. Similarly, contusions, sprains, and strains have common principles of healing and treatment regardless of location.

Ankle/Foot Injuries

Ankle and foot injuries are among the most common problems in a running and kicking sport like soccer. By far the most common injury in this area is the ankle sprain. Fractures and sprains to toes may also exist.

Ankle Sprains: Ankle sprains may occur on either the inner (medial side) of the ankle or outer (lateral side). Lateral sprains are more common, and usually result from an inversion (roll out) or twisting type injury to the area on the outside. Medial side sprains occur from an eversion (roll in), twisting maneuver. The ankle sprain is an injury to the ligaments that provide support to this joint. Muscles surrounding the ankle provide little additional support to ankle stability.

Several ligaments exist on the outside of the ankle. These are injured to varying degrees with lateral sprains. Mild sprains usually injure only one or two, while more serious sprains may damage all ligaments. Typical ankle sprain treatment begins with immediate ice and compression application. All but the most simple ankle sprain should be x-rayed to insure that an ankle fracture is not present. Functional rehabilitation with bracing or tape support usually allows for more prompt return to soccer activity. Full range of motion, diminished swelling, and improved proprioceptive (spatial awareness) training is necessary to achieve full recovery. Recurrent ankle sprains may infrequently need surgical reconstruction. Simple ankle sprains allow return to activity within days.

An especially problematic ankle sprain is the "high ankle sprain." This is an injury to the lateral ankle ligaments and involves an associated sprain of the supporting structures between the tibia and fibula, the large bones of the lower leg.

Mark Adams and Mia Hamm during the Olympics

Photo by J. Brett Whitesell

PRE-PARTICIPATION EVALUATION

BY DR. MARK ADAMS

A pre-participation medical evaluation is designed to enhance and protect the health and safety of athletes. It's not a punitive effort meant to disqualify athletes from participation. Rather, the goals are to detect any condition that may limit participation, to detect any condition that predisposes the athlete to injury, to determine the general health of the athlete, and to meet legal and insurance requirements of participation.

Most states now require yearly examination to participate at the interscholastic level. College athletes are usually not allowed to participate without pre-participation examination. Every national team player has been through a comprehensive pre-participation evaluation that includes eye, dental and general physical examination. Any soccer athlete should be examined before participating in the rigors of this sport at any level.

A pre-participation evaluation is also a good time to question physicians on health maintenance issues. These include proper nutrition, physical conditioning, drug use, and weight control. Eye and dental exams may also be included. If a problem is found in the physical examination, one must decide whether the problem places the athlete at increased risk of injury. The American Academy of Pediatrics has published guidelines that determine whether or not it's safe to allow athletes with medical conditions to participate in sports. It's rare, however, to be totally disqualified from sports based on the physical examination.

The pre-participation evaluation is generally conducted individually at a physician's office, or by mass team-screening utilizing multiple stations. The use of mass screening and the multiple station format has several advantages, including the use of specialized personnel, fitness testing, multiple examinations in a less time-consuming format, and greater communication with the coaching and training staff.

Recording the medical history is the first step in the pre-participation physical process. The medical history has been shown to identify sixty-three to seventy-four percent of problems affecting athletes. It's best completed by the parents of children or adolescent athletes. For elite women soccer athletes, a menstrual history is also important. This history should include age of menarche, frequency and duration of menstrual periods, date of last menstrual period, and any birth control or hormonal therapy use.

The pre-participation physical examination should be all inclusive. Evaluation of the heart, lungs, abdomen, genitalia and skin are as important as the musculoskeletal evaluation. Eye and dental exams may also be included.

The mechanism of injury is an externally directed rotational force. Tenderness, swelling and bruising may be evident on the outside of the leg higher than the typical ankle location. Pain is generally present with attempts to "push off" running. This problematic sprain takes longer recovery time.

Maybe you remember the sight of Mia Hamm down on the field during the first round 1996 Olympic game with Sweden. Mia sustained a painful ankle sprain requiring her to miss the next game against China. Mia immediately began a rehabilitation program, first directed to control swelling and pain, and then progressing to return of motion and strength. Patty Marchak, the women's national team trainer, began rehabilitation immediately. Mia was able to return to play the semifinal game against Norway, and was back to her usual full strength in the gold medal victory against China. Her dedicated rehabilitation effort allowed her to recover quickly from a serious and painful ankle sprain.

Dr. Mark Adams, took Mia to the pool every day for treatment and rehabilitation. Each day they would do water walking and exercises designed to work on her range of motion, strength and keep her as fit as possible. This was active rehabilitation. It allowed Mia to be back by our semifinal match against Norway. Dr. Adams realized that he and Mia could take control of certain aspects of her comeback and seized the opportunity to maximize her safe return.

The incidence of ankle sprains may be reduced by stretching the Achilles tendon, strengthening muscles surrounding the ankle, and participating in a proprioceptive training program. Athletic taping may provide additional support to the ankle ligaments, and may be necessary with the vigorous pivoting and cutting type maneuvers associated with soccer. Most players have trouble wearing large ankle braces or other forms of orthotics.

Turf Toe: Turf toe is a hyperextension injury to the first or "big toe," metatarsal phalangeal joint. This is the "ball" of the big toe. This injury has become more prevalent as soccer footwear has become more flexible. The development of artificial surfaces has also increased sprain to this area.

A typical turf-toe injury shows swelling, tenderness and limitation of motion in the region of the big toe. You may have trouble pushing off while running. As with other sprain-type injuries, rest, ice, compression, elevation and anti-inflammatory medication may provide early symptomatic support. This injury can be especially hard to come back from since the full weight of the body is transmitted through this joint with all running or cutting activities. A stiffer sole soccer shoe helps resist the hyperextension force to this joint, and may be necessary upon return to activity.

Knee Injuries

Historically, knee injuries have been the most common — and potentially debilitating — of all sports medicine problems. Acute knee injuries certainly make the most headlines, but overuse injuries can also keep you on the sidelines. Common injuries to the knee include various ligament sprains, cartilage tears, and patella dislocations. Strains and contusions may also occur in the area around the knee.

Improved surgical techniques now make it possible for the injured athlete to return to competition from knee injuries. Many promising athletic careers have been curtailed in the past by knee injuries. New methods of treatment, however, make it possible for most athletes to return to full function. There are several well-known players on the Women's National Team who have enjoyed very successful careers despite previous knee injuries.

ACL Injuries: The anterior cruciate ligament, or ACL, helps control pivoting or deceleration-type movements of the knee. Historically, this was felt to be a rare injury in the woman athlete. The advent of arthroscopy revealed that ACL injuries occurred much more commonly than previously recognized. We now know that non-contact turning or sudden stopping places a stress on this ligament, and that the female athlete is especially prone to this type of injury mechanism. Studies now show that women soccer players may suffer ACL injuries two to four times as frequently as men when injury rates are examined. There are many theories as to why this injury is seen more commonly in women, but to date there is no firm indication as to why women are so affected.

The common history associated with ACL injury is that of a non-contact, twisting, giving-way injury to the knee. You may even hear a "pop." There may be little or no swelling early, yet the next day a stiff, swollen knee may be evident. Pain may be present early, but this diminishes over the course of the first week. Athletic trainers, therapists, and sports' medicine physicians are usually adept at making the diagnosis of anterior cruciate ligament injury.

Early treatment consists of rest, ice, compression, and elevation. Crutches may be necessary, but generally the need for ambulatory aids diminishes over the first week. Associated cartilage tears may prolong the need for crutch support. Surgical reconstruction is usually necessary for the elite soccer athlete. The physical demands of constant pivoting and twisting usually require the support of an anterior cruciate ligament. Specific braces for ACL support may at times allow continued participation in the minor ACL injury. Many physicians use braces to complement surgical reconstruction.

MCL Injuries: Sprain of the medial collateral ligament, or MCL, is a common soccer knee injury. This usually occurs from an outside blow to the knee with a resultant stretch of the inner knee ligament. The athlete feels pain along the inside of the knee, and may have swelling associated with this area. Limitation of motion is usually present. Minor sprains of this ligament may allow an early return to soccer activities. Major sprains, or complete tears, of this ligament need additional recovery time, and in certain circumstances, surgical repair or reconstruction. Combined MCL/ACL type injuries are problematic to the athlete in that two of the four supporting ligaments of the knee are damaged.

Initial treatment consists of rest, ice or cryotherapy, compression wrapping, and elevation for swelling control. Early movement with isometric strengthening may speed recovery.

Brandi Chastain sustained a severe sprain of the medial collateral ligament during the 1996 Summer Olympic Games. The injury occurred during the first half of the semifinal game against Norway, yet with adequate bracing and taping, Brandi was able to complete that game. Vigorous rehabilitation with early swimming pool running, icing treatments, and gentle range of motion allowed Brandi to return in time for the gold medal game. Thank goodness!

It's important to ask your doctor first what is safe, and, second, what can help you stay fit during the healing phase.

"Doc Adams was in the pool with us two hours every day," recalls Brandi. "He was instrumental in getting me back on the field. I don't know if I could have done it. I couldn't practice after the Norway game. In the pool, we did a lot of bending, squatting, and walking to get used to the feel of my knee. Three days in the pool definitely helped."

TWELVE SURGERIES AND STILL KICKING

Michelle Akers believes the number is twelve, but she can't really be sure. She's lost track of how many times she has had knee surgery. But she insists it is at least a dozen. Michelle has learned to take her rehabilitation seriously and listen to her physical therapists and doctors. She has also found ways to improve her game while injured.

"I injured my right knee so many times, I would sometimes play for weeks just one-footed, using only my left foot," Michelle says. "That could have been a frustrating thing, but I kind of learned to ask myself, 'Okay, how can I play around this.' I look back now and I am a much more capable player because of those things."

Cartilage Injuries: Cartilage, or menisci, provide padding and support to the knee joint. They occupy the space between the femur and tibia, and re-distribute the force between these bones. They have been described as the "shock absorbers" of the knee.

Acute cartilage tears generally occur as a specific event. You may have a sudden twisting movement to the knee, with the feeling of a "tearing sensation" within the joint. This feeling may lead to a fall and subsequent difficulty in straightening the knee. Swelling is common within twenty-four hours. Focal tenderness is usually present at the joint line, either medially (inside) or laterally (outside). Physical examination may also reveal a painful "pop" secondary to the torn tissue displacement.

Cartilage tears are generally treated operatively with the arthroscope. Otherwise, the mechanical limitation associated with displaced cartilage tears may prevent sports activity. There has been an increased emphasis on operative repair rather than removal. It's thought that repairing cartilage may lead to less degenerative stresses later in life. Cartilage injury may occur in combination with ligament injuries within the knee.

Patella Instability: The patella, or kneecap, is a knee structure that can be subjected to a dislocation force, driving it from its normal position. The injury occurs more frequently in females than in males, and almost always occurs in a lateral (outside) direction. A first-time dislocation may be very scary to the athlete, as significant deformity is usually present. The kneecap sits off to the side of the knee, and creates severe pain. Most dislocations spontaneously reduce when the knee is taken from its flexed position to full extension.

This injury creates immediate pain and disability. Most athletes can recount the appearance and feeling of this injury quite easily to the medical professional. Even the first-time dislocation should be referred to an orthopaedic surgeon. Generally, immobilization with ice and compressive wrapping will be utilized with early isometric quadriceps contractions beginning as soon as symptoms allow. A patella stabilizing brace should be worn upon return to athletic activities. Recurrent dislocations, or even subluxations, may necessitate surgical intervention.

Hip/Thigh Injuries

Most injuries to the hip and thigh region are either contusions or strains to the muscle groups surrounding this large joint. Soccer skills require these muscles to participate in speed and quick cutting moves, and injuries to the hip and thigh muscles can markedly limit your performance. It's important to work on strength and flexibility to the hip and thigh to prevent injury.

Quadriceps Contusion: A direct blow or compression force to the muscle on the front of the thigh is also known as a "charley horse." The severity of quad muscle contusion is graded by the degree of knee bend (flexion) you can obtain twenty-four hours after the injury. If you have flexion greater than ninety degrees, this is a mild contusion. Less flexion indicates higher grades of muscle contusion injury. Icing in a prone position with the knee bent is beneficial in maintaining motion and lessening swelling. Exercises to achieve full flexibility should never include forced flexion movement. This may stretch the injured muscle tissue and delay recovery. Time away from competition is dependent upon severity of the contusion.

Quadriceps/Rectus Strain: The quadriceps is the large muscle on the front part of the thigh that works to actively straighten the knee, while the hip flexors assist in the bending of the hip joint. This group of muscle and musculotendinous unit injuries are seen in soccer players who are hit as they attempt to kick the ball. It creates a hyperextension type force to the hip flexors or quadriceps itself. These muscles provide force to the kicking motion, and injury to this group may be quite debilitating .

Pain, swelling, and loss of function are common signs of muscle strain in the thigh and hip area. Non-operative care is generally employed, and it's rare to need surgical treatment of injury to these muscles. Rest, ice, compression with an elastic bandage, and elevation are early treatment activities. Physical therapy modalities — electrical stimulation, ice, etc. — to speed recovery may be of benefit.

Hip Adductor Strain: Injury to this muscle is also commonly known as a "groin pull." Pain and injury to the upper muscles of the inner thigh are common in soccer activities. Swelling, bruising, and tenderness may be present in this area. Pain is especially noted with resistance to adduction, or pull of the inner thigh muscles. Strengthening and stretching of the adductor may prevent injury to this region. Groin stretch activity should be a part of any soccer athlete's warm-up routine.

Osteitis Pubis: This is an uncommon sports injury, but may on occasion be seen in the soccer player or other kicking type athlete. It occurs from repetitive overuse of the adductor muscles of the upper inner thigh. It has a rather gradual onset as opposed to the acute injury seen in groin strain. Pain occurs with running, and occasionally the athlete may complain of a "popping" sensation while kicking.

This tenderness may at times be confused with a hernia or other sources of groin pain. Focal tenderness at the pubic bone is present, while x-ray studies and bone scans by medical professionals assist in making the diagnosis. Treatment consists of rest, anti-inflammatory medication, and adductor muscle strengthening and stretching. Local steroid injection has occasionally been used to alleviate the pain associated with this problem.

Shoulder Injuries

The shoulder is not as commonly injured in soccer as it is in other sports. Football, with its upper extremity contact nature, has many shoulder injuries, and throwing sports like baseball or softball, also see their share of shoulder problems. Most injuries to the shoulder in soccer occur from a fall on an outstretched arm, or direct contact to the shoulder while you are in the air. Fractures, contusions, sprains, and dislocations can occur in the shoulder area. Several of the more common shoulder injuries in soccer will be explored.

Clavicular Fracture: This is a fracture that happens to the "collar bone." It's the most common fracture of the shoulder and usually occurs secondary to a fall on the lateral (outside) shoulder. This may be a function-limiting injury, yet is most commonly treated only with the support of a Figure 8 strap or sling. Healing generally occurs in six to ten weeks and contact is usually limited until complete bone healing has occurred. This injury is more common in younger soccer players. It's a rare injury in the adult or elite soccer athlete.

AC Separation: The acromioclavicular joint is the small joint on the top of the shoulder. Technically, an AC separation is a sprain-type injury to the ligaments supporting this joint.

Separations usually occur from a direct blow to the outside of the shoulder with resultant pain, loss of limb function, and possible deformity at the AC joint on the top of the shoulder. Most of the time, non-operative treatment is employed for this injury. Those with significant displacement (Grade III), however, may need surgical intervention. Minor grade injuries to this area heal within a couple of weeks, while higher grade injuries may need more time. High grade injuries may result in degenerative changes in the AC joint with recurrent pain and tenderness with activity.

Shoulder Instability: Shoulder instability may range from minor forms of subluxation all the way to the complete dislocation. The shoulder joint is the most mobile joint in our body and balances the need between functional mobility and adequate stability. Shoulder motion is a complex interaction of static and dynamic forces that allow the greatest range of motion of any of our joints.

The first time, complete dislocation is a painful and frightening event to a player. It may be difficult to distinguish a complete dislocation from a fracture, and x-ray examination is usually necessary. Various forces can direct the dislocation in an anterior (front), inferior (downward), or posterior (back) direction. The anterior, or frontal, dislocation is by far the most common. Initial treatment is directed at placing the joint back into normal alignment. Immobilization for comfort, swelling control, and healing then usually occurs. Generally, three to six weeks is necessary to allow a healthy response. Episodes of recurrent dislocation may require surgical intervention.

Head Injuries and Concussions

Head injuries and concussions can be a source of problems to the soccer player. It's important to identify players with a head injury or concussion, since there has been increased concern about a persistent neurologic condition from cumulative head trauma.

The term concussion describes a syndrome characterized by "impairment of neuro function, such as alteration of consciousness, disturbance of vision, equilibrium, etc., caused by mechanical forces."

Concussions are classified according to level of confusion, association of amnesia, and duration of loss of consciousness. Specific grading criteria are beyond the scope of this book. Any of you who experience symptoms of confusion, amnesia, or headache with injury to the head, should be removed from practice or competition and referred to an appropriate physician. Loss of consciousness on the field must be treated as if a neck injury may be present. Spine board treatment of the athlete and emergent transport to a medical facility is necessary in this circumstance.

It is not unusual for athletes to have extended symptoms following even mild concussive events. Headache, especially upon exertion, fatigue, irritability, and impaired memory are not uncommon. The athlete may have difficulty concentrating for a period of time. Return to competition for any head or neck injury must be deferred until all symptoms are gone and appropriate diagnostic studies show no signs of injury. After the initial concussion event, the chance of recurrence may be increased as much as four-fold. Second or third concussions that occur after return to play are especially worrisome and warrant removal from soccer activity and further medical evaluation.

Overuse Injuries

Overuse injuries are quite common in sports activities, and may account for a high percentage of the injuries that affect any team. They can affect any part of the musculoskeletal system, including muscles, tendons, ligaments, and bones. Overuse injuries generally result from repetitive micro trauma to the musculoskeletal system. There may not be one event that leads to pain or injury, and you may notice a gradual onset of tenderness and decreased function.

Stress Fractures: Stress fractures are also known as "fatigue fractures," and they were first described in untrained military recruits. Bone usually adapts to increasing loads of athletic or physical stress. When a bone is loaded and stressed, it becomes stronger and more dense. Athletes may get into situations, however, where even normal loads are applied so frequently that the bone's adaptive process cannot occur quickly enough. Under those circumstances a stress fracture may result.

Any bone subjected to repetitive stress is subject to fracture. In soccer, the lower extremities are more commonly affected. Fractures of the pelvis, hip, tibia or "lower leg", and foot have all been described.

You should not attempt to train through pain that seemingly is located in the region of a bone. The best treatment for a stress fracture is early recognition of the injury and a change in the training program. Early in the process, rest may be necessary to decrease pain. However, it's usually possible to institute non-weight bearing training to shorten the recovery phase of the stress fracture.

It's not uncommon for a stress fracture to have negative x-rays. It may be necessary for the medical care provider to perform a bone scan to find the abnormality in affected bone. The fracture is healed when you no longer have tenderness to palpation at the fracture site. At that time, you are usually able to tolerate impact. It's important to begin a gradual, progressive return to full soccer activity.

Patellofemoral Pain: One of the most common overuse complaints of active soccer players is anterior, or frontal, knee pain. It's especially common in female athletes and can be quite difficult to diagnosis and treat. The main cause is chronic overloading of the structures in the front of the knee.

Pain is usually described as vague, non-specific, and is usually related to soccer activity. Overuse problems in this area usually begin quite gradually but may increase with activities like stair climbing, stair descent, uphill running, or prolonged kicking. The tenderness may even lead to feelings of "giving way."

The physical examination may show tenderness around the knee cap and the surrounding soft tissues. There may even be grinding, with knee flexion and extension. Subtle forms of knee cap instability may be present.

Patella tendinitis is especially common in high-impact running sports like soccer. Tenderness is common at the lower end of the knee cap, right where the soft tissues join to hold the knee cap in it's normal position. Slight swelling may be present in this area, and some degree of grinding may be noticed with movement.

Overuse problems of the knee cap, or patellofemoral joint, are initially treated with non-operative methods. The goal is to decrease pain, increase strength, and control symptoms associated with this problem. It's usually possible to continue an active lifestyle, yet other forms

Linda Hamilton, 1991 World Champion, treats her battle wounds.

of training (cross-training) may be necessary. Ice is especially beneficial, as is anti-inflammatory medicine use. Generally, a flexibility program directed to the hamstrings is beneficial. Athletic trainers or physical therapists can usually be of great assistance in the recovery from anterior knee pain. Surgical treatment may be necessary if conservative means are unsuccessful.

Rehabilitation

It must be understood that rehabilitation of the injured soccer player is a team effort involving the athlete, athletic trainer or physical therapist, physician, coach, and many times the athlete's parents. Each of these team members has an important part to play in the rehabilitation process.

You must understand that you are the one most affected by the injury. Dedication and resolve are necessary for full recovery. It's important that you show up for scheduled rehabilitation sessions, and follow rehabilitation instructions closely. You must also give feedback to the physician or trainer, explaining what seems to help and

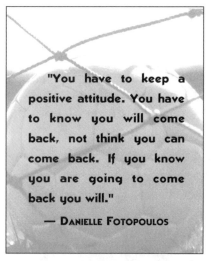

"You have to keep a positive attitude. You have to know you will come back, not think you can come back. If you know you are going to come back you will."

— DANIELLE FOTOPOULOS

what creates further pain. If anti-inflammatory medication is prescribed, make sure to follow the schedule closely. In summary, you must have the proper attitude and attention to detail to enhance the rehabilitation process.

The athletic trainer or physical therapist has a unique role in the injury recovery process. They may interact with the athlete on a daily basis and become part psychologist, part coach, and part cheerleader, as well as rehabilitation specialist. They must understand the psyche of the injured athlete and continue to encourage and educate her. No elite soccer player likes to sit on the sideline during big games, and it's important for the trainer to help you through these difficult times. The athletic trainer should help with communication between athlete and coaching staff.

Physicians are responsible for making a correct diagnosis and overview of the rehabilitation process. They must take into account your general health, as well as the diagnosis and treatment of the injury. Specialized tests like x-rays, bone scans, and MRIs are ordered by the physician. Any use of medication for the healing process should be under a physician's direction.

Coaches must work with you during the injury-recognition phase and the recovery process. Through proper training techniques, they also help prevent injury to members of their team. They may help design special training needs as the athlete returns to the field. For instance, the coach may avoid long-ball kicking situations as you return from a groin pull. Coaches must be kept informed as to the true physical and emotional picture of the player.

Finally, parents and family provide emotional support during times of injury and rehabilitation. Family members many times know their daughter better than anyone and may be the first to recognize a change in their athletic performance. Parents play the role of advocate quite well for their child, and provide resources to make adequate rehabilitation possible. Young soccer players need the soothing guidance that parents or family member can provide. Even national team players turn to their parents, husband, or other family members when injury occurs.

It's not within the scope of this book to provide detailed rehabilitation for each body part. General principles exist, however, that may be utilized regardless of the site that is injured. Minor acute injuries generally respond to the RICE techniques. This stands for Rest, Ice, Compression, and Elevation.

Relative rest means removal from the activity that created the injury. This is generally done until adequate evaluation is done by the trainer, therapist, or physician. The sprained ankle, strained quadriceps, and bruised elbow all do well with ice application. Heat should not be used early in the injury process. It's best to use ice alone in the first seventy-two hours of any acute injury, and it's also useful in chronic overuse problems.

Compression refers to gentle pressure, usually provided by an elastic bandage or other mild pressure device. Elevation should be aimed at placing the injured extremity slightly higher than the athlete's heart. This helps with swelling control, and allows movement of fluid away from the injured joint.

Rehabilitation of the soccer player begins the moment the injury occurs. Proper use of these techniques can lead to full recovery. Criteria for return to play are:

1. Normal range of motion of the injured area
2. No, or minimal, pain at the injury site
3. No, or controlled swelling
4. Strength ninety percent of the opposite side

Special Topics

Heat Problems/Hyperthermia: Since soccer is primarily played outdoors, heat can play a significant part in your ability to compete. Heat exposure can lead to diminished performance in the non-acclimated athlete and can lead to various forms of heat illness. Mild forms of heat stress can present themselves as cramps, light-headedness and exhaustion. But more serious forms can be life threatening.

Danielle Fotopoulos suffered a serious knee injury in April of 1997. She diligently worked on her rehab, and two years later she was playing in the World Cup.

The untrained athlete is certainly at higher risk for heat-related emergency. Other factors may lead to various levels of increased risk. Various drugs may lead to problems with heat dissipation, as can improper clothing coverage. Beverages that promote urinary frequency like coffee, tea and caffeinated beverages, can also lead to increased water loss. In small children this, combined with the loss from sweating, can lead to dehydration.

Heat cramps are usually secondary to the loss of salt in sweating. Muscle spasms and cramps, especially in the lower limbs, may be present. The athlete may also feel total body

---

TIPS FOR THE INJURED ATHLETE

1. When you see a sports medicine physician, bring a list of questions to ask.

2. Ask the doctor to write down your injury, a treatment plan and what your follow-up should be.

3. Ask what you can do to stay fit during your recovery from your injury — "Can I go in the pool? Can I ride a stationary bike," and so on.

4. Work with an athletic trainer or a sports physical therapist for the rehabilitation process.

5. Stay involved with your team. Go to training and show your teammates you support the team.

6. Learn from watching training. You can be a student of the game while injured.

7. Stay positive. Believe you will be back.

8. Visualize your return to the field.

weakness, fatigue, and nausea. Treatment is aimed at removal from the heat, mild cooling, stretching, and icing as necessary for the affected muscles. Athletes who have cramps during heat activities should carefully rehydrate with an electrolyte solution. Various sport drinks are good choices to replenish the body's water supply.

Heat exhaustion can be characterized by light-headedness, weakness, profuse sweating, headache, and nausea and vomiting. This is a more serious problem and may even show core temperature elevation. If you are showing these symptoms, it's important to immediately begin a cooling process. Sweaty clothing should be removed and immediate oral hydration begun. It may be necessary to cool down with fans and to bath in lukewarm water to lower the core temperature.

The heat stroke is the most serious of all problems and should be treated as a true emergency. This can be characterized by changes in mental status and should be cause for immediate hospitalization.

Heat illness is preventable. Coaches and athletes must recognize high-risk conditions and take steps to prevent problems associated with this environmental exposure. You should wear light, permeable clothing during times of risk, and you should concentrate on pre-hydration before exercise. Time should be spent getting acclimated to heat before intensive exposure. Women's National Team members monitor their weight before and after practice, and greater than three percent of body weight loss indicates dehydration. Every effort should be made to insure adequate hydration during practices and games.

Unique Female Issues: As the number of women participating in soccer and sports continues to grow, medical professionals have become aware of several unique problems that face women. These include special problems of menstrual dysfunction and nutritional problems. These gender-specific problems must be understood to ensure you receive proper medical support. Other medical problems can occur if these issues are ignored.

Exercise And The Menstrual Cycle: The U.S. average for onset of menses is about twelve-and-a-half years with the range generally occurring between nine and seventeen years of age. This coincides quite closely with the beginnings of high-level soccer training in many young women. It has been shown that menstrual cycle irregularities can exist in athletes, especially those who are training at intense levels. Menstrual problems include delayed menarche, and exercise associated amenorrhea.

Delayed menarche, also known as primary amenorrhea, is the failure of menses to begin by sixteen years of age. Intense training in the years leading up to this event has been thought to be related to delayed onset. It's believed that the low body weight associated with intense exercise may disrupt the female brain-ovary endocrine cycle. The consequences of a delayed menarche may be a mildly increased risk of stress fractures, and delayed appearance of breast growth and other signs of female maturation.

Young athletes who have not begun menstruation by sixteen years of age may need medical evaluation. The physical examination and clinical testing usually reveals no abnormalities. When the delay relates to the levels of exercise, the physician may suggest exercise reduction and increase in body weight and fat to induce menstruation. It's important to consult with a physician to discuss the possible causes and appropriate management if this occurs.

Exercise associated amenorrhea is occurring with increased frequency as young women participate in sports at ever higher intensity levels. Women participating in all sports are subject to this unique problem. This problem occurs when a normal menstrual function suddenly stops, and the athlete no longer experiences a regular cycle.

Several factors may predispose the soccer athlete to exercise associated amenorrhea. This includes problems with late menarche, training prior to menarche, high-level training, decreased body weight, and poor nutrition.

"Fitness tests make statements about the ability of the body to generate and use various energy systems or factors of physical fitness necessary for exercise."
— Don Kirkendall, Ph.D.

CHAPTER XI
FITNESS TESTING

Before 1994, there was no current test data on women soccer players. During the 1995 residency camp prior to the World Cup, the women's national team was put through a series of tests, which measured speed, agility, endurance, power and aerobic capacity. Don Kirkendall assisted the national team staff with the testing and data. These are on-going tests which the team is put through two or three times a year. (3) Now there is finally test data not only for coaches, but for our young athletes to measure themselves against.

"Physical fitness is an umbrella term for a number of factors including, among others:

▲ Agility: The ability to accurately change position and direction
▲ Speed: The time it takes to travel a total distance
▲ Power: The rate at which work is performed (work/time)
▲ Endurance: The time limit of a person's ability to sustain work
▲ Local Muscle endurance: The endurance of a specific muscle group

Because soccer fitness is a mixture of these, you must develop in each of these areas."
— From *Fitness Assessment of the U.S. Women's National Team*
By Don Kirkendall

When testing your physical conditioning, it is important to remember to go into your testing fresh and rested in order to get pure measurements. Also, you cannot perform too many different tests on the same day or even over back to back days. No one fitness test can be used to assess a soccer player. Be sure to pick an example in each area, and then, schedule the tests in a way that minimizes performing one test back to back with another test that could influence your results. For example, if you run the three-hundred-yard shuttle and then try to perform the three-hop test, you will shred your muscles and affect your data. Adequate recovery after testing must be factored into your schedule. If you have an important game coming up within that week, now might not be the best time. Testing periods are typically done during the pre-season, mid-season, post-season and off-season time frames.

Fitness is an important part of the equation. It factors into your technical level, tactical execution and your psychological dimension. The following tests and standards will serve as guides for your training for excellence in the physical pillar. You must also appreciate, though,that you cannot only train this dimension and be the best player you can.

PHYSICAL TESTING OPTIONS

TESTING AGILITY

Purpose: Agility tests measure your ability to accelerate, decelerate and change direction.

▲ ▲ ▲ ▲ 20-Yard Agility Test ▲ ▲ ▲ ▲

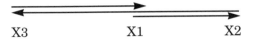

Set-up: Place a cone or a shoe as a center marker. Measure out five yards in both directions from the middle marker. Place the cone so the center of the cone is at the end of the five- yard distance (If you don't have a cone, use tape or a shoe.)

Method:

1. Start by straddling the center-line with your feet equal distance from the center spot (X1). Face forward so the wide cones are on your right and left.
2. Start with your hand on the cone or line.
3. On the word *"go"* run toward the cone of your choice (for example, X2), touch it with your foot.
4. Change direction and run past the center cone to the opposite cone (X3) and touch inside the boundaries of the cone or touch the line, turn and sprint past the center cone.
5. The total distance then is 20 yards.
6. Perform three times and record your best score.

Considerations:

The time to run this test is so short that determining differences between athletes is difficult.

Standards

20-Yard Agility (sec)					
	TEAM AVG	**GK**	**MF**	**FWD**	**DEF**
WNT					
Apr '96	4.75	4.97	4.68	4.71	4.73
Mar '98	4.35	4.41	4.39	4.32	4.30
Sep '98	4.34	4.40	4.33	4.38	4.30
Jan '99	4.24	4.28	4.24	4.20	4.23
U-21					
Jan '99	4.57	4.69	4.66	4.56	4.47
CLUB '97					
U-12	5.85				
U-13	5.88				
U-14	5.45				
U-15	5.49				
U-16	5.34				
U-18	5.55				
U-18	5.22				

▲ ▲ ▲ ▲ The T-Agility Test ▲ ▲ ▲ ▲

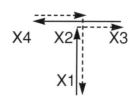

Set-up: Place a cone (tape or a shoe) down as a marker. Walk out ten yards. Place another cone. From the high cone, place a marker out five yards on each side. It should look like a T.

Method:
1. Start at the base of the T (X1).
2. Sprint out to the middle cone (X2), go past it and shuffle to the cone on the right (X3).
3. Do not cross feet while shuffling. Hit the marker on the right side, turn and sprint to the cone on the opposite side (X4).
4. Then shuffle just past the center cone, and then, back peddle to the start point.
5. Hit your watch when you leave, or if someone is timing you, have them start the watch when you initiate the test and then stop it after you cross over the starting point.

*Note there are other T Tests. Be sure if you make comparisons they are from the same test types.

Standards

T-Agility Test (sec)					
	TEAM AVG	GK	MF	FWD	DEF
WNT					
Mar '98	9.02	9.53	9.15	8.74	8.83
Sep '98	9.16	9.34	9.18	9.14	9.08
Jan '99	9.10	9.39	9.15	9.00	8.95
U-21 WNT					
Jan '99	9.32	9.55	9.62	9.31	9.08

▲ ▲ ▲ ▲ Illinois Agility Test ▲ ▲ ▲ ▲

Set-up: Measure out the course in a 10-yard square. Use cones for start/finish "gate." Place flags at the top two corners of the grid, and at the five-yard mark on the top and bottom of the grid. Next, place two flags down the middle of the grid — every ten feet. To create a slalom.

Method:

1. Player starts by lying on their stomach with their hands at the chest level (should not be supporting any body weight with their hands) and both legs extended without their cleats being "dug in."
2. On the "start" command, the player scrambles to their feet and runs the course as fast as possible.
3. Player runs from X1 around X2 and heads to X3. At X3 the player zig zags up and back around the flags.
4. Next, head from X3 to X4, around and sprint across at X5.
5. Take the average of the 2 fastest trials.

Considerations:

1. Because this agility test is longer (65 yards) it serves as a better marker.
2. There is a huge potential to tear up the grass in this test. Rotate the test course by trading the start/finish locations with the first and last flag; turn the course 90 degrees, then 180 degrees; move the course completely.
3. It is best if you have options for moving the course planned ahead of time to minimize time to re-set the course.
4. Players may try to cheat the start by bearing weight on their hands and feet.
5. There is a bit of a learning effect, so the final run is frequently the best.
6. Remember that the clock starts at the tester's command.
7. Players may start from either start/finish gate.

Standards

Illinois Agility Test (sec)					
	TEAM AVG	GK	MF	FWD	DEF
WNT					
Feb '98	15.64	16.50	15.40	15.54	15.52
U-21 WNT					
Feb '99	16.44	16.89	16.41	16.25	16.30
May '98	16.50	16.05	16.88	16.67	16.21
COLLEGE	TEAM +GK	TEAM Only	GK Only		
'98 PRE	17.61	--	--		
FALL '98	17.79	17.63	18.47		
SPRING '99	17.26	17.16	17.80		
CLUB '98					
U-13	18.71				
U-14	19.11				
U-15	17.79				
U-16	18.62				
U-18	18.57				
U-18	19.22				

TESTING ACCELERATION AND SPEED

Purpose: Although a soccer player really only sprints (at full speed) a short time over the duration of a match, the ability to sprint or perform short, high speed runs can be a factor in victory. There is explosive speed or acceleration and then pure speed which can be measured over a forty-yard run.

▲ ▲ ▲ ▲ 20-Yard — 40-Yard Dash ▲ ▲ ▲ ▲

Set-up: Place a marker or cone at the start point. Take a tape measure and mark off a 20-yard distance. Place a marker. Continue walking out with the measure tape and place markers at the forty-yard mark.

Method:

1. Be thoroughly warmed-up and stretched.
2. Perform a few pick-up runs to ensure warmup and familiarize yourself with the distance.
3. Have someone stand at the twenty-yard marker and then at the forty-yard marker.
4. Start with one foot on the start line. Sprint as fast as you can past the twenty-yard marker and continue past the forty-yard marker. If you have only one timer repeat for both the twenty and the forty.
5. Decelerate slowly over an additional twenty yards. This is important in injury prevention. Repeat 2-3 times.
6. Record your best time.

Considerations:

1. This can be performed using an electric eye. This is an electronic device that has a photo-electric cell attached to a timer.
2. If you give yourself a 3-5 yard run to start the forty, then this is referred to as a "flying" forty versus a stand start. Either is fine but be careful in comparing times as they will be different.

Standards

20-Yard Acceleration (sec)					
	TEAM AVG	GK	MF	FWD	DEF
WNT					
Mar '98	3.11	3.16	3.21	3.04	3.06
Sep '98	3.03	3.14	3.06	3.03	2.96
Jan '99	2.93	2.96	2.97	2.88	2.91
U-21 WNT					
May '98	3.23	3.24	3.31	3.23	3.13
Jan '99	3.03	3.12	3.19	3.06	2.89
CLUB '98					
U-13	3.70				
U-14	3.39				
U-15	3.36				
U-16	3.57				
U-18	3.31				
U-18	3.81				

Standards

40-Yard Dash: Standing start (sec)					
	TEAM AVG	**GK**	**MF**	**FWD**	**DEF**
WNT					
Mar '98	5.38	5.57	5.51	5.26	5.29
Sep '98	5.20	5.45	5.24	5.18	5.11
Jan '99	5.36	5.55	5.49	5.23	5.26
U-21 WNT					
Jan '99	5.32	5.53	5.37	5.27	5.24
CLUB '97					
U-13	6.48				
U-14	6.54				
U-15	6.13				
U-16	6.28				
U-18	5.97				
U-18	6.13				

40-Yard Dash: Flying start-electric eye (sec)					
	TEAM AVG	**GK**	**MF**	**FWD**	**DEF**
WNT					
Feb '98	4.84	5.03	4.94	4.72	4.72
Apr '96	4.99	5.20	4.95	4.91	5.04
U-21 WNT					
May '98	4.700	4.86	4.72	4.51	4.73
COLLEGE	**TEAM +GK**	**TEAM Only**	**GK Only**		
Spring '99	5.10	5.01	5.59		

TESTING POWER

Purpose: As a soccer player, we are most interested in the power of your lower body. Power is the rate at which work is performed. There are a few ways to measure the power in your lower body. One is to measure your vertical jump. This is your ability to jump high. A second way is to perform three consecutive double leg jumps or three-hop. It is in essence a standing long jump three times in a row without stopping in between jumps.

▲ ▲ ▲ ▲ Vertical Jump ▲ ▲ ▲ ▲

Set-up: Take a tape measure and mark off distances up a wall starting at head height. This measurement should extend at least two feet above your arm's reach.

Method:
1. Stand next to a wall sideways. Reach up as far as you can with that one arm.
2. Mark your reach.
3. For a standing jump measurement, jump as high as you can, touch the wall at the highest point possible.
4. Mark your jump and touch.
5. Measure the distance between your highest reach and your jump and reach.
6. This is your vertical jump.
7. Repeat this with a rock step or one step jump. Keep both results.

Considerations:
1. If your team or school has access to a "Vertex" you can measure your jump this way more effectively.
2. Note the testing standards for vertical jump are with a Vertex and include both one step and no-step vertical jump distances.

Standards

Vertical Jump: No step (inches)					
	TEAM AVG	GK	MF	FWD	DEF
WNT					
Apr '96	21.73	21.5	21.8	21.6	21.4
Mar '98	22.70	22.4	21.9	23.6	23.0
Jan '99	22.18	22.4	21.0	23.3	22.3

Standards (cont.)

Vertical Jump: One step (inches)					
	TEAM AVG	**GK**	**MF**	**FWD**	**DEF**
WNT					
Mar '98	24.6	24.3	23.6	24.6	25.7
Jan '99	23.72	24.4	22.4	24.7	23.9
U-21 WNT					
Mar '97	20.78	21.17	20.70	19.75	21.33
May '98	20.81	21.00	19.58	21.70	21.08
COLLEGE	**TEAM +GK**	**TEAM Only**	**GK Only**		
'98 PRE	22.75	--	--		
FALL '98	22.10	21.63	24.00		
SPRING '99	20.29	20.09	21.33		
CLUB '97					
U-12	15.85				
U-13	16.27				
U-14	17.97				
U-15	17.46				
U-16	18.79				
U-18	20.35				
U-18	18.04				
CLUB '98					
U-13	15.89				
U-14	15.75				
U-15	17.89				
U-16	17.07				
U-18	18.63				
U-18	15.86				

▲ ▲ ▲ ▲ Three-Hop or Reciprocal Double-Leg Jumps ▲ ▲ ▲ ▲

Purpose: This is another means by which to measure your leg power. It gives you information on your explosiveness or power.

Set-up: Have a measure tape laid out. Place target markers at or near your anticipated jump distance.

Method:
1. Be sure to be warmed up and stretched.
2. Perform three consecutive double-leg jumps.
3. Do not stop and rest after each jump. Hit and go.
4. Mark where your heel hits on your third jump.
5. Repeat three times and keep best result.

Considerations:

Be careful to not repeat more than the recommended number of times as these can cause you to pull your leg muscles.

Standards

Three-Hop (feet-inches)					
	TEAM AVG	**GK**	**MF**	**FWD**	**DEF**
WNT					
Apr '96	21'6"	21'5"	21'8"	21'6"	21'4"
Mar '98	22'6"	23'	21'10"	22'7"	23'1"
Sep '98	22'3"	23'6"	21'9"	22'11"	21'8"
Jan '99	22'4"	22'8"	22'1"	22'2"	22'7"
U-21 WNT					
Apr '98	21'7"	22'	21'2"	21'9"	22'2"
Jan '99	22'3"	22'	21'2"	21'9"	22'2"

TESTING YOUR LACTATE SYSTEM

Purpose: These tests are designed to measure your ability to run at high intensity for a sustained period of time. Because the game is not always played on straight lines, we test this energy system with a change of direction. Studies have shown that as a soccer player you run at a high speed every 30-45 seconds. For example, an all-out 300 tests your ability to sustain a high-energy requirement. We have created a few tests that also involve change of direction.

▲ ▲ ▲ ▲ 300-Yard Shuttle ▲ ▲ ▲ ▲

Set-up: Place a marker for a start line and another marker out 25 yards.

Method:
1. Run out and back to the marker six times.
2. Record your time.
3. Rest five minutes and repeat.
   This gives you an idea what your base is. If your time on the second run is significantly different from the first, then your base needs work. As you get fitter, you should decrease the rest period between the two runs.

Considerations:
The times included here have been done by averaging the two times.

Standards

300-Yard Shuttle (sec)					
	TEAM AVG	**GK**	**MF**	**FWD**	**DEF**
WNT					
Apr '96	59.80	62.20	58.50	59.84	58.67
Mar '98	60.60	63.75	60.25	60.50	59.75
Sep '98	61.30	63.50	61.40	60.30	61.30
Jan '99	58.60	61.60	58.40	58.40	57.40
U-21 WNT					
Jan '99	63.37	66.50	64.17	61.80	62.57
COLLEGE					
'98 PRE	68.08				

▲ ▲ ▲ ▲ Stinkers — 240-Yard Run ▲ ▲ ▲ ▲

Set-up: Place a start marker and a marker 40 yards from the start.

Method:
1. Run out to the marker and back three times.
2. Record best time.
3. Rest one minute.
4. Repeat three times.
5. Combine total time.

Standards

Stinkers (sec)					
	TEAM AVG	GK	MF	FWD	DEF
WNT					
Apr '96	191.9	199.9	188.9	191.4	187.2

▲ ▲ ▲ ▲ 300-Meter Shuttle ▲ ▲ ▲ ▲

Set-up: Place flags at 0,10, 20, 30, 40 and 50 meters from the start.

Method:
1. Run out and around each flag and back continuously.
2. Start with the first flag.
3. Record time.

Standards

300-Meter Shuttle with Flags (sec)					
	TEAM AVG	GK	MF	FWD	DEF
U-21 WNT					
May '98	68.09	71.64	68.97	67.16	65.79
CLUB '97					
U-13	76.26				
U-14	79.54				
U-15	73.93				
U-16	75.84				
U-18	72.99				
U-18	72.35				
CLUB '98					
U-13	77.17				
U-14	77.34				
U-15	71.93				
U-16	76.08				
U-18	75.07				
U-18	77.99				

TESTING ENDURANCE

Purpose: Endurance testing gives you information about your ability to sustain work. Cardiovascularly and within muscle groups. There are many ways to measure your endurance. There are two standardized "Beep Tests" that serve to test your endurance. One, is a continuous test without recovery periods (standard beep test) and the other has built in recovery (intermittent yo-yo). Both tests pace you by a cassette tape that has set time intervals. You must have a boom box. Over time the pace you are asked to run at increases until you cannot run any more.

BEEP TESTS

▲ ▲ ▲ ▲ Standard Beep Test ▲ ▲ ▲ ▲

Purpose: It is a pure steady state endurance test. There is no rest period. It is useful to see what your base is early in the year or season. It is important to have a good base to build on. The running pace increases with repetitions.

Set-up: Mark a starting point and place a marker 20 meters from this point. You need a boom box to play the audio cassette that paces the players. The standard beep test has a continuous out and back cycle (20 meters out and 20 meters back).

Method:
1. Run out and back to markers at pace established by audio cassette.
2. Increase pace as indicated.
3. Test is over when you fail to keep up with the pace over two consecutive repetitions.
4. Partner helps keep track of your level on a recording sheet provided.
5. Each level reached corresponds to the distance covered.

Standards

Beep Test (level)					
	TEAM AVG	**GK**	**MF**	**FWD**	**DEF**
WNT					
Mar '98	10.3	9.0	11.1	10.6	10.3
Sep '98	11.5	9.6	12.1	11.6	11.6
Jan '99	11.7	9.6	12.2	11.8	12.4

▲ ▲ ▲ ▲ Intermittent Yo-Yo Recovery Beep Test ▲ ▲ ▲ ▲

Purpose: The Intermittent Yo-Yo is designed to test your endurance. It has a standard recovery phase built into the running program. It tests endurance and recovery from moderate to high intensity exercise.

Set-up: Mark a starting point and a marker 20 meters from this point. Place another marker five meters behind the starting marker. Get a boom box to play the audio that paces you.

Method:

1. You run out and back to a marker 20 meters out.
2. Each time you are given 10 seconds to walk/jog around a cone 5 meters behind the start marker.
3. You continue repeating the out and back cycle, with recovery.
4. The pace of the interval gradually increases. At each speed, there are eight repetitions.
5. The test is over when two consecutive runs are missed.

Standards

Intermittent Yo-Yo (level, meters)					
	TEAM AVG	GK	MF	FWD	DEF
WNT					
Apr '96	16.8 (1394.55)	15.6 (1000)	17.3 (1520)	16.2 (1160)	16.7 (1360)
U-21 WNT					
May '98	16.6 (1302.73)	15.15 (820)	16.6 (1326.67)	17.15 (1460.00)	17.1 (1443.33)
COLLEGE	**TEAM +GK**	**TEAM Only**	**GK Only**		
'98 PRE	16.1 (1133.00)	--	--		
FALL '98	15.8 (1074.67)	16.2 (1176.67)	14.6 (666.67)		
SPRING '99	16.6 (1338.89)	16.3 (1206.67)	15.1 (800.00)		
CLUB '97					
U-12	14.20 (528)				
U-13	14.10 (472)				
U-14	14.50 (640)				
U-15	14.45 (620)				
U-16	14.40 (589)				
U-18	14.40 (592)				
U-18	14.40 (585)				
CLUB '98					
U-13	14.40 (589)				
U-14	14.20 (533)				
U-15	15.30 (891)				
U-16	14.60 (663)				
U-18	14.60 (675)				
U-18	14.10 (486)				

LOCAL MUSCLE ENDURANCE

Purpose: To test the endurance or ability of muscle groups to perform sustained work. Two simple ways you can test this are push-ups and sit-ups.

▲ ▲ ▲ ▲ Push-Ups ▲ ▲ ▲ ▲

Set-up: Place a shoe on its side. Or have a partner place their fist down on the ground.

Method:
1. Perform the push-up so your chest hits the shoe.
2. If you put your knees down or you need to arch your back up to rest you are done.
3. Do as many push-ups as you can in one minute.

Considerations:

If you haven't been doing a strength program then perhaps 30 seconds would be a better starting point.

Standards

Push-Ups (per minute)				
	TEAM AVG	**GK**	**MF**	**FWD**	**DEF**
WNT					
Apr '96	46	41	53	43	52
Mar '98	45	47	45	41	47
Sep '98	47	36	50	41	48
Jan '99	51	43	62	40	56
U-21 WNT					
Mar '97	42	54	32	40	48
Apr '98	47	38	53	43	51
May '98	48	40	49	49	52
Jan '99	38	27	39	35	44

▲ ▲ ▲ ▲ Sit-Ups ▲ ▲ ▲ ▲

Set-up: Have someone hold your feet down (or use an object to put your feet under), keep knees bent.

Method:

1. Cross your arms and place them against your body.
2. Perform a sit-up.
3. Come up and touch your elbows to your knees (upper thighs) without your arms coming off your body.
4. Go down until your shoulder blades hit the ground.
5. Perform as many sit-ups as possible in a minute.

Considerations:

If you haven't been doing a strength program then perhaps 30 seconds would be a better starting point.

Standards

Sit-Ups (per minute)					
	TEAM AVG	GK	MF	FWD	DEF
WNT					
Apr '96	57	55	58	53	61
Mar '98	58	57	55	58	60
Sep '98	58	63	55	56	62
Jan '99	62	57	65	59	62
U-21 WNT					
Mar '97	57	69	52	53	57
Apr '98	47	45	49	53	57
May '98	56	55	53	56	58
Jan '99	51	43	54	49	54

Advanced Anaerobic Fitness Test

Purpose: Soccer players need to have very good anaerobic capacity. Creating a test more specific to the demands of the game is an ongoing process. The limitations of this test are in the fact that it requires a photo-electric cell or electric eye to measure the speed of the athlete over 30 meters, seven different runs.

Set-up: Place the photo-electric eye over a thirty meters distance. Have a recorder ready to keep time intervals.

Method:
1. From a standing start, the player sprints the thirty meters.
2. Then you have 25 seconds to return to the starting line.
3. The timer should count down the last 3-5 seconds for you to the next start.
4. Every run should be done as fast as possible.
5. The ideal standard is that your first is fastest.
6. You are trying to have a fast first thirty-meter and repeat that time over and over for the seven trials.

Results/Discussion:

The data that is collected includes:

1) **PURE SPEED** — compute the fastest run.

2) **SPEED ENDURANCE** — Average the times for all seven runs.

3) **FATIGUE** — Determine the percent decline of the fastest to the slowest. Obviously looking for the lowest percent decline.

It is important to take all three variables into account: your fastest speed, your ability to repeat at or near that speed over the seven repetitions and have as little as possible decline from your fastest time to your slowest. It is necessary to take all of these variables into account for the following scenarios:

1) If you were a slower player or didn't run as hard as you could for your first time, then it would be easy for you to sustain the slower time over and over. This would lead to a small, if at all, decline in your performances, providing misleading data by itself.

2) To only look at your actual fastest speed would only favor the fastest player. Therefore, it would not give you information about your speed endurance — your ability to run over and over at, or near, your maximum. Sprint training and interval training are two different entities, not to be confused. This test helps measure your speed endurance or your sprinting ability. Faster players tend to fatigue quicker than endurance athletes. The information gives you an idea of whether or not you can improve your ability to sprint with less recovery.

Here are two examples of data collected on two collegiate women's soccer players:

PLAYER 1	**PLAYER 2**
Time 1 4.48	Time 1 5.10
Time 2 4.67	Time 2 5.17
Time 3 4.85	Time 3 5.09
Time 4 4.82	Time 4 5.11
Time 5 4.86	Time 5 5.17
Time 6 4.89	Time 6 5.17
Time 7 4.91	Time 7 5.21

Results Player 1

Fastest time = 4.48

Average speed = 4.78

Percent decline = 9.5

Results Player 2

Fastest time = 5.09

Average speed = 5.15

Percent decline = 2.16

As you can see if you only looked at speed, player 1 would be favored. If you only looked at percent decline, player 2 would be favored. But look at each simultaneously and see that player 2 had more endurance at or near her maximum which was significantly slower than player 1. In turn, player 1, was able to sustain an overall lower average for all of her runs than player 2. Application would be to work on improving base speed in player 2 and reducing the decline of player 1's ability to sustain her top speed over time by training speed endurance. We would work on the player's ability to recover from performing high intensity work to perform it again and again.

Data courtesy of Don Kirkendall (UNC) and Patty Marchak (Duke), Steve Slain, Dave Oliver (Sports Specific Training, Orlando, Fla). Data collection was made possible by Grants from Nike, INC and USOC Sports Science and Technology and the Women's National Team Staff.

Thanks to the support of Carolina Utd.SC for their participation in the youth aspects of this project.

Technical Section

"As a kid, I was always messing around with the ball, or playing pickup. I didn't just play at practice. I didn't realize how important it was then, but now I can see that it was very important."
— **Tisha Venturini**

CHAPTER I
THE TOOLS OF THE GAME

There is a saying — no technique, no tactics. If the players on a team cannot perform the basic skills or techniques, all the tactics in the world won't help. The players you admire as skillful have earned your respect by working countless hours perfecting their talents. Some of you will have some skills that are better than others. Some of you will feel more natural with the ball than others. Regardless, you can become better at any of these areas through practice.

The techniques used in a soccer game are heading, shooting, passing, dribbling and receiving. It's critical that you spend time developing these skills. Good technique combined with adequate practice time and repetition can result in the skills you need to reach your goals. Although I will not go into the proper motions and analyze technique, I want to give you suggestions for taking your game to another level. I want to sell you on the process of becoming a champion. The tools shared here can be implemented even if you have no one with whom to train. You can always find someone that can give you a few on-site tips, but the bulk of the responsibility belongs to you.

It isn't enough to just train these individual techniques. It isn't enough to perform repetitions and expect proficiency. Technical training is tied to the training mentality we established in the first section of this book. How you train, even technically, will determine how you evolve as a player. Do you do what is comfortable, or do you go outside your comfort zone to get to the next level?

I know everyone admires how Michelle Akers can strike a ball. Everywhere I go, I tell players like yourself that Michelle spends hours and hours a week shooting. Whether it's against the wall or

Photo by J. Brett Whitesell

with a partner serving her balls, she repeats basic shooting techniques over and over with precision and with an edge.

Mia Hamm is one of the fastest players in the world with the ball at her feet. Certainly, she is fast. But not all fast players have her speed with the ball — what we call "technical speed." The other magical aspect of Mia's game is her ability to change direction while running full speed at players. That doesn't just happen. She trains that quality. In her personal technical training, Mia is constantly defying her limits. There is always more to be done and more ground to gain. She works that much harder to set new standards for herself.

"When I made the national team, it was a big eye-opener," says Mia. "Before that, my speed made up for a lot of technical shortcomings. That's how I would beat people, with speed. When I made the national team, I realized I wasn't technical enough. I quickly found out that everybody was fast. Then you play against Norway and Germany and everybody has pretty good speed. So I had to learn other ways to beat people — technically, tactically. When you start playing against players who are fast, you have to beat them in other ways. You just can't rely on your ability to run past them anymore. You have to go laterally, and get balls played into space."

Carla Overbeck, the anchor of the national team's defense, and Julie Foudy, Brandi Chastain, Tisha Venturini and Michelle Akers, our central midfielders, can serve a ball fifty yards with either foot. After practice, they are often looking for each other to practice hitting long balls. Because of its importance to the game, we actually started making long-ball service one of the national team's standards, in addition to fitness, that we test during each camp. Like heading, long-ball service is one of the first skills you lose if you don't work on it.

All great players can attest to the fact that you can improve your technique on your own. As always, be creative when you are working on your skills. Lorrie Fair and her twin sister Ronnie spent a great deal of time playing little games with the soccer ball. "It started on the garage door, and we had a field very close to our house," says Lorrie. "We'd drag anyone we could find out with us. There was also a tennis court near our house, and my sister, our best friends and I would go out until about nine o'clock playing soccer tennis until our legs fell off. Then we'd bike home and find out our mom had been searching for us everywhere. By the time we got home, we'd be almost falling asleep."

Photo by PAM / ISI

Lorrie Fair and her twin sister, Ronnie, spent hours playing pickup games as youngsters.

Going to a racquetball court or using a wall is one of the best ways to work on a variety of technical skills when you don't have a training partner. Repetition is so vital to mastering any technical skill, and the number of repetitions you can do in twenty minutes in a racquetball court is tremendous. There are many ways you can use a racquetball or squash court, or any wall, to train many aspects of the technical pillar. Tisha Venturini is so clean technically, she can head, has a great first touch, can shoot and volley anything. Her ability comes from preparation.

"I really don't have a lot of people to play with," says Tisha Venturini. "So I'll go into the racquetball court a lot and do ball-handling for thirty minutes or so. I'll finish up by striking balls against the wall using proper technique. I try to get into a rhythm, and I'll work on turning and shooting against the far wall. In the racquetball courts, with the slick floor, it makes it harder so it's a better workout. And with all of the ball-handling I do, the ball moves faster and it makes you work harder."

Adds Julie Foudy, "I do a lot of stuff by myself. I go to the high school near my home and get on the racquetball courts and do shooting. I work on bending the ball against the racquetball court wall."

A key ingredient to training yourself is the ability to self-monitor or self-coach. For example, you should be able to feel the difference between when you volley the ball correctly and when you don't. The challenge is to be able to learn how to make adjustments. If the ball goes up instead of on a more even path, you should start asking yourself questions and learn how to make corrections on your own. That's essential to self-coaching. It doesn't mean you do not ask your coach for advice on specific techniques. Even the best still look for feedback. But the feedback is then stored so that when you are on your own, you can recall the tips and help yourself train.

You must realize that your dreams and aspirations may be different than many of your friends and teammates, meaning you must be able to get it done sometimes by yourself. "We didn't have all the opportunities players have today," says Tracey Bates Leone. "The ODP program was just beginning and the national teams were paper teams. European trips were not even considered. But I think there were many benefits to our situation. I went out with my older sister or by myself everyday and played with the ball for hours — in the back yard or against a wall (our poor neighbors), just making things up and loving it. There weren't as many organized practices back then, maybe two-to-three times a week, so we played indoor soccer at the recreation center down the street with neighborhood kids everyday after school and everyday in the summer. Even before practice. We played soccer tennis at night under lit tennis courts. Many of our friends were guys, so we played with and against guys growing up, many of them older. The Bates girls and some of our friends were the only girls.

"It was a social event for me and my sisters," Tracey adds. "There was nothing I would rather have been doing. All that really helped my technical ability and speed of play."

There is no secret to why the technical players possess the skill they do. They spend time with the ball, enjoy it and are creative in the ways they find to train technique.

CHAPTER II
DRIBBLING

Dribbling needs to be a regular part of your training. There are many different ways to dribble. Speed dribbling is the most popular, and that's what April did and what Tiffeny Milbrett, Shannon MacMillan and Mia Hamm do so terrifyingly well. Not many of you could run without the ball as fast as they can with the ball. Defenders absolutely hate to have to mark them. Mia can also change direction with the ball better than anyone in the world at top speed. On Mia's first goal against England in 1997, she beat a player not once but three times, and by the time the ball had gone in the net, four defenders were eliminated. Mia has a sixth sense of a defender's balance and offsets them by design.

"Everything has to be based on the situation," says Mia. "If they are playing good defense on you, what you hope to do is keep the ball moving and watch to see if they try to change their feet to step, and then you hope to get them off-balance. If they get off-balance, then maybe you can put the ball past them at that moment and cut it past them. Those are all things that come with experience, repetition and confidence." Tracey Bates Leone had the nickname in 1991 of Willamena Coerver, the female counterpart to Weil Coerver who has developed many

Tiffeny Milbrett utilizes sharp and explosive cuts when she dribbles.

Photo by J. Brett Whitesell

tools to help you learn movements with the ball that we use frequently. Well, Tracey had spent so much time with the ball, she could perform Coervers quicker than anyone else on the team. It wasn't a mystery why. Tracey practiced these religiously. She recalls how she became such a good dribbler in a tight space.

"You must spend time with the ball — you and a ball," says Tracey. "And you must absolutely master it. What's awesome is that it's so much fun. What I'm learning more and more as college coach is that great technical ability sometimes takes years and years to develop."

We used to have a saying: "Is the ball your friend?" Each player knew what we meant. Had they been spending time making friends with the ball. "In soccer, to be deceptive and creative with the ball is critical," says April Heinrichs. "To be competent with the ball, spend a lot of time working with it. Be creative. You can dribble around your living room to work on simple changes of directions — you get to the end table that's a defender. Change directions. You get to the couch, another defender. Change directions."

A great place to become friendly with the ball is in a racquetball court. Also, before every practice get there a few minutes early. During that time, warm up with the ball. Too often, players sit around waiting for the coach to arrive. By spending that five to fifteen minutes making friends with the ball, you can become magical with it. Not surprisingly, the players that are good on the ball, spend time playing with the ball. You must be willing to embrace the areas that are less comfortable for you, and the time to start is now. The longer you wait, the less likely you will be to start over on the basics.

Photo by J. Brett Whitesell

Before the 1999 World Cup, Mia Hamm became the world's all-time leading goal-scorer, tallying her 108th against Brazil on May 22, 1999.

Mia is always spending time with the ball. She often does throw the cones down as she describes here. They are much closer than you would think possible. Yet, because Mia accelerates so fast and has such great ability to change direction, she rarely hits a cone. Give it a try.

"I do little dribbling things around cones, just like eight year olds do," says Mia. "When I dribble through cones, I try to do it as fast as I can with as few mistakes as possible. It's amazing what you think of when you are by yourself. When I'm dribbling by myself, I like to throw five or six cones down, probably two yards apart in a big mess. They are all defenders. All I do is touch the ball to accelerate, and once I accelerate I'm at another cone, so I have to cut the ball and accelerate in another direction. I do that until I feel tired. I have to prepare it and shoot. I put cones in the goal about a yard or yard and a half from each post, and that's where I have to shoot.

"I do that drill for the same reason you shoot free throws at the end of a practice in basketball — because you're tired," she adds. "Usually in soccer, you are shooting at the end of a long run or after you've beaten someone. After a long run, it's hard to have that concentration and focus."

Dribbling is a skill that can differentiate you from other players. There are different types of dribbling: speed dribbling, creative dribbling, take-on or explosive dribbling, dribbling to solve pressure. In all of these circumstances, you must develop a comfort level with the ball. We actually took several of the Coerver moves and created a routine that we use and often teach young players. It's easy to remember, and it teaches you to use different surfaces of your feet in dribbling. Remember you might not actually use all of these moves while competing, but they teach you how to move like a soccer player. Invest in the Coerver tapes or one of the books listed in the back of this book for more ideas.

We took some of the moves in Weil Coerver's book *Soccer Fundamentals for Players and Coaches* (1) and adapted them to have three touches. We renamed them "Chinese Coervers." The Chinese always took an extra touch. One touch is to eliminate the defender. The second quick touch is to prepare the ball, and the third is to execute. Their adaptation was the small second touch that was used to get a hold of the ball. This series primarily varies the first touch. You can cut (or chop) the ball, pull it (using the ball of your foot), cut behind your standing leg and roll it (using more of your foot than the pull, which really only uses the sole of your foot; rolling it can use the bottom of your foot).

These movements and time spent practicing dribbling, cutting and changing direction, teach you to move like a soccer player. They can help you work on lowering your center of gravity, which helps you change direction better and avoid being bumped off the ball. Practicing these movements also will develop your local muscle endurance. You will feel it in your calf muscles as you practice. Remember, once you have a comfort level, try to go up a notch and do it more quickly or more explosively. We do the following series for quickness first, then, after being warmed up, for explosiveness.

Cutting the Ball

You can begin by first trying to just cut the ball back and forth on a line. Use a sharp precise motion using the inside of your foot. You can also practice cutting with the outside of your foot. Mia is awesome at cutting the ball. She likes to make her defender believe she is going one way, even adds a fake in that direction, then cut. The defender usually ends up on the ground, and Mia looks to shoot, pass or take the ball in the other direction.

Cut Inside, Outside-Outside: Cut the ball with the inside of one foot, and touch it with the outside of the opposite foot with a little touch, then bigger touch; then cut with that foot and then the outside of opposite foot, little and big. The little touch we use in these sequences is a preparatory touch, then the next touch in a game would be to take-on, to shoot to pass, etc.

Cut Inside, Inside-Outside: Cut inside right, touch inside left, touch outside left. Cut inside left ... and repeat.

ADDING VARIETY TO YOUR GAME

"The Coervers helped me develop confidence with all different surfaces of my feet," says Mia Hamm. "You can't always use the inside or outside of your foot. Sometimes, you have to pull the ball back. Sometimes you have to chop it behind your standing leg, or lift it. All these things go hand in hand. If you work on them all the time, it becomes instinctual. You won't have to think about it.

"Repetition is also very important," adds Mia. "I work on my dribbling all the time, trying to find different ways to do things."

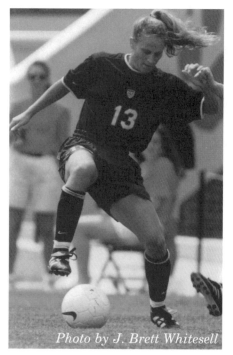
Photo by J. Brett Whitesell

Pulling the Ball

Pulling the ball uses the sole of the foot (the pad below your toes).

Pull, Outside-Outside: Pull the ball (using sole of your foot) under your body, then touch outside, outside with opposite foot. It's almost like drawing a V. The ball is out in front of you. A defender goes to tackle it. You pull it back away from them as they step at you, touch it with the outside of the opposite foot, then push it penetratively forward to eliminate them with your touch. Remember, the second touch is small and designed to get the ball under control and prepare it to do something else.

Pull, Inside-Outside: Pull the ball under your body with one leg and touch it with the inside of the opposite foot, followed by the outside of that foot. Again, draw a V. Keep it going side to side.

Cut Behind Standing Leg

This again is a cutting action behind the leg you are standing on. As you get comfortable with this, try to keep your foot off the ground between the second and third touches.

Cut Behind, Outside-Outside: In order to cut behind your standing leg, it helps to step past the ball slightly with your plant foot. Then cut the ball with one foot, catch up to it with the outside of your other foot, and outside again. Repeat back and forth.

Cut Behind, Inside-Outside: This is an agility challenge. After you cut the ball behind your standing leg, you need to get your hip opened up and catch it with the inside of the opposite foot, followed by outside again. Repeat back and forth.

Again, this is a simple pattern that varies which surface you use to perform your first touch. Then, you perform each using the outside of the opposite twice, or the inside-outside combination.

Dribbling Tips
▲ Practice, practice, practice
▲ Be creative
▲ Develop one or two favorite moves
▲ Coervers - maybe invest in a book or tape
▲ You have two feet, use both of them
▲ Insides .... outsides ... sole ... toes.. heel
▲ Touch for quickness
▲ Touch for explosiveness
▲ Change direction
▲ Change your pace
▲ Use feints or fakes
▲ Make the ball your friend
▲ Train on your edge. If it feels comfortable, train harder.
▲ Stay low so you can change direction, accelerate and avoid being bumped off the ball.

Carin (Jennings) Gabarra, one of the world's all-time great dribblers

CHAPTER III
PASSING

Shannon Higgins Cirovski served both assists in the final of the first Women's World Cup in China, 1991. We won 2-1. The attention to detail she speaks of is the difference between being an average player and a great player. Passing the ball may be the most important technique in soccer. If you can't pass the ball from Point A to Point B, you are going to have trouble playing the game. Like all techniques, passing can be improved with practice on your own. It's important to start using both feet as young as possible. In addition, I would recommend that you challenge yourself to use different surfaces of your feet. Can you pass with the inside of your foot, outside of your foot, on the laces (or instep), or your heel?

If you watch the elite teams play, you can pick out many players with tremendous passing ability. Michelle Akers, for example, is one of the best passers in the world. She can use all four surfaces very well, inside and outside of both feet. She can, therefore, "paint the field" with her distribution. Brandi Chastain played a critical role for us after becoming a defender for us and helped us win a Gold medal. With her technical ability and her ability to playmake and set play out of the back, she set a new standard for defenders.

Photo by J. Brett Whitesell

Excellent passing is just one element of Mia Hamm's offensive arsenal.

One of the great qualities I like about the Brazilian men's team is they can slice a defense with a pass. It stems from their ability, and subsequent confidence, to bend, texture and serve different types of balls. They can get players in the box with what we term a "final pass." A final pass is a ball that puts a player into dangerous positions in the final third. Julie Foudy had a brilliant final pass with perfect pace to Shannon MacMillan for the Golden Goal in the Olympic semifinal win over Norway. The timing and the weight of the pass were such that Shannon ran on to it, never broke stride and knocked it one-time into the goal and put us into the gold medal game.

Keepers Have to Play

The ability to pass the ball is not only critical for field players, but for goalkeepers, too.

"We jump into games all the time," says national team goalkeeper Tracy Ducar. "You have to be able to play with your feet. A lot young keepers say they hate playing on the field. I tell them, 'Get used to it. You need all those skills.' Some players will play once or twice, and they don't see any improvement so they stop doing it. It takes time. It took me a whole season to develop my goal kicks. I never took goal kicks in high school or in college. I spent a lot of time on them, and now, I wouldn't say it is a strength, but it's no longer a weakness."

PASSING

PASSING TIPS
▲ Repetition.
▲ Strike the ball cleanly by keeping your ankle locked.
▲ Follow through with your kicking foot.
▲ Properly weight the pass — is it too hard or too soft?
▲ First touch preparation when playing two touch.
▲ Make your teammate look good.
▲ Use all surfaces of both feet.
▲ Find a wall no one minds you using!

QUICKNESS
Do thirty to fifty touches with the following surfaces of your feet a short distance from the wall. (Repeat same quick-touch repetition using two touches)
▲ Instep, or on your laces
▲ Outsides of your feet
▲ Insides of your feet
▲ Two touch, alternating feet — touch right, pass left.
▲ Two touch, same foot — touch right, pass right.

ONE TOUCH SERIES
▲ Work about 8-10 yards from wall.
▲ Strike the ball with the inside of your foot.
▲ Repeat using alternating feet.
▲ Repeat one touch passing with all four surfaces of your feet.

TWO-TOUCH SERIES
▲ Pass the ball off the wall, receive ball off the wall, with one touch serve with the second touch.
▲ Receive the ball with the outside of one foot, return the pass with same foot.
▲ Receive the ball with one foot, return the pass with the opposite foot.
▲ Vary the surface you receive the ball with, and the surface with which you return the ball to the wall.

GOOD PLAYERS CAN COME IN SMALL PACKAGES

One of the most appealing things about soccer is that a person of any size can play it, and play it very well. Some of the best players in the history of the game were most likely too small to play other sports. In soccer, a small, quick player can be devastating to opposing teams.

"The beauty of soccer is that you don't have to be six-feet tall to be good at it, even at a high level," says Tracey Bates Leone, who was under five-feet tall when she played for the U.S. "There are so many dimensions to soccer that you can master to become a high-level player. Size is really not a limiting factor."

"I was really a small kid," adds Kate Sobrero. "I was 4-11 and 85 pounds as a freshman in high school. My junior year, I ended up being 5-6 and 110. I was a scrawny kid. I would get pushed a lot, but I just kept working hard. I never quit. I didn't care if I was hurt, I was going to play through it. I have never quit."

Kate has become one of the best defenders ever for the U.S.

Cindy Parlow, 5'10" and Tracey Bates Leone, 4'11" share two things — their love of the game and how good they are at playing it.

*"I was going to measure my success by
how I pursued excellence."*
— Amanda Cromwell

CHAPTER IV
RECEIVING

Receiving the ball means the same thing as the term "trapping" the ball. We use the term first touch. It is a more active state than trapping. We no longer just stop the ball. Now we prepare it. Your first touch when receiving the ball is critical. The ability to receive a ball well allows you more options. Your first touch should put you in position to do what you want or need to do. It can eliminate a defender. It can prepare you to shoot. It can help you see the field or require you to have to put your head down and recover from a poor first touch.

"Speed of play is the critical element in a player's tactical development," says Anson Dorrance. "Speed of play is your ability to do things quickly with a soccer ball. A four-year-old can stop a soccer ball, but does that mean this particular four-year-old player can trap a ball? No. This four-year-old can't trap a ball on a full run when another player is trying to cut her off at the kneecaps. As you go from one level to the next technically, you are required to be able to do things so much faster — shoot under pressure, do things with the ball without time and space, to do things with one touch, with more efficiency."

One of my funniest memories was in 1991 when we were warming up for a game during the FIFA Women's World Cup. There was Michelle Akers, April Heinrichs and Carin (Jennings) Gabarra warming up together before we started our formal team warmup. They were only a few yards apart and were drilling the ball at each other. I asked, "What are you guys doing?" One replied, "We're warming up for the types of balls we get in the game. We are working on cleaning up difficult balls." Basically, at this point we weren't as proficient delivering quality passes to our front-runners. So, as a consequence, they had to be very good at receiving difficult balls.

First touch involves receiving balls on the ground as well as balls in the air. Again, your comfort level here can be developed through repetition and confidence that your first touch is going where you want it. In order to know where you

Photo by J. Brett Whitesell

should touch it, you must always take a look before you receive the ball. This will allow you to see your teammates and your defender, giving you valuable information as to what you should do with your first touch.

You can work on receiving the ball in a squash court or off a wall. The number of times the ball comes back to you is remarkable. I do a lot of two-touch shooting in a racquetball court," says Tiff Roberts. "I shoot, then trap it and get a shot off as soon as I can. I practice my heading in there, and also passing. You can get a lot done in a racquetball court."

We have included some ideas for you regarding receiving the ball. Certainly, you can take the passing series and put the emphasis on your first touch and ability to return the ball efficiently when the ball is on the ground. In turn, we have provided a sequence for you to practice when the ball is coming off the wall in the air. This will train your ability to collect it and clean it up with the first touch, then either dribble away, pass, shoot, or turn with it. After time, you will be able to create your own workouts, by improvising and modifying your training based upon what *your* game needs. As you develop confidence in receiving the ball, add a change of pace to your movements to get to the ball. When checking to the ball, you want to always accelerate first to try to leave your defender. Then, decelerate as the ball approaches you to absorb the defender and make it easier to receive the ball and execute your next move.

Aly Wagner, one of the young stars for the national team, developed an outstanding first touch, in part, by juggling ... and juggling ... and juggling. "When I was little, maybe eight or nine years old, I juggled all the time, and I could do over a hundred before I was ten years old," Aly says. "That really helped with my touch on the ball. Our club team had a juggling ladder, and I always wanted to be on top. Once when I was twelve, I entered a juggling contest, and I got something like fifteen hundred. I was getting dizzy."

First-Touch Preparation — in the air or on the ground

You can work on your first-touch preparation by striking balls off the wall and cleaning them up. In addition, you can work on receiving or preparing balls off the wall in the air. If you are comfortable with your first-touch preparation, the next level is to add a fake or a feint before receiving the ball, or after receiving it and before serving it again.

1. Throw the ball up against the wall.

2. Prepare it with your chest one way.

3. Collect it against the ground and dribble off.

4. Repeat to both sides.

5. Next, repeat using both thighs and both feet.

6. Drive the ball off the wall.

7. Check to it, clean it up with your first touch and return it.

8. Practice your first touch with both feet.

9. Vary the surface you use on your first-touch preparation.

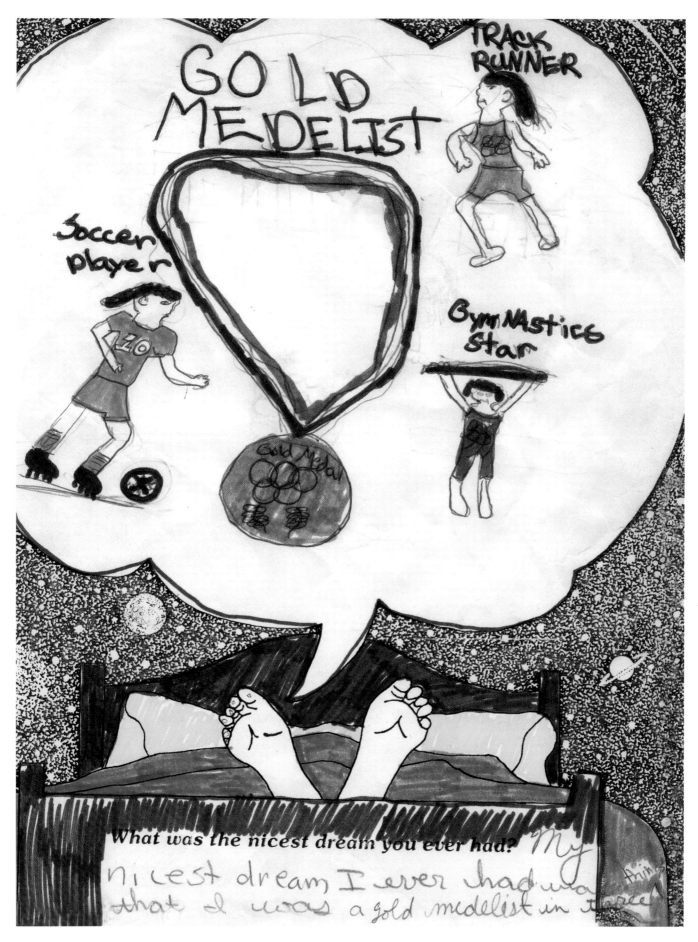

Tiffany Roberts

Photo by J. Brett Whitesell

First-ever Olympic Gold Medal Team: (Bottom left to right) Team coordinator Michelle Jolicouer, Tiffeny Milbrett, Staci Wilson, Carin Gabarra, Tiffany Roberts, Carla Overbeck, Mary Harvey, Tisha Venturini, trainer Patty Marchak, Lauren Gregg, alternate Amanda Cromwell. Second Row: alternate Jen Streiffer, alternate Thori Staples. Third Row: Shannon MacMillan, Brandi Chastain, Kristine Lilly, Julie Foudy, Michelle Akers, Cindy Parlow, Bri Scurry, Joy Fawcett, Katelyn Fawcett, Mia Hamm, April Heinrichs, Colleen Hacker, alternate Saskia Webber. Back Row: Heather Kashner, Steve Slain, team physician Dr. Mark Adams, team director Pam Perkins.

Historic Night: U.S. National Anthem before the 1991 World Cup Final — U.S. vs. Norway in China.

Photo by Phil Stephens

Photo by J. Brett Whitesell

Gold Medal Staff: The coaches for the first-ever Olympic Gold Medal women's soccer team — April Heinrichs (l), Tony DiCicco and Lauren Gregg (r).

Photo by J. Brett Whitesell

Golden Moment

Family: Being part of a team is being part of a family.
Here is part of our extended family.

Carin Gabarra with son, Tyler

Carla Overbeck with son, Jackson

Joy Fawcett with daughters, Katey and Carli

Around the World: Two countries I have found most interesting
are Haiti and China.

Young Stars: Aly Wagner (top right) and Susan Bush (top left) were the two youngest players in the '99 residency training camp. **First World Cup:** Sara Whalen (bottom left) and Danielle Fotopoulos (bottom right) made their first World Cup team in 1999.

Photo by Phil Stephens

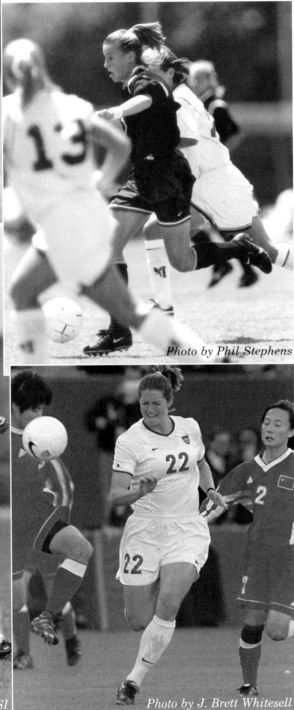

Photo by Phil Stephens

Photo by PAM / ISI

Photo by J. Brett Whitesell

The Future: The U.S. Under-20 Women's National Team, 1997 Nordic Cup Champions. Front row left to right: Jen Grubb, Michelle French, Tiffany Roberts, Lorrie Fair, Ronnie Fair and Laurie Schwoy. Back row left to right: Kristy Whelchel, Rebekah McDowell, Lakeysia Beene, Meredith Florance, Meotis Erikson, Kate Sobrero, Robin Confer, Lauren Gregg and Siri Mullinix. Not shown: Cindy Parlow and Jen Streiffer.

Success vs. Excellence

By Amanda Cromwell

"I have learned that success is to be measured not so much by the position that one had reached in life as by the obstacles which one has overcome while trying to succeed."
— Booker T. Washington

I've been thinking about my definition of what a champion is and what a champion does. And to me, champions believe in themselves when the pressure is on and when the odds are against them. Champions aren't afraid to dream, even if it means possible failure. The potential gain from a dream realized is so much greater than the perceived loss in failure, because even in failure something is always learned through the process of reaching for that goal. When something is learned, a champion sees it as a positive gain and a worthwhile venture. Champions can't accept not trying.

This brings me to the idea of Success vs. Excellence. I thought success was reaching a goal, some type of favorable result — winning a game, acing a test, etc. And I thought being successful, in the public's eye, was enough. I had success in high school, winning state championships, earning All-America honors. I had success playing for Lauren Gregg at the University of Virginia with a scholarship, playing at a big-time school, getting to tryout for the national team.

After we lost a playoff game at Virginia, I knew something was wrong with my thinking and my ambitions. Lauren helped me realize I could do more. She helped me realize what striving for excellence was all about. From that point on, I was going to measure my success by how I pursued excellence. To me, excellence is challenging the limits, going beyond setting goals, and trying to be greater than your perceived potential. I was learning that by striving for excellence I couldn't help but have success along the way.

My dream as a young girl was to someday be in the Olympics. As I earned my spot on the national team, I wasn't satisfied with just making it. I wanted to reach my dream of the Olympics and beyond. As I look back, if making the team was my only goal, I wouldn't have lasted as long as I have. I played in the 1995 World Cup in Sweden, and I kept striving to be better. In '96, I tore my ACL six months prior to the Olympics. The irony of the situation was that I had come back from being cut and the coaches thought I was playing well. I knew the road ahead would be hard but the door wasn't quite closed on my dream. At the very least, I would try. After three months of rehab, I made it back to training camp. Although I didn't have enough time to be considered for the roster of sixteen, I was selected as an alternate. I didn't reach my exact goal, because I didn't play. But I know I didn't fail for one reason — I didn't quit. If my old definition of success was in place, not playing and not receiving an Olympic Gold Medal would have been devastating. I was disappointed sure, but I tried something no one thought was possible. I pursued excellence, and I learned incredible things about myself, my teammates, and my coaches. Through that whole experience, maybe, just maybe, I inspired someone out on that field. I find myself again in period of uncertainty, but I can rest assured knowing that God "Is able to do immeasurably more than all we ask or imagine, according to his power that is at work within us." (Ephesians 4:20)

To me, striving for excellence is all about going beyond what you imagined possible or even better, going beyond what you have imagined at all, period. I know there are risks and possible disappointments, but I would never want to look back and say "What if?" I have learned that success is continuing that quest for excellence after others have let go.

CHAPTER V
TURNING

C ertainly, one of your choices as you receive the ball is to turn with it. It's important to work on turning, with and without pressure. You should work on how to shape your body up to see your defender, the quality and efficiency of your touch, as well as how to play with your back to an opponent or to the goal. Playing with your back to the goal — when you have less time and space to negotiate — is an aspect of the game you will experience as you play against better and better players.

When you receive the ball there will, obviously, be times when your decision is to shield the ball or spin out of pressure. Many times, however, players turn their backs to pressure and lose sight of the field when it's not necessary. Often, that reflects their poor comfort level on the ball. Your ability to technically receive the ball under pressure gives you the confidence you call on to use the spectrum of options available to you.

There are a variety of ways to turn with the ball, and I recommend practicing many different ways. The moment of the game will dictate the best option to use. Sometimes, players have a preconceived idea about what they are going to do with the ball which is independent of the situation. You have to respond to the game situation. An important step toward incorporating the decision-making process is a comfort level with what we call the "Three-Look Theory."

Shannon MacMillan spins out of pressure against China.

Photo by J. Brett Whitesell

Three-Look Theory

You have to train the habit of "taking looks." The term "three-look" refers to the looks you take before, during and after you receive the ball. The three-look theory gives you the information to decide whether you are going to face up, double pass, dummy it, or something else. In order to know your options, it's important to develop the ability to locate your defender. If you watch elite players, they are always looking around the field, especially before they receive the ball. This allows them to make the best decision.

1. Take looks before, during and after you receive ball. This means, before you leave to check for the ball, take a look and notice your defender's position. This will put a thought process in place. Next, look again as you are coming to the ball to reassess the situation. Lastly, look as you receive it to make final adjustments.

2. I recommend practicing just this basic habit of what we call "taking looks" or "head on a swivel." It becomes much easier to perform all subsequent movements based upon the information you gather by taking looks.

3. Knock the ball against the wall (or with a partner). As you go to receive the ball, practice the three looks. This should eventually become second nature.

Turning Series

"Soccer is a simple game," Detmar Cramer reminded us in our national "A" coaching license course, and that phrase is a good reminder to always revisit the fundamentals. Being able to turn with the ball is a basic soccer movement, and you'll find you can be more efficient if you practice turning. First, just work on the technique of turning, then add in a passive defender who forces you to choose the correct turn based on the situation.

There are countless ways to turn and receive the ball. Some will come more naturally to you than others. Remember as you develop one or two turns, make sure your choice is dependent on the game. Some players tend to decide what they are going to do before the ball comes. They aren't flexible, and by the time the ball arrives, their plan won't work. But they try it anyway. Let the game tell you what to do.

Photo by Tony Quinn

Knowing where your defender is gives you important information before receiving the ball.

Playing Back to Goal and Receiving Balls Under Pressure

Being able to play with your back to the goal becomes more important as you go to higher and higher levels. It means having the ability to receive or turn with the ball when you have defensive pressure. Back to goal turns include:

Facing Up: This turn requires that you continue checking to the ball. When you arrive at the ball, open up with your body and let the ball come across your body. Prepare it with the inside of your front foot. It's a very basic movement. The challenge is to make it as efficient as possible while maintaining all your options. You must have time and space to use this turn.

Cut Against the Grain: If you are about to receive a ball and a defender is running up your back, you can cut the ball with either the inside of the foot farthest from the defender or the outside of your other foot and use the defender's momentum against her. Usually, the ball served to you is wide of you or at least away from the defender.

Dummying the Ball: Use the same scenario as cutting against the grain. However, instead of cutting the ball, you fake as if you are going to go inside, and you let the ball go past you on the outside. If there is too much pace on the ball, you may have to guide it in such a way as to slow it down.

Receiving with the Outside of Your Foot: Believe it or not, it's important to practice what appears to be the simplest of things — receiving the ball. Ideally, you want to receive the ball "side-on," meaning your body is almost perpendicular to the defender. This body shape allows you to see your defender and penetrative options. When you are under pressure, receive the ball with the foot furthest from the defender using the outside of that foot.

Self-Pass: This means exactly what it says. You actually pass yourself the ball. Perhaps on your check to the ball, you notice you have some room but not enough to fully get around the ball and face the field. So as the ball is coming to you, try knocking it two to three yards with the inside of your foot nearest the defender, or the outside of the foot farthest from the defender. As you pass it to yourself, work on getting around the ball and facing your defender.

All of these turns and any others you can come up with — because there are limitless ways to receive or turn the ball and numerous variables that influence how and why — can be practiced against a wall. Knock it off the front wall, check to receive it, turn with it and knock it off the back wall. Take your looks to develop or maintain good habits. Remember to change pace when you check for the ball. Train the habit of accelerating to go to the ball and decelerate when you receive the ball. Then, put it into practice during training and matches.

Once you are comfortable, add a feign or a fake. Trick your defender into thinking that you are going to do one thing and then do the opposite. Don't be predictable. A simple fake will often provide you with an extra split-second, which can make all the difference in the world.

Spin Turns

Spin turns are your ability to solve pressure or change direction without exposing the ball to your opponent. There are many ways to perform this move. You can step past the ball with your right foot and then turn it away with the outside of that same foot and "spin" out. (Be sure to practice with each foot.) You can step past it with your right foot and then use the inside of your left foot to cut it away from the opponent. And lastly, you can step on the top of the ball and pull it away, putting your body between the ball and your opponent. It's important to pick your head up as you come out of any turn.

In your training or in games, you will encounter the need to spin out in different directions. For example, a front-runner may be sprinting toward the end line with the ball, and her defender gets there first. She may need to spin out on a forty-five degree angle and find someone at the top of the box. Or a flank midfielder or flank defender may be penetrating down one side of the field, and her passing options close down. The best choice may be for her to spin out, "reload" and go out the other side. This spin turn would almost be a 180-degree turn.

Following are some easy environments to practice the technique of spin-turning. These turns, if done at speed and with sharp changes of direction, are good conditioning exercises. They functionally train strength, change of direction and acceleration. If you perform these turns for thirty seconds as hard as you can, they are exhausting. For this reason, they are very good for developing local muscle endurance. A simple series is included here.

Spin Turn Series

180 Degree Turns

1. Dribble at one cone, spin out, accelerate out of the turn toward the other cone. (10-12 yards)
2. Decelerate, spin turn and repeat.
3. Try to vary the turn used each time.
4. Repeat continuously for thirty seconds.

90 Degree Turns

1. Make a square with four cones.
2. Dribble at any cone, spin out at a 90 degree angle and head to next cone.
3. You will be forming a square.
4. Be sure to change directions.
5. Vary technique used to turn.
6. Repeat for thirty seconds.
7. You can use same grid to zig-zag.
8. Make up patterns, repeat for 30 seconds.

45 Degree Turns

1. Make a triangle with three cones
2. Dribble at any cone and spin out at a 45 degree angle.
3. You will be forming a triangle.
4. Vary direction and technique.
6. Repeat for thirty seconds.

Photo by J. Brett Whitesell

Tisha Venturini developed her exceptional technical ability through hours of hard work alone with the ball.

BE SURE TO BALANCE TECHNIQUE WITH TACTICS

Certainly, working with the ball is very important. However, it's important to understand that ball work alone is not enough. You need to balance your skill work with the other pillars of the game.

"I think if a player has desire and is training by themselves, that's very important," says Laurie Schwoy. "You can't really teach a player to have desire. But I've realized lately that training on your own is not enough by itself. During my junior and senior years in high school, I'd try to play about three hours a day. But now I wish I had had more structured training. I always figured the more I was touching the ball, the better player I would become. That was enough in high school. Once you get to the higher levels, you realize touch isn't everything. The tactical parts of the game come into play a lot more, and that's the weakest part of my game because I spent so much time just with the ball.

"Getting in good competitive games is so hard for everyone, especially me because I always thought I could do it on my own and become the best player I could be," Laurie adds. "After my first year in college and playing with the national team, I realize how important games are. I get in situations I am not used to, and the best way to learn is to get into those situations more and more. I recommend that players get into as many games as possible. You have to learn to make technical and tactical decisions under pressure. Find top competition and just play."

Turning Tips

▲ Respond to what the situation requires.
▲ Take looks and know where your defender is.
▲ Face the field if you can, rather than turning your back to it.
▲ Be efficient with your body movement and your touches.
▲ Keep as many options open as possible.
▲ Use a fake or feint and sell your defender.
▲ Change speed when checking to the ball.
▲ After you come out of a turn, pick your head up and reassess the situation.

Remember, be creative and develop new games to practice your ball skills. Trust that a consistent approach to all of your ball skills will show great results, and you'll find they can be fun to work on. Certainly, some areas will become your strengths and others will become sufficient to play at the level to which you are aspiring. I bet the ball even becomes your friend!

CHAPTER VI
SHOOTING

In my career, I was referred to at the time as one of the top finishing midfielders in the United States. Without question, my work in the squash court was a significant factor in developing this ability. When your team does shooting, count how many times you actually get to shoot. Next time you go to a wall or racquetball court, see how many shots you get in twenty minutes. It's a remarkable difference. Some of our best shooters do a tremendous amount of work against a wall. Tisha Venturini and Michelle Akers are two to mention. Their strike of the ball is extremely clean. They know practice translates into confidence and ability when they are out on the field. They have trained their muscles, and it has become a habit almost ingrained in them. We will speak of this process in the Physical Section. It is termed "muscle memory."

Below are a few shooting patterns you can follow. The emphasis can be on repetition, good technique, power vs placement, bent vs driven, volleys, turning and shooting, or receiving and shooting. Great finishers make choices when they shoot.

Midfielder Julie Foudy is a goal-scorer for the U.S.

Photo by J. Brett Whitesell

Shooting Tips

▲ Repetition of good technique.

▲ Practice driving balls with your instep (using your laces).

▲ Use the outsides of your feet as well.

▲ Work on bending balls by striking the outside part of the ball .

▲ Place tape squares on the wall (if permitted!) to work on placement.

▲ Keep the ball down.

▲ Follow through and land on your kicking foot.

▲ Keep your ankle locked and toe down.

▲ Practice shooting one touch.

▲ Two-touch shooting is practiced by receiving balls off the wall and preparing them before returning the ball back against the wall.

Volleying

Volleying is when you shoot the ball out of the air. Good clean contact is the key. The tendency when volleying is to swing too hard at the ball. A firm ankle, short follow-through and lower-leg "punch" are important. To keep the ball down you must get your knee over the ball on a front-volley and even with the height of the ball on a side-volley. Tisha Venturini scored our first goal in the 1996 Olympic Games off a side-volley from a throw-in by Brandi Chastain. It was text book. It didn't surprise me, because I know Tisha spends time in the racquetball courts working on this.

Volleying With a Wall

1. Practice volleying the ball back against the wall.

2. First start close to the wall, drop the ball from your hands to your feet and volley it back, catch the ball off the wall and repeat.

3. Back up and throw or kick the ball against the wall and volley it back against the wall.

4. Throw the ball in front of you or to your side and practice a clean strike of the ball.

5. You can practice half-volleys as well.

6. See if you can juggle the ball continuously back and forth against the wall.

Volleying Tips

▲ Concentrate on keeping your head, knee and shoulders over the ball.

▲ Shorten your swing and strike the ball with a lower-leg punch.

▲ Less swing, less movement, clean contact are keys!

▲ Try to hit the ball on its way down not on the way up.

Side-Volleying

This is when you are taking the ball out of the air off to the side of your body. To get the full extension in your lower leg (which gives you the snap), you often will see players almost fall away from the shot. If the ball is high, you may need to drop your opposite shoulder to get your shooting leg even with the height of the ball. This will allow you to strike through the ball and have better success keeping it on goal. Adjusting your feet early to the flight of the ball can be important. This allows you to be set and balanced when you go to strike the ball, even if you need to fall out of it.

Side-Volleying in a Racquetball Court

1. Face the side wall. Bounce the ball in front of you and try to side-volley the ball off the front wall.

2. When you feel confident with your technique, toss the ball off the side wall and side-volley it to the front wall.

3. Side-volleying requires good movement of your feet to set your stance.

4. It's important to drop your opposite shoulder in order to get your leg even with the height of the ball when you strike it. Otherwise, it will pop up and probably result in a poor shot or go over the goal. Sometimes getting your leg even with the ball requires that you fall away on your shot, which means landing on the ground.

5. As always, practice using both feet.

JUST YOU AND A RACQUETBALL COURT

By Michelle Akers

When I was a kid — and I'd get in so much trouble doing this — I used the garage door, the side of the house, the fence, the hedge ... anything that would either stop the ball or send it back to me. Or I would go down to the elementary school, which had a three-way enclosed court. I'd hit balls by myself or with friends. I would also use a hill or a big embankment to hit balls at, so they would roll back to me.

Now, I use a racquetball court. Since I've been injured so many times, I have a rhythm of getting back into things. Often, I had to start out with a volleyball and work up to the weight of a soccer ball. In the racquetball court, I would just hit balls and work on receiving them and preparing them to shoot again, just working on hitting that sweet spot.

Usually, when I am working out in a racquetball court, it's my first step toward getting back on the field from an injury. First, I hit the ball with the inside of my foot, not hard, but just hard enough so it comes back to me, and then I hit it again, and again, and again. I hit it first-time or take a touch and then hit it again. I work on perfect technique, and having a perfect first touch. And I'm always working on my balance — how does my body look, how is the ball coming off my foot. Those things are always in my head. I also pay attention to where the ball is going after it hits the wall. That will tell me what kind of spin I'm putting on it. That will go a long way toward showing you if you are hitting it properly.

After I'm done hitting it straight ahead, I hit it at the front wall and when it comes back to me, I'll prepare it to go left — forty-five degrees off the side wall. Then I'll hit it at that wall, turn and hit it off the back wall. This helps me with my quarter-turns. After I've gone completely around to the front wall again, I do it the other way, turning to my right.

Then, I'll put it in the air. I'll hit it in the air off the wall and turn and hit it off the next wall without the ball touching the ground, and go all the way around like that. Then, I'll take it down off my chest and hit it off each wall that way. Then I'll take it off the wall out of the air and juggle a few times and work on my side-volleys. After you make a complete turn, going to all four walls, if you are still standing in the middle of the court, you know your touch and pace are pretty good. So it's really a great chance to work on everything.

"Heading is something that is so overlooked.
It's so important. I think there could
be a lot more attention paid to it."
— Sara Whalen

CHAPTER VII
HEADING

We have a tendency to avoid the things at which we are not good, and most players do not have much desire to head the ball. To a large extent, it's because it has been ignored or not even taught to players. But you have to embrace this skill the same way you do any other. You will be surprised at how much you can improve. That's the great thing about most technical training — the more you do, the better you'll get!

While the technique of heading with your feet on the ground as well as when you are in the air are similar, you might wonder why you can't head the ball out of the air. Two reasons. One, you lose your technique when you jump, forgetting to arch back, to follow through, to keep your neck tight and watch the ball — all the things you felt you had mastered on the ground. Hence, problem number two — we don't jump well. Jumping requires a vertical translation of your momentum. Most of you will jump from one spot and come down a few feet away from where you had taken off. So too much of your momentum went forward not up.

The most common problem for girls heading the ball is what I call "early disease." If you are too eager and jump too early, the ball will often hit you on top of your head, or you will miss it altogether. If you jump too early, the ball will find you on the way down. You want to time your jump so you can jump and head through the center of the ball, the sweet spot.

Another element in heading is your courage. You must make a decision to be good in the air. You risk physical injury. It's a moment of confrontation on which players with a dueling mentality thrive. Putting it all together, though, isn't easy. But a sure way to not develop this skill is to ignore it and hope no one will notice.

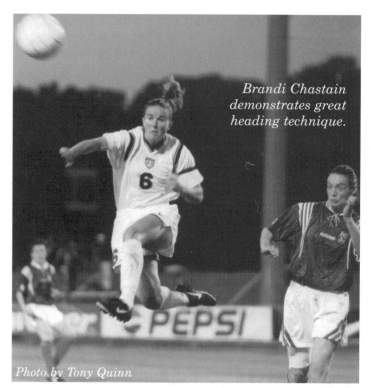

Brandi Chastain demonstrates great heading technique.

Photo by Tony Quinn

"Heading is something that is so overlooked, but at this level it's so important," says Sara Whalen. "Growing up, I always played sweeper, and I never really had to work on combative heading. I had done heading to clear the ball but never combative. I had no idea what to do, where to stand, how to jump, and that is very sad.

"There are players who still don't know how to head," adds Sara. "I think there could be a lot more attention paid to it. Growing up, when we worked on heading in practice, it was very non-game like. We did head-catch games and little things like that. But it's very important to work on combative heading. It doesn't happen in a game a lot, but when it does it is vital. I grew up with all my heading being defensive heading. Defensive heading is up and out, as hard and as high as you can. Then, when I came to the national team, I had to learn to head down at goal. I couldn't do it. It was so frustrating. I can't explain how uncomfortable it was for me to try to learn after all these years. It felt awkward. Thinking back, every time I went to regional camp or national camp, my evaluation said I needed to learn to head down. It was obvious for so long. It's something I wish I had developed earlier. But I've worked on it now."

Like any other technical skill, heading can be improved in a racquetball court. Although it doesn't exactly replicate what you will see in the game, it will allow you to improve your technique and allow you to learn how to correct yourself. If the ball is going straight up after you head it, you must be getting underneath it too much and doing what we call "spearheading" it. Your adjustment then must be to hit more in the middle of the ball and meet the ball with your forehead later in its arc.

Since a racquetball or squash court offers a controlled environment, you can develop confidence. And don't underestimate the courage you can gain through mastery of the technique. It will hurt less, you'll have done it more than you would have with your team, and, hopefully, you'll see improvement and develop the ability to coach yourself a bit during a game or training if you do make a mistake.

The next level would be to get a partner to work on combative heading. Start by having your partner simply shadow you and distract you, but not challenge you for the headers. The next step is to compete with your partner in the air for the head ball. You will need someone to toss, punt or serve balls while you and your partner battle to win the header.

Heading with a Wall

1. Head juggle as a warmup.
2. Gently stretch your neck muscles in all directions.
3. Stand about ten feet from the wall, throw ball against the wall and head it back for power.
4. Head high and away for defensive clearing.
5. Head down for offensive heading.
6. Move back and punt the ball off the wall, jump up and head it back.
7. Try juggling with the wall as your partner.

CHAPTER VIII
LONG-BALL SERVICE

This skill is, along with heading, the least attended to in the women's game, and both are the first to disappear if you do not practice them. It was our inability to solve Norway's condense defense that led us to attend and now take pride in our long-ball service. The great aspect of both of these technical skills is that they improve dramatically with training. Carla Overbeck, our captain, must be able to serve long balls as our central defender. She always hones this craft away from our training camps to stay sharp. Her ability to distribute long balls is critical to our offense.

"The key is to make sure you are warmed up properly before you practice hitting long balls," Carla says. "I usually do a Coerver warmup, and then serve some balls easily — not serving them as far as I can at first — to get in the proper motion. Gradually, I serve longer balls.

"Then I get five balls and go to a net or a wall," Carla adds. "I just serve them into the net or against the wall. I also try to pick out a spot on a fence or the cord in the middle of the goal and try to get it over that line. Anything like that helps. That's all I do. I don't even care about the distance. You know when you hit a ball well, and you can guess the yardage. I do twenty-five to thirty a day with each leg, and it's amazing how quickly you'll improve. It's a good idea to have someone video tape you to see your motion, your plant foot and your follow through."

Another way to train long-ball service is to practice serving balls over the net. Start a certain distance from the net. At first just work on getting the ball over the net. Then move your service distance back further and further. If you have a partner you can create a competition out of this exercise. Start five yards back from the goal on each side. You succeed by getting the ball over to your partner. After successfully accomplishing this drill, each player backs up a little more, and so on.

It isn't as much fun on your own because you have to chase your own ball, but you can make it into a game. I used to incorporate long-ball training into my fitness training. I would serve a long ball and then sprint after it. Serve and sprint for twenty minutes. By the end, you've hit a lot of balls and have done some interval training. Michelle French developed an outstanding long-ball service by working with her older sister who liked to hit long balls. "I used to play with my older sister, and she had a great long service with her right foot," says Michelle. "We used to kick a lot of long balls back and forth. I also used to go to a wall and hit the ball off it for hours." If your older sibling wants to kick long balls, the only way to get it back to them is to hit a long ball yourself.

Before you know it, your high school football coach may be calling you to place kick. Jen Grubb's did. Jen started in the defense for the U-20 National Team that captured the prestigious Nordic Cup in 1997. Her ability to serve long balls is world class at any level. She developed a good quality into a strength. "I did a lot of stuff on my own because I didn't have a lot of people in the neighborhood who played soccer," Jen explains. "I would just be out there in my back yard all alone playing games with myself. I would try to knock things over to work on driving the ball as hard as I could.

"I played a lot on boys' teams, especially when I got to high school," adds Jen. "I place-kicked for my high school. The defensive coach was also the girls' high school soccer coach. He came and asked "How would you like to make history?" I didn't know what he was talking about. When he explained, I immediately said no. He asked if I would think about it, so I decided I would at least try it and see how I did. I went out after school, kicked a few field goals, and he said I could play for them. The next day, the captain came to me and said they really needed a kicker and they'd love to have me join the team. Having their support really helped, because I wasn't trying to prove anything."

Just so you know, Jen's longest field goal, hit during a warmup, was 51 yards.

Michelle French can serve long balls with either foot accurately over forty-five yards.

Long-Ball Service Tips

▲ Be warmed-up.

▲ Plant foot slightly away from and behind the ball.

▲ Lean back, follow through.

▲ Use both legs.

▲ Repetition.

▲ Do not serve too many in a row or you will pull your quadriceps muscle.

▲ Concentrate on technique first, distance later.

▲ If you are having trouble flighting a stationary ball, you can have someone roll a ball to you and practice hitting it long.

Michelle Akers was the Golden Boot Winner in the 1991 Women's World Cup, awarded to the leading scorer — 10 goals.

"It never hurts to make technical training more entertaining."

CHAPTER IX
TECHNICAL WORK CAN BE FUN

For many of you, working on technique alone will be boring. It never hurts to make training more entertaining, so we've included some games, most of which incorporate technique into fun, competitive games.

Soccer Squash: This is a game that was invented at my alma mater, the University of North Carolina. It's one of the best games for developing a good first touch, volleying, and shooting. You can play one against one or two against two. Soccer squash, when played well, can also be very tiring. The crucial point with soccer squash is to not give up on yourself. At first, you'll be awkward and balls will hit off you in all directions. With time, you will be reading balls better, receiving and preparing them better. Eventually, you'll take it to the next level where strategy is being used. So, be patient. With time you can do it.

One-v-One Squash

1. The ball is served from behind the serving line of a squash/racquetball court. This line should be about half-way between the front wall and the back wall. The serve is a short chip against the wall starting with the ball on the ground. I recommend a minimum height that the serve must reach (like having a net in tennis). This allows more opportunities to return the serve.

2. Once the ball is put into play you have one, two or three touches to return the ball against the wall. During that time, the ball may bounce once. So, you could volley the ball directly out of the air against the wall, or prepare the ball and volley it back. A higher level variation is to not allow the ball to touch the ground once you have chosen to take it out of the air.

3. You continue back and forth in that fashion until one player fails to return the ball against the front wall.

4. You also lose the serve or the point by hitting the ball against the ceiling. Obviously, we are working on shooting so any ball that goes that high probably would miss the net!

5. Points are scored only while you are serving.

6. Play a game to eleven or fifteen.

7. If one player gets to seven before the other player gets a point, they win. They have skunked their opponent.

8. Other variations include allowing no head returns to force preparation touches.

9. You can hit it off the back wall to get it to the front wall.

Partner Squash

1. Here you play two against two.

2. Unlike tennis, you must play the ball between you and your partner before returning the ball against the wall. In other words, you must pass it to your partner in the air for them to hit it back. You may use your touches and bounce any way you choose. You may take two touches and your partner may use one, or vice versa. Or each might only use one touch.

3. Alternate which player serves each time you regain the ball.

Soccer Tennis: Soccer tennis is a great game for technique and, specifically, first touch. Initially, you can play on a tennis court and use the singles lines. Play it like tennis. The ball can bounce once, and you have three touches to return it. You can score points only on your serve. We play the game to fifteen points. As you progress, reduce the size of the court. This game can be played as singles or doubles like soccer squash.

It is a great game for goalkeepers as well. Mary Harvey has her version of soccer tennis.

"Every goalkeeper should be playing soccer tennis like there is no tomorrow," says Mary, a veteran of the 1991 and 1995 World Cups as well as the 1996 Olympics. "You get comfortable with moving your feet to prepare a ball. I've found it's good to play doubles on a regular tennis court, not the doubles court."

One-v-One: One-v-one and two-v-two are designed to work on your dribbling technique, passing and finishing. In addition, they can be an incredible workout. One-v-one in the squash court is exhausting because the ball is never out of bounds. The play is continuous, so it is a great anaerobic and aerobic workout.

Actually, one-v-one is perhaps the best game you can play to incorporate all four pillars of soccer (indoors and out).

To get started, place a pair of shoes one yard apart at each end of the court. Play for no more than ten minutes without a break because it is very demanding, and the shorter games (3-6 minutes) ensure quality.

Two-v-Two Tournament: If you can find a few friends or teammates to play, another great game is two-v-two. In two-v-two, make the goals slightly bigger than you use in one-v-one, and play three 10-minute matches.

To create a mini-tournament, change partners each match you are playing with someone new. Record each player's win-loss-tie record. This way you can figure out who factors into winning most.

Tactical Section

"The way in which we won in 1991 — with such dominance, attacking flare and personality — drew attention around the world to women's soccer."

"This was the critical period during which we laid the foundation of self-coaching."

CHAPTER I
THE EARLY YEARS

It's hard to believe that women's soccer in the United States at the national and international level has only existed since the mid-1980s. The standard the United States has set is phenomenal. To a large degree, this standard stems from the incredible commitment of the players, coaches and supporters of our sport. Another significant factor is the growth of the game around the world. Since winning the first-ever Women's World Cup in 1991 in China — where the American women set the stage for what women could do in the soccer arena — many of the traditionally elite soccer nations around the world went to work to find answers to our early and unexpected dominance.

The tactical evolution of the game has been, in many ways, a by-product of our early success. In 1995, the Norwegian women claimed the world championship, setting a new standard. In the wings, not far behind either world champion, were the teams from China, Denmark, France, Germany, Holland, Italy and Sweden. Each had made commitments to compete in the world arena. For the United States, our 1-0 loss to Norway in the 1995 Women's World Cup gave us incentive to lay down a new foundation with many changes and improvements to our team. Still, inherent in this process were the roots of our early success. It was a unique challenge to reconstruct our style without losing the features that were unique to American women's soccer. Just as our victories and excellence had been the impetus for growth around the world, we re-evaluated ourselves in the face of defeat.

"Just watching the game and taking in information as you play is so important. I have always been fit and technically okay, but all my coaches have always told me I need a lot of work tactically. I'll watch games on TV and learn about different options in different situations. Believe it or not, you'll remember them during games and do the things that work."
— SARA WHALEN

In 1996, the first-ever Olympic Gold Medal match for women's soccer took place in Athens, Ga. The event, yet again, demonstrated that the ascension of the women's game was far from over. The level of play was at an all-time high. Countries had spent resources and embraced change. The margins of victory grew slimmer. The ante had been upped one more time in a mere decade of our existence. The growing popularity of our team and the women's game was demonstrated by the nearly 77,000 fans that attended the final between the United States and China. We won 2-1 to claim the first-ever Olympic Gold Medal for women's soccer. Since then, countries around the world revamped their existing programs. Professional leagues of varying degrees were formed in many countries.

Throughout each of these major growth periods, new systems and styles emerged. The tactical sophistication of the women's game — now light years from its infancy just over a decade ago — will make the 1999 Women's World Cup the best ever. Held in the United States, it promised to be an event that few will forget and that will endure in stature with time. Clearly, a breakthrough event for women's sports.

As in each section, my focus has been on the process of becoming a cham-

> ### TIPS FOR TACTICAL UNDERSTANDING
>
> 1. Play the game
> 2. Watch the game in person or on TV
> 3. Watch players in your position
> 4. Watch yourself play
> 5. Coach
> 6. Ask questions
> 7. Play different positions

pion. Here, in the Tactical Section, you will hear the yet untold story about the process of our becoming world champions. You will be shown how in victory, as well as defeat, we went after another level. You will learn to appreciate that victories would not become resting places but beginnings. Just as I have tried to challenge you to never be satisfied and to always find another level inside, we strove for an unseen, unparalleled standard of excellence.

The tactical evolution of the United States will be told through the stories, anecdotes and major moments which influenced the cutting edge of our game. The challenges our opponents pose, as well as what we are able to learn from them, are vital assets in this evolutionary process. Each moment will be brought to life through the decisions and the directions we took.

Shannon Higgins, Lauren Gregg and Mary Harvey hold "The Cup" shortly after winning the first-ever FIFA Women's World Cup, 1991.

The United States Women's National Team program has seen tremendous evolution over the last decade. In 1986, when Anson Dorrance took over the team from Mike Ryan, the program's first coach, who served for the 1985 year, we developed a system that combined man-to-man and zonal defense. We played with a sweeper back. Because most of our opponents played with two forwards, our predominant system of play was a 3-4-3. We played with three backs, two of which were marking backs, and a sweeper. We played four midfielders. Up front, we never wavered in our commitment to play with three front-runners. No other team in the world played with three front-runners, and this made playing against us very different for our opponents.

The system we played, and our style in that system, to a large degree was the most feasible given the nature of our program in the early years. Our system had to be devised around the fact that we did not spend a lot of time together training as a team. In 1986, we had one event the entire year, the North America Cup. In 1989, we had one match, and in 1990, six. Our preparation was very limited. This was the period during which we laid down the foundation of self-coaching. Our players had to organize their environment away from our scheduled events.

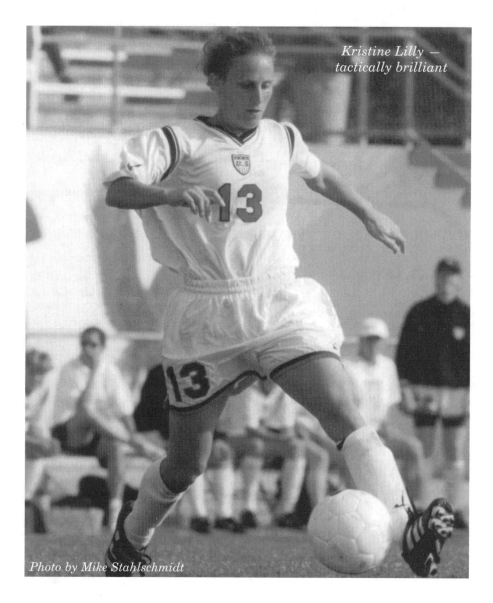

Kristine Lilly —
tactically brilliant

Photo by Mike Stahlschmidt

Without time together, we decided it was best to play a combination of zone and man-to-man. Because we had such limited time with our players, this defensive system was easier conceptually to teach and to organize in short periods of time. It didn't require as much time or integration of players as a zone in the back would have, and it allowed us to bring out our competitive spirit. Equally important, we felt that this system played into the strengths of our defensive personalities at the time — Linda Hamilton, Debbie Belkin, Joy (Biefeld) Fawcett and Lori Henry. Also, we had a phenomenal sweeper back, Carla (Werden) Overbeck. They took tremendous pride in their individual defending and loved to "duel." During these early years, the concept of a dueling personality was formed. We also worked to foster a competitive fury. What developed were the origins of what is now called, "USA Mentality." The mentality was "Refuse to Lose." It was hard, took risk on both sides of the ball, and was vital to our success.

"As a forward, defensively, you want to force the other team," says Shannon MacMillan. "You want to force them to make it predictable. You are not so much trying to win the ball. When you do, it's nice, but your main job is to make it predictable for the rest of your team. For instance, you have to work hard to force it inside ... if that's what the game calls for. If it does get played through your side, you can turn and double back and help out. Our defense creates our offense."

Photo by J. Brett Whitesell

Mia Hamm takes pride, not only in scoring goals, but in her defensive effort.

OFFENSIVE ADVANTAGES OF A THREE-FRONT

1. More players forward in attacking positions: Since there are three forwards in this system, you have an attacking shape instantly.

2. A penetrative option is usually omnipresent. Because there are three forwards, it usually allows you to keep one in a high position.

3. A balance of support is easier to have with three forwards than with two. In other words, when a team regains the ball and plays it forward, odds are they have a player in support.

4. Less work: The workload is shared. If one player has made a death run, a second or third runner is ready to go.

5. The pressure a three-front puts onto a defense is greater than with two front-runners.

6. Potentially causes confusion for defenses: If a team is in a man-to-man defense, a three-front pulls their shape apart if your team floods one side. If the team is in a zone there is less chance for defensive cover because three or four of the four backs are occupied in their zone with an attacker. If the defense plays with a sweeper, a three-front can engage the sweeper with one attacker and still have two other players to show, get wide, etc.

   We find internationally that a three-front forces an opponent to play differently. For example, if an opponent is used to having five players in midfield and three in the defense, then they must adjust and drop a player back. Or they might be forced to take a player out and substitute a true defender in the back.

7. Three players high also allows a team to keep their width better in attack, especially in the final third. This system doesn't require a deeper player to get forward in order to create width.

8. When you get to the endline, it's easier to fill the necessary runs in the box. By virtue of this system, you have more players available and committed naturally to attacking.

DEFENSIVE ADVANTAGES OF A THREE-FRONT

1. Three players high allows you to press your opponent higher in their own end. Three front-runners can make it more difficult for the defense to get out of their end than two front-runners can.

2. Typically, your pressure is more effective because it is harder to relieve pressure because the ratios are smaller between attackers and defenders.

3. It is easier to create an even-numbers defensive situation. With three front-runners one can eliminate the option of one defender and then create a three-against-three situation.

4. It shares the workload and distances to track opponents are shorter. With three forwards, the distance between them is smaller than if there were only two.

5. It creates more opportunity to double-team back into midfield.

6. As mentioned in the attacking advantages, it usually forces the other team to change the way they are comfortable playing in the back, not only to absorb the attacking numbers, but to aid them in getting the ball forward from the defense.

DISADVANTAGES OF A THREE-FRONT

1. In a three-front, it is often difficult to get greater numbers behind the ball defensively.

2. One long ball plays them out of position, especially pertinent to the United States against the direct attacking style we face playing the Nordic teams. It's hard to establish shape before they have played the ball long.

3. If you play three in the defense in order to be able to play three players up top, you lose some defensive security (see comparison of three- vs four-back defenses). The ratio of your defenders to their attackers in a three-front, three-back defensive system is low.

The decisions for defenders in a man-to-man system are simpler, as well. We marked with our backs and played a sweeper behind them. The role of the sweeper, Carla Werden, in our system was to create a two-versus-one advantage. Carla's decisions of when to leave the middle were predicated on whether she could get to the player who had the ball before that player was able to serve it. If not, her job was to try to create a numbers-up situation in the box. Because getting the first touch on a ball served into the box is so critical, we asked our players to mark tight and deny the attackers the first touch. In the box and around the eighteen-yard area, the sweeper became a marking personality. This general rule of thumb still exists today — we mark in and around the box. We feel this makes it easier for the goalkeeper to sort out and make decisions.

In the midfield and up front, we played a combination of zone and man-to-man. When a player entered your zone, you marked them. Simple as that. Runs that were vertical out of our opponent's back line or midfield line were also tracked. However, we would pass on runs that were across the field as long as the player in the next zone was not engaged with another player. We asked a tremendous amount from our players defensively. The job of our front-runners was to close service. This was — and still is — an instrumental part of our defensive scheme. Our defensive effort begins with our forwards. Their commitment to defense would set the tone for our game. While they were not always the ones that actually dispossessed the opponent, their ability to apply pressure and close service would make the next ball more predictable and of lesser quality, thus giving the next line of our defense more opportunity to regain possession.

Offensively, the system we used played into the attacking personality of our players. We had dominant front-runners. In the women's game, playing three front-runners helped the forwards play together more, cover more ground, and put the defense under more pressure simply by virtue of our numbers. This quality was, and has remained, one of the unique tactical dimensions of the United States. The front line that became our starting unit in the first World Cup featured three of the most amazing forwards the world may ever see. And certainly, as a unit, they were lethal. They would become known as the "Triple-Edged Sword." They were April Heinrichs, Carin (Jennings) Gabarra, and Michelle Akers. What made them so dangerous? They were all goal-scorers. They were athletic. Each player was very different in their method of assault.

April was a devastating one-v-one personality. Her mentality to take-on was unrelenting. Her leadership was invaluable to our success as a country, and she helped lay the foundation of the USA Mentality.

THE TRIPLE-EDGED SWORD

Front-runners must be dynamic, creative and mobile. They must possess the mentality that makes them thrive in one-v-one situations, yet they must combine well with their teammates. But most of all they must have the goal-scorers mind-set. Carin Jennings was awarded the Golden Ball, deeming her the best player in the 1991 World Cup. Michelle Akers was awarded the Golden Boot, the top goal-scorer award, having scored ten goals. The Triple-Edged Sword — April Heinrichs, Carin Jennings and Michelle Akers — combined for a devastating twenty of the USA's twenty-five goals, more than earning their title.

Carin, nicknamed, "crazy legs" for her brilliant dribbling ability, could upend any defender and find any player anywhere in the box. She had an incredible final pass inside the eighteen-yard box. "I remember watching the game tape of the Sweden game, the first game in the 1991 World Championship," says Mary Harvey. "And there's Carin dribbling into the box making three Swedish defenders — one after another — sit down. Then, she caps it off by making the goalkeeper sit down. They should have respected her."

Michelle gave us a physical presence. She was dangerous in the air, could finish and hold the ball under the most arduous of circumstances. It was their complement of each other's personalities that also lent to the magnitude of their impact.

Our midfield was also a wonderful balance of personalities. Julie Foudy and Shannon Higgins were technical geniuses. Their distribution and ability to get into our attacking box were their primary offensive responsibilities. Our flank midfielders, Kristine Lilly and Mia Hamm, had an incredible end-to-end responsibility. As we discussed, defensively they often had to track all the way back. Offensively, we asked them to get to the end line for us. In this system, since our front-runners played very close together, the flank midfielders often had the responsibility to give us width in our attacking third. Each of these players had excellent speed and flank service. Without question, this was the most demanding position in our system.

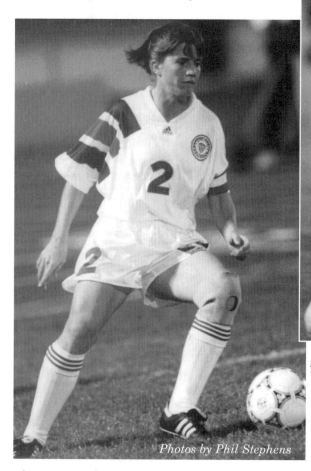

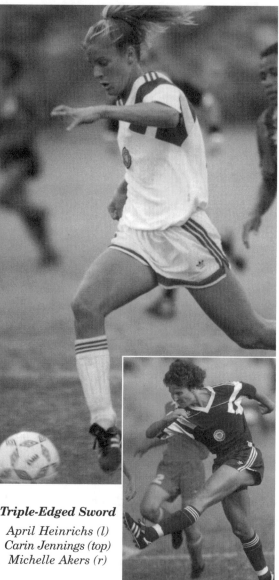

Triple-Edged Sword
April Heinrichs (l)
Carin Jennings (top)
Michelle Akers (r)

Photos by Phil Stephens

CHAPTER II
1991: AMERICAN WOMEN SET STANDARD

In preparation for the first-ever Women's World Cup in 1991, we had a brief training camp in Chapel Hill, N.C., for several weeks. Many players had jobs and were there on a part-time basis. We traveled from Chapel Hill to play various matches, one of which was against China. It was an important marker for us, as it gave us critical information for our polishing touches down the stretch. We played a 3-4-3. Most teams played with only two forwards. Staying with the three-forward alignment was a bit of a gamble, and we needed to be well-prepared in case a team played with three forwards against us. If that were to happen, we would have dropped one of our midfielders back into the defense or tried to absorb the attack of this player by our shape or sweeper back.

We gathered information for the final details of our World Cup preparation. Certainly, much of the room for growth was centered around a lack of tactical sophistication. We just weren't in high-level environments to learn these lessons. Lessons such as holding a lead, the use of restarts and solving bunkers were discussed on paper not in practice. Initial scouting and our preparation matches had told us that most of our opponents played a 4-4-2. Many teams during this early phase of the evolution of our sport played with a sweeper. They played with either a zone in front of a sweeper or a marking system with a sweeper.

Our opponents in the 1991 Women's World Cup were Sweden, Brazil, Japan, Taiwan, Germany and Norway. Our first match with Sweden was a lesson in tactical naivete. We were up 3-0 in the second half. Yet, we almost let the match be tied in the closing minutes and barely held onto a 3-2 win. We had not been in a situation where teams could get back into the game. Instead of recognizing how to hold the lead, we continued to attack and lost possession too often, allowing them opportunities to come back. We knew only one way to play, and that was to attack relentlessly. It was certainly one of our strengths, but it would need to be massaged in a way to use the clock, keep possession, probe a bit more and recognize when to go forward again.

**Lineup
1991 Women's World Cup
3-4-3**

Jennings   Akers   Heinrichs

Lilly   Higgins   Hamm
Foudy

Hamilton   Biefeld

Werden

Harvey

Mary Harvey our goalkeeper saved us, literally, against Sweden. Not only did she do her job and make saves, she helped us win. She was a personality player for us. A personality player, by definition, is a player that can impact in the outcome of the game. She was vital and did, in fact, help us win.

Our second match was against Brazil. Clearly, Brazil is the team that has most improved since 1991. We expect them to be a force in the world arena in the next decade. In 1991, however, their country hadn't really supported their women's program. In Brazil, as in many other parts of the world, soccer was a game played by men. Women really weren't accepted as football players — yet. In that match, we felt our challenge was to play with an intensity, but not emotion, as we felt that would play into their style. Brazil was very good at drawing fouls. We made a point of playing solid defense and avoiding unnecessary fouls. Overall, our match was fairly one-sided. Our experience and athleticism just dominated the less-experienced group from Brazil. The final result was 5-0.

In our third match, it took us some time to solve Japan. They were very technical and liked to spring players out of midfield. We played a mix of our starters and our non-starters in that game. Japan was an organized team, and they were dangerous because they sent players forward out of their midfield. Because our defensive make-up was based on a more naive man-to-man system, we were having a hard time sorting out who should pick up what runs. The challenge Japan posed us was in their formation. They played a 4-5-1, which looked like a 4-4-2 at times, and we weren't as versed in how to keep shape against different systems and styles. We had to make adjustments during the course of play to gain control. While their system and style slightly exposed our defense, our dominance in so many other areas more than made up for it and overpowered any weaknesses. We won 3-0.

We faced Taiwan in the quarterfinals and had another lesson — teams would foul us to try to win. Any hint that we were getting in behind them and they would take us down. They had no other way to stay with us. With all the fouls, the value of restarts would begin to come into focus. Against Taiwan, we scored five of our seven goals off restarts (and seven of twenty-five overall off restarts). We did a great job of capitalizing on our restarts. Michelle Akers had an absolutely brilliant performance scoring five goals, a record that may endure forever.

Prior to our semifinal match against Germany, we reviewed our performances to date. Since our early years we have had a protocol to review our performance as a team after every game. We evaluate what we did well, and then what we need to improve going into the next match. We zeroed in on a few areas on which to focus. We felt we were doing several things well, and we reinforced them with the team. We do this as a staff and then together with our team.

What we were doing well:
1. Box organization
2. Restarts becoming very effective
3. Rhythm continuing to improve
4. Improvements holding the ball since our first match
5. Variety in our attack
6. Making teams play us
7. Defensive shape improved
8. Commitment from players to take-on around the box and on the flanks

We always take one game at a time, and all of these were things we wanted to see going into the semifinals. Despite our success, we felt we still needed to improve a few aspects of our game to win against Germany and advance to the finals.

What we needed to improve:
1. Finding the feet of our front-runners
2. Keeping our shape in midfield
3. Always following up shots — now termed "framing the goal"
4. Free kicks outside shooting range — placement of service behind the line
5. Finding a patience — knowing when to not force it
6. Dictating how the game is played — slowing up the pace, etc.
7. Review our defensive shell or organization when holding a lead
8. Staying mobile

Our semifinal match was against Germany. I was sent to scout Germany's match against Denmark. A trip I will never forget. We were staying in Panyu, a small town outside of Guangzhou, China, the site of the opening and final matches. I had explained to our translator that I would need to see this match. She told me she would arrange transportation and to meet her at the entrance to the hotel early the next morning. Upon arriving, she spoke in Chinese for several minutes with the "taxi driver" — a Chinese man in a small car. She turned to me and said, "You're all set." I got into the car and realized as the cab pulled away that she wasn't coming with me. Chinese is not like any romance language. My limited French would not do any good. I was completely at his mercy. We could not communicate in the slightest. Nodding and smiling was the extent of our dialogue. Hours went by. The more time that passed, the smaller the roads became. There were only a few signs of civilian life. Three hours later, we were going down a one-lane dirt road. At this point, I was really beginning to wonder if I was ever going to see my team again, let alone the game I was sent to see. But sure enough, almost four hours later, we came through an opening in the woods and low and behold, there was a magnificent stadium in the middle of nowhere. The Chinese government had three brand new stadiums built for the World Cup, each about thirty million dollars. The next challenge was to communicate with my driver when and where to pick me up. Immediately following this game, I was to head off to our own game against Sweden. Another four-hour ride to endure to yet another town unknown. Boy, was I glad to see my teammates that night.

Watching Germany and Denmark play was fascinating. Their styles were vastly different. Denmark was like Norway, a very direct team that liked the ball in the air. They were hard and combative. The Germans, on the other hand, were brilliant on the ball. Their combination play was amazing. Religiously, they formed small triangles all over the field, always taking up good supporting positions for each other. Technically proficient at this stage in the women's game, they were clean and precise. Like a surgeon they dissected the defense. But the physical style wasn't appealing to them and served to disrupt their ability to possess the ball out of the back. By putting Germany under pressure, Denmark was able to dispossess them. Their match ended in a 1-1 tie that went to penalty kicks. Watching the Germans, it became clear that they wanted to always build out of the back. Each time it went through the goalkeeper, including goal kicks, and they would build it out of the back. Methodically, they would pass and pass with remarkable patience. And it became clear that if you didn't organize well defensively, they could pass circles around you.

Scouting, as I discussed, is useful to see what systems teams play, how they defend as a group, how they attack, and identifying their key personalities. The key to scouting or match analysis is what you do with the information you get ... if anything. My notes on Germany clearly showed a pronounced desire to build through short passing. We conferred as a coaching staff and decided we would high-pressure them all over the field, basically lock them in their end through our pressure in hopes of disrupting their rhythm. Giving them too much time and space would have been risky. But we didn't know what they would do in response.

Germany played a marking system in the back with a sweeper. They had a tremendous attacking personality, Heidi Mohr. She was very dangerous. She loved to be sprung and worked very hard off the ball. Similar to the forwards for the United States, she was intent on taking you on and scoring goals. Like most teams who played us, Germany would have to drop another player into the defense to play against our three forwards. This was clearly a big reason we liked the three-front. Teams were constantly adjusting to us.

The tactical choice of pressuring them in their end worked. They were so committed to build their attacks from the back, that they couldn't or wouldn't change. Even though we had scored two goals off of our defensive work rate and organization, they continued to set play from the goalkeeper working it out to one of their backs. They were determined to play their style at all costs — including losing by, in their eyes, an embarrassing 5-2 margin. The work rate of our front-runners was relentless, and the offensive performance by Carin (Jennings) Gabarra was one of the best I have ever seen by an individual player. She scored three gorgeous goals and was a constant presence for us throughout the match. We advanced to play Norway in the final.

Germany, a great soccer nation, was in shock, both by our sound victory as well as our physical play and hardness. As with every game, we evaluated our performance. Even with one game left, we needed to find any opportunity to improve. Factoring in Norway's strengths, we honed in on a few key areas on both sides of the ball.

Our defensive keys revolved around our commitment to team defense. We wanted to keep our defensive shape. We knew we had to be prepared to track midfielders coming forward, an integral part of Norway's attack. We put Joy Biefeld on Linda Medalen, a tremendous target player. We had to compete and win as many air duels as possible. And lastly, we had to avoid fouling Hege Riise, as she was clever in drawing penalty kicks for her team.

Offensively, we knew it would be important to find the feet of our forwards against Norway. In turn, our forwards needed to hold the ball for us so we could establish a rhythm against their style. Because Norway played with a sweeper, it would be important to engage and eliminate her when we were in the final third. Tactically, we had to be prepared to solve whatever they threw at us. For example, they pulled an offside trap well. We needed to be able to solve this through long-balls over the top from the opposite side, second runs, and by possessing the ball.

More importantly, we wanted our players to play with confidence and to trust their preparation. We were doing many things well at this point. Our double-team mentality was tremendous, as demonstrated in the resounding win over Germany. Our finishing and box organization was better than our earlier games. We were dictating how opponents had to play as well as setting the pace of the game. And there was such an intense desire and commitment to succeed. There is an expression that captures this confidence — "Many have the will to win, few have the will to prepare to win." We had prepared for victory, not just in those moments together but more importantly, perhaps, in those moments when we weren't together. A champion trains when no one is looking.

We faced Norway in the final. They were, and are still, a very organized long ball or direct offensive team. Defensively, they were hard, organized and played out of a 3-5-2 formation.

How to Scout a Game

After establishing the system of play (i.e., 4-4-2 — four defenders, four midfielders, two forwards), look at the team's defensive and offensive tendencies.

Ways to look at defensive tendencies

1. Are they playing a zone, or are they marking man-to-man?
2. Is it some combination of both?
3. In which parts of the field do they mark man-to man? Zone?
4. Where do they initiate pressure?
5. What is the shape of the defense on the weak side or the side away from the ball?
6. Is there a sweeper? Does the sweeper tend to stay central, or does she come ball side?
7. How are goals scored against them?
8. What do they do on defensive set pieces?

Ways to look at offensive tendencies

1. How do they attack?
2. Are they direct and move forward quickly?
3. Do they play indirectly with a more patiently built attack?
4. Do they play up one side more than the other?
5. Who sets the play for them? Who are their play-makers?
6. What types of runs do their forwards make?
7. How do they score goals?
8. What do they do on offensive set pieces?

Positional play of various lines

After making note of the overall tendencies of the team, you should watch the various lines of the team. For example, if you are a defender, watch how defenders play both offensively and defensively. As a forward, watch how they solve pressure, the types of runs they make, individual moves or combination play between them, how they score goals, and how final passes are made.

In the midfield, watch how they serve as a link between the defense and the offense, how do they dissect defenses with their passes, what types of movements are made to get the ball, what skills are necessary to be a midfielder on this team, what qualities set them apart.

Strengths and weaknesses

At the same time, I evaluate what works for an opponent and what does not work. This gives me information on what strengths we may need to contend with, or how we may make adjustments to counter them. In turn, I become aware of how we can exploit them as a team, and individually, certain players.

Translating what you see into useful information

The most important aspect of scouting is not necessarily what information you get but what you do with the information you have. That is the art of it all.

Because we played with three front-runners, it caused a match-up problem for Norway, and they pulled back another player defensively. They had a dominant personality and an icon in international women's soccer, Heidi Stoere. She was absolutely a professional in all respects, retiring after playing in over 150 matches for her country in 1996.

Offensively, Norway is always one pass away from scoring a goal. They are very direct, but not direct in the way we would think about direct soccer. They do it in a calculated, organized and effective way. Linda Medalen was one of the best target players ever to play the game. Any ball of any quality delivered in her vicinity became a pass. She was an extremely dangerous finisher in the air. We knew it would be important to be very organized defensively because they played in a way that wears you down. They just went at you for ninety minutes and banked on forcing you to make a mistake. They also were very tactical. They understood how to play for corner kicks, and their dominance in the air made them very effective on corners. They were the kind of team that you could never relax against. One ball into the box could result in a goal. They could expertly draw fouls for their advantage on plays that our players wouldn't have even thought were fouls. The deadly nature of their restarts, as well as their intent to draw fouls, would be a lesson we would take from the Norwegians in 1991, and again in 1995.

As we expected, the game came down to the slimmest margin. Re-starts played a major role in the game. One of the areas we identified as needing improvement throughout the Cup, was our service on free kicks. We went up 1-0 on a free kick. Shannon Higgins sent a perfectly driven ball to the back post. Michelle Akers had drifted there, seemingly unnoticed, and headed a brilliant ball to the back post. Moments later, though, Norway was on the board. They converted a free kick they received just inside the midline. They played the free kick to the point of our goalkeeper's range and caused a miscue between our goalkeeper and our defenders. They redirected it into the back of the net for the equalizer.

Overall, we never really found a good rhythm in the game. That, we would come to appreciate, would be an essential but difficult challenge of playing against the Norwegians. At half time, I remember our comments as coaches, and those of our captain, April Heinrichs, being reassuring. Despite having horrible pain in her knee and being unable to impact the game at her usual high level, she stirred the unit in a profound way through her leadership. We needed to fight through the nature of the game, find ways to get a hold of the ball and not let their style eliminate our strengths. We would have to find ways to win while exhausted, and in some ways, uncertain of which way the game was going. We had to refuse to lose and find a way to win.

The goal that won the game and the Cup came less than two-and-a-half minutes from the end of the match off a great individual effort by Michelle Akers. Shannon Higgins took a free kick around midfield for us. On the service, Michelle closed in on the loose ball and forced their defender to play it back to their keeper. Under Michelle's pressure, the defender miss-hit it, and Michelle went in one-on-one with the goalkeeper. She touched it around her as the keeper went down, and placed it into the back of the net. The last two minutes took an eternity. Norway pumped ball after ball into our penalty box. But the final whistle blew and we were the first-ever World Champions in women's soccer. The small group of family and friends were all we needed to share in the moment for which we had waited and trained a lifetime.

Photo by Phil Stephens

World Champions
Carin Jennings, Golden Ball winner for her spectacular play in the 1991 World Cup

LESSONS FROM 1991

"What we call results are only beginnings."
— Ralph Waldo Emerson

There were many tactical lessons from 1991. Each country showed us new levels of the game in different areas. And we weren't averse to borrowing and incorporating what we could from them. Winning could not be a resting place but rather a stepping stone for us.

1. Our opponents didn't need nearly as many chances to score as we did. They were used to having fewer scoring opportunities, and they put them away. We, on the other hand, generated so many more opportunities and finished a significantly lower percentage.

2. Sweden and Germany were extremely effective at counter-attacking. In fact, they were brutally dangerous on *our* offensive corner kicks. We needed to pay attention to our defensive shape while we were on attack. Both countries were excellent at execution.

3. Norway's prowess on free kicks. Their ability in the air was tremendous, and they were physically dominant. Their direct style was one pass away from a goal all the time. It taught us the importance of closing service. We learned to compete in the air. But one very important lesson was that we were more tired in the final than they had been. There were two explanations. One was the demand we put on our front-runners by asking them to play so much defense. Second, we took a critical look at our preparation and conditioning. We discerned that we needed to be doing more sprint work, more repetitive, hard runs (anaerobic) and develop more what we term, "speed endurance" — the ability to run at or near maximum speed as often as you need throughout the game. We needed to develop new conditioning parameters to prepare for the grueling event. *(See Physical Section)*

4. We needed to be more sophisticated. We didn't know how to draw a foul. In fact, we didn't know how to get calls even when we were fouled. We would often fight to not fall over. That was a by-product of the culture we had created — don't complain; stay on your feet. We needed to know when and how to play for corner kicks. We needed to let the clock work for us, salting a lead. We needed to grab the ball as it went out of bounds as if it were our possession. Often it was our throw in, but the other team would get to it first and get the ball.

Final Rankings After the 1991 Women's World Cup

1. USA
2. Norway
3. Sweden
4. Germany
5. China
6. Italy
7. Denmark
8. Chinese Taipei (Taiwan)
9. Brazil
10. Nigeria
11. New Zealand
12. Japan

CHAPTER III
WORLD RESPONDS TO U.S. DOMINANCE

The way in which we won — with such dominance, attacking flare and personality — drew attention around the world to women's football. In many ways, other soccer countries paid more attention than did the United States. The fact that the United States won in the world's sport was like a nagging toothache. Changes began. Over the next few years, the rest of the world worked to analyze their teams and personnel to make up ground.

My favorite analogy is what happened with the four-minute mile. Once thought impossible and unobtainable, it's now the standard. After Roger Bannister ran a mile in under four minutes, others followed. Well, once we showed that women could play the game, it somehow gave permission to so many countries to invest in their programs. In many ways, this trend was born because it was unacceptable for the United States to succeed in soccer.

Still, for years we saw a direct correlation between women's stature in a particular culture and how much support they received as soccer players. The Scandinavian teams, for example, were strong, as were women in their societies. An exception at the time was China. Certainly, their political and social status at the time did not hold the Chinese women in high regard. But their prominence in women's soccer came from a national pride. Whatever endeavor the Chinese undertake, they do so fully. The government was committed to their success in the world arena and supported their team's efforts. Not winning or doing as well as was expected was very painful for the Chinese people.

The evolutionary process began. Teams around the world began organizing their teams to beat the United States. From 1991 to 1995, there was an evolution in defensive systems utilized in the women's game. We saw a significant rise in the use of zones in the back, replacing the more traditional marking and sweeper systems. The predominant international defensive system in the back became some form of a four-back zone.

The Norwegians, as did many of the Scandinavian teams, went to a zonal defense after 1991. They played a 4-4-2 with a four-back zone They developed the best flat-back four in the women's game. We studied them for a few years, but really didn't have an understanding of the ways to break down this system until 1994. Norway's evolution forced our growth as well. In addition to playing a very rigid zone in the back, they condensed their unit both horizontally and vertically, trying to make the space in which their opponents play into about a forty by forty-yard grid at best. At a glance, it would appear that you could break them down by playing over

The mobility of the U.S. attack resulted in many teams switching to a zonal defense.

Photo by Mike Stahlschmidt

the top of their zone. However, at the same time Norway moved into a flat-back four, they evolved the role of the women's goalkeeper, playing their keeper very extended off her line behind their zone. This requires that the goalkeeper has exceptional ability with her feet. Secondly, you must be able to serve a ball that can get over the zone or you have to change the point of attack on them. We weren't able to consistently serve that long ball. As a result, we developed a long-ball proficiency and standard.

Germany remained in a 4-4-2 with a sweeper. Germany slowly progressed into having a better balance of direct and indirect play. They worked to accomplish this without sacrificing their tremendous combination play. After 1991, China was in a 4-4-2 with a four-back zone. They did not play a rigid flat-back four like the Norwegian system, though. In fact, they played it with one player actually dropping in the flow of play to provide cover. The Chinese went into a residency period in preparation for the 1995 World Cup. They remained very similar in style — exceptionally technical, physically gifted with speed and quickness, and organized.

We had very little activity for the first two years after the World Cup. In 1994, after we qualified for the '95 World Cup, by winning CONCACAF, Anson Dorrance resigned. The United States Soccer Federation recognized that the position of head coach of the U.S. Women's National Team needed to be full time. The level of play and the developments that were taking place around the world necessitated that we go in this direction. Because of his family and his love for his program at North Carolina, Anson decided to stay in Chapel Hill full-time. I, too, wanted to stay in my full-time coaching at the University of Virginia. Tony DiCicco, also an assistant coach since 1991, took over. Tony and I had been a great team, doing many hours of

ADVANTAGES OF A FOUR-BACK ZONE

1. Spacing is narrower between players. The zone or area for which each defender is responsible is smaller.
2. It's more secure defensively. Less space makes it harder for the attacking team to penetrate. In addition, there are defenders more naturally available for cover in breakdown situations.
3. When you regain the ball, you are in a better shape. The likelihood that once you have regained the ball you are able to possess it due to numbers and inherent shape is significantly increased with a four-back zone.
4. It's easier to possess the ball because you are often up one or two players. It's much harder for the attacking team to defend two against four.
5. Flank midfielders usually are required to pinch in but not drop all the way into the back line to provide balance. Therefore, this system spares flank midfielders tracking all the way back on a consistent basis.
6. Can track runs out of midfield more easily. The shape and numbers in the back provide a cushion defensively.
7. The formation naturally takes up attacking space. Less room for attackers to find gaps or holes in the defense.
8. Because the defense is already flat, if they wanted to trap, it's easier to coordinate the few steps necessary to put a player in an offside position.
9. In this system, you could change in and out of trapping throughout the game — without changing your system — because of the inherent shape of the back line.

DISADVANTAGES OF A FOUR-BACK DEFENSIVE ZONE

1. It takes players away from the attack, because you have committed one more player to your defensive scheme.
2. If you play a four-back zone with three in midfield, you will potentially be out-numbered in midfield. You concede space on the field to protect a deeper defensive area.
3. Sorting out responsibility for opposing attackers can be difficult. Often, our players are more decisive in the three-back, because the choices are more concrete. Communication and early decisions becomes paramount.
4. It's harder to provide support when you go forward because fewer numbers are forward. There are naturally more players in defensive positions. Therefore, on attack — especially in quick transition — you will attack with fewer players.

IMPLICATIONS FOR THE KEEPER

The flat-back four is extremely popular among the teams we face internationally. Because of the flat shape and by using the offside rule, teams who utilize this system can really condense the space in front of them. Consequently, this changes how the keeper plays behind them. If there is no space in front of the flat-back four, the space is behind. The goalkeeper is responsible for the space between the last defender and the goal. She has to make decisions on balls that are played over the defense — whether to come for them or not. Starting positions for the keeper are the key to playing this space effectively. Remember, though, the keeper still has responsibility to organize and communicate in addition to adjusting their starting position.

editing, match analysis and scouting together. In 1995, with Tony as head coach and myself and April Heinrichs as assistants, we had our first residency program ever.

We continued with the man-to-man system that the program had been built around. Going into the 1995 World Cup, our lineup showed slight changes from the '91 team. April Heinrichs, Shannon Higgins and Kim Maslin were retired now. Mia Hamm moved permanently to her home on the front line. Tisha Venturini replaced Shannon Higgins, in the center of midfield. Thori Staples came on board and developed into a possible starter in the back, allowing us to consider putting Joy Fawcett in our midfield. Thori was the best athlete we ever had in our national team program. We often used her in a marking role against the Chinese, because of their tremendous athletic ability. Young Briana Scurry also came onto the scene. She challenged starter Mary Harvey and backup Amy Allmann for the starting role. Mary Harvey had suffered two devastating injuries, to her knee and back, that she was overcoming leading up to the World Cup. By the time of the Cup, Bri Scurry had earned a starting position. At age sixteen, Tiffany Roberts was first introduced to our program. She brought an unparalleled tenacity to our team. This dimension earned her a position on the 1995 World Cup roster. So, our biggest changes were in personnel. Overall, we kept our system of play the same as well as our style. Most of the tactical changes Tony made were centered around developing a sophistication in our players and game. The task was difficult because the environment in which most of our players trained — in college or out of college — didn't replicate the international game.

We made adjustments to prepare for the world powers of that time — Norway, Germany and China. For Norway, we spent time solving flat defenses, increasing our range of service and focusing on what we came to term "first and second ball mentality." This is simply putting yourself in position to win the first ball and organizing to win the second ball. Against a team like Norway, where the ball spends so much time in the air, winning either the first heading duel or the second is vital to regaining possession and decreasing their opportunities to score. We spent time on our restarts on both sides of the ball. We appreciated the narrowing margin of victory we knew we would experience in the 1995 Women's World Cup.

CHAPTER IV
1995: THE WAKE-UP CALL

We opened the 1995 Women's World Cup against China. Despite a 3-1 lead, they tied us 3-3. It was obvious we were still showing a lack of sophistication with our inability to hold a lead. This stemmed in part from an inability to hold the ball both technically and with tactical decisions. The Chinese were incredibly mobile. We had a hard time keeping our shape on both sides of the ball. They were brilliant at getting players forward out of the midfield. Their speed of play was tremendous both on and off the ball. They were athletic and had great personalities. We had a major setback in the opening minutes of the first match. Michelle Akers suffered a serious injury that, in essence, would put her out the rest of the Cup. Tiffeny Milbrett, went from a reserve player to a starter in a split-second. Although she was quite nervous, she was ready and came into the game and scored our first goal. Tiffeny's ability to jump into the game is another great example of how you must prepare yourself for every game with the same approach, regardless of opponent or your status as a starter or a reserve. You cannot expect to just turn it on. In this case, Tiffeny was able to step in and get the job done for us. Carin Gabarra had suffered a back injury leading up to the World Cup, and despite a tremendously courageous effort, she was unable to give us the quality minutes we all would have hoped for.

Photo by Mike Stahlschmidt

Norway celebrates capturing the World Cup, 1995.

USA Lineup
1995 Women's World Cup
3-4-3

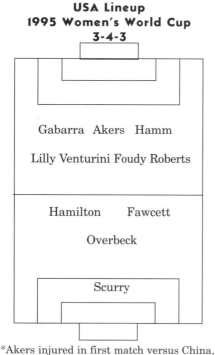

Gabarra Akers Hamm

Lilly Venturini Foudy Roberts

Hamilton   Fawcett

Overbeck

Scurry

*Akers injured in first match versus China,
replaced by Tiffeny Milbrett

The Chinese had layered an exceptional quality into their game — very effective flank play. We have since adapted their flank play into our game. Their patented serve is the early bent ball behind the defense. Because of their quickness and acceleration, they were good at getting in behind teams on the flanks. Instead of always going to the end line to serve, they would hit a hard, curving ball behind the defense. It's a very dangerous ball because it splits the distance between the defense and the goalkeeper, making it very hard for the keeper to play. And it's served at the moment when the defense is turning and running back at their own goal. It's impossible to knock back up field and often results in a corner kick or an own goal.

After tying China in our first match of the first round, we faced Denmark and Australia. Denmark is much like Norway in their style and choice of system. They play a 4-4-2 and were very direct and combative. Overall, they weren't as athletic or as effective at this system as the Norwegians. Their flat-back was more like China, not as rigid, and it featured a covering player. We won the game soundly by a 2-0 margin. The last match of the first round was against Australia. After some early difficulty scoring, we went on to win in rather dramatic fashion. Julie Foudy and Debbie Keller added the go-ahead and insurance goals in the 4-1 win.

The semifinals placed China against Germany and the United States against rival Norway. Norway came out in a 4-4-2 as we expected. We played our 3-4-3 (still with two marking backs and a sweeper on defense).

Julie Foudy looks to frame U.S. free kick.

Photo by Mike Stahlschmidt

Norway's Lineup
1995 Women's World Cup
4-5-1

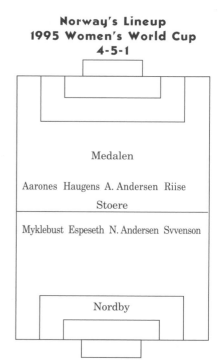

Medalen

Aarones Haugens A. Andersen Riise

Stoere

Myklebust Espeseth N. Andersen Svvenson

Nordby

Hege Riise and Heidi Stoere were two dominant midfield personalities for the Norwegians. Hege was extremely tactical in the quality and timing of her runs out of midfield. Because we were in a man-to-man defense in the back, her mobility gave us a lot of trouble. She tended to come off the right center of midfield. Unlike in a zone, where you have players more naturally in the spaces where the opponents like to attack, we had big holes behind our outside midfielders. As a result, they would organize their attack up one side, playing very direct up their left side, for example. But the area they were ultimately going to attack often was the opposite side. Their weak-side runs off the ball were timed perfectly. So while our defenders were tracking their front-runners up one side, they would release a midfielder, often Riise from the other side. This required our outside midfielder, in this case Kristine Lilly, to do a lot of work defensively to track that space. Kristine is so responsible, we didn't have to worry about her commitment to track those runs. In fact, because Kristine Lilly is so tactically smart, she is given free reign on the field. However, the bigger issue was we didn't get Kristine on attack enough, in part because of the man-to-man defensive system we played.

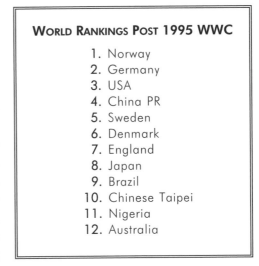

WORLD RANKINGS POST 1995 WWC

1. Norway
2. Germany
3. USA
4. China PR
5. Sweden
6. Denmark
7. England
8. Japan
9. Brazil
10. Chinese Taipei
11. Nigeria
12. Australia

Up front, they played to their target personality, Linda Medalen. Supporting her out of midfield, or at times as a front-runner, was an emerging personality on the international scene, Ann Aarones. Both Medalen and Aarones are tremendous attacking players. Aarones is especially dangerous because of her six-foot-two inch frame. Marianne Petterson, coming out of the midfield, posed another attacking threat for the Norwegians. In goal, Bente Nordby had shown us another level for goalkeeping in the women's game. Her high starting positions behind her defense and her kicking game were becoming factors in Norway's success and a new marker for the women's game.

ADVANTAGES OF MAN-TO-MAN DEFENSE

1. You can select your matchups: For example a fast defender with a fast forward.
2. You could put a strong player against a weaker player and try to dominate the matchup.
3. It is easier to demonstrate players' "dueling" mentality in a man-to-man system.
4. Roles are well-defined and decisions are simpler for the less-experienced player.

DISADVANTAGES OF MAN-TO-MAN DEFENSE

1. The other team's movement can take your team completely out of shape.
2. When you regain the ball your team shape may not lend itself to possessing the ball well.
3. The work required of the players can be greater than in a zonal system.

IMPLICATIONS FOR THE GOALKEEPER

In a man-to-man system, the keeper must be ready for runs out of midfield, and she has to be prepared to organize her teammates to track those runs. Communication skills are, therefore, very important, as is the keeper's ability to read the game. She is also responsible for organizing the weak-side shape of her team.

In addition, we gave the ball away too much. The more you give it away the more you give your opponent the potential to score. It was hard for us to hold it in the back partly because of our lack of shape, and also, because we hadn't demanded it of our defenders before. The ability of our defenders to hold the ball would be critical because other teams started to lower their restraining line, meaning instead of putting pressure on us in our own defensive end (or "high"), they would drop off and let our defenders carry it out and set play. We were still at a point in time where our defenders were mostly defensive players because of their marking responsibilities. Marking was primarily what we had asked of them. Norway drew a patented corner kick, less than twenty minutes into the match. They scored to go up 1-0. Aarones, a tremendous personality in the air, headed a ball in from our six. That would be the only score of the game. We had been dethroned as world champions.

While you have heard me recount some tactical concerns exposed by this match, there was also something less tangible, but perhaps as telling to the outcome. There was an air of unease beyond what one would expect going into a world championship semifinal. We played from a place of uncertainty. We played without the USA Mentality. If there is one team you had better show up to play, it's the Norwegians. You must play with complete conviction, with resolve and a sense of abandon. We didn't have it. With fifteen minutes left you could feel our tentativeness lift. We rallied and hit three shots off the crossbar, but it was too late. Norway had just knocked us off the top of the world by a narrow 1-0 margin. They went on to defeat Germany 2-0 in the Cup finals, while we would re-face China for the bronze medal. Although this was a difficult challenge, we were able to re-group, play with pride and defeat China 2-0.

1995 Women's World Cup Review

Reviewing a season or tournament or match is a key part of development. This is an example of how to do it. The second part of any analysis is what you do with the information you get.

THINGS WE DID WELL:

OFFENSIVELY

✓ Scored fifteen goals; eight different players scored, six goals from set pieces
✓ Displayed great one-v-one mentality
✓ Scored from low restraining line, high pressure defense while protecting a lead
✓ Played some excellent direct soccer
✓ Speed of play was outstanding at times

DEFENSIVELY

✓ Played different defenses successfully
✓ Condensed the game from the back and horizontally well
✓ Three shutouts, gave up two goals in five games
✓ In every game, extended periods of relentless pressure
✓ Successful at regaining possession by forcing players towards the center
✓ Overall best defensive shape, except China first game
✓ Double-team successful when used

OVERALL

✓ Overcame adversity throughout the Cup
✓ Won our group (the toughest group)
✓ Players came off the bench consistently well
✓ Overall team heading presence
✓ Our team displayed great leadership and personality
✓ Poise under questionable refereeing
✓ Overall team sophistication improved during the Cup
✓ The ability to play directly or indirectly successfully

THINGS WE NEED TO IMPROVE:

OFFENSIVELY

✓ Using width in attack and then recreating width
✓ Possession: Understanding when to take the chance and when to keep the ball
✓ Dictating the style of the game (against Norway, the game was played for too long in their style)
✓ Not enough long balls to feet, to set up through ball
✓ Finishing quality chances
✓ Finding seams, players in seams or looking far post
✓ Looking before receiving the ball and better and quicker support

DEFENSIVELY

✓ Consistent pressure and elimination of options by front-runners
✓ Honest defense via pressure — cover and balance from all lines of the team
✓ Consistent compacting from the back to eliminate space in midfield
✓ Goalkeeper starting position must cover space behind the defense
✓ Midfield condensing and communication among each other and to front-runners
✓ Double teaming mentality

OVERALL

✓ Tackling presence inconsistent
✓ Heading needs to continue to improve
✓ Overall a team 'softness'
✓ More sophistication needed to avoid giving up corners, but to gain corners and throw-ins
✓ Doing more with our throw-ins
✓ Using our defenders to keep possession
✓ Recycling (swinging the ball back around through the defense to keep a lead)
✓ Winning the second ball: That must be our trademark (Norway dominated second balls)

Chapter V
CHANGE

The loss to Norway set the stage for growth. We identified several key areas on which to focus in our preparation to win the 1996 Olympic Gold Medal. Tactically, we specifically needed to address the following areas:

1. Examine our current system and the possibility of being capable of playing more than one system.
2. We needed to at least be able to play a zone in the back, if not adopt that as our primary defensive scheme.
3. Offensively, we had to be better on the ball and keep possession.
4. We needed to continue to layer in a deeper overall sophistication.

We had many non-tactical adjustments, too, the most important being recommitting to our self-training and USA Mentality. Our depth, on a whole, was not adequate to win at this level. We would need to expand our player pool and augment our youth national teams' programming.

In 1996, we evolved from a marking man-for-man system with a sweeper to a zonal defense. The impetus for this change came in part from our World Cup loss and in part from the overall growth in the level of our international competition. After the 1995 World Cup, we realized the game had become sophisticated. Teams around the world had players and styles that were mobile and left us responding to our opponents too often. We realized we needed a system that kept its shape, both from a defensive standpoint but also, offensively.

OBJECTIVES FOR SPRING 1996

As with the review of a single game, match analysis, scouting report or a review of an event or tournament, it's important to use what you have learned. What do you want to reinforce and keep in your team's style and what needs to be changed or improved? After these questions are answered, they become objectives going forward. Here are the objectives we set forth after 1995 in preparation for the Olympic Games in 1996.

▲ Evolution of a zonal defense

▲ Decision between three back and four back

▲ Varying the restraining line by our forwards

▲ Balance of our runs by forwards; introduction of the "unbalancing run"

▲ More comfortable playing different systems

▲ Possession with less time and space

▲ Transition from our defensive fury to composure and speed of play going forward

▲ Quality of final pass

▲ Getting out defensively

▲ Re-establish our mentality

▲ Get our one-v-one flair back

THREE-BACK ZONE

In a man-to-man defense, attacking players are tracked (or followed) by their defenders all over the field. That includes across the field as well as into another third of the field' — wherever you go, I go. This defensive system is easier for players to understand because you only have one responsibility as a defender — to decrease the effectiveness of the player you are marking. High level man-to-man marking backs understand how to contribute to team defensive shape while marking a player out of the game.

Zone defense is a defensive system that requires players to be responsible for players in their area or zone of the field, but also, for providing defensive shape for their team. There is a balance between playing space and playing the player. Zones typically allow your team to keep a better shape defensively because runs are tracked more often for shorter distances before being able to engage your teammate's help (on horizontal runs in front of the defense). Vertical runs and runs behind the zone are often tracked based upon your team's policy. There is a great deal more decision-making for you as a player in a zone versus marking man-to-man.

ADVANTAGES OF THREE-BACK ZONE

1. Allows you to play more players in natural attacking positions.
2. Gives you more double-team options from the midfield. The greater numbers in midfield allows you to double down and help the defense.
3. Need to have certain characteristics in your players to play three-back successfully. Typically speed on the outsides is important. You need good individual defenders, very good athletes in the flank positions, and tactical players in order to only play with three defenders. The central defender needs to read the game well and have the ability and confidence to track the space behind the flank defenders.

DISADVANTAGES OF A THREE-BACK ZONE

1. In a three-back zone, players are asked to cover a lot of ground and often find themselves without cover. In a four-back zone, cover is more naturally present.
2. The three-back zone forces a flank midfielder to track more space to provide balance. Because there are only three defenders, the midfielders have a responsibility to provide cover, especially on the weak (non-ball) side.
3. There is more space to occupy in the zone. The spacing between the three defenders in the back is greater, requiring the defenders to have a greater responsibility.
4. Players have limited or selective roles when attacking; runs must be highly selective and ensure success because of the possibility of being dispossessed; penetration is usually by a passing option from back.

IMPLICATIONS FOR THE KEEPER

In three-back zones, cover is created by balancing the weak side defender. The goalkeeper must always use communication to help position this defender on the weak side. The goalkeeper must always be ready to win through balls that are well placed behind the zone. The space behind the defense must be dominated by the goalkeeper.

DEFENSIVE EVOLUTION

By Carla Overbeck

For so long, we played with marking backs with a sweeper. Every team figured out how we played because we had one style and that was it. Now, the game has evolved to incorporate the goalkeeper more in a flat-back zone. The sweeper system was good and bad. You had cover all the time, because it's the sweeper job to provide cover. And on every breakdown, you knew whose job it was to pick up that breakdown.

The bad part was that the other team could dictate your shape. If their front-runner goes down the sideline, your shape gets pulled all out of whack. The good thing about a flat-back is I know exactly where my two backs are, and the speed at which you can attack is so much quicker. You don't have to wait for your teammates to get into position for a pass. They are there immediately. I like it a lot better. I feel I'm more involved. The transition I have to make is going from someone who always provided cover, to stepping up and knowing that someone is going to cover for me.

Photo by Mike Stahlschmidt

Carla Overbeck has anchored the U.S. defense to a World Cup and an Olympic Gold Medal.

During the beginning of our six-month residency period, we experimented with a four-back zone. We traveled to Brazil in early 1996 and played a 4-4-2 for part of the tournament. We discovered that a four-back zone created a more defensive mindset. We wrestled with the fact that we were keeping an extra player on defense. It would make our system similar to the majority of the teams we would face. The beauty of our usual system is that everyone has to adjust to us, especially when we play with three forwards. At that time, we didn't embrace the 4-4-2. We began investing in a three-back zone.

In order to play a three-back zone, certain qualities are necessary in the players you choose to fill those roles. First, there must be a dominant central defender. This player must have a good tactical understanding of the game, be confident in her decisions, able to read service and be a good individual defender (in a four-back zone, the central defenders can share the role and are naturally in position to cover for each other). It's important for the flank defenders to have speed, be good individual defenders and understand team defense — when and how to provide cover for the other two backs. All three must be willing to have marking responsibilities. In addition, the role of a goalkeeper playing behind a zone is different from playing with a sweeper in front of them. They have an increased role reading balls behind the defense, providing some of the cover that is now missing with the absence of a sweeper.

Carla Overbeck was that dominant central defender. She has a tremendous tactical sense of the game. She was a leader and could organize her teammates and had their respect. On the flanks, we had Joy Fawcett as one back. Her speed, commitment to defense and attacking ability made her a prime candidate for right back. We had to develop or find another back.

Brandi Chastain, who had been playing professionally in Japan for the past few years, wanted an opportunity to play for the national team again. We told her a position was open at left back. She wanted to give it a try. Brandi was a front-runner on the championship team in 1991. Yet Brandi just maybe could answer one of our concerns illuminated in 1995. We needed defenders who wanted the ball and could play-make for us. So here was Brandi, a savvy, skillful attacking personality, ready to learn a new position to help the team and find a role for herself. With time, Brandi became a tremendous defender. She is such a student of the game that she embraced her new position and weathered the ups and downs of being on the other side of the ball. Offensively though, Brandi, Carla and Joy became our first defensive unit that could really keep possession of the ball. They could set play and come forward, helping us create numerical advantages. They shared the offensive responsibility with the front seven.

Our challenge, as I have noticed with many teams and players, was to convert marking defenders to defenders in a zone. When making this transition, players initially feel lost, exposed and uncertain of their decisions. When marking, their decisions are more simple — deny your player the ball, shut your mark out of the game. They could assess their performance based upon the level of impact their particular player had in the match. In reality, a top-level man-to-man marker contributes to team defense while accomplishing her individual assignment. The objective has to be to translate a player's individual marking abilities into a system that requires a greater contribution to team defense and overall team defensive shape.

The difficulties for the individual defenders in a zone tend to be when to track runs, both back to the ball and into space. If a run back to the ball is tracked, there is the obvious space behind this player that becomes vulnerable to a second run. The central defender in the system must read when the pass is about to be made and be able to track that space behind the defender who has left their zone. Like a man-to-man defense, it's important not to chase a "dummy run." A dummy run is designed not to get the ball, but rather to serve as a decoy to pull a defender out of their space. It's not always easy to discern whether or not a run is viable. My advice is to track only as long as necessary and then re-absorb your shape. Sometimes reading body cues of the player on the ball can give you information. If she starts shaping her body up to hit the ball long, she is probably going to serve past the checking player into the space you are leaving. Also, you need to decide whether the player getting the ball is more dangerous than a ball being played into the space.

Zones we face are very different with regard to how they treat runs. Some zones are very committed to their shape first, like Norway. On the other hand, China and Sweden, are more willing to be pulled out of shape and maintain more of a marking mentality within the zonal concept. Another point of difference comes from how teams that play a zone solve breakdowns — step or retreat.

We play our three-back zone on a diagonal. The amount of pressure on the ball determines the degree of balance by our weak-side defender, as does the location of the ball on the field. The closer to our penalty area, the less balance. Around the eighteen-yard box, we flatten out entirely because at that point we have tied in our goalkeeper and she becomes our cover. Our weak-side back (side away from the ball) provides balance for our defense. The critical factor is that we do not over-balance or else we give the opponent too much penetration. The positioning of the weak-side defender also allows this player to track runs in behind our central defender. As a very general rule, we track runs behind the zone and don't track runs in front of the zone.

It's important for the weak-side defender to know when to step a player offside, as well. Overall, we are not an offside-trapping team. However, based upon the run and the pressure on the player serving the ball, we will step players offside. In addition, this player must organize their flank midfielder. Flank midfielders have a tremendous amount of defensive responsibility in our system. The zone helps absorb some of the runs and shape they were asked to play in a man-to-man defense. In a flat zone — three-back or four-back — the goal-keeper provides cover higher on the field.

The offensive roles of the players in a zone became another important piece to our overall plan to work on possessing the ball better. The beauty of the zone for us was that it kept us in a better overall shape. Our new shape could absorb the mobility of China. When we would regain possession of the ball, we would be naturally in a better offensive shape. The zone allows a greater freedom offensively for flank midfielders, especially in a four-back zone. The space behind them is always protected. For our team, this was an important benefit. We want to attack with our flank midfielders, and the zone provides greater freedom to do that. Obviously, in a three-back zone, it's important to have players that can handle the ball offensively, because they are typically playing three-v-two instead of four-v-two as they would be doing with four backs.

TECHNICAL QUALITIES OF A GOALKEEPER

The role of the goalkeeper is, obviously, to stop shots and to save goals. However, they also need to provide cover for the defense and start the attack. They, too, must be soccer players. Your technical ability will influence your tactical decisions and positioning.

Technically, the keeper needs to have soft hands, clean catching ability, a good technique on boxing, tipping, diving and smother saves. And they absolutely have to have good foot skills. Don't confuse foot skills with foot work. Foot skills refers to your technical ability with the ball at your feet. It's so important that as a goalkeeper you work on your ball skills.

Briana Scurry remembers when she was growing up that often her foot skills were overlooked because she could get by with her athleticism. That changed when she went to the next level. "Nowadays, a goalkeeper has to be more like a field player, so don't neglect that part of it," advises Bri.

This increased responsibility on the ball includes the goalkeeper. In many ways, the keeper becomes like a sweeper in a more traditional system. She becomes an outlet for the defenders and must possess technical ability and confidence with the ball at her feet. The starting position of the goalkeeper is crucial on both sides of the ball. Bri Scurry took on the challenge and made her kicking game an essential part of her training. Siri Mullinix, Saskia Webber and Tracy Ducar have begun to set a new standard for our country's goalkeepers. Their comfort level on the ball has allowed them to play higher in the space behind our defense and be more of a factor in our attack.

Possession became a key focus. In 1991 and again in 1995, we relied on our defensive commitment to get the ball back. As teams became more technical, we realized we couldn't always regain the ball by working hard. So we needed not to give it away as easily. Our ability as a team to hold the ball related to our shape, our technical level, our ability to read the situation and the tactical decision-making necessary to execute.

We made a simple adjustment in training to help replicate international competition. In small-sided games, we almost always utilized an offside line. This made the game more like what we see internationally. The space is condensed, eliminating time and space, necessitating good ball skills and execution. Furthermore, the offside line required our runs to be well-timed and the quality of our final passes more exact. The

Photo by Mike Stahlschmidt

In 1996, Cindy Parlow became the youngest gold medalist ever in soccer at the age of 18.

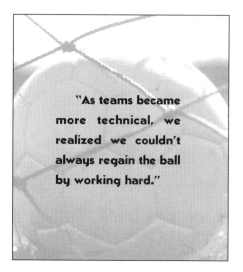

"As teams became more technical, we realized we couldn't always regain the ball by working hard."

use of an offside line was also an important training tool for our defenders. Even though we were not generally a trapping team, we like to use the rule to our advantage. It allowed us to work on condensing and dropping. The Norwegians are tremendous at condensing and then dropping to win the serve. They read service very well.

We needed to learn to solve breakdowns within a zonal defense. Because of the lack of cover and the amount of space covered by the zone's three players, there are two basic ways in which breakdowns are handled. When there is a breakdown, the defenders in the zone must distinguish which is more important, the man on the ball or the space. There will be times when defenders should delay and choose to protect the space initially. The critical factor is that whatever way you choose to play, all of your defenders must be on the same page. For example, if an opponent gets in behind the midfield, the defensive zone must either step together and condense the offensive team or retreat as a unit. As a general rule, we retreat when a team gets in behind our midfield. We do this for two reasons. First, it buys time and allows recovery of our other players. Second, we retreat only until the point where we can engage our goalkeeper as cover. Norway will retreat as long as possible before committing a defender.

In preparation for the Olympic games we evolved the 3-4-3 with a zone in the back as our principle system. Within this system, we played the formation two ways. What we came to term a "3-4-3 traditional." This meant a three-back zone in the defense, four midfielders and three high forwards. We also played a "3-4-3 inverted." This meant that instead of the three forwards all playing high, we played one in the middle beneath the other two. This would more naturally place one forward in the high seam in front of defenses, specifically in front of Norway's flat-back four defense. This, we felt, would prevent all three of our forwards from being marked out of the game by virtue of our shape.

We also wanted to have options and a level of comfort with more than one system, a luxury we didn't have in 1995. We spent time with the 3-5-2 as well. This system gives you more numbers through the midfield, making it hard for opponents to get through. The system plays with only two front-runners, increasing the responsibility of the flank players. They have to get forward to keep the width in the final third and maintain our flank play. With Shannon MacMillan and Kristine Lilly, on our flanks in midfield, we felt we had the personnel to use this system as an option. In addition, Joy Fawcett is a phenomenal flank midfielder and we could rotate her into that position and play Tiffany Roberts or Staci Wilson in the back line. Both Tiffany and Staci brought an incredible psychological dimension to the field. They were hard and loved to defend. Lastly, we spent some time on a 4-4-2, a more defensive system, we felt, but possibly useful to protect a lead, rest our front-runners and get more possession in the back because of the obviously superior numerical advantage. In addition, we anticipated possibly needing Michelle Akers' heading presence in midfield. Since we wanted to have our best players on the field, we could play Julie Foudy wide. This would keep Tisha Venturini, another world-class header, and Michelle inside, with Julie and Kristine Lilly wide. We introduced everything that may come to fruition down the road, well in advance.

One other significant "tactical" adjustment was to bring in Colleen Hacker on a semi-permanent basis. Although I addressed her role with us in the Psychological Section, it would be remiss not to mention her here, as well. I have told you throughout the book that you cannot talk about one aspect of your development without the others. We cannot think about discussing our tactical evolution without touching on the psychological aspects of both embracing these changes and its impact on each player and the team. It would be misleading to say these changes alone were enough. We believe that how you train is not divorced from training itself. Our mental preparation and psychological skill work was paramount to our cause. Colleen facilitated and maximized this, and she helped to harmonize our efforts to implement change.

*"Tactics are wonderful, but the biggest difference
between the 1995 World Cup and the
Olympics was our mentality."*
— *Tony DiCicco*

CHAPTER VI
THE OLYMPIC GAMES

We opened the Olympic Games against Denmark, a team that we had split with a year earlier. If you recall, our last two opening games in world events had not been at the level we had hoped. In 1995, we ended up 3-3 with China and pulled out a 3-2 win against Sweden, in 1991. So we had the formidable task of playing our first-ever Olympic match — in our own country — and to set the stage for the Games. We needed to start strong because our task of winning the gold medal necessitated that we continue to evolve throughout the games. We had to get better. We wanted a good platform on which to build.

Shannon MacMillan earned a starting role only six months after being cut from the initial residency roster. Her story, which is told in full in the Team Section, was a remarkable one of perseverance. It shows the character and heart of the players in this program. Not only did she not fold under this decision, when asked to come back she embraced a new position in order to have an opportunity to make this team. She and Kristine Lilly were two fast, attacking personalities for us on the flank. Shannon and Kristine both flagged the attacking unit comprised of Mia Hamm, Michelle Akers and Tiffeny Milbrett and central midfielders, Tisha Venturini and Julie Foudy. As always we were an attacking team with a number of ways to beat teams. The new defense of Brandi Chastain, Carla Overbeck, Joy Fawcett and Briana Scurry would prove almost impenetrable. And they had started new eras for their positions. They were no longer just defenders, but rather critical starting points for every attack.

The rest of our roster was full of possibilities. Who is on our bench is as important to us as who starts for us. We knew we would need everyone to win. Carin (Jennings) Gabarra and young star Cindy Parlow would be our options up front. Cindy would go on to become the youngest soccer player, male or female, to win a gold medal. In the midfield, we had Tiffany Roberts, nicknamed, the "Little Animal" because of her tenacity. She made the team because she had an exceptional quality. Her strength and her fighting power could help us win. Staci Wilson would be our defensive option. She was also a fierce player and a great tackler. In goal, we had veteran Mary Harvey. Mary battled back after major injuries to make the Olympic roster. We knew if we needed her at any point, she would be ready and would help us win. Her leadership for us, particularly with the reserve group, was a critical factor in our staying on target and our players being ready to step in when called upon.

Denmark, played a 4-4-2. They are always a very hard, physical team like Norway. They, too, played with a four-back, but this time it featured a cover personality, Kamma Flaeng behind the defensive line. When they condensed or came forward, she would flatten out her shape and become part of the line. In and around their box, she stayed deeper to provide cover, like a sweeper. She stayed very central. They organized their strength right up the middle of the field. Tactically, Denmark organized with a low restraining line, meaning they didn't pressure us coming out of the back until we reached midfield. This wasn't a bunker, rather a calculated counter-attack style. They sat in there and tried to nip something and attack quickly and directly.

It was a brutally hot day. Close to 100 degrees and 100 percent humidity. We thrived in that environment because of our residency training in Orlando the past six months. Over the course of the game, the heat definitely took its toll on

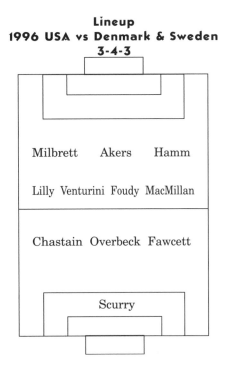

Lineup
1996 USA vs Denmark & Sweden
3-4-3

Milbrett   Akers   Hamm

Lilly Venturini Foudy MacMillan

Chastain Overbeck Fawcett

Scurry

Denmark. If you recall, we instituted the Water Brigade. We trained ourselves to want water more regularly, and we had a system in place to get players water during the game. Once we went up a couple of goals, our ability to hold the ball — one of the areas targeted for improvement after the 1995 loss — proved valuable in that first game. Denmark couldn't chase because of the heat, and we didn't give it away unnecessarily as we had in the past. Furthermore, we showed a greater game savvy, never letting them back in the game. We went on to win 3-0. This starting point was a dramatic improvement to our start in either of the first two World Cups.

Our second match of the Olympics was against Sweden. After one game, Sweden was already in a must-win situation to avoid elimination. Sweden is not a team you want to face when they need to win. They are fighters to the end. They are hard, know the game, and are always well-organized. We had defeated them twice earlier in 1996, and we were concerned about having to beat them a third time under these circumstances. "They play their best soccer when their backs are against the wall," Tony told the team. He reminded us of 1995 when they had lost their opening game to Brazil. In their second game against Germany, they were behind 2-0, but went on to win 3-2.

Sweden, too, had made changes since 1995. They replaced some of their more possession-oriented players with more direct attacking personalities up top. In the spring of 1996, I went to Spain to scout them. I remember charting the types of balls they served. There were distinct types of services and certain areas of the field they liked to play from. Overall, they liked to come forward, working the ball out of the back up the left side through Kristin Bengtsson. She was a world class, left-sided defender. In fact, because she was so dominant and because so much of the play went through her, we organized our defense to force them to play out of the back in ways other than through her to make it less comfortable for them.

Once they were able to get the ball around the midline, they liked to spring players on the flank, find a front-runner on an inside to wide run or flight the ball into the box. They had

HOW TO WATCH A GAME
by Brandi Chastain

There are a lot of different ways to watch a game. I take different information in as a fan, just to enjoy the game. As a coach, I try to take what is happening in the game and explain it. As a player, I look to see if I was in a particular role, how would I set myself up to handle certain situations.

Watching it on TV is hard. You can't see everything off the ball. If you want to get better and become a tactician, you should watch games in person. When we were in residency training in Orlando in 1995, I would drive hundreds of miles to watch the Tampa Bay Mutiny play.

Coming to an understanding of tactics doesn't happen all at once. It's an evolution. You start by taking a piece of paper. You note the formation or the type of pattern teams play. Then you look for one player in that system and see how they play it — both offensively and defensively. There are several things you should try to discover — who's the play-maker, who touches the ball the most. Look at how

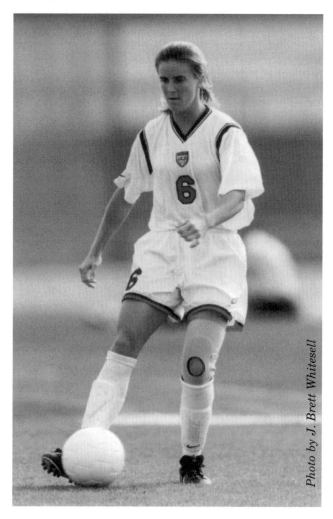

Photo by J. Brett Whitesell

players work together. For example, check how the center back and wide backs work together. Then check the relationship between center back and central midfielder. How can each player help the other one get into a better position? How will a better pass make that player more open?

I also learned from watching from the sideline when I was injured. I had never watched a game because I was always on the field. It really helped me to be able to see it from a different perspective and a different angle. I knew what the coach had been talking about because I could see it. When he was saying that to me, I thought, "No way." Now it is obvious.

If you are looking at the game tactically, you can break it down into nine grids. First, separate the game into the three "thirds" of the field — attacking third, midfield third, and the defensive third. Then, split it into channels. What do you see that left back doing in the defensive third that you don't see them doing in the attacking third. How does it change? Just because you are the left back, doesn't mean you can't do left midfield things or forward things. A lot of kids who play left back, stay back there and say, "I am in my position, I must be doing my job."

very good flank service and box organization, and their fighting mentality in the air made those balls hard to handle. It was important for us to compete in the air and fight to get the first touch on the ball served into the box.

We played a 3-4-3 against Sweden. But in games like this, where Sweden had to win to stay alive, tactics sometimes mean less than fighting power. Never underestimate your psychological dimension in performance, both individually and as a team. The game with Sweden was much like we expected. It was a war. They were as physical a team as we had seen in the international arena. My favorite goal of the Olympics, was our first goal against Sweden. Tisha Venturini, in classic form, scored on a beautiful diving header. Mia Hamm served a lofted ball into the box, and Tiffeny Milbrett worked to get inside her defender to get the first touch on the ball. She redirected it behind her. Tisha, who is brilliant with her runs into the box, unbalanced her run to get back post and dove to head in the goal. An unbalancing run is a term we use to define a run that stretches a defense. Often, it is a run that exploits the weak side of the field. In this case, the play was developing up the left side of the field. Our players and Sweden's were all on the left side. Instead of going to the ball, Tisha made a run away from the crowded area, to the weak-side of the field or unbalanced. Michelle Akers and Tisha are the best in the world at this run. Our young stars of the future, Laurie Schwoy and Aly Wagner are also very dangerous making this run out of midfield. The run can be made to get the ball or to just stretch the defense. Tisha also took an incredible physical risk to get to the ball and give us the lead. Tisha had a defender closing in on her and the goalkeeper coming out.

Shannon MacMillan gave us a 2-0 lead, but Sweden fought back behind their veteran leader Pia Sundhage and drew a foul on the left side outside our penalty area. Their shot hit off one of our defenders and deflected in. After that, every ball was served at our defensive restraining line or into our box. Briana Scurry earned her weight in gold by dominating on those through balls behind our defense and dominating on the flighted balls into the box. We weathered an outstanding team to win by a 2-1 margin.

The last game of the first round paired us with China. Each of us had been assured a spot in the next round with six points. Mia Hamm had been injured in the closing minutes of the Sweden game and was sidelined for this match. Both teams' legs were a bit tired as we were on an every other day rhythm, which is extremely difficult at this level. China's midfield defense was the best in the world. They would invite you to play into them, and then look to dispossess you and strike. Their system of play was a 4-4-2 like most of our opponents. They played with a four-back zone with a covering player. Her job was not as pronounced as Denmark's Flaeng's, but she clearly would drop in the flow of play to provide cover for her teammates.

Of any team, China most resembles the United States, athletically, and in that they had several personalities on the field, beginning with their goalkeeper Gao Hong, one of the best in the world. China was dangerous on the flanks. Zhao Lihong was an awesome left-sided player. She, like Kristine Lilly, impacted the game from the flank, not only by getting up and down the field, but also by coming inside with the ball, and by virtue of her overall mobility. Sun Wen and Liu Ailing were dominant international figures. They were precise and deadly in their passes and runs. Liu Ailing was a tremendous distributor and the engine for their team in many ways. Sun Wen was such a schemer, always having a sense of where and what the game needed from her, and she could score goals. China is so dangerous because of their speed, technical and tactical level, and their mobility. One of our reasons for advancing our defensive system to a zone was, in part, to accommodate the mobility of the Chinese midfield, specifically and overall.

Because the goal differential was in China's favor, they only had to tie to win our group. So at halftime, with the game knotted in a scoreless tie, they were content to sit back and clog our space and look to counter-attack. We had to be careful pressing in from our end to get a goal. This would have left us vulnerable in the back. Because they find your weak spot immediately, it was vital to keep our shape and remain disciplined against the Chinese. Carla Overbeck, Joy Fawcett and Brandi Chastain kept us secure in the back. Because of Briana's organization and communication, China had very few opportunities to shoot. Despite some terrific soccer played by both teams, and several crossbars by us, the game ended 0-0. This meant we would face Norway once again in the semifinals. China would play Brazil.

Norway was a team with which we were all too familiar. I had scouted them in Oslo, Norway, one last time prior to the Olympics. They were very direct, still in the 4-4-2. In fact, Norway is clearly a country who picks players for their system not a system for their players. Boys and girls play a 4-4-2 with a rigid, flat-back four and a direct style of attack. In Norway, they actually select players for their national team program that can play inside right back or outside left defense. This system, built around the defense, led Norway in the Olympics to replace Carlson, a key defender for them who had been ejected, with Aarones. Aarones is a key offensive personality for them. So based on their philosophy, the obvious adjustment was to put her in the back. However, from our standpoint she was also one of their top attacking players. This was a mistake, I believe, for them but shows their orientation and rigid design.

In my scouting report on Norway to our team, I isolated three personalities to discuss: Medalen, their target up front; Riise, their central attacking midfielder; and Nordby their goalkeeper. Remember, it is important not just to get information on your opponents, but more so what you do with it and how it is presented. Medalen was a veteran of two World Cups. She was a tremendous target, and the player through which most of their attack went. She could make any ball a good pass. She was dangerous in the air and had an aggressive mentality around the box to score. Riise, was the best player in the world in 1995. She could victimize any defense with her passes as well as her movement off the ball. And she was lethal on free kicks. Next was Nordby. It's very unusual for me to select a goalkeeper as one of the personalities to discuss with our team. But I did so because I felt we could use that information to our benefit. She has two qualities that distinguish her. One, her kicking game is the best in the world. Two, her starting position behind her back line is very aggressive and makes playing over the top very difficult for us.

SCOUTING NORWAY

OFFENSIVE TENDENCIES

▲ Direct and then re-direct for second attacker or midfielder coming through
▲ Very organized attack off the long-ball service into Medalen, their target
▲ Looked to serve into the box from the flank when they were just inside their midline
▲ Worked for corner kicks, long throw-ins, and free kicks
▲ Capable of combining around the top of the eighteen

DEFENSIVE TENDENCIES

▲ They are hard
▲ Strong tackling and heading presence
▲ Played with rigid flat back four; condensed and dropped very effectively
▲ Zoned in midfield with invite; closed hard when ball is delivered into attacker
▲ Forwards pressurized in different parts of field; varied restraining line
▲ Zone stayed together in breakdowns until forced to commit to the ball, especially on the dribble

What did we do with this information? First let's look at Medalen. Her ability in the air and her importance to her team simply meant that we needed to have a good defensive shape in the back. When she was competing for a ball in the air, we needed to have good shape around the player competing with her so we could pick up the second ball. We could not leave her unmarked in and around the box. We challenged our front-runners to deny service — or at least pressure service — so the quality of the passes delivered to her would not be as precise.

Second, utilizing the information on Nordby would be important. The adjustments we made from the information I had on Nordby were to figure out her service range and have our best heading personalities on the end of it. For example, on goal kicks we had Michelle Akers and Tisha Venturini stationed at her service range to win the heading duels. This was a similar strategy to what we used against Denmark. This resulted in our first goal against Denmark when Michelle won a head ball and Mia ran onto it and put it away. In addition, when playing against Nordby in goal, we had to ensure that the quality of our service over the top would eliminate her. This meant avoiding playing up the middle. We had to utilized the flanks more when playing over the top of the defense.

Our biggest adjustment came from our decision on how to play Riise. So much of their attack went through her that we decided to play ten against ten and mark her one-on-one. Making this adjustment could really throw off your team or an individual player if you are not prepared for it. There could have been a sense of concern if our players felt these changes were being made because the opponent was better than we were. Since marking Riise one-on-one was something we had entertained, and did in the U.S. Cup the year before, we felt we could do it again without any psychological ramifications to our players. If you recall, we also had asked Julie Foudy to play on the flank during our lead-up to the Olympics. This said, "We can beat you ten on ten." So we put Tiffany Roberts* on Riise, and she did a marvelous job. More importantly, it freed up Kristine Lilly to attack. Remember one of the problems we had against Norway in 1995 was that Kristine was engaged defensively too much with Riise. With Tiff Roberts marking Riise all over the field, Kristine was free to do damage.

"We were changing our team," says Tony DiCicco. "The United States was changing because of an opponent, and no coach likes to do that. They would rather say, 'They have to play us. They have to figure us out.' But at the same time, we as coaches, can be too stubborn. In this case, I conceded that we had to stop a portion of what Norway does so we could play our game. And putting Roberts on Riise, freed up Kristine Lilly. She gave us that third attacker and she gave us that wide presence on the flank. Yes, we conceded something, but at the same time we created something with that concession."

Preparing for your opponents at this level is vital. In preparation for Norway, we did a lot of scout-team training, where we would have the reserves playing a mock flat-back four. Solving this organized, disciplined, flat defense was a challenge. A critical thing to realize is that female players in the United States see very similar styles.

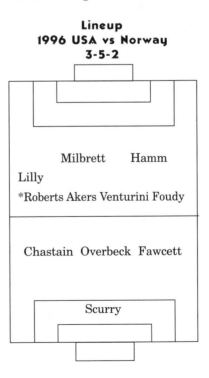

Lineup
1996 USA vs Norway
3-5-2

Milbrett   Hamm

Lilly

*Roberts Akers Venturini Foudy

Chastain Overbeck Fawcett

Scurry

The spacing between Norway's midfield and the flat-back four is the "seam" where we wanted to possess the ball.

Even though teams may play 4-4-2 or a 3-5-2 or a 3-4-3 our styles are not drastically different. As a result, we seldom see the styles other countries play. That posed a challenge unto itself. Norway, in particular, evolved their flat-back four zone and overall system, in part, as a means to beat the United States. They clogged the space up the middle with the equivalent of a four-player wall. They took the space away behind us by playing their goalkeeper high like a sweeper. They condensed the space we had to play in. As a result, we spent a considerable amount of time studying and solving this system. The lessons we learned and incorporated into our preparation were as follows.

First, we had to find areas in which to hold the ball against this system. The design of the 4-4-2 as the way Norway played it was on rigid lines. If, for example, the ball is at the feet of our right back, then Norway condenses from the back up and horizontally. The spacing between the two lines of defense is such that you can hold the ball there. We call the space between the two lines of defense "seams." So there is a seam between their forwards and their midfielders, one between their midfielders and their defenders and on down the opposite flank, or weak-side flank. In the above photo you see our forwards (in white) in the "seam" in front of their defense (in dark).

In our match against Norway, we were very prepared and confident. In the locker room, you could sense a tremendous focus with positive energy. "The mood was very different from 1995," says Tisha Venturini. "We knew we were going to win. There was never any doubt." Even though we had spent much of our Spring preparation focusing on changes in our system of play, we knew one thing to be true — our mentality would decide the outcome of the game. Our mentality on both sides of the ball would be the margin. Remember in 1995, we felt it was missing. As always, during our pre-game meeting, we review our keys to victory offensively and defensively. When we faced Norway, we had mentality on the top of each list of objectives. Our offensive mentality was our willingness to take risks, go one-v-one, and take shots. Defensively, it was our fighting mentality, our commitment to first and second balls, our heading and tackling presence. Without our mentality against a team like Norway, you could almost throw all of the tactical preparation out the window. It must be the foundation. From that place — our technical, tactical and physical prowess would be unleashed.

Tony echoed these sentiments after the win to a reporter. "Tactics are wonderful, but the biggest difference between the 1995 World Cup and the Olympics was our mentality going into the game. Our mentality was too tentative in 1995. We were like, 'What are they going to do, and what do we need to do to stop them?' In this game, it was our mentality that was going to prevail. If you look at the semifinal, Norway was trying to stop us most of the game. They were still dangerous. But most of the game, they were trying to stop what we were doing, and that was a complete turnaround from the '95 World Cup."

At the same time, we knew we had to work hard not to make the game a fifty-fifty game with the ball always in the air. We asked the players to keep working to get a hold of the ball and keep possession. The more the ball is in the air against Norway the more the game plays into their favor. "We have a lot of respect for the Norwegians," says Tony DiCicco. "Evan Pellerud, their coach, is an honorable man and an excellent coach. And his teams always project his style and competitiveness. We knew it was going to be a difficult game, and we knew the way we had to play to beat Norway. We knew if we let the game get into a direct-style game where we were constantly competing for air balls, it would be a difficult game. They are so disciplined in picking up second balls and surrounding target areas of long balls, and from there they have players already attacking the goal. If we played that style, we knew it would be to their benefit."

During the warmup, April and I were trying to slow our players down. There was such energy to play, we knew we were ready. We didn't want to expend all our energy on warming up. Although on the inside, April and I were pleased to see the mentality we so much needed to win.

The game began in a flurry. The crowd was in for a thrill. We got in early and had some tremendous chances. Early in the game, Brandi Chastain suffered an injury to her medial collateral ligament, but she was able to return and continue playing. Her ability to serve balls with different surfaces of her feet allowed her to protect her injury and still remain a factor for us.

USA vs. Norway "Keys to Victory" Olympic Semifinal, July 28, 1996

Mia Hamm and Tiffeny Milbrett were getting behind the Norwegian defense. We were off to the kind of start we had hoped for. Less than twenty minutes in, though, Norway was on the board. With Brandi on the sideline receiving treatment for her MCL injury, we had miss-cleared a ball out of the defense. They pounced on it and in our attempts to pressure them, we over ran a second runner, Linda Medalen, coming in. We had come out in a "V" formation. The center of our defense ran out and the flank defenders kept Medalen on-sides. They played the ball past us and she went in one-on-one with Bri Scurry. Bri came to close Medalen on the serve into the box but was unable to prevent the goal.

Trailing to Norway was a familiar early position for us, but this time it would prove different. We were still confident. We had been getting in on their defense and knew we would continue to get chances. When half-time came, it served only to remind our players we had time. "We were as confident that we would score two goals as we were that we would score one," says Kristine Lilly. "We were totally confident." Our preparation — all aspects — was the root of this confidence.

Late into the second half, Norway committed a handball in the box trying to deflect a service off course. Michelle Akers looked to the bench, asking to take the kick. That's a champion. She wanted the responsibility for victory to rest with her. "I wanted that kick," says Michelle, who realized that if she missed, her team would probably lose. "How many times in your life do you get a chance like that. To be faced with that kind of challenge and make it ... what an incredible feeling." She stepped up and with authority, drilled the ball to the opposite side-netting from where Nordby guessed. It was a 1-1 ballgame. At the end of regulation, the score remained 1-1. The tie-breaker began with two fifteen-minute periods of golden goal — the first team that scores wins. Doc Adams, Steve Slain, Patty Marchak, the coaches and reserves were helping players stretch and doing massages and getting hydrated. Tony said, 'sudden victory.' Usually you hear the more familiar term — 'sudden death.' For us it was about sudden victory. Just the words provoke very different feelings. When you hear sudden death, it's a bit more frightening and creates a fear of failure. We chose to view it as sudden victory. That evoked a positive response in our players. We went onto the field with a commitment by everyone to an aggressive mentality. We would accept only one outcome.

Midway through the first overtime period, we decided that we needed a boost. If you recall we sat Shannon MacMillan out to use Tiffany Roberts to mark Riise. Shannon, accepting what was best for the team, had been warming up and down throughout the end of the game. She stayed focused and ready, awaiting any opportunity to get in. Had she not been in such a good frame of mind, she would never have answered her calling the way she did. The time came. We put her in for Tiffeny Milbrett. First, Joy Fawcett won a long ball in the air and headed it. Julie Foudy, reading the first ball (Joy's header), won the second ball. She received the ball in the seam right in front of the defense. She dribbled from the right flank, right at the heart of the defense. The key is to get a player from the defensive line to commit. Julie did this by dribbling at them. As they stepped to her, Shannon made a brilliant run along the restraining line. With perfect execution, Julie found Shannon in behind the defense by playing a ball into the space the defender had just vacated. The weight on Julie's final pass was perfect. Nordy came to play it, but the pass was so well paced by Julie that Shannon was able to get the first touch. Without breaking stride, Shannon slipped it past the keeper as she went down. Shannon's second touch of the game was the golden goal. It was a classic finish and punctuation to all the ways we worked to beat them.

Photo by Tony Quinn

Julie Foudy sets the pace for the U.S. team.

MIDFIELDERS: THE ENGINES

Midfielders are the engines of the team. They have to be intrinsically hard workers and enjoy dueling. A good midfielder has a combative attitude, and they take pride in being a ball-winner.

Technical qualities essential to a good midfielder include having a strong heading presence and being an effective tackler. They must be able to distribute the ball with all surfaces of both feet and have a good shot. Long-ball service is an important quality.

Physically, midfielders need a tremendous conditioning base, both aerobic and anaerobic. They must possess the upper- and lower-body strength to win physical battles for ninety minutes.

Mentally, midfielders are players that seek a duel. They are aggressive and have the desire to out-work their opponent. They pride themselves on being among the fittest players on the field. They are confident in their fitness and ability. They have a ball-winning mentality which is unwavering. And most of all, they are a team leader who serves as a quarterback or a coach on the field.

TACTICAL ASPECTS OF CENTRAL MIDFIELDERS

1. Play-making
2. Finding players' feet vs finding space
3. Final pass or "getting a teammate in"
4. Changing the point of attack
5. When to go forward — with the ball; without the ball
6. First defender responsibilities (closing, denying penetration)
7. Second defender responsibilities (providing cover)
8. When to track runs

Flank Midfielders: 120-Yard Responsibility

Kristine Lilly is one of the best flank midfielders the world has ever seen. Her work-rate, fitness, dueler's mentality, tactical awareness and overall consistency are virtually unparalleled. Over the years, Kristine has developed a great understanding of her position.

"Playing on the outside, you have to be patient and wait for the ball," she says. "You can't go into the middle just because your teammates aren't passing it outside to you. But when I played other positions, I realized how hard it is to get it outside sometimes. When Julie Foudy started playing on the flank, she couldn't believe she never got the ball. Then she realized when she was in the middle, she was the one who was supposed to be putting it out there."

Kristine explains the perfect midfield mentality of combining patience with the desire to get forward. "I realize I have a role," she says. "I have to be patient and wait for the ball, and when I get the ball, I want to make something happen. If I get half a chance to take someone on or do a quick one-two to get down the flank, I certainly will."

Shannon MacMillan learned to play flank midfielder prior to the 1996 Olympics. She understands the physical demands of flank midfielders, as well as the offensive and defensive responsibilities of the position.

"We have a 120-yard role," Shannon says. "We have to get up on attack and get crosses off, or we might have to be at the end of a cross from the opposite flank. But we must always get back on defense. If we don't, we are going to put our defense in trouble. So when we don't have the ball we must be balanced back a bit. The decisions then become how far back. You are not always even with the backs, but if our defensive line is stretched then we may need to get back and provide cover, cleaning up anything that goes through. Playing flank midfield you're all over the place. You are not necessarily a straight up-and-down player."

Both Shannon and Kristine can be considered goal-scorers. They entered 1999 with 75 international goals between them.

"Scoring is for everybody," says Shannon. "Midfielders tend to set up more, but they certainly can be goal-scorers. When I see Lil breaking in, I'm busting to get to the far post for anything that might come skipping over. The whole team carries the burden of scoring."

Tactical Aspects of Flank Midfielders

1. When to run to get behind a defense
2. When to withdraw back to the ball
3. Recognizing opportunity to initiate the change of point of attack
4. Recycling the ball, avoiding the "not on" syndrome
5. Quality flank service
6. Getting into the box
7. Closing, providing cover
8. When to balance on defense: and how far

Shannon MacMillan scores the Golden Goal, putting the USA in the Olympic Gold Medal Game.

Photo by Mike Stahlschmidt

It was over. We had won. The crowd erupted in a deafening roar. We sprinted out and piled on top of each other. We were in the Olympic Final. For a few moments, we savored the victory. But soon, we were task-oriented, moving on to the challenge of facing China for the gold medal. China had narrowly defeated Brazil (3-2) in the closing minutes of the other semifinal.

At that moment, I found myself reflecting on many of the team-building activities we had done just a month before. There was one simple one. We were in small groups of about eight or so. The exercise was to get this little ball touched by everyone in the group without a break in contact between the ball and the player, in as little time as possible. Sounds simple. Well at first, it was a competition between the two groups. Then, it became an internal battle as well. Each time, we would lower our score. And then, they would ask us to cut our time in half. At first, it almost felt impossible. But we kept at it. We would accomplish marker after marker. Just when we would wonder if we could do it any better, they would say we had to beat our time again. We employed new strategies. But it required something else — a sense that there is always room to improve. There can be no limit. And we now found ourselves having beaten Norway, the defending world champions. We had left everything on the field, played some of the best soccer we had played in the Olympics to date. Now, we were faced with having to be even better just three days later. That small team activity showed us to never define our limits. There must always be the possibility of being even better. Our best had gotten us to the final. We knew we could be better, and we had to be to win it all.

CHAPTER VII
GOLD

China posed different challenges. We looked at what we needed to do differently this game to win. We knew them inside and out. Our discussion as a coaching staff came to the same conclusions. This game was about us. We needed to be healthy, rested and focused on executing. Tactically, we needed to keep possession and our defensive organization was vital.

The game opened up in front of a crowd of 76,461, the largest ever to see a women's sporting event ... anywhere. It was so loud the players couldn't hear me shout out the warmup. I had to use hand signals. The atmosphere was breathtaking. A thousand emotions were running through everyone. Dreams of a lifetime were unfolding before us. The Olympic music was playing, serving to remind us that we were really here. But we weren't ready to be merely content to be there. We wanted to win. That was our only goal. Nothing short of that would be enough. We were very confident going into this game. There is no better feeling than knowing you are prepared — in every respect.

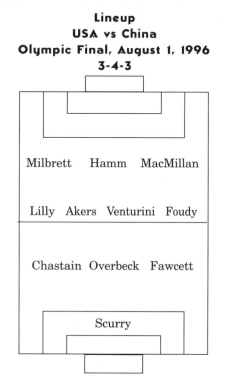

Lineup
USA vs China
Olympic Final, August 1, 1996
3-4-3

Milbrett   Hamm   MacMillan

Lilly   Akers   Venturini   Foudy

Chastain   Overbeck   Fawcett

Scurry

The pace was fast, as is to be expected when playing the Chinese. In many ways, we were playing too fast in the beginning. We weren't really holding the ball as much as we would have liked. Against China, if you give the ball up you have to spend a lot of energy working to get it back. The game ebbed and flowed for awhile. But we were confident early because we had developed some very good scoring opportunities. The first goal was a textbook picture of so many elements we had focused on this past year. The play started with our goalkeeper, Briana Scurry. Bri made this awesome save at one end, distributed it, and on the same possession, we went down and scored at the other end.

What was so amazing about this goal is how it involved almost our whole team. It was initiated by a change in the point of attack. Tiffeny Milbrett got the ball and decided it was too congested on that side of the field. She played it back into Michelle Akers who had come in support of the ball.

Michelle found Kristine Lilly patiently waiting on the left flank. Kristine attacked the end line and bent a beautiful ball to the back post. Shannon MacMillan had made a near post run. Mia sprinted into the box to fill the slot, and with a sliding volley, hit a ball on goal. Gao, the Chinese keeper made a tremendous first save, knocking the ball wide, and it careened off the goal post. Shannon who had made the near-post run, turned and framed the goal. (Framing the goal is the act of keeping balls alive on shots. It's running a player at each post and into the goal mouth to keep shots alive and make the frame of the goal larger). Shannon nailed the rebound back at the goal past Gao. We were up 1-0. After scoring, Shannon did her patented "dive and slide," and for an instant the team celebrated the moment. Then, back to business.

**China's Lineup
Olympic Final
4-4-2**

The Chinese were still getting in on us. They were sending players forward from midfield and creating too many opportunities against our defense. Joy Fawcett was outstanding at providing cover behind our line. She would sweep across the back of the defense thwarting trouble numerous times. Joy had been, in our opinion, one of the MVP's for the Games. She not only dominated her zone, but she provided great cover behind our defense, and she was getting forward for us out of the back. Joy, Carla and Brandi absorbed this situation well. In fact Briana, who on the stat sheet didn't have many recorded saves, was huge in denying scoring opportunities because of her positioning and mentality. Bri was outstanding at playing the through ball and was snuffing balls at attackers feet before they even were able to get a shot off. "We were running at the Chinese player with the ball, and they were one-touching around us or beating us with dribbles," says Tony. "Luckily, though, we were playing with great recovery. We were sprinting back, and our back three and Bri were solving a lot of problems."

Later in the first half, China served a ball over the top of our defense. We hadn't read service well, and they got in behind us. They cleaned the ball up and scored, as Briana came to make the play. This was only the third goal we had given up in five games. We went into halftime 1-1. My halftime remarks were to keep doing what we were doing. That only forty-five minutes were between us and our goal. The only tactical adjustment we made was to put Michelle Akers in a deeper seam defensively in midfield. We needed to clog the middle of the field where they were getting through us too easily, either through a penetrative pass or run. We accomplished this by pulling Shannon back to flank midfield and pushing Julie Foudy inside. So, we went into a 3-5-2 formation at the start of the second half.

This adjustment really took away the space into which they wanted to play. Julie and Shannon did a great job on the flank making Zhao play them. She is a dangerous attacking left-sided midfielder who was forced to play more defense because of our offensive commitment from this position. We did less chasing in the second half and kept possession better than in the first half. Midway through the half, we regained a ball in the midfield third. Shannon

SPECIAL QUALITIES OF FRONT-RUNNERS

"The role of a forward first of all is to put the ball in the back of the net," says Tiffeny Milbrett. "I believe it takes a special something to be a forward. There is something you can't teach. When you are a forward, you have a knack for scoring goals, and you feel good when you score goals. Honestly, when we don't score, we don't feel good. We get upset. That's a natural part of being a striker."

The front-runner must possess certain technical qualities. Of course, they must be able to put the ball in the net. They must be able to finish with both feet and all the surfaces of both feet. They have to be able to turn the ball quickly and efficiently. And they have to have an excellent first touch which allows them to receive the ball so as to leave as many options open as possible.

Perhaps more than any other position, the front-runner has to be strong psychologically.

"The beauty of our team is all our front-runners want to score," says Shannon MacMillan. "When we get the ball, we're looking to go goal. I remember one time when we played Japan. One of their front-runners got in on us, and she was like, 'I don't know if I want to go it alone.' That's not us. We want to score. You definitely have to take a defender on every time you can. You might lose it, but you're wearing that player down. The more you take on, the more you put your stamp on the game. Let that defender know, 'Hey, I'm coming after you!' It makes your job a bit easier in the long run."

Front-runners not only have to have the ability to go one-on-one, they have to have the willingness to do so. They are risk-takers by nature, who want the ball every time down the field. The physical qualities needed are speed, upper- and lower-body strength, explosive acceleration and change of pace, change of direction, and anaerobic and aerobic conditioning

Front-runners also have to be students of the game. They need to understand the nuances of the game, knowing when to shoot and when to pass. One thing that makes Brandi Chastain such an incredible player and so much fun to watch is her sense of the smallest moments in the game. She appreciates the sophistication with which the game can be played.

"My grandfather used to pay me a dollar if I scored a goal," Brandi says. "If I got an assist, I got a $1.50. He thought helping someone else score a goal was important. I started thinking it was really fun setting up a goal. Then, I moved into thinking, 'What if I make my defender run away so someone can run into that space.' As a forward, that was big for me. That was really fun. Sometimes I make a run and someone will follow me, and I just laugh because I fooled them into thinking I'm going to get the ball. And I was setting her up the whole time. I think that's something that is really underrated.

"Scoring goals is awesome, but it's the little stuff that makes the goals happen. It isn't always about the ball and who has the ball. It's about what's happening away from the ball each time."

TACTICAL ASPECTS OF FRONT-RUNNERS

1. When to take on; when to pass
2. What type of run to make
3. When to come to the ball; when to go away from the ball
4. When to face up with the defender; when to play back
5. Back to goal decisions
6. When to pressure the ball on defense; where to force the ball

found Joy who played it into Mia. Joy went to the inside of Mia, and Mia threaded a perfect pass back to her. Joy, one of the fastest defenders in the world, overlapped and accelerated to goal. She carried the ball just long enough to keep the goalkeeper engaged at the near post. Just like an exercise we did the day before the final. She carried it just long enough and then laid this perfect pass to Tiffeny Milbrett who had sprinted in with her. Tiffeny just tucked it away. The timing was impeccable.

The game ended 2-1. We were the first-ever Olympic Gold Medalists in women's soccer. "What is a credit to our team is that the first two games against Denmark and Sweden, we played the same lineup," says Tony DiCicco. "And that was the last time you saw that lineup. The first time against China, when Mia was out, the lineup was different. The Norway game was different. I think other teams had a hard time figuring

---

FLANK DEFENDERS: OFFENSIVE WEAPONS

Offensively, defenders have to have an understanding of how to attack.

The flank defender's offensive responsibility does not end once they have served the ball to a teammate. "If we make a run forward, we may not always get the ball, but it may free up someone else," Lorrie Fair says. "For instance, if I have the ball at left back, and Lil's in front of me — if she is wide early, and her player is playing off of her, I can serve the ball out to her. If she takes it inside, it gives me a chance to overlap around her. If they fail to mark me, I can get the ball from a center midfielder, a forward or even the opposite side. When I get the ball I can serve a cross, or I might have a one-v-one there.

---

out what we were doing. Now, when they see Michelle Akers, they have seen her in the midfield, and they have seen her up front. I think China figured she was going to be in the center of our attack. But for the first time the world saw, Mia Hamm, Tiffeny Milbrett and Shannon MacMillan up front, Michelle Akers in the center of midfield and Julie Foudy on the right flank. China has never played against that system. We played with only one acceptable outcome. You could see it on their faces. They handled the pressure of being at home and being one of the favorites. And they found a way to win."

What is critical to remember is that we didn't introduce anything new during the games. We had explored all of these changes to some degree in advance. This was important to our players' confidence and buying into what we were doing. If changes are made unexpectedly, players will read the wrong things into them, or be left uncertain as to why such decisions were made. If an understanding of the possibility of change is introduced, then there is less room for mis-interpretation. For example, Julie Foudy's willingness to play outside on the flank during the Olympics when we needed her to was crucial. This allowed us to play the players and the system and style we felt was going to help us win. And it wasn't always the same. While we didn't make huge adjustments, we were willing to make the little adjustments that suited us, and they helped us win. We were flexible to a point. But you must introduce the possibility of change ahead of time.

In turn, I hope you appreciate the willingness of all of our players to do what is best for the team. Whether that meant playing a new position, not starting or being on our bench, the team's success always came first.

Tiffeny Milbrett scores the game-winning goal for the United States in first-ever Olympic Gold Medal match for women's soccer.

Photo by Michael Allen

"We felt our preparation for the 1999 World Cup should involve developing a more secure defensive system."

CHAPTER VIII
RIPPLES THROUGH THE WORLD

In 1997 and 1998, everywhere in the world teams were re-examining their players, their systems and styles, trying to discover what they needed to do in preparation for the 1999 Women's World Cup. Germany consolidated their thirty-six-team league down to a twelve-team Bundesliga to create an environment that would be more competitive for their players. Brazil, who had finished a remarkable fourth, narrowly losing to China in the semifinals and losing a very respectable 2-0 game to Norway in the bronze medal game, had also begun a new league for women. They had drawn attention to themselves. Now what they needed was their country's support. Expect Brazil to be a possible contender in 1999. We were no exception. We re-examined our performances in the Olympics and after the Olympics. We studied the directions in which the women's game was going. We saw the retirement of two of the games greatest players, Mary Harvey and Carin (Jennings) Gabarra, both world champions and Olympic Gold Medalists. The national team pool of players would be re-formed and many young faces would complement our veteran core.

Norway continues to be the best team in the world at finding the most penetrative options as soon as possible. They are able to play forward on their interception, and therefore, can punish your mistakes. Norway made some personnel changes but also some subtle changes to the types of players they are using in their system, which remains the same. They continue to get personalities in their midfield. Mainstay, Linda Medalen has found a new home in the defense.

Germany will play a 4-4-2 in 1999. They will play with a sweeper, Stephanie Jones and a three-back zone in front of her. Bettina Wiegmann, back after a serious knee injury, will be a key component to their success. They will continue to play with a mobile midfield. Their dominant offensive scheme is to counter-attack. They drop their defensive restraining line set by their forwards and look to counter-attack. And they are very good at it. They have evolved under the new leadership of Tina Theune-Meyer, the long-time assistant coach for the Germans. She has brought a balance between the classic, inter-passing and combination style team to a more direct counter-attacking team. It is a very dangerous and enjoyable style to watch. The consolidated league has helped them make tremendous ground in the international arena. They have developed a fighting mentality since their disappointing result against the United States in the 1991 World Cup. European Champions in 1997, Germany will be one of the top teams in the 1999 Women's World Cup.

China, although they revamped their team after qualifying for the World Cup, is still one of the most athletic teams in the world. They have begun to expand the personalities of players they are selecting. For the first time, they have attacking players that have the ability to play in the air. The balance of veterans and young players makes them a dangerous team. Once China truly supports their women as athletes and they evolve the confidence and psychological hardness of a Norway or a United States, they will be deadly. Other teams around the world that have shown resurgence are Italy, and Denmark.

For the United States, we feel our preparation for the 1999 World Cup should involve developing a more secure defensive system. Three in the back has worked for us but we wanted at least the option of greater numbers in defense and a system that would allow us to play three front-runners. We remain the predominant team in the world that plays with three front-runners.

How could we accomplish this? The only way to play with three forwards high and four in the back would be to play three in the midfield. At this level, to play three across our midfield would not work. Teams would always out number us and get through the defense too easily. Also, we had dominant central midfielders. So, the decision was to play with three central midfielders — making the predominant system for the U.S. in the 1999 Women's World Cup a 4-3-3. The decision came from balancing out the direction in which we felt our team needed to go to stay more secure in the back, due to the rising level of the women's game, as well as what system would maximize the personalities we have.

The 4-3-3, like every system, affords you things and takes away others. Offensively, it gives us the chance to play three players high. We want to maintain this characteristic not just because of its uniqueness, but also because we have many dominant attacking personalities. Mia Hamm, Tiffeny Milbrett, Cindy Parlow and Shannon MacMillan give us incredible speed and mobility up top. The system puts front-runners in one-v-one positions which is an environment we thrive in. In addition, the system plays with three central midfielders, two of which play high, underneath the front line. This plays nicely into the attacking nature of our midfielders, Julie Foudy, Tisha Venturini, Brandi Chastain, Kristine Lilly, Michelle Akers and new stars for the U.S., Alyson Wagner and Laurie Schwoy, and more naturally puts them into higher shape offensively.

Since we also have defenders that can get forward — Joy Fawcett for example — this system, because there are four defenders instead of three, allows one defender to go forward without as much risk to the defense. Because we have four defenders, our shape in the back when we regain the ball is more conducive to possessing it. The emergence of Kate Sobrero as a defensive force, makes the center of our defense tough to penetrate.

One area on which we need to concentrate is ensuring we still have our patented flank play. Because you do not play with flank midfielders in this system, we need to develop habits from all three lines to create and re-create width. Up front, while we are used to playing all three front-runners in closer proximity to each other, this system requires more discipline with regard to staying wide, especially on the weak side. At times the third front-runner almost disassociates from the other two to keep our shape on the weak-side.

As I mentioned, the responsibility of keeping our width, both ball-side and weak-side, is shared by all three lines. In the midfield, ball-side, the high midfielders can withdraw to the touchline to create width. On the weak-side, the high midfielder can make an unbalancing run to create width or get herself into the attack. But it requires tactical recognition and timing to be effective. If the runs are too early, the defense is sitting in the space. If it's too late, the player on the ball may be closed down before you have given them an option. If width is not provided, it allows a team to condense you and make you play over a smaller area of the field, which plays into their game, not ours.

Lastly, the third main option to create or re-create width is from the flank defenders coming forward. A great environment for this to happen in is when the play is being changed from one side to the other. The defender is brought into the game with a pass. Joy Fawcett, Brandi Chastain, Lorrie Fair, Christie Pearce and Sara Whalen are outstanding at coming forward from the back, and this system gives them that freedom.

Another area offensively we need to work on is to maintain our mobility up top. Mia Hamm, Cindy Parlow and Tiffeny Milbrett are players who are incredibly mobile and dynamic. In some ways this system is very mobile, by virtue of the fact that players can come forward easily out of it. In other ways, it asks our front-runners to take up good positioning rather than always running, which makes us dangerous. For these players, that works against years of running together and playing in their more natural, narrower shape.

Defensively, with the personalities we have in the back, this system keeps us very secure. It also clogs the center of the field. We have two defenders, Carla Overbeck and Kate Sobrero in the middle, as well as Michelle Akers in the holding midfielder position. Remember, we moved Michelle into that position against China in the Gold Medal Game. This helps deny penetration up the middle of our defense. By keeping three front-runners, we still get the work rate and defensive commitment by our front-runners, which is important to our overall defense.

Defending opponents' flank midfielders or players coming forward on the flank out of the back is shared by the flank defenders, the central midfielders and the front-runners. When the play evolves up one side, it is solved either by the holding midfielder sliding out to the ball, a rotation from the back player into the midfield or a front-runner tracking the space. In this system, as in any flat-back four system or a variation of a flat-back four, the goalkeeper's role defensively is increased. She is responsible for the space over the top or behind our defense. When we played with three in the back, the weak-side defender balanced more to provide cover. In this system, we are asking Bri to help share the responsibility of defending the space in behind our defenders.

The areas that we need to keep addressing in this system are the rotation of the defense into the midfield, the increased role of the goalkeeper on both sides of the ball, and our defensive shape with three central midfielders. If we can accomplish these things we will be very secure and will maintain our classic attacking style. In turn, we will be best prepared to absorb the changes and improvements of the best teams in the world. Since we are also comfortable playing out of the systems that won us a gold medal, we will be versatile enough to make adjustments, as we did in 1996 to win.

CHAPTER IX
THE FUTURE OF THE WOMEN'S GAME

The future of our game is bright. On one hand, we have seen an exponential growth in women's soccer, not only in the United States, but around the world. On the other hand, historically, we have only begun. Most countries have played the game for less than twenty-five years. But it's hard to remember the day a world cup for women didn't exist. As a country, we won the first, and in 1999, hosted the largest women's sporting event ever — the FIFA Women's World Cup. The 1996 Olympics drew over 76,000 fans to see China and the United States pair off in a thrilling match for the first-ever Gold Medal.

In my lifetime the sport has gone from having no collegiate national championship, no Women's World Cup, and no women's soccer in the Olympics. Today, we have collegiate national championships, national championships for clubs, youth national teams for girls, the Olympics and the World Cup. Now, on the horizon, a women's professional league is not only necessary, but what is right for the growth of our game. In your lifetime, you will have the opportunity to play some level of professional soccer. Leagues have sprung up all over the world. While not all are what you may envision a professional team to be, they are providing financial compensation for playing soccer, are helping players develop and advancing the level at which women's soccer is played.

My goals are to see a women's professional league in the United States come to be, and in turn, to help establish FIFA youth world championships for girls in at least two age groups. Project Gold is a long-term plan to ensure the ongoing success of women's soccer in the United States. It will encompass an infrastructure on all levels: player development, coaching and referee development, programming for our national teams, a professional league and an administrative structure to support this plan.

It is exciting to see countries break down barriers, not only for women's soccer, but for women in sports. While it may be hard to appreciate that in some countries, it is not the norm for girls to play sports, that's the case. What I love about soccer is that anyone can play the game. The future of soccer must reach out its arms to those girls and women that have not been allowed to play. The battles some pioneers faced, that enable us now to have the opportunities we do, still exist for many girls and women around the world. It's my hope that we can influence the lives of others by opening the doors, to show that women and girls can play — and play well.

Photo by J. Brett Whitesell

The wonderful place which women's soccer is now in, means you have role models in your sport. Many of our current heroes had to break barriers. They found training partners — often a brother or a friend — watched men's soccer or other sports in order to have someone to learn from. One year, I had our U-20 women's national team fill out questionnaires about themselves. One question I asked was, "Do you have a role model? If so, what is it about that player that you admire?" I was pleased at the number of women's national team players that were listed as their role models. I encourage you to watch your favorite players.

The United States women's soccer program has established itself as one of the best in the world. Many of our players, some for over a decade, are some of the best to ever play the game — Michelle Akers, Joy Fawcett, Julie Foudy, Mia Hamm, Kristine Lilly and Carla Overbeck have played in three consecutive world cups (1991, 1995, 1999) and in a fourth world event — the 1996 Olympic games. They are remarkable players and people who have set the standard for the sport. We are closing in on the end of an era. Some may retire after the Sydney 2000 Olympics, their fifth world event.

Briana Scurry, Shannon MacMillan, Brandi Chastain, Tiffeny Milbrett and Tisha Venturini have played in two world cups and an Olympics; Cindy Parlow, a world cup and an Olympics at age 21. They all have had illustrious careers already and give us stability into the next era. In addition to these seasoned players, we had many key players in our residency camp (twenty-six) leading up to the 1999 Women's World Cup. We had Lorrie Fair, Michelle French, Jen Grubb, Christie Pearce, Kate Sobrero and Sara Whalen on defense, Tracy Ducar, Siri Mullinix and Saskia Webber in goal, and Laurie Schwoy and Aly Wagner at midfield. Up front we had our youngest member, Susan Bush, and career NCAA scoring leader, Danielle Fotopoulos. Outside our allotted twenty-six, there are many more players that will help lead the United States in the tradition of excellence.

Who are the next great players? Are you one? My hope is that someday you will possess the qualities of our greatest — the take-on ability of Mia Hamm or Tiffeny Milbrett, the leadership and mental toughness of Carla Overbeck, the work ethic of Kristine Lilly, the heading presence of Michelle Akers or Tisha Venturini, the defensive mentality of Kate Sobrero, the shot of Shannon MacMillan, the fighting power of Tiffany Roberts or the athleticism of Briana Scurry. Remember, there are no limits unless you set them for yourself.

"I hope that kids aren't trying to be the next Mia Hamm, says Mia. "My hope is that they will be better than me."

Goalkeeping Section

By Tony DiCicco

With Chris Ducar

"It's all about organizing your environment and then having the ability to follow through and get it done. That's the common denominator of all the great goalkeepers."
— Tony DiCicco

CHAPTER I
SELF-TRAINING CHALLENGES

By Lauren Gregg

The goalkeeper position is the most specialized position on a soccer team, and as a goalkeeper, the self-training model offers you a unique challenge. While there are many things you can do on your own, organizing your environment needs special attention. We have been fortunate to have had very disciplined goalkeepers who understood the concept of organizing their environments away from events. For example, Mary Harvey was a 1991 World Champion and Olympic Gold Medalist because she was a great goalkeeper who could organize her life and training in a way that enabled her to be one of the best in the world. In some areas, you will need to train someone to train you if you don't have access to a goalkeeper coach.

It's important to remember that you are a soccer player first, with very specific demands and talents relative to your position. Too often, I feel, young goalkeepers are secluded in training and separated from the team. For that reason, much of this book can be a valuable resource for you. The technical training can help your foot skills. First touch, passing, long ball service, clearing and even shot-handling techniques can be done in a squash court, if necessary. Understanding the process of conditioning for a soccer player is addressed in the Physical Section. Tactically, you need to understand your position, but also the demands of the other positions, as well as the tactical nature of the game itself. Psychologically, all aspects apply as much to you as they do any field player. The Psychological Section helps you appreciate the importance of a good training mentality. It provides you with an understanding of psychological skills and gives you ways to apply them. The Team Section offers you insights into all aspects of being part of a team which are common to all players regardless of position.

For the areas where your training differs, we have included specific information for you here. This section of the book, by Tony DiCicco, begins with a discussion on organizing your environment. Following this, each pillar of a soccer player will be specifically addressed relative to the demands of your position as a goalkeeper.

The technical skills of a goalkeeper include shot-saving techniques, handling of crosses and high balls, and distribution with your hands and feet. The necessary footwork, pre-stretch and stance to perform these techniques will be addressed. In addition to providing an understanding of these areas, we have included ideas on how to train them, as well as supplemental training tools you may want to explore. Technique is fundamental to your performance.

Your ability to save shots, handle crosses and eliminate scoring opportunities by your opponents can be maximized through your tactical understanding of your position. In the Tactical Section, we provide you with a lot of information on understanding the game and the evolution of your position. The tactical chapter for goalkeepers in this section will provide details on using this information, beginning with your starting positions on the field relative to the ball, your teammates and your opponents. We hope

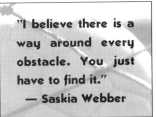

"I believe there is a way around every obstacle. You just have to find it."
— Saskia Webber

that by understanding your ability to read the game, you can improve your positioning. We will address general positioning, the ball line, angle arc, vertical and horizontal positioning. We will help you with starting position and three-goal situations. Your tactical understanding of the game will allow you to communicate more effectively with the team. Communication and organization are some of the most important tactical roles a goalkeeper can play for their team.

The physical pillar for a goalkeeper, like any position in soccer, is critical to your success. It's a mistake to feel that you don't need to be fit because you don't run for ninety minutes. You do need to be fit and focused on different physical dimensions than a field player. Being a goalkeeper is no reason to be unfit. Tracy Ducar shares with you how she prides herself in being fit. She trains herself in such a way that she is attending to her position-specific demands physically, but also, in many ways, to the degree a field player is fit. The physical dimensions of a goalkeeper are strength and power (or explosive strength), speed (goalkeeper speed is different than a field player's speed), agility, and quickness. Briana Scurry, has tremendous explosive strength. With an almost thirty-inch vertical jump, she is one of the most athletic goalkeepers in the world.

There are exercises developed for the physical aspects of goalkeeping that are more position-specific, termed Pressure Training Exercises. We have included several of these in Chapter VII — Physical Dimension, of this section. For additional information on physical training, you may also refer to the Physical Section for exercises that will help your conditioning as an athlete and soccer player.

The psychological dimension of a goalkeeper is crucial to success. This is true with any player. Unique to your position, though, is the potential to have what you do directly impact your team. Our keepers have provided you with insights into how they handle mistakes, or the fact that goals are going to be scored on you. Briana Scurry is so composed in goal that she evokes confidence in her teammates no matter what the game is like. In turn, reading the Psychological Section is directly applicable to you as an athlete and a soccer player.

*"Organizing your environment means looking around
you, and finding or creating the absolute
best possible training environment."*

CHAPTER 11
ORGANIZING YOUR ENVIRONMENT

Goalkeepers, like field players, that aspire to get to the next level cannot always count on having a coach available to train them. Obviously, the ideal situation is to have an experienced person available to coach you, even if it's only once a week. The coach can assist you with shortcuts that will help you to get from one level to the next much quicker than a player without one. If you have someone to coach you, they will be able to determine what needs improvement, then design a training environment for that particular area. This will not be available to most of you on a consistent basis. But don't use this as an excuse not to go out and do most of the hard work on your own.

There are times when you must be your own coach, which is the challenge any great player is often faced with. You are going to have to get it done by yourself through clever organization of your environment. You just have to get your best friend out of the house to help you train. It's a bargaining process. Figure out ways so your partner's needs are met as well. Ask her to give you all the shots, crosses etc., exactly the way you want them served for a half hour so you can train your technique. In return, let her blast all the shots she wants for the other half of the session. Pretty soon, great competitions start to form. Challenges like: "How many can you score from outside the eighteen?" ... "I challenge you to the MLS Shootout!"

Since there is no coach watching over your every mistake, now you have to think and analyze things that are going wrong and take responsibility for making them right again. Organizing your environment means taking a look around you and finding or creating the absolute best possible training environment. Sometimes that simply means asking other people for what you need.

We've had some wonderful players who have had the incredible ability to organize their environment. One of the best examples is Mary Harvey. In 1994, Mary was coming off knee surgery and back surgery. She needed to get her game back together or she was not going to be playing for the United States anymore. So how does she organize her environment? She trains with the men's World Cup team in Mission Viejo, Calif. Most people wouldn't even consider that, but she knew she needed the best possible training environment, so she said, 'Where is it? It's in Mission Viejo.' So she trained with the men's goalkeepers who were preparing to play in the '94 World Cup. I'm sure there were people shaking their heads and rolling their eyes. But she didn't care. She knew how to create her own environment. She needed games, so she went to Germany, got a job and joined a club team. Then she went to Sweden. I remember her calling me up from Sweden, and coming back to the U.S. a week early, staying at my house so she could get a week of training in. Of course, we made her baby-sit and everything, but I have a lot of respect for someone like that. It's not easy to go to Bora Milutinovic, the men's national team coach at the time, and say, 'I need to train. I'll try to stay out of the way, but can I train with your team?'

Saskia Webber was on the national team in 1995 and played one game in the '95 World Cup. A knee injury caused her to fall out of the national team picture shortly after that. Saskia determined she needed to play in games in order to get her sharpness back.

"After I was cut at a 1995 training camp, I decided to go to Japan," she says. "They were getting ready to pick the residency camp for the '96 Olympics, and I was told I wasn't as sharp as I needed to be. I attributed it to not having enough games. I was out of college, and it's hard for a goalkeeper to get in games. But I wasn't ready to give up. I made some contacts in Japan and signed with Oki. I got thirty-five games a season."

Saskia was added to the 1996 Olympic team as an alternate. "It's out there," she says. "You just have to go find it. I had to exercise every option to make myself a better soccer player. I wanted to do everything in my power. I believe there is a way around every obstacle. You just have to find it."

FIND THE BEST COMPETITION
By Chris Ducar

I was playing for the San Francisco Bay Blackhawks in 1991 and didn't know much about women's soccer or goalkeeping in the women's game. My first introduction to the women's game really was when our goalkeeper coach brought Mary Harvey out to one of our training sessions. She was from the Bay area and was preparing for the 1991 World Cup. The session for the day was a six-v-six tournament, and she was overpowered against the likes of Eric Wynalda, Paul Bravo, Marcelo Balboa and Dominic Kinnear. But she made some great saves and never showed any outward signs of intimidation. She came out to train with us whenever she could. From that time on, I had the greatest respect for what she was trying to achieve, and I sought her out as much as she did me in order to prepare each other for our upcoming events.

Tracy Ducar also had a chance to train in with some high level men. When she would visit me while I lived in California, I would take her out to my training session with the San Jose Oaks, a team comprised mostly of former professional players. The Oaks won the U.S. Open Cup in 1992. Most of our sessions were small-sided games to full sized goals and the winning team would stay on. One night, out of four teams, Tracy's came in second, and the boys never let me forget that I came in third. Tracy received many great compliments for her play and toughness. I think that gave her great confidence going into her senior collegiate season.

Both of these women found a way to make something out of nothing and were able to stretch their own development to the maximum.

PILLARS OF THE POSITION

For the goalkeeping position, there are four distinct dimensions:

1. **Technical:** The "how to" of making the save. For example, in the technique of catching, you want to have your hands with your palms facing the ball; your fingers slightly bent to mimic the contour of the ball, and finally make contact with the fingertips.

2. **Tactical:** The cerebral side of the game. Having a plan for a certain situation. For example, if your team has possession in the other team's half, should you be on your goal line or should you be outside the eighteen ready to communicate with your defenders and be in a good position to win a through ball?

3. **Physical:** Strength, power, speed, agility and quickness

4. **Psychological:** The great separating dimension. How does a keeper deal with small mistakes or costly errors? Can it be dismissed and fixed or just become a negative spiral? Do you give your team confidence?

While each is an independent entity, all four are uniquely interdependent when it comes to developing the best possible player for this position. Most great players will have at least one exceptional quality — the rare player — more than one exceptional dimension. But the other areas should be above average as well. No player will succeed in the long term if one of these areas is severely neglected.

Photo by Michael Allen

Briana Scurry has several world-class dimensions.

CHAPTER III
TECHNICAL FOUNDATION

The goalkeeper position has many technical demands. There are the ways of handling shots through catching — basket, contour, side contour and high contour. For the shots that you must dive to save, there are the techniques related to diving. In a game, there will be times when you cannot catch the ball and need to employ one of the following techniques to keep the ball out of the net — tipping, parrying, punching or boxing. Prior to saving the shot or fielding a cross, you must utilize two additional techniques: your pre-stretch or stance and good footwork. We need to stress the importance of your distribution as a goalkeeper. This requires foot skills, such as clearing, passing, punting, half-volleying and so on. You need to train the techniques associated with hand distribution, too. This will allow you to contribute to your team's efforts offensively as well as defensively.

Good goalkeepers pick up hints and clues about what may happen next in a certain situation. To improve on shot-saving, learning to read the rhythm of the shooter will help you the most. In order to be set at the proper time, a goalkeeper needs to recognize when a shot will be taken. What are the common cues that let us know a player is going to shoot the ball? Look for a touch forward to prepare the ball, the shooter's head going down, arms out, and the leg in a back swing. Upon seeing that rhythm, you generally should be moving towards the striker and getting set for the shot. The set position or stance in preparing for a shot has the goalkeeper with the legs about shoulder width apart, the knees bent, the chest slightly forward, and bent at the waist, and the arms in a relaxed "gunslinger" shape. This allows a goalkeeper to be balanced and ready to react in any direction.

Getting to that stance, a keeper uses what is called a pre-stretch. Pre-stretch is a biomechanical term many keepers don't believe or know they use until they see themselves on video. Simply put, a pre-stretch position is when a keeper, reading that the striker is about to shoot, takes a little hop to load their muscles in order to react effectively. As the ball is hit, you are in contact with the ground, but you are in a very un-weighted state, therefore using very little muscular activity to move your body. Rather than being anchored, where you are stationary and need a lot of muscle contraction to overcome inertia, the pre-stretch creates a mobile, dynamic, but stable stance to respond to a shot.

When balls are flying past you and hitting the back of the net way out of your reach, then you have to look at your positioning and pre-stretch. You should have the feeling that the shots taken are within reach. You should be thinking, 'One step this way, and I have this post covered.' You will have confidence that you don't need to fly and dive for shots.

Now that you have put yourself in a good position and recognize that a shot is coming, it's time to make some saves. The following are types of saves that a keeper will make in the "Control Zone." The control zone consists of all the saves a keeper is responsible for saving on a high percentage basis. They are all the saves from your stance (the ground up) and one step in either direction. If you position yourself properly for shots inside the eighteen-yard box, this will be the zone in which you will save balls most frequently.

TECHNICAL HANDLING OF SHOTS

1. Basket catching is for low (ground to waist height) shots. Prepare your arms in front of your body with the fingers pointed to the ground and your palms out. Your arms should be parallel so when the ball makes contact with the forearm above the wrist, it will not go through and hit your stomach or chest.

2. Contour catching is just a way of preparing your fingers to catch the shape of the ball. This type of catching is for shots hit right at you, or when you use good footwork to get behind the ball. Contour catching is usually used for shots chest height or higher.

3. Side contour catches are for dives that you cannot get all of your body behind, or when the ball is hit wide of your body. Hold the ball outside your body and go into a collapse dive.

4. High contour catches are for crosses and high shots. The hand position is the same as the contour, but you don't have the luxury of having your body behind the ball.

Photo by J. Brett Whitesell

Briana Scurry uses the basket catch to save a shot.

Diving

For all goalkeepers, this is the fun stuff! Magazine cover shots! Highlight tapes! Game saving acrobatics! Remember, diving is only used when you cannot get a shot without diving. Some of the best goalkeepers make everything they do look easy through good positioning and good footwork. But there will be the times when you cannot get there without diving.

A collapse dive is a save that's used when the ball is hit outside of your immediate stance and you don't have time for footwork to get your body behind the shot. This is still a part of your control zone. Take a step into the path of the ball. After catching it in the side contour position, take the ball to the ground and land softly on your side. Your feet should never leave the ground and you should not land like a ton of bricks after each save. If the ball is inside the penalty area, you should be creating a control zone. This doesn't mean you won't dive, but it's a different type of dive, more of a collapse dive. The sequence for a collapse dive is step, reach, catch and take the ball to the ground.

Flying and diving types of saves are generally done for shots taken outside the penalty area. When the ball is outside the penalty area, your positioning has to be closer to the goal line so balls don't go over your head and you have more time to cover the distance to the posts. By being closer to the goal line, the goal is bigger to the shooter, and you have a smaller control zone. To get to balls hit well and to the corners, you must use footwork and extension.

Extension diving is the flash of goal-keeping. When used properly, a keeper will dive for a shot that's heading to the post or corner using a little footwork, but mostly power. When the ball is hit, you need to generate momentum in the direction the ball is headed. Momentum is developed from the leg nearest the ball (your push off leg), the opposite leg (knee drive) and the arms. With extension diving, the feet leave the ground and then the ball is caught. The landing sequence starts with the ball touching the ground first followed by the arms, chest, thigh and feet. For most young keepers extension diving is as common as a basket catch. We have all gone through the phase where we will dive for anything, even if it is right at us, in order to hear the "oohs" and "ahs" of our teammates and parents. Pretty soon, the body starts to ache a little too often, and we look for a smoother and more comfortable alternative. Professional keepers only extend for saves for which they absolutely must dive. The theory of "less is more" fits perfectly for goalkeepers when it comes to making diving saves.

Photo by J. Brett Whitesell

Mary Harvey demonstrates excellent extension dive technique.

Breakaway Saves

A breakaway save is often thought of as any time the striker is going to have the ball behind the defense where she could literally dribble the ball into the goal if the keeper wasn't there. That can happen from midfield or inside the six-yard box.

Once you understand the choices of the striker, then the breakaway save becomes easier to sort out. During a breakaway, the ideal high-percentage save for a goalkeeper is to win the ball before the shot. You could win a through ball, or smother a bad touch from the player with the ball. If the player is advancing toward you, you need to come out under control (stealing ground/stalking) and wait for your chance to win it outright. Assess each touch from the striker, and if one touch is overplayed, that's your cue to attack it. The second most advantageous breakaway save is the smother save — where the keeper and striker meet the ball at same time. This is actually more of a mentality than a technique. To perform it safely, go in hard and low with your hands leading. Make sure your head is behind your hands and behind the ball. You actually block the shot with your forearms, and your hands go around the outside of the ball so it cannot be pulled away. The smother save needs training to overcome natural reactions to not put your body in that risky situation. You smother the ball as it is hit. It's actually more of a block. This keeps the striker from following through. And if you get to the ball just as it's hit, the shot isn't as strong. This save takes courage. You can begin by practicing smothering a ball as someone shoots a stationary ball. Then work into playing against a moving partner and ball and so on. In the Olympic semifinal against Norway, we were behind Norway 1-0, and they had a ball spring free to their best striker five yards from goal. As this striker went to kick the ball, Briana Scurry dove out and smothered the shot and held the ball. It was a critical play at a crucial time in the game. These saves change game momentum and also win the big games.

The goalkeeper's third and least effective alternative is to get in the best possible position and concede possession because the striker has firm control of the ball. With your positioning and body position you are saying, "Beat me if you can." They are going to get a shot off, and you must deal with it. Keep your body weight forward, be patient, stay up, make yourself big, then respond to the shot. Make the striker earn the goal. Briana Scurry is excellent at this. She stays up and makes herself into an imposing figure that takes up the whole goal. The striker ends up playing the ball past her and wide of the goal or ends up hitting it into her. Briana had this presence for us throughout the Olympics. She made a clear breakaway save in our first-round game against China by keeping her shape, standing the Chinese player up, and preserving our 0-0 outcome. She is very good at standing players up.

Distribution

The modern game demands that goalkeepers be proficient with their feet. The type of defense that we play on the national team is a zone, sometimes with three in the back, and at other times four. The job of the zone is to compress the attack into a small space as far away from the goal as possible.

The drawback is that it exposes a lot of space behind the defense and in front of the goal-keeper. The goalkeeper must be responsible for that space. Keepers are not expected to be one-v-one artists. They must, however, be able to kick a goal kick over adequate distance and to play through balls from the opponent or back passes with their feet with one or two touches. They also have to be able to make the correct tactical decision to play possession, or to clear it out of danger. You need to constantly work on and develop these skills. Oftentimes, keepers specialize too soon and forget about the importance of field play. When they compete for a starting position later on against someone who can play with their feet, they struggle.

You need to understand how the game is played and be able to play it. You must be able to receive balls, kick left and right and do so with distance and accuracy. Just play like a soccer player, so when you are called upon to play with your feet in goal, it's not that big a deal. Here are some things to keep in mind when you are training foot distribution from the ground.

▲ Prepare (or touch) the ball away from pressure and keep it in motion.

▲ Taking two touches makes sense because it keeps the ball out of the striker's reach, and it's still rolling forward letting you run on to it to kick with more power.

▲ Always shape up your body to kick it first time. If there is no pressure, then you can play possession through one of your teammates. If you are not prepared, you end up kicking a terrible ball that the other team intercepts, or even worse, they strip the ball from you outright and score a goal.

The other types of foot distribution are the volley (punting) and half volley (drop kick) and the goal kick. Each keeper has her own preferences and techniques here. The bottom line is distance and accuracy. Many keepers today are earning first and second assists with their quality distribution.

Like anything in your bag of techniques, kicking should be practiced every day! Practice a little each day at the beginning or ending of training. By yourself, it's easy to get a few balls and blast them into the net. Your legs will get stronger from the repetition and you will make little adjustments in your technique that will make you more consistent. With a partner you can practice distance and accuracy. Make two twenty-by-twenty yard grids, twenty to thirty yards apart. If you can kick the ball into your partner's area and they catch it, you get a point. If they drop it or it hits inside the grid, you get two points. If you do not make it inside the grid and your partner catches it outside, she gets a point. Play for any number of rounds you like, add up the score, and declare a winner. Make sure you work on the different types of foot distribution.

TECHNIQUES THAT KEEP THE BALL OUT OF THE NET

1. **Tipping:** Tip the ball over the goal or around the post using your fingertips. This works well for softer shots that you are guiding to safety. Have a partner shoot on you from inside the eighteen at different angles and tell them to aim for the posts. Anything you cannot catch, deflect.

2. **Parrying:** Use the heel of the hand. If you try to tip a hard shot, you may not have enough strength to change the direction of the ball, and it will find the back of the net. By using the heel of your hand (the hard, bony surface), I guarantee it will not go past you into the net. Plus, it usually goes farther away from your goal than a tip would, giving you time to recover back to your feet and get into a good position.

3. **Punching/boxing** crossed balls: Punching, sometimes referred to as boxing, should be used as a last resort. Catch it if you can. But sometimes you have to go up, over or even through somebody to break up the play. When you feel you cannot catch the ball comfortably, punch. When you do decide to box the ball, it must be hit with authority. Sending the ball outside the penalty area is a good clearance, and it allows you to get back into a good position to save any shots. Boxing is an important part of controlling flank attacks. If you have to box, you are controlling your area at a slightly higher level. This technique may be used when the ball is wet and trying to catch it is too dangerous.

Hand Distribution

Distributing by hand is a lost art. Distance and accuracy are the areas on which you should concentrate. Hand distribution is most effective when you want to get a ball to your backs or midfielders who are twenty or thirty yards away, but you don't want to risk kicking it. This is where the medicine ball (described later in Supplemental Training Tools Chapter) comes into play to build strength (only if you are over fifteen years old).

Begin by throwing the regulation ball over ten to fifteen yards with the sling or javelin style throw. Make sure you get side-on to your target, pointing your shoulder at the intended target. Then step toward the target, and bring the ball straight over the top of your head and follow through with your back leg. If there is perfect backspin, you have done it right. If it swerves and has side-spin, you will lose accuracy and probably possession. Keep trying. After five minutes a day, I guarantee you will be better.

Bowling distribution is great for accuracy over short distances. The biggest problem we find is that keepers often take its simplicity for granted. When bowling a ball, it should be to a player in or around your eighteen. Make sure you get low to the ground and follow through so the ball does not bounce to your player. Here are some subtle tips:

▲ Serve the ball to your teammate's lead foot (the one farthest from you). This will allow them to face the field when preparing the ball. If you throw it behind them, they are facing you and cannot gauge pressure, putting them in a dangerous situation.

▲ If your teammate is standing, play it to them directly, don't lead them!

▲ If they are running up field, lead them.

▲ To test yourself, set up cone goals twenty-five yards away and throw for accuracy. How many can you hit out of ten from twenty yards away? How quickly can you get the ball there?

Photo by J. Brett Whitesell

Briana Scurry starts a USA attack with bowling distribution

Footwork

This aspect of your position is extremely important. The way you move will dictate whether you will even be in a good balanced position to actually make a save. Goalkeepers use a variety of footwork to get the job done — quick lateral mini-shuffles (left or right), crossover steps (laterally and recovering back to the goal), sprints, and backpedaling.

One of the major laws of goalkeeping is you must try to get as much of your body behind the ball as possible. Quick and agile movement with your feet will help you accomplish this. One quick lateral shuffle will help you make a basket catch save, or a step-and-a-half will get you into a good position to make a collapse dive save. Good angle play and positioning gets you away from the goal line, so you need to learn how to get back to the goal line quickly. Turning and running back to the goal will be the fastest, but you lose sight of ball. You could backpedal, but it's slow for distances over two or three yards. A side-on run is quick and in a distance of ten yards, you can still see the ball and make adjustments, if necessary.

To work on your footwork options, get a partner to stand outside the penalty area with a pile of balls. Have her play a ball into your area, but outside the six-yard box. You must save these shots breakaway style. Get up quickly and recover back to your line while your partner tries to kick (or throw) the ball to the crossbar. Try substituting a punched ball instead of the breakaway for variety. These exercises will train foot-work back to the bar, and you will increase your comfort level in making these difficult saves.

Footwork during a breakaway save is very important. Picture the MLS shootout tie breaker: a player is thirty-five yards away from goal with a ball and that player has five seconds to take a shot. Now think of what the goalkeeper does. Most will steal ground on the first and second touch of the ball. Stealing ground means that you use fast running steps to close the striker down when they touch the ball forward. When the striker catches up to the ball, their options are now decreased. If they stop the ball or try to fake you out with some moves, you need to stalk them. Stalking means forward mini-steps that are tight and quick, allowing you to stay balanced and able to react to a shot. Your upper-body is hunched over with your arms outside and in front of the legs. The palms are facing the ball. Since you are close to the striker, you need to guard the low areas and know that a chip is a low-percentage shot from this distance.

TECHNICAL QUALITIES OF A GOALKEEPER
1. Soft hands
2. Clean catching ability
3. Boxing technique
4. Tipping
5. Diving
6. Smother saves
7. Breakaway saves
8. Foot skills
9. Footwork

KEEPERS' ONE-V-ONE OR KEEPER WAR

Just like with field players, goalkeepers can play games of one-v-one to incorporate a wide-range of skills needed for soccer. "We set the goals up just like a one-v-one match-up, about twenty yards apart," says Tracy Ducar. "I start with my hand on the ball, and you start about an arm's length away from me in a stalking stance, and I try to score on you on your goal. You have to do whatever you can do to keep the ball out of the net — kick saves, shot saves, smothers. If you save it, then you go at me. It's a battle back and forth. It's a lot of fun. And you can do it two-v-two, three-v-three, whatever."

ON YOUR OWN

BY TIM NASH

Without a doubt, goalkeepers can train themselves, and this section of the book illustrates a variety of ways to go about it. As many of you begin the process of working on your own, you will discover that finding someone to workout with can be difficult.

Field players really only need one training partner — the ball. Goalkeepers can also do a tremendous amount of work using only a ball and a wall. Eventually, however, you are going to need someone to shoot at you, serve crosses and field your punts and goal kicks. Obviously, the person you most often drag out on the field with you is not going to be a high-level goalkeeper trainer. This person can be a great help to you, though.

"Be patient," advises Mary Harvey. "It's hard, very hard. When you go from an environment where they know what they are doing to an environment where you have to show somebody how to train you, it can be frustrating."

If you are training with someone who is not well-versed in what you want to accomplish, you have to show that person how to help you. "The best way to do that is to let them be the goalkeeper first," says Bri Scurry. "Show them a drill so they know where you want the ball served because service is key. If you are chasing the ball for twenty of the thirty minutes you are playing, it's not doing you any good. First, they have to know what bad and good service is so they can give you good services. After they understand what you want, switch places and let them serve to you.

"You have to be to sure to tell them exactly what you want," adds Bri. "If you are working on getting up and down quickly, you have to say, 'Wait until I get off the ground before you hit it to the left post.' Or say, 'Wait until I say go before you hit it here.' You have to communicate what you want to them."

Tracy Ducar believes you can gain something from any workout. "I actually dragged my mom out there once," she says. "If you are out there with an inexperienced player who can't serve you balls consistently, have them throw it to you. Repetition is what's important. You can get a decent workout if you try. It might not be game-like or a realistic shot, but at least you are getting repetition.

Ideally, you will have a friend who is a field player and wants to work on shooting or serving crosses. It's important to make sure you both get the workout you desire.

"It's good to do a combination of both sometimes," says Tracy. "The shooter does what she wants for a while and then does what the keeper wants. A lot of times, the shooter will go for a while, and then I'll say, 'I need some crosses.' Or I might want to work on tipping it back to the bar.

"But first," Tracy adds, "you need to get a good warmup. Hit balls at me, not into the corner. Close range is good so you get a lot of handling, a lot of repetition. You should do a lot of collapse dives, and gradually build it up so you are being challenged, not buried."

Mary Harvey has found it easy to incorporate what the shooter wants to do with what she needs. "If you are working with someone who wants to work on their shooting, there are some drills you can do that can be very beneficial to both of you," Mary says. "For instance, dead ball drills require them to hit the ball to a certain place time after time. And you can have them hit it in a certain way. It can be a great exercise for field players to hit you in the hands every time."

It can be easy to acquire bad habits if you don't have a goalkeeper trainer to correct your technical flaws. Bri Scurry suggests that you compare your technique to high-level goalkeepers. "Get a video camera out and tape yourself," she says. "You can show it to a goalkeeper coach and ask for advice, or you can buy a video of great goalkeepers and compare your tape to what you see them doing. You might want to tape yourself early in the season and then again later in the season to see if you are making any progress."

*"Playing racquetball, you have to time the ball.
The ball is moving very fast, so it
can be good for your reflexes."*
— Mary Harvey

CHAPTER IV
SUPPLEMENTARY TRAINING TOOLS

In the soccer industry, there are hundreds of gimmicks that will supposedly improve performance. We have found a few tools that have proven to help goalkeepers at all levels. They can be used in training to help vary your workouts to keep things fresh and fun.

Medicine Ball: The Kwik Goal medicine ball is one of the greatest training tools ever developed for goalkeepers. We actually helped to design it. You should only use this if you are over the age of fifteen. It bounces and does everything a soccer ball does, but it's heavier. It builds strength in the hands and the arms for catching, and throwing distance is increased as well. This ball instantly exposes poor technique and will help you gain greater focus as you must concentrate intensely on each save. But be careful! You definitely should not kick or head it.

What makes it great is that it bounces and you can handle it just like a regular soccer ball when it's thrown at you. It's great for handling shots from close range, too. It's especially good for technical training and building confidence. It takes a few minutes getting accustomed to because it's heavier than the regular ball. By your fifteenth catch, it feels really heavy!

This ball helps you to focus on the catch because if you relax for a second, it will rebound off of you. After you successfully catch this ball for awhile, then you revert back to training with a regular ball, it's like catching a nerf ball. If you can catch a med ball, you can catch anything! This is definitely not recommended if you have a hand or wrist injury, so be smart.

Mini-ball: We usually use a mini-ball — about a size two. Some keeper coaches use tennis balls. When a mini-ball is thrown or kicked at you, you must concentrate just as when you train with a medicine ball. It forces you to move your feet quicker to get behind the ball and to use perfect technique so it will not go through your hands or legs.

It's much harder to save than a regular ball. Because it's so small, it really helps your diving and tipping skills. It almost seems like you are playing in a bigger goal.

Weighted Jump Ropes: These will benefit you by the jumping itself, but also by strengthening your arms and shoulders, translating into better catching and throwing. Regular jump ropes are good for foot quickness, too.

Staples: Staples are like over-sized wickets in croquet. Roll the ball under one, jump over the staple and make a breakaway save. Put four in a row and use your imagination! This can help with power, quickness and agility. But be certain not to overtrain by doing too many jumps or bounds. Check with a conditioning coach.

WALL WORK

A wall is a great training tool. You can serve a ball off a wall and work on your handling. Then you can hit it against the wall, turn and handle it. Use your imagination. Roll the ball off the wall, do a forward roll (if you are on grass) and then get the ball. You can stand ten yards away from the wall, serve it and catch it. The ball is coming off the wall at different heights and angles.

A corner is even better. If you can find a corner where there is grass, you can get some diving practice in. You kick a ball into the corner and play the ricochet.

"If you have a wall, you can get creative — shoot and catch," says Tracy Ducar. "You can get in a racquetball court and work on a lot of reaction stuff. You can hit the ball with a volley or half-volley. Obviously, you don't want to do a whole lot of diving. Just be creative."

Mary Harvey used a racquetball court to actually play racquetball. She'd found that the hand-eye reaction work benefitted her as a keeper. "Playing racquetball, you have to time the ball. The ball is moving very fast, so it can be good for your reflexes."

As a young keeper, Tony DiCicco played handball because it's two-handed, very quick and great for hand-eye coordination.

Viper Cords: These are devices that you put around your waist and attach to the goalpost or have a friend hold. Run forward eight to ten yards and dive on a ball. The cord stretches, and the resistance makes it harder to run, increasing your first step speed and leg strength.

Kick Back Net: The newest addition to our equipment arsenal is the kick back net. It's great for solo training. It has two sides and different angles. Practice your throwing accuracy and catch the rebound. Or start off to one side, throw at the net, and make a diving save. If you really want to challenge yourself, kick it off the rebounder and see if you can react to the shot. If you don't want to spend any money, go find a wall. Practice your kicking and then make the save as the ball comes back to you. The closer you get to the wall, the less reaction time you have and the more challenging it becomes.

MEDICINE BALL TRAINING

"A medicine ball is very good for throwing and catching," says Mary Harvey. "With a partner, you can start off ten yards apart and sling throw it to each other as a warmup. You should be trying to hit your partner in the numbers so it has to be caught. After warming up, you throw it harder at each other. You should try to do twenty in a row without dropping it or making a bad throw. If you drop it or miss-throw it, you have to start over again.

"After you do twenty, you do the same thing with a soccer ball," adds Mary. "A regular soccer ball is nothing after doing twenty med ball throws and catches. You can build terrific strength in your arms and your back. After a period of weeks, you will really notice the difference and you will be really winging it at each other."

When Mary Harvey was coming back from her knee surgery in 1995, we would be on the road in some hotel and she would call me at midnight and say, "Tony, I found a conference room, can you hit me some med ball shots." And for the next hour she would just handle medicine and regulation balls from a seated or kneeling position. That's why she was one of the best at handling. Remember, being injured doesn't mean you can't keep developing!

Photo by Stephen Slade

Tracy Ducar's training mentality has translated into her success on the international level.

Chapter V
Tactical Responsibilities of Goalkeepers

Once you have your technical abilities honed, you can now combine them with your tactical responsibilities. Reading the game is one of the most important dimensions of the goalkeeper. The information you gather from reading the flow of the game will influence many subsequent decisions. The better the information you get, the better your decisions and movements will be. Learning to read the game takes time, but can be worked on every time you play. Over time, you can learn to recognize cues that give you valuable information. This information will greatly influence your positioning on the field.

First, we'll talk about general positioning, beginning with the ball line. Figure 1 is an imaginary line from ball to center of goal. Generally you are straddling this line as the ball moves about the field. There are times, however, when you are not on the ball line. For example, during corner kicks and wall situations or sometimes even crossed balls, you might need to sneak off the ball line because of where the ball is probably going to be played. Do your experimenting in practice. In shooting situations, generally you want to straddle the ball line, which enables you to cover both posts.

The other concept that works closely with the ball line is the angle arc (Figure 2). The angle arc is an imaginary arc from just outside one post. It arcs up and touches the six-yard line, and then arcs back and touches the other post. This arc is perfectly symmetrical, and it gives you the guideline on the maximum angle. For example, when the ball is in the middle on

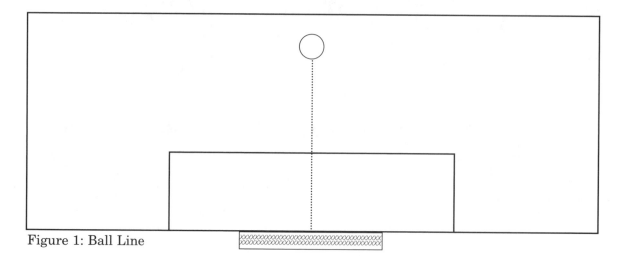

Figure 1: Ball Line

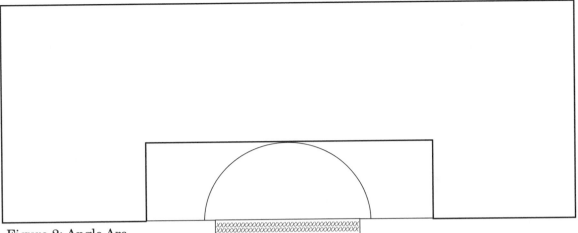

Figure 2: Angle Arc

the eighteen-yard line, the keeper should be on top of the six at the top of the arc when the ball is shot. This requires footwork and getting on the rhythm of the shooter, so when they look up, you are positioned at the two or three yard line. When the shot is taken, you are saving at the six. When the ball is off to one side, say the near-post side, the arc is very close to the goal line. In this situation, you don't need to be out beyond the arc. You are just slightly in front of the near post, and you have the near post covered. A common problem for young keepers is to go way out and end up eliminating their reaction time. The other consequence for coming out too far is that if the ball is played centrally, then you are now four or five steps outside the post and can't get back into a good position. The angles around shot-saving are based upon those two concepts: Ball line and Angle Arc (Figure 3).

Vertical positioning means up and down the field. When the ball is at the opposite end of the field, your positioning should be around the eighteen or above. With this positioning, if the ball is played over the defense, you will be in a good position to come out and clean it up. A second reason is for communicating with and organizing your defenders. If you are all the way back, your defenders cannot hear you as well. Lastly, this closer-support positioning gives you a better view of the game, and that will translate into better plays on your part.

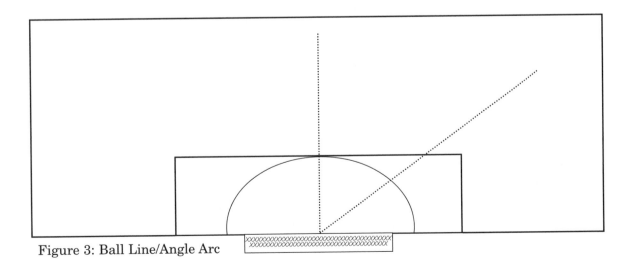

Figure 3: Ball Line/Angle Arc

THE EVOLUTION OF THE POSITION

The most important tactical responsibility of a goalkeeper is an understanding the game. At the same time, keepers must have an understanding of their starting position and the organization of their defense. They must also provide good communication and initiate attacks for their team. A goalkeeper can impact the tactics of her team and opponents by how she plays, and can change the pace of the game by having the play come through her.

In the past decade we have seen significant evolution in the role of the goalkeeper in the women's game. Because of the differences in the physical dimension of women keepers, positioning is very important.

"The keeper's role has changed because teams are playing more zone defenses," says Siri Mullinix. "In that system, the keeper has to play higher. A lot of our responsibility then becomes to eliminate shots."

The goalkeeper's start position is higher in order to read the space behind the defense. The Norwegian keeper, Bente Nordby, set the standard around the world. Her aggressive starting position made playing balls in behind the Norwegian defense very difficult. In order to play higher behind your defense, you will need to have good foot skills to play the balls that comes through or over the top. This had a large impact on the evolution of the position. Siri has become very good at playing high behind our defense, due mainly to strong foot skills and the ability to read the game.

Goalkeepers are always working on starting positions. It isn't easy. One keeper may be able to play six yards off her line because of strong physical dimensions, such as speed and height. Another keeper may have to be more conservative and play closer to the line. Ask yourself this question when you are in the game: "How far can I go away from my goal line in this situation and still be able to cover any shot taken over my head?"

You don't want to be too far out or too far in. You want a combination of aggressive positions when the ball is far from the goal and tactical, conservative positions when the ball is in shooting range. Because of size and athletic ability, it's easier for girls to be scored on over the top. Here is something you can try with your teammates. Have them take shots on goal from the midfield line. You start at the top of the eighteen. Give them twenty tries. If they can't score on you, then perhaps when the ball is in that general area during the game, you can be confident that you are in a solid but safe starting position.

If a keeper has a good, aggressive starting position and comes out to win through passes or passes over the top of the defense, it will change the way your opponent has to play. It makes them serve into different areas that aren't as dangerous. Starting positions are the key to putting pressure on the other team to find different areas — with lower scoring percentages — from which to get their scoring chances. When the ball reaches midfield and your defense is somewhere halfway between the top of the eighteen and the midline, the goalkeeper needs to be around twelve yards from the goal. Top-level goalkeepers may be a bit above the twelve, depending on how much pressure your team puts on the player with the ball. With the ball this far away, you are not really in a situation where you will face a shot. It may happen but it's unlikely. You are in a position where the first attacker is trying to get the ball in behind the defense. Here, your starting position and starting stance (a sprinter's stance) are essential as you constantly assess the alternatives of the attacker. It's imperative to be tied into the defense in order to maximize the space in which you make saves.

When the ball is in the final third, the goalkeeper has to be in position to deal with shots and balls placed behind the defense. Depending on the pressure on the ball, you should be anywhere from a stride to three or four strides above the goal line. No more than that. Now rely on your ball line/angle arc positioning. Stay aware of the striker's options — are they going to shoot, pass, play the ball through, or continue to dribble? These options are constantly and rapidly changing, and if you read them properly, you will be in a great position to get set and make the save.

Keepers should be working on reading the game every time they are in the net. Each time you practice, focus on reading the physical cues of a striker to decipher their intent. To help you learn to recognize the striker's alternatives, train with two of your friends. Put a pile of balls inside the "D". If a player were to take a shot from there, you would be roughly one stride off your goal line. The other partner needs to be outside the eighteen and even with the player with the ball, so she is on-sides. If the player with the ball chooses to shoot, you can pick up on her physical cues, and you are in a good position to make the save. If she chooses to pass it into the penalty area as a through ball, you now must try to play the ball in the space between the goal and the attacker. As you steal ground, you can decide to win the ball outright or if the striker gets to it first, you should be in a good angle-play position to deal with the shot. Those are the only two alternatives for which you are looking. Usually, by watching the striker, you can pick up their intent and the movements around the ball. If somebody is breaking in behind the defense and has some space, they are probably going to slot the ball. With this type of practice you are already looking for and anticipating the shot. As the ball is slotted, you are already moving into that space and ready to make the big play.

Horizontal Positioning is when the ball is closer to the sidelines. Your positioning again is based upon the alternatives of the striker. If the ball were at the midline, and close to the touchline, you would still be more "vertically" positioned. But when it gets closer to the final third, it's your horizontal positioning that matters. For example, if the ball is around the corner kick spot, you are going to position yourself at the front post. Covering the front post is your first priority. "Can I get to my front post if the ball is miss-kicked there or intentionally driven into my front-post area?"

After you've determined that your front post is adequately protected, you want to assess whether or not you can cover space in front of your goal. Can you put a lot of the goal in front of you so all your movements are forward? That's how you start to extend that range. As they get closer to the goal from the flank and start penetrating the penalty area, you have to come closer to the front post and square up to the ball.

There are organizational implications, too. Your mentality has to be to protect the near post first and foremost. If the ball is then played into the center of the goal, you must get into position to protect the goal when the ball is in the center. And if it gets played to the far post on a chip, that's your third priority. If a chip occurs, you'll need to get over to the far post as best you can. A lot of times, keepers are almost more concerned with the far post and they are already cheating to the far post when the ball is driven to the near post, and they cannot respond. Remember, a near post goal is almost always the goalkeeper's fault.

TACTICAL RESPONSIBILITIES

▲ Read the game

▲ Communication

▲ Organize defense

▲ Understand starting position

▲ Initiate attack

▲ Control tempo of the game

Three-Goal Situation

This situation arises when the ball is on the flank and your opponent has beaten your defense. They are inside the penalty area and are at or near the six-yard box. This is a serious defensive situation. The goalkeeper needs to know her positional priorities as well as the alternatives of the striker

Being prepared for a shot on goal is the keeper's first priority (Figure 4). Any goal scored between the near post and the goalkeeper is the goalkeeper's responsibility. Start one step in front of the near post and an arm length away from the post. Even deflections from hard shots will go out of bounds and not in the goal. You don't want to give up goals from this angle!

The second "goal" in the three-goal situation is a goal scored off a pass across your box (Figure 5). This is the ball that's played from that flank on the ground into the space between you and the top of the six-yard box. If the ball gets past you in this space to an attacking player, it's going to be a pretty easy shot and goal. There is a range here and the better keepers will cover a bigger range. Don't let it go through there easily. Dive and catch or at least deflect it. Keep it away from anyone in front of the goal.

We can start to see different levels of keepers by how they deal with the second goal. High level goalkeepers have the ability to look solid on first and cheat a bit to win in the 2nd goal but remember; no near post goals.

The third goal or last priority is the ball that is played over the top of the keeper to the far post (Figure 6). Many great saves in history arise out of this situation. The ultimate third goal save was the memorable Gordon Banks save against Pele. The ball was served from the flank to Pele at the back post. When England's Banks saw that it was not winnable, he left his near post and ran to the far post. Pele exploded into the air and drove a header down to the far post. Banks' quick feet put him into a great position to react and he parried the ball, off the bounce, over the bar. Truly an amazing sequence of events and a save many regard as the greatest ever.

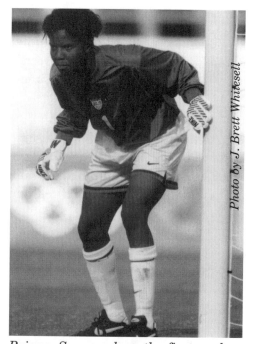

Briana Scurry plays the first goal — protecting the near post.

The third goal has to be organized by looking quickly to the far post and getting a player to compete for that ball. The responsibility of the keeper is to organize the back post with specific communication so there is competition for the ball. Tisha Venturini has made a career out of scoring far-post goals. If you don't have the far post organized, you're going to make some great saves but there are going to be a lot of goals scored. We work on this with the women's national team quite a bit. Remember your priorities: Even if there is someone wide open on the back post, the front post is always your responsibility.

The most important aspect of this situation is patience. You will get into trouble if you charge at the player with the ball. The shooting angle is poor so there is no need to leave that position unless the ball is over-touched and you win it outright. If you do leave, you absolutely must get the ball. Otherwise, the goal is left wide open and there is little or no hope of recovering when the ball is played past you.

As the player gets closer, a keeper's reaction time is cut down a bit, but it decreases the number of options they now have to find teammates. Your shape needs to be so solid that they feel that there is no way to score at the front post. When they put their head down, the keeper can then cheat out a bit. Many players live off aggression alone. If you learn to balance your patience and aggression, you will become a better player. Gao Hong, the Chinese National Team goalkeeper, is tremendous at the three-goal situation. The second goal of the Olympic Final, she almost made the save on Tiffeny Milbrett's shot. Joy Fawcett, who overlapped out of the back, carried the ball long enough that Gao Hong had to honor the near post. She laid the ball across the box at just the right time. Her pass was weighted so the talented Gao Hong, just missed getting to the ball at the second goal.

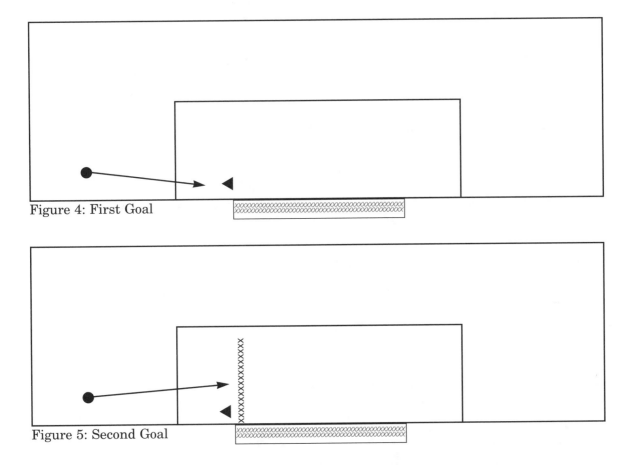

Figure 4: First Goal

Figure 5: Second Goal

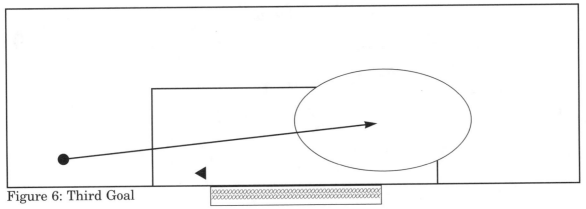

Figure 6: Third Goal

*"If you can make it look like your mother
can play goal, you've done your job."*
— *Briana Scurry*

CHAPTER VI
COMMUNICATION AND ORGANIZATION

Communicating with and organizing your defense effectively is as important as any other aspect of the position. At most levels of play, keepers believe a great game is one with a ton of action and saves. In all fairness, they may have done well to stop many shots with their technical or athletic ability. However, when a goalkeeper progresses in age, experience, tactical maturity and ability, the stakes of winning are higher. Tons of action on goal is hardly welcome. Part of your evolution will be in organizing your defense to eliminate your opponent's opportunities.

Many professional goalkeepers rate their performance by how many shots were taken on goal. The fewer the shots, the better they were able to tactically organize their team so the opponent's attacks were ineffective. Everyone wants to be the hero and pull off the point-blank breakaway save or the diving save on a screaming knuckler hit to the post. But ask yourself, "If I was in the state cup final, what type of situation would I like to be put in?" Dealing with back passes, some long crosses, and some forced through balls would be preferable than facing high-percentage scoring opportunities. Keepers need to use their voice to make saves, not always their hands. A knowledgeable goalkeeper who is able to read the game can place her players in positions where the attack can be stopped before reaching the goal, or force the attacking team to play poor percentage shots and services.

Why do goalkeepers have to take this responsibility? It helps establish confidence and leadership. Goalkeepers are the last line of defense and have better vision of the field. You can see how attacks develop. If you don't take the responsibility, you are the one who must pick

*Mary Harvey organizes the
USA defense.*

Photo by J. Brett Whitesell

the ball out of the net. How do you communicate with your team? Your voice should be loud, calm, and clear, and your words should be concise. You must develop a glossary of terms of which you and your team can understand the exact meaning. Examples:

▲ Keeper
▲ Away
▲ Contain
▲ Push left/right
▲ Stand her up
▲ Tackle
▲ Don't dive in
▲ Pressure ball
▲ Cover
▲ Balance
▲ Track your runner
▲ Push up/out
▲ Drop
▲ Step up

The information you give must be specific, not general. In order to eliminate confusion, it's imperative to put your player's name to a specific job. For example: "Jill, get goal side of number ten!" Telling Jill exactly what to do is much better than simply saying, "Mark up!" Using the term "mark up" is so general that players will not always know what they are supposed to do. Be specific.

Here's a practical example. The other team has the ball and is counter-attacking inside your half. You have two defenders who are the same distance from the player with the ball. What do you say? First you must organize who is going to pressure the ball. It's up to you to decide who goes to pressure the player with the ball. If you don't make the decision and Kim thinks that Jen is going to step up to pressure and vice-versa, then the attacker only has to beat one of them to get a prime scoring opportunity. In this situation, the goalkeeper should put a name to a specific job: "Kim, pressure ball!"

Now that you have organized Kim, and she has put pressure on the ball and Jen is in a good covering position behind her and to her right, you can help make the rest of the play predictable. You can instruct Kim to "Push her right!" And if she gets beat by a touch or a dribble, then Jen is there to cover.

We've given you some examples of good communication, but it's also helpful to have examples of bad communication. Here are some things to avoid.

1. Cheerleading is not productive and can be annoying to defenders, which may ultimately cause them to tune you out. Learn what is effective with your teammates.

2. Yelling at your teammates. You need to give support to your teammates in order to get them to work for you, not the other way around. If you find it necessary to bark at a player, do so sparingly. Think of how you would like your teammates to speak to you after giving up a soft goal.

3. Don't assume anything. It's always a good idea to double-check with teammates on their positioning or marking assignments. To assume that they "had" someone could be costly. Most defenders come to expect and appreciate a goalkeeper who keeps them focused and on their toes.

COMMUNICATION CAN STOP SHOTS

Organization is a vital role the goalkeeper plays for her team. Good tactical knowledge allows keepers to read the game and make good decisions for herself and her teammates. Goalkeepers need to be able to take charge and let their teammates know what is happening around them. Good communication prevents shots, and every breakdown that can be prevented is one less scoring opportunity. Keepers have to be involved every time the ball moves, and their positioning and the organization of their defense should adjust as the ball moves.

Keeping your house in order requires tremendous concentration. Even if you are rarely called upon in a game, you come off the field exhausted. If you are a goalkeeper you know what I mean. You become mentally drained from focusing on your job — as well as every other player's job — for ninety minutes. The relationship between the goalkeeper and the defenders is a critical one. You absolutely must be on the same page, and communication is the basis for this relationship to work.

"Up until my second year on this team I didn't say a word," says Briana Scurry. "In college, I didn't say anything. I think back now, and if I just spoke a little bit I could have prevented so many goals. That's the key to communication — preventing a shot from even being taken. The key is getting your people into the right positions, kind of like chess. If you can do that and never have to make a save you are better than anybody flying around into the corners left and right. If you can make it look like your mother can do it, you have done your job.

"It is something you develop," adds Bri. "A lot of kids are shy, and they are afraid of offending their defenders. I don't care. But when I first joined this team, I hardly said a word. Carla, came to me and said, 'Bri, you gotta do what you've gotta do.' That was all I needed to hear. I started talking more, and now I say whatever to anybody. But how you say it is important. If I say it nicely one time and you don't hear me, I will have to say it another way the next time. My job is to keep the ball out of the net, and it can be cut-throat here. If you don't do it right, I am going to have to raise my voice a little bit to get you to hear me. Sometimes you have to do that. Don't take it personally. It's part of the game."

Communication is an art form, and it takes work. Remembering that there are different ways to talk to different people is helpful.

"Sure, it's difficult," says Bri. "You have to know how to talk to each different player. Some players, like Joy, would prefer me to yell at her, whereas another player might not. I need to tap into the psychology of each player and adjust accordingly. If I'm yelling at some player like I yell at Joy, they might shut me off. If you are doing your job properly, I will use a softer tone. But if you're not, then I have to somehow spur you on a little bit because I'm not just going to be nice and let them come down your side every other attack just to spare your feelings."

Tracy Ducar has found that communication not only helps her teammates, it also keeps her alert and in the game, even when the action is at the other end of the field.

"Communication is my big thing," says Tracy. "I'm constantly checking in with my defenders — 'Watch number five on your left, step up, drop off.' That keeps me in the game. I also adjust my positioning, I move with the ball. Even if the ball is down at the other end, I'll move from side to side as the ball moves, just so I am always cued in to what's going on and not checking out the crowd or the bench or counting clouds."

*"For our position, being able to jump quickly and
get off the ground quickly is key, so you should
do lot of speed work and agility work."*
— Briana Scurry

CHAPTER VII
PHYSICAL DIMENSION

Physical preparation in the modern game is paramount. However, most goalkeepers are never pushed to maximize their physical potential. All too often, coaches in youth practice sessions have the team working out incredibly hard, yet the goalkeepers are asked to go aside to play catch. Unless a goalkeeper is self-motivated, she will gladly skip any uncomfortable session.

Goalkeepers' fitness standards have to be different than the field players. There are days when we do fitness with the field players and there are days when we do goalkeeper fitness — exercises like coming out to win the ball and getting back to your line and repeating and repeating and repeating until your legs are burning. The goalkeeper has to pride herself on keeping an aerobic fitness base. But from that point on, most of their fitness is different. You have to be able to get off the ground, quick forward, quick back, quick laterally. That is where you should be spending the time. You don't really need to be making 120-yard fitness standards.

If a goalkeeper is not included in team fitness sessions, it's important to have an alternate plan of position-specific fitness that will help her reach the goals she has set. Participating in team fitness has another positive benefit — camaraderie. No one respects a person who does not put in her fair share of work. By participating in the fitness sessions that are relevant, it has a positive effect on leadership and team chemistry, as well as the primary fitness aspect.

Why should fitness training for a goalkeeper be different than for a field player? Think of the movements a keeper will make during the course of a game — sprinting forward, backpedaling, shuffles, crossover steps, and jumping, diving, getting up quick. You can design exercises with and without the ball that focus on sprinting, backpedaling, shuffles, cross-over steps and jumping. Make economical use of your time and train two aspects at once. In this case, the physical and the technical aspects are combined. Recall in the Physical Section, the discussion on position-specific training.

"For our position, being able to jump quickly and get off the ground quickly is key, so you should do a lot of speed work and agility work," says Briana Scurry. "You don't need to do a bunch of running. The longest distance you should do is maybe two miles. When you run long distance, you are training a muscle fiber that you don't really want to train for your position. You are training the wrong fibers, so you are hindering yourself by running long distance."

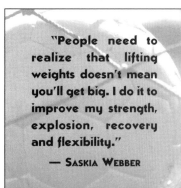

Most speed and strength specialists agree that long distance running works against what a goalkeeper wants to build. We are concerned with power and agility, and distance running eliminates that. Circuit training can help a goalkeeper build strength, endurance and power. Many athletes use weight training to enhance an already solid strength base. If you are just starting out, try this leg circuit. It would be best if you were able to consult a strength specialist before trying any type of program. Here are four exercises.

Note: For Foundation Strength-training Program, see the Physical Section.

Leg Circuits

1. **Body weight squats:** Hands behind your head, legs about shoulder width apart and your heels on the ground. Keeping your back as straight as possible, squat until your legs reach a ninety degree angle, then power back up quickly. Do this as quickly as is comfortable for your fitness level. Do not sacrifice good technique for speed.

2. **Lunges:** Hands on your hips, back straight, take a big step forward until your leg is bent to ninety degrees and push back to your starting position and then alternate legs.

3. **Step-ups:** Find a box or bench that is about knee height, step up with one leg, come to a stand, step down. Alternate legs, or repeat all with one leg, then the other leg.

4. **Skaters:** Stand on your left leg, push off or jump laterally and land on your right leg and bend low. Immediately, push off and land on your left leg. The arm and body movements mimic that of a power ice skater.

Photo by J. Brett Whitesell

Agility

A goalkeeper needs agility. The position is a lot about getting from down positions to up positions quickly and with balance. These movements are performed in relatively tight spaces.

Example: After a corner kick is taken, the ball is pinging around the area like it's in a pinball machine. The goalkeeper is crouched for the shot and starts to lean as the ball comes off the striker's foot. The deflection sends it slightly behind the leaning keeper. The keeper changes directions to make the diving save. But she could not catch it, and it bounces three yards away, and there's a forward four yards beyond that. Can that keeper scramble off the ground and beat that player to the ball? This is a situation that many keepers are faced with over the course of a season. While it's difficult to replicate every possible situation, goalkeepers can use their own creativity when training alone to make some outstanding saves with no one around. It's about efficiency of motion.

> ## PHYSICAL QUALITIES OF A GOALKEEPER
>
> ▲ Flexibility
> ▲ Agility
> ▲ Quickness
> ▲ Explosive strength
> ▲ Speed: Goalkeeper speed is different than field player speed. Keepers need reaction speed, first-step speed, vertical-leap speed, change-of-direction speed, five- to ten-yard stride speed, visual speed, decision-making speed.
>
> *(adapted from Tony DiCicco's and Paul Cacolice's Training Manual for Goalkeepers) (1)*

Many of the pressure training exercises we have included have an agility component to them. In the Physical Section we have included several agility tests you can perform to measure your agility.

Speed

Speed is going from point A to point B as quickly as possible. While keepers don't run the distance of a midfielder, they would be well-served to prepare and attempt to match the speed of a striker. Over the course of the game, a keeper may stand relatively idle for extended periods of time. While concentration is a factor, the actual burst of speed on demand over, say, a twelve-yard area, may mean the difference in a goal, or not. While we inherit, to a large degree, our pure speed, you can maximize what you have been given and even improve on it through appropriate training.

Quickness

Quick feet. Quick hands. Quick wit. Reactions using all body parts. This is a somewhat subjective area, but we sure know the difference between a keeper who is and isn't quick. Again, you can train yourself to be quicker. You can do reaction exercises. This involves doing fast footwork, hand quickness activities, and being put into situations that require putting it all together. The pressure training exercises detailed later in this chapter help push a goalkeeper to be quicker. If you are training by yourself and you are able to shuffle between two cones four yards apart twenty-six times in thirty seconds, you can now set your goal to be two repetitions better the next time. If you have a partner, compete to see who can get the most repetitions out of each exercise.

Power

The area of fitness training for goalkeepers that is most neglected is power. The easiest way to measure this is vertical jump. Most keepers are exposed to power exercises when they reach a collegiate level. Unfortunately, for many this is too late, as power takes quite a while to develop and maintain. Those who are exposed to the proper training in high school or fully committed to it in college, reap huge rewards. Briana has the best vertical jump of all of our goalkeepers (29 inches). She has great power in her legs. Power allows you to dive farther, jump higher and get places more explosively. You can improve this physical dimension through training. Weight-resistance training, as well as functional activities, such as the specific Pressure Training exercises, are tools to enhance this physical dimension.

Photo by J. Brett Whitesell

Leg power helps Saskia Webber dominate in the air.

CHAPTER VIII
PRESSURE TRAINING

Pressure training exercises are quick movements and technical saves at intense training levels. It should be exhausting. It's all done with the soccer ball performing basic goalkeeping technique. The goal is to keep your technique clean throughout the whole exercise.

At the national team level, we train for forty-five seconds and then rest for forty-five seconds. Don't forget that these keepers are extremely fit and have built up to this. At a youth level try training for twenty to thirty seconds with an equal amount of rest (or more if you need it) depending upon your current fitness level.

Here are some examples covering a wide range of techniques with and without a partner Pressure Training/Circuit Training.

SOLO TRAINING

Breakaways

The fitness components trained here center on agility and first-step speed.

1. Start lying down on your stomach with a ball in your hands. Toss the ball over your head and get off the ground as fast as you can and make the save breakaway style.
2. Lay on your side with the ball (like you just made a diving save) and throw the ball away about five to seven yards, reload as quickly as possible and sprint to make the breakaway save.
3. Bounce the ball off of your foot, and chase the "rebound."
4. Serve the ball through your legs and save as quickly as possible (front or back).

Collapse Dive

The fitness components trained here center on agility and quick footwork.

1. On your side with both hands on the ball, toss it to the opposite side in the air, reload to a standing position and collapse dive within one or two bounces.
2. Start standing with the ball in your right hand (palm up, level with shoulder, parallel to the ground). Rotate your body to the right (as far as possible) and drop the ball. Quickly spin and then, using good footwork, save the ball in a contour catch and take it to the ground.

3. Start five yards away from a line. Toss your ball straight up then shuffle to the line, and touch it with your nearest foot. Then make the save before the second bounce.

4. With the ball in one hand, toss it forward and at an angle then step to catch it in the side contour position and finish with a collapse dive.

High balls

The fitness components trained here center on agility and power.

1. Start in a seated position with the ball in your hands. Toss the ball up as high as possible, jump and catch it above your head. Sit quickly and repeat.

2. Toss the ball up, drop to the ground and do a push up, then attempt to catch the ball above your head before it bounces, or after bouncing only once.

3. From a seated position, box the ball (two-handed) above your head, get up quickly and attempt to catch the ball before it hits the ground.

4. Toss the ball in the air, do a forward roll, and catch the ball above your head, if possible.

WITH A PARTNER: BOTH WORKING

The fitness components trained here center on agility and first-step speed.

Breakaway

1. The bridge: One person starts in a push-up position and the other with a ball in her hand. The person with the ball bowls (rolls) it underneath the "bridge" (no more than 10 yards) then the "bridge" makes a breakaway save while server follows. The server becomes the bridge and then makes the breakaway on the next service.

2. Place two balls four yards apart. Face your partner so that you both have a ball on the left and the right. You act as leader and initiate a breakaway save. Your partner makes the save on the other ball. Reload and make as many saves as possible.

Collapse Dive

The fitness components trained here center on agility and quickness.

1. Cross court/Down the line. You need one ball. Start facing your partner about four yards away. Serve the ball underhand to your partner's right side. She will make the collapse dive save then throw the ball from the ground (like a throw in) to your left. She will reload to her feet and wait for the next serve. When you make the save, serve the same ball "cross court" to your partner's left side. She will then serve "down the line" to your right. Repeat the pattern.

2. Start facing your partner. You are standing with the ball; your partner is on the ground in a collapse dive. Start by tossing the ball straight up (about head height). Your partner must reload from the ground and catch the ball in the basket before it hits the ground. After serving the ball, you drop quickly to the ground and reload for the ball that she is tossing. Do this as quickly as possible.

3. Face your partner about five yards apart. You each have a ball. You both toss your ball to the left at same time. You will both save to your right in a collapse dive. Reload with the ball in your hands then repeat.

WITH A PARTNER: ONE WORKING ONE SERVING

Collapse Dive

1. Your partner serves you a firm ball that is either on the ground or waist high. Make as many collapse dive saves as possible. Switch and serve your partner after your time is up.

Combination

1. Here is the pattern: Front smother/collapse dive/high ball. Your partner starts about six yards away from you and bowls the ball hard right at you. Attack the ball and finish in a front smother. Get the ball back to your partner and make a collapse dive save. Then get the ball back to her, and she will toss the ball up in the air for you to win like a cross. Repeat the pattern and switch the sides that you dive to and catch the high ball on.

2. Start in a seated position. Your server tosses ball up and you get to your feet as quickly as possible, then catch the ball above your head.

3. Lie on your back. Your partner tosses the ball near you. You cannot move until the ball bounces, then get up and make the quickest save possible.

Quick feet

1. Small steps, move 360 degrees around one ball. Reach starting point, change direction.

2. Figure eight around two balls. Distance can vary, but should not be further apart than three yards.

3. Two ways: Front to back or side to side.

4. Balls three yards apart. Start with body behind ball, hands touching bottom of the ball. Shuffle to second ball and show same shape before going back to the other ball.

*"I'm always striving to be perfect. But I realize
that nobody is going to be perfect, so
I can't hammer myself about it."*
— *Tracy Ducar*

CHAPTER IX
DEVELOPING A PSYCHOLOGICAL DIMENSION

Many promising young goalkeepers, and even some top keepers struggle, because they can't dismiss mistakes. When things aren't going their way, they cannot maintain a workable level of confidence. They are not capable of staying calm when the game is getting hectic.

It's a close game, going down to the wire. You're holding onto a one-goal lead, the other team is throwing everything at you, and you are trying to hold on. Some goalkeepers get caught up in that frenzy, and they become part of the problem rather than the solution. Composure, concentration and some mental-skills work help create a psychological dimension that will be a positive influence to your play. Some of it is developing mental skills. For example, how do you dismiss a mistake? We use "cue" words. You might say a word — "Focus" ... "play" ... "relax" or something that helps get you back into the present.

The best goalkeepers can make a mistake. Confident goalkeepers might go out for a crossed ball, misjudge it and it goes over their head. Then, it's gathered on the other side and served back in and they go out again and gather it. Not a big problem. On the other hand, a young or less confident goalkeeper will misjudge the first ball and is afraid to go back after it on the next cross. That's a difference between goalkeepers that are established and those that are not strong enough yet in the psychological dimension.

Many players feel it's the coach's total responsibility to build confidence, and that's hard on the coach and player. Take responsibility for your own confidence. The coach does have a role, however, and needs to impact positively on it. Keepers have to understand what impacts confidence. What do you do when you lose confidence? How do you get it back? Is it just going to show up again some day? As a goalkeeper, you may never have a chance to get out of a slump. You might be on the bench. When I talk to youth coaches, I tell them I'm looking for athletes that have the right mental skills. We define those mental skills as work ethic, leadership, composure, confidence, and the ability to deal with mistakes. If you have those qualities, you can learn tactics and technique.

Keepers build confidence by their training method, intensity and habits, like field players. If you train hard and with a plan, you give yourself the right to play well. There is no secret there. If you are low in confidence, then get out and train. That's where you build confidence. If you are a field player and get into a game and are lacking confidence, then maybe, during the course of the game, you can run that out of your system. By making some good plays you get your confidence back. But as a keeper you may not be able to work the kinks out during the game and you might be put in a position to make a big play on the first shot. You have to come into the game confident in order to perform properly.

"In practice, I think it's important for goalkeepers to be able to deal with disappointment and deal with giving up goals ... all the time," says Tracy Ducar. "If you can't deal with that, you're in the wrong position because it's going to happen. You have to be able to deal with nightmare days, and also deal professionally with the great days. I think it's important to keep an even keel. You have to come up with some mental tactics that work for you. If you are in a rut, what can you do to overcome that. If you feel yourself slipping during a game, maybe you have a mental cue or a marker that is going to keep you focused.

PSYCHOLOGICAL QUALITIES OF A GOALKEEPER
▲ Confident
▲ Willing to lead
▲ Good training mentality
▲ Good under pressure
▲ Consistent and dependable
▲ Can recover from making a mistake

"I want to be perfect every day," Tracy adds. "I get mad when I drop a ball. I'm always striving to be perfect. But I realize that nobody is going to be perfect, so I know I can't hammer myself about it. I accept it when a ball goes in, but I would rather have it go in a corner than through my legs. If a ball goes through my legs, I will be furious. Be upset about what's savable. If a ball goes into the upper corner, I can't be mad about that because it will be a goal on any given day."

A keeper's ability to deal with failure and to put mistakes behind her is something we all have to grow into. As a rule, goalkeepers set very high standards. They want to play the perfect game every time they step on the pitch. That goal is unrealistic. The demands we place on ourselves, and the expectations that those around us are placing on us, make for a pressure-filled combination. No other player is singled out for failure as frequently as the goalkeeper. This is something you must come to terms with early in your career and devise strategies to deal with it.

First of all, when things go wrong, do not let it show in your actions. Kicking or punching the post is only going to injure you and prove nothing. What will send a stronger signal to your coaching staff and teammates is to get the ball out of the back of the net as quickly as possible, get together with your defenders or your whole team, and unite in an effort to get that goal back. If you did make a mistake — a small one or a huge blunder — it's not the end of the world.

Goalkeepers should rely on positive self talk to get their focus back. Say something to yourself like, "Okay, I messed up. Now I need to make a big play." If you start beating yourself up mentally with negatives, there is a good chance you will still be berating yourself as the next goal goes whizzing by you. Without a strategy to refocus and get on with the game, one mistake turns into two, and so on.

Whenever you feel down about letting in some goals, pop a "Greatest Goals" video into your VCR. Almost all of them have a section on goalkeepers' blunders. This will point out that even the greatest goalkeepers have their nightmarish moments. Pretty soon, your mistakes don't look so bad. Use a key word or phrase to get back on track; because you are in the game for a reason, and your team needs you to make the big play.

Imagery is good preparation work. Many players will visualize making a perfect technical save, over and over again. This stimulates the brain to have a similar response when the actual event occurs. As a keeper, you can image goals that you have given up, or you can image the positives and the great plays. When we daydream, most of us relive and replay exciting games in our minds, moments in which we made a huge impact. Image diving for shots, taking crosses in a crowd, and organizing your defense. Let yourself be perfect, be the hero. When used consistently, you will see the benefits of this powerful, but little used, tool. Imagery is relevant for all positions, but it's especially important for the goalkeeper and her confidence.

Although you have a specialized position, the psychological skills field players use are the same for you as a goalkeeper. The Psychological Section earlier in this book is a reference for applying psychological skills training and ideas to improve your psychological state and overall performance. Developing a training mentality is paramount to your success. Be sure to refer to all of the other sections of the book to enhance all aspects of your development.

Remember to consider yourself a soccer player first. You are a player that has special talents and needs like a midfielder or a forward. So utilize this book to develop as a soccer player first, and use this section to focus your training when and where it's necessary. The stories and lessons throughout the book are important resources to a player in any position. The process of becoming a champion remains the same. Taking responsibility for your development begins with organizing your environment. Making choices, staying motivated and eager to learn and grow as a player are fundamental to achieving your dreams.

Team Section

"If you don't make an effort to be a good teammate, you'll never make it on this team, even if you're the best player in the world."
— Julie Foudy

Photo by Michael Allen

Photo by Mike Stahlschmidt

The four pillars of a soccer player — technical, tactical, physiological and psychological — have been addressed. There is another pillar that I believe is critical to your development and success as a player, and that's being part of a team and maximizing your contributions to your team. Clearly, with a team, you will accomplish things you could never do on your own. This section will look at the important attitudes and responsibilities that need your attention. Once you commit to soccer, you commit to being part of a team. It all comes down to a simple phrase we live by: "Team before I."

CHAPTER I
MAKING THE TEAM

All of you have been faced with the challenge of getting to the next level, the challenge of making the team. And, most likely, you have all been nervous about the process. You start thinking, "What can I do to make the coach notice me? What is the coach looking for?"

"Going through a tryout can be a very humbling experience," says Mia Hamm. "First of all, it's very easy to be intimidated, and it's okay to feel that way. But you have to remember, you were invited to try out for a reason, and you have to make the most of it. You have to use your strengths as much as you can. And it's okay to display your strengths. That's what the coach wants to see."

As a coach, I'm often asked what I look for in a player. Well, that's not an easy question to answer. Players make teams for a myriad of reasons. Coaches look for personalities, someone who impacts on the outcome of a game. Do you affect the outcome of the game? Do you play in a way that makes a difference for your team? It's common for players to play in a way that ensures they will not make mistakes. That's a sure way not to advance to the next level. Players who play safe rarely impact on the game. There is a great passage from Marianne Williamson's book *A Return to Love* that I think describes this feeling very well:

> *It is our light not our darkness that most frightens us.*
> *We ask ourselves who am I to be gorgeous, talented, fabulous?*
> *Who are you not to be? You are a child of God.*
> *Your playing small does not serve the world.*
> *There is nothing enlightening about shrinking*
> *so that other people don't feel insecure around you.*
> *We were born to manifest the glory of God that is within us.*
> *It is not just in some of us; it is in everyone.*
> *As we let our own light shine,*
> *we unconsciously give other people permission to do the same.*
> *As we are liberated from our fear, our presence automatically liberates others.*

Every one of you has a quality that sets you apart, and as Mia said, be sure to highlight that quality. You will hear the same advice from everyone who has successfully undergone a tryout situation. "You must be outstanding in one of the pillars," says Shannon Higgins

Cirovski. "There has to be something about you that gets you to the next level. There are a lot of really good players that are pretty well-rounded, but they have to have that one special thing."

Adds Carin Gabarra, "Players have to evaluate their strengths and determine what they are. They all have one solid reason why they will make a team. You have to work on that one area because that's what makes you special. For me, it was my dribbling."

Many times, skill is just a part of it. Sometimes players make a team because of combined qualities they possess as a player and as a person. Some players contribute to the chemistry of the team; some are exceptional leaders. "You have to incorporate everything, but still show your best stuff," explains Cindy Parlow. "Everyone on the national team has a unique quality. You have to bring everything else in, while keeping your unique qualities."

In 1998, Susan Bush made a rapid rise from her regional ODP team to the U.S. U-21 National Team and then was invited into the residency training camp to try to earn a roster spot for the 1999 Women's World Cup. "Every time I went up a level, I had to play faster and think more," says Susan. "The biggest jump for me was from regional to the U-21s, where everyone was really good, and they all had the same goal. The training sessions with the U-21s were a lot faster and much more intense. But I liked it that way. You just have to have confidence in yourself. At the national team level, everyone is so good, and they expect a lot from you. You have to give 100 percent all the time. I had to try to stay confident."

As you move to the next level, you go from being the best player on your team or in your town, to suddenly being among players that are all great. Your challenge is to set yourself apart. Getting to the next level begins with a decision. It's a decision to go after it. It's a decision to make the commitment, a decision to go beyond what is comfortable. It's all about taking risks. Trying to make the next level — no matter what level to which you aspire — is about all of those things.

Says Lorrie Fair, "When anybody who is the best player in their particular community comes to a setting where all those best players meet, they have to decide for themselves —'Am I going to step up to this challenge,' or say, 'I'm the best player in my community,' and leave it at that. It's all mental. Sure, there are aspects of everyone's game that need to be improved in order to be the best. But it's really a decision you make. It's something you have to motivate yourself to do, because maybe at home in your own community you won't have to work so hard to be the best."

How you respond to your mistakes can be a factor in making a team. Do you get down on yourself or hang your head, or do you work hard to rectify your error? The game is full of mistakes, but how you respond to them may be what sets you apart. It's easy to get caught up in what others say, but all you really can be responsible for is yourself. You have to assume accountability for your training and make it impossible for someone to leave you off the field or off the team. In the end, if you have given everything you possibly can — even if you don't make a team or win a championship — you will have a sense of satisfaction about yourself. If you can honestly tell yourself you gave it your all, you will never look back and regret any part of the experience.

Every year, I speak to the players in our Olympic Development Programs. I remind them that only a handful will ever go on to make the national team or the Olympic team. I tell them this not to discourage them, but to remind them of why they are playing — to be the best they can be — also, to enjoy the process. The quest is often more satisfying than the destination.

At the same time, I announce that someone in that room may very well be on our next Olympic team. I want those words to send chills down their spines. I want to look in each of their eyes to see who is screaming out inside, 'That's going to be me!' Next, I tell them about the process you have read here — how becoming great is up to them. The critical factor is who is really going to do the work to make that dream a reality. I remind them that, to me as a coach, how they respond to adversity is as important as how they respond to success. If they are cut one year, do they cry politics, or do they come back out and make it impossible for the coach to cut them again. Remember, if doing great things was easy, everyone would be doing them.

What if you don't make the team? Have you ever been cut? Some of you are nodding yes, and some of you are getting that sick feeling in your stomach all over again. And perhaps some of you are saying, 'I am too good to ever get cut.' If you are cut, you have a couple of choices. One, blame your coach. Another would be to give up on soccer and stop believing in yourself. Or, you can become determined to make the team and do everything in your power to never get cut again. Shannon MacMillan and Brandi Chastain are two players who, at one point in their careers, were cut from the national team. Shannon, although disappointed, decided to train even harder. She knew she had to be prepared if she got another opportunity. She loved the game, her motivations were sincere, and she wasn't going to give up on her dreams just because she didn't get invited back into a training camp.

Sure enough, shortly after Shannon had been cut, circumstances changed, and she was needed to come in for a tour to Brazil. If she had not been training on her own, or if she had given up, she would have been unprepared when the opportunity arose. Instead, she was not only ready, she was even better than before. She made it hard — and over time, impossible — to ignore her contributions to our team. If you recall, Shannon went on to score the Golden Goal against Norway in the 1996 Olympics to catapult us into the gold medal game, where she scored our first goal in a 2-1 win over China.

Part of the reason Shannon was able to make such a huge contribution to the Olympic team was that she gladly accepted a position switch. A striker in college, Shannon was asked to play right midfield. Her attitude was, "If that's what I need to do, fine." In addition to being willing to change positions, it is important to keep believing in yourself and not give up. The easy way out is to quit or blame someone else.

"I know what it's like to be disappointed," says Brandi Chastain. "I played on the best team in the world. I had what I thought was everything going for me in my soccer career. Then, somehow it didn't work out. I never stopped believing in myself. I never stopped playing soccer, and I used it as a learning experience. I asked myself, 'What are the things I can change or improve?'"

Brandi went to Japan for two years where she played and trained. She didn't let being left off a roster determine her love for the game or her tenure as a player. So whether you make a team or get cut, you can choose how to respond. That's the critical lesson — you determine your response to situations. It's important not to internalize not making a team as a reflection on your self-worth. Not making the team, or not getting enough playing time, doesn't mean you aren't good. It may mean you need to work on some aspect of your game. Never lose sight of your love of the game.

Shannon's Comeback

By Tim Nash

The 1995 college season ended with Shannon MacMillan as the consensus choice as national player of the year. A speedy and dynamic striker, Shannon was playing the best soccer of her career. She was healthy. She was fit. She was confident.

Then, she was cut.

After college, Shannon joined the U.S. National Team at the training camp near Orlando, Fla., where the team was preparing for the Olympics. For Shannon, this was the next logical step in her career. Excited by the prospect of continuing her playing days, Shannon went to Orlando, nervous but determined. When coach Tony DiCicco whittled the squad down for a trip to Brazil, Shannon was not on the team. It hit her hard. "That's it?" she thought. "I can't be finished already." It seemed she was.

"It completely devastated me," Shannon says. "But Clive Charles, my college coach, told me that I had to keep working and keep proving myself until it gets to the point where they can't turn me down. I was like, 'Yeah, whatever.' But I walked out of his office and got to thinking that maybe he was right. So I just went back out there and tried twice as hard. I did the little things over and over. A lot of it is mental and a lot has to come from your heart."

So Shannon went back to work ... on her own. "I worked on my fitness and my ball touch, all the little things. I wanted to make sure that when I got the call to come back in, I would be ready. I didn't want to just hang out, mope around and waste my next chance by going into camp completely out of shape. I didn't want to give them reason to say, 'See, we were right.' I wanted them to say, 'Well, maybe we need to bring her back in again.'"

The call came. The national team needed players for the Brazil trip after all. But there was a catch. As has been the case throughout its history, the national team was loaded with forwards, Shannon's natural position. Tony DiCicco asked her to try outside midfield. Shannon got her second chance. She was impressive enough in Brazil to earn a permanent position in residency.

"I had played almost eighteen years, and I had always been a forward," Shannon explains. "I was faster and quicker than most players growing up, so my coaches always put me up front. Moving to midfield was just a complete learning experience, but it was neat. In the first game I was getting beat all over the place. Fortunately, I had Kristine Lilly playing across from me. I had watched her for years, and I finally figured out that I could learn from her because I was playing the same position now. I really had to learn from scratch. I was fortunate because I already had the attacking mentality, so I could focus on the defensive side of the game. I've always had a love for the game. It's never really been all about scoring."

Six months later, Shannon walked onto the field as a starter for the first-ever Olympic women's soccer match. In the semifinals, she eagerly sat on the bench through a tense match with Norway. Then, five minutes and twenty-three seconds into sudden-death overtime, Tony DiCicco sent Shannon in. Four minutes and nine seconds after she entered the game, Shannon ended it by slotting a Julie Foudy pass perfectly into the corner of the Norwegian net. It was her second touch of the game.

"I saw Foudy making this run, and there was an opening, and that's really all I remember. I watched the tape and said, 'So that's what happened.' I just took off, and it was the best pass I've ever received. If it was any harder, it would have been swallowed up. If it was any softer, I would have had to stop."

Some players always seem to be in the right place at the right time, but Shannon MacMillan did everything in her power to put herself in the right place.

Shannon MacMillan, after her Golden Goal in the 1996 Olympic Semifinal

Photo by Mike Stahlschmidt

*"If you can only play one position, you'd better
be the absolute best at that position."*
— Christie Pearce

Chapter II
Playing a New Position

Do you put the interests of your team before yourself? Are you willing to do whatever it will take for your team to succeed? This is very important, as I mentioned, to the success of your team. One example of how this may present itself is when you are asked to play a new position. Your team may need you to learn to play some place where you are not comfortable. Are you willing to take on this assignment and embrace the needs of the team before your own desires? You will come to see that flexibility can benefit you as well as your team.

A year before the Olympics, Brandi Chastain was given another chance with the national team. The provision was that she would try out as a defender. Brandi had been an attacking player all her life. However, the new direction of the international game required that we put more skillful players in the defense. So Brandi had an opportunity to play in the Olympics ... if she was willing and able to become a defender. Brandi is incredibly savvy on the ball, and her challenge was to learn the elements of defense and bring her strengths as a player to a new position. She did everything asked of her and much more. Now, Brandi is a tremendously versatile player who can play a number of different roles for us.

If you are ever faced with playing a new position to help your team or to make a team, realize that from whatever position you are playing you can always bring your strengths. One year when I was playing in an Olympic Festival, my team needed defenders, and I was put at right back. I was by nature a midfielder — not exceptionally fast, but I was fit and loved to attack. At defense, I worried if my speed would be enough to handle the likes of the players I would come up against. Then, I thought about what I had that would pose a problem to my player. I loved to attack, and I could run all day. So my challenge was to read the game well, not get exposed speed-wise, and then make my player play me. I made runs forward at every opportunity. I knew the last thing a front-runner wanted to do was chase.

Justi Baumgardt, a former All-American at the University of Portland, relates why she, or any of you, should be willing to do what it takes, for the team, and to preserve your own dreams. "This is a team sport and not an individual sport," Justi says. "You have to accept your role if you want to play on a team. A lot of people may look at it as 'Oh poor me, I have to play midfield or defender.' But you can't look at it that way. If you have to do something to better the team, you'd better do it. Shannon is a perfect example. She could have easily said, 'No, I'm not going to play outside midfield.' That would have been ridiculous. She would have been wasting her whole dream.

"It's the same concept at any level," continues Justi. "I went through ODP — state and regional — and if the state coach put me at outside mid or left back, I would have done it in a heartbeat. The coach may think a particular position is the best place for me to show my strengths, which may get me to the next level."

It's important to remember we can't always see what good is in store for us when things don't go well. If it is really what you want you must fight through the disappointment and do everything in your control to make it happen. Put the team first and things often fall in place. Be true to your heart and never give up on yourself.

"I think it took getting cut for the coaches to try me at another position ... and for me to accept it," says Shannon MacMillan. "I was completely open to the switch because I was so eager to make the team. It's not that I would have said no to playing midfield, but I wouldn't have been as open to it if I hadn't been cut. I truly believe you have to be willing to do anything for the team. You have to put the team ahead of yourself. When Tony approached me and said they needed a flank mid-fielder, I just said, 'Okay, I'll try it.'"

There is an old adage — "The more you give, the more you get." Similarly, the beauty of putting the team first is, more often than not, it will ultimately benefit you. For it is only with each other that you can accomplish greatness as a team.

Christie Pearce has made a successful switch from forward to defender.

Photo by PAM / ISI

*"The great thing about attitude is,
you have complete control over it."*
— Tracey Bates Leone

CHAPTER III
TEAM CHEMISTRY

Chemistry is an active process. It is in a constant state of flux. It's an attitude and atmosphere to which the players and staff commit so everyone operates for the good of the team. And being a positive influence on your team is entirely in your control.

"If you have a positive attitude, then you are going to have a more positive experience yourself," says Tracey Leone. "And anyone would much rather have a positive experience than a negative one. If you remain positive and have that kind of affect on people, you have to accept that as one of your roles, just like a forward or a goalkeeper accepts her role in certain parts of a game. The whole thing about having a positive voice is, if you accept that role, you're accountable for it.

"The rewards come from visibly seeing the effect on people," Tracey adds. "It excites you and makes you feel good. It could come from one person's comment to you, or seeing someone smile. It's the little things, like someone having a nightmare week and you're helping them play really well, and you know that you helped them."

Team chemistry is an energy that exists both on and off the field, and at the national team level, we place a very high value

Tracey Bates had the complete respect and admiration of her teammates during the 1991 Women's World Cup.

on it. If it comes down to two players of relatively equal ability, we will clearly choose the one who most contributes to positive team chemistry. There are many ways to affect the chemistry of your team:

1. Be positive.
2. Get to know your teammates.
3. Pick someone up who's had a tough day.
4. Break the ice with a new player.
5. Dismiss negative talk.
6. Always speak highly about your teammates and staff.
7. Find something fun in a bad situation.
8. Relate to everyone on the team and eliminate cliques.
9. Focus on others' needs, as well as your own.
10. Keep working at it — it is an active process.

We've been so lucky to have traveled all over the world in soccer. Seeing the countries, learning some of the culture and meeting people all over the world has been a remarkable reward of soccer. We are grateful for these experiences. Many of our early trips brought unique challenges. Each posed an opportunity to learn and grow. While they weren't always easy — you'll see for most of us, they became memories for a lifetime, and the stories that endure. Not because of any real hardship, but rather in what we shared and how we viewed them. We knew they were cherished times, and that helped us realize how fortunate we were.

Here are some of the stories:

In the early days of the national team, the team adopted a saying: "Deal with it." For example, in 1991, we went to Haiti to qualify for the World Cup. In our hotel, there was electricity and running water only a few hours a day. It became a joke for us to see how quickly we could get in and out of the shower. Too slow and you risked having the electricity go off and water stop while your hair was lathered with shampoo. A scream would go across the courtyard of our hotel, and we knew one of us was caught. We laughed and dealt with it. That's just one story. Another is the bubble gum soda we drank at halftime in China — warm bubble gum soda because they didn't have any refrigeration at the time. None. But we dealt with it. Every national team veteran has dozens of anecdotes about dealing with it.

"When we went to China in 1987, I can remember our accommodations were a little bit less than adequate, to put it nicely," says Shannon Higgins Cirovski. "I remember hopping on coal trains in the middle of the afternoon. It was hot so the windows were open, and the coal would come in the windows. We rode seventeen hours on a coal train in rural China, and by the time we arrived, coal was stuck to our faces, just sticking to our faces. Down the hall, there was a little hole in the corner of the room. That was the bathroom ... just this little hole, and it would go right out onto the tracks.

"In Bulgaria, we had meat for every meal," Shannon continues. "It was a loaf, but you really didn't know what kind of meat it was. It was meat for breakfast, and they would do something different with that same meat for lunch, and then meat for dinner. Lori Henry was the taste tester, with April Heinrichs. April would try to figure out what we were eating. Bulgaria was crazy. On the Bulgarian airlines, they stuck all the bags down the aisle. There were bags all over. The second the plane took off, almost everyone but us lit up a cigarette.

I had my hands cupped over my mouth so I could breathe. Flights were always an adventure. In China, we were taking off and the whole inside of the exit door fell off onto a woman. We didn't fly more than a mile high the whole time. I thought we were dodging cows and stuff, we were so low. It was a propeller plane, and you'd be thinking, 'At any time, this thing can go down.' It definitely made us stronger as people. We learned the value of what we had.

"In Germany, we stayed in barracks," remembers Shannon. "We had this little tiny bus, and we had to fit twenty-five people in there. That very day the men's U-23 team came strolling down in a big bus. We were both going into Paris that day, and they asked if we could take some of their luggage, as a joke. We knew, in order to do what we had come to do, we had to try to take everything in a positive light. We began to appreciate what we did have, much, much more. We just had to live that way because complaints just spread like wild fire, and then you have a problem."

It's a fact of life that things aren't always going to go the way we hope or expect. But it's remarkable to realize that the very situation that's negative for some, is minor for others. It's just something to deal with. "When we travel, we act professional," says Julie Foudy. "We adapt to things. We've stayed in some of the worst places imaginable, and it's easy to have something like that become a negative. You just have to deal with it and remain positive."

Over the course of traveling to some twenty-plus countries, you can imagine how many situations we have run into that could go either way. But we have an unwritten rule to make the best of everything. When we went to foreign countries, our players often lost weight because of the food. It's easy to unite around negatives when something is different or doesn't go according to plan. Or in turn, if someone is being critical, it's easier to go along than to stand up for what may be better for the chemistry of the team overall. Now, we bring a snack trunk!

"We always have a meeting before every trip," says Kristine Lilly. "We tell the new players that the conditions are not always going to be great, whether it's the fields, the hotels, the food, or whatever. But you deal with it. And we never seem to have a problem. The reason is that younger players see the veterans dealing with it and it filters down. When you have something coming from the top, people seem to respond to it better."

Without question, one of the most positive people I have ever known is Tracey Bates Leone. Tracey was a member of the 1991 World Championship team. And she was always smiling. Even though she was a reserve, we couldn't have won without her. She was also my assistant coach for the youth national team. Anson Dorrance, our former coach, refers to Tracey as a *positive life force*.

"It takes work on everybody's part not to let that negative voice grow and expand to other people," Tracey says. "If someone is telling a story about other team members, and you know the story is negative to your team, you have to have the courage to stand up and say, 'I don't want that representing our team. We don't need that.' It takes a lot of courage. But having that kind of positive approach is crucial to your team's success. You can turn it all around."

A good example of framing the situation is when we were in Italy several years ago. We traveled forever to get there, and as we were driving to the hotel, we noticed what appeared to be a soccer field. The only difference was there was only gravel for a surface. The players were joking, "Hey, bet that's where we are going to play." It was! That was our practice field. After two practices we had to get new cleats because they were all worn down. Our first game, though, would be on a completely dirt field. It was so much better than our gravel practice field, we were all happy. That's how we chose to feel.

The preceding examples illustrate why we deem team chemistry an active process. Teams don't just have good chemistry — it's worked on. And the quality of people comprising the team determines it. Be the type of player who influences team chemistry in a positive direction.

OLYMPIC CHEMISTRY

Leading up to the Olympics, we all knew we had an obligation for the team to remain positive and united. Colleen Hacker played a major role in creating positive team chemistry. She did a myriad of exercises with us to remind us how valuable each player was to the team and how we need everyone to get the job done. You cannot play the game by yourself, and she showed us that the beauty of being part of a team is that what you can accomplish together far exceeds what you can achieve on your own. Maybe you can work to have your team participate in team-building activities, or talk with your coach about ways to help your team appreciate the uniqueness of being part of a team. There are many simple activities that require teamwork, where you can come to appreciate each other.

"The main thing Colleen Hacker helped with was team chemistry," says Tiff Roberts. "She played a huge role in how close our team became. We worked in small groups and had to accomplish a goal. Afterward, we realized we never would have gotten that done without teamwork. She taught us what it takes to be supportive of ourselves. When we did a team-bonding exercise, Joy Fawcett would really stand out. Joy listened to everyone's opinion, and then she'd put them all together. Through the exercise everybody got to point out something good about everybody else. It might seem rather trivial that you need somebody to say you did a good job, but everybody needs that. And when it comes from these people, it really means something, because they have to count on you everyday.

"Each one of the players on our team has something special," adds Tiffany. "And when you put them all together, it's awesome. It's really unique to teams like ours who are at such an elite level because if everybody had it, everybody would be doing it."

Good team chemistry is difficult to touch, and it's important for us to understand that. Sometimes we can lose sight of our team as a unit and see it only as a collection of individuals. We have to hold on to chemistry, preserve it and really take care of it. We can't just let it go by the wayside. Remember, it's an active process and choice.

"Team chemistry ranks up there with the four pillars," says Shannon Higgins Cirovski. "It's hard to be successful if your team doesn't get along. If you're in it for yourself, that is not the right reason."

*"Leadership takes many forms. It's important
to develop your own leadership style. Know
your strengths, and lead from there."*

Chapter IV
LEADERSHIP

Leadership on any team is critical to success. All of you have been on teams that have had very good leadership, and I am sure you have been on some teams without it. Often, leadership is awarded by being elected captain by your teammates or selected by the coaching staff. However, not all leaders are also captains, and just because you are not a captain doesn't mean you cannot lead. Leadership isn't defined by a position, necessarily. It's indicative of the person more than the position, and it can take many forms. People lead in a variety of ways, and it's important to remember that leadership means different things for different people. I want to challenge you to embrace leadership as a valuable skill that will serve you throughout your lifetime in many environments outside of soccer. We must strive to develop more leaders and people with leadership qualities.

There are many ways to lead. But there are some basic tenets that are important in many positions of leadership, as well as moments of leadership. The examples we will share here illustrate some consistent messages about effective leadership.

Lead from your place of strength

Be who you are. Knowing yourself gives you a good starting point. In turn, knowing your strengths as a person gives you information from which to lead. Lead from this place of confidence.

"First and foremost you have to be yourself," says Kristine Lilly, considered a leader by all the national team players. "Come out and show people who you are. And you should do little things for your teammates. For example, if they left their shoes some place, pick them up and bring them to that person. Don't leave them and say 'Oh, by the way your shoes are out there.'"

Carla Overbeck, long-time captain of the national team, is a tremendous leader, both vocally and by example.

Photo by Mike Stahlschmidt

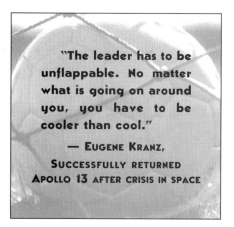

"The leader has to be unflappable. No matter what is going on around you, you have to be cooler than cool."

— EUGENE KRANZ, SUCCESSFULLY RETURNED APOLLO 13 AFTER CRISIS IN SPACE

One of the best leaders I have ever had the fortune of coaching was April Heinrichs, who captained the 1991 World Championship squad. April led in a variety of ways. First, she led through her incredible command on the field. Everyone tried to keep pace with her standards and mentality. That's the definition of leading by example. "April had the mentality that made you want to beat her all the time," says Kristine Lilly.

April had a reputation that came from how she embraced her training. This consistent standard earned her credibility and respect from her teammates. She didn't ask one thing and do another. She led from her place of strength — her psychological dimension. Her leadership impacted the future leadership we would receive from Carla Overbeck, April's successor in the captain's role. Carla has become an invaluable leader for our program, upholding the high standard and expectations for our team.

LAYING THE GROUNDWORK

Leaders need to recognize the moments in which their leadership is needed. Although this is an art in and of itself, much of the groundwork for a leader's effectiveness is established well in advance of any critical moment with which they are faced. A leader may have the ability to recognize when they need their team or staff to respond to their leadership. However, if they haven't developed necessary relationships with critical members of their team well in advance of needing their support, it's often too late.

April had set a standard for our program. This was established through the way she played, conducted herself and in her relationships with the starters, as well as the reserves. This was very important for us in establishing a tone in training and a mentality in our games, but also, when we were vulnerable. In the 1991 Women's World Cup, she helped us in the final match despite a disappointing knee injury that left her unable to physically impact the games, as she had for us all along. The process of gaining this trust and her ability to impact during halftime of the final was grounded long before.

"April evolved as a leader," says Shannon Higgins Cirovski, also a 1991 World Champion. "She didn't worry about how she was playing as much as how the team was playing. And she learned how to be outside of herself as a leader. She was in a lot of pain in those last games, basically heating up her knee so she could play. Without the injury, she could have torn it up, absolutely torn it up. She wasn't able to do what she could do, or wanted to do, for her team. But she was able to come out of herself and figure out what she needed to do for the team, perhaps just be there for us. She found a way to do what was going to help us win.

"I recall in '91 playing in the final against Norway," continues Shannon. "It was not a pretty game. We were just running. We couldn't get a hold of the ball. We couldn't string more than two passes together, and I remember April getting us all together during a stoppage of play and saying, 'Listen, we're good. Think about it. We're good!' I remember going back and saying 'Yeah, we are good. We aren't showing it right now, but we're good.' You can't let your lack of confidence kill you when you have been playing for eighty minutes and you haven't put two passes together. You can either look at what is going on and look into yourself, or you can emerge. April was telling us to emerge."

Leaders are able to lead because of their relationships with their players. They have a pulse on the team. This doesn't mean they are best friends with everyone. It means they know everyone and they understand what will be effective in working with them. Our leaders give the coaches invaluable input on the team's morale, energy, enthusiasm, burnout and motivation. This information is critical for us to factor into our own perceptions. It helps us with what we may want to do in practices, which players need feedback, and the timing of our hard days and days off. Great leaders develop trust among the people they work with, and this foundation must be put into place well in advance.

> "The most important thing is to listen to your peers and understand what is being asked of you. You have to understand that someone has identified you as a leader, and it's your responsibility to accept that and act on it."
> — APRIL HEINRICHS

CREATING A COHESIVE UNIT

The dynamics of any team or organization are instrumental in the viability of that team. Understanding the personalities on your team is essential to knowing how to listen, to provide alternative views, and to lead them to action. This, too, is an important foundation. You can't wait until you need your teammates to respond to you. First, you need to know what makes them tick and how they are going to respond to a situation. All of your interactions then become important early steps. Cohesiveness is worked at and must be in place. Knowing your personnel allows you to better lead the unit. Then, the integration of these personalities must become central to a leader's mission.

Carla Overbeck, Julie Foudy and Kristine Lilly are tremendous leaders. They take the time to welcome new players and make them feel part of the team. "You just have to get to know every player," says Julie. "A sure thing to break down a team is little cliques. It's easy to have younger players in one group and the older players in another group. On any trip we go on, the veterans make a point of just sitting with the younger players and talking with them. It would be so easy to stay in our comfort zone and hang out with the people we've been playing with for ten years. So we sit with the younger players at lunch and talk with them. It's easy after you've broken the ice."

Adds Kristine, "We spend so much time together, we want to know about everyone's lives and enjoy them and have fun with them. And to me, that translates on to the field. If you don't care about your teammates, you aren't going to work as hard. I don't care what anybody says, you might work hard, but you are going to work harder if you care about the people you are playing with. If players get so caught up in themselves, it affects team chemistry."

Tracey Bates Leone, 1991 World Champion, points out that each player is unique and thus requires a different

EVALUATING YOUR LEADERSHIP DECISIONS

It is important to re-examine decisions you've made, or actions you've taken, individually as a leader or as a team. This information will reinforce effective leadership or give you new information which will impact future actions. Michael Useem wrote the book, *The Leadership Moment*, an invaluable resource for anyone. (1) He provides four basic questions to help you look at your leadership.

1. What we (I) did right?
2. What was our (my) biggest mistake?
3. What we (I) wish we had done ahead of time?
4. What is the most enduring lesson for my actions now?

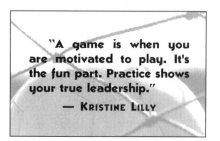

"A game is when you are motivated to play. It's the fun part. Practice shows your true leadership."

— KRISTINE LILLY

approach. Do your groundwork to better appreciate how to reach each person. It's a mistake not to be flexible and to try to lead just one way. "You reach people differently," Tracey explains. "If one person is down, you might go up to them and just try to help them or get something off their mind. With someone else, you might joke around and try to get their mind off of it. A lot of it is just paying attention to people and caring about them."

LEADING BY EXAMPLE

What you do should speak louder than any words you could use. There are many different ways to lead through example. "One of them is work," says Tracey Bates Leone. "Work gains a lot of respect." Your work ethic makes a statement to your teammates.

At the University of Virginia, I can remember a few of my players in our program who became incredible leaders through their work ethic. Amanda Cromwell and Gayle Smith always set our practice tone. Players followed their lead, and our whole practice intensity went up. We were able to build a program from scratch in only a few short years to be a national championship contender because of some of the great leadership Amanda gave us. She helped us establish a tradition of excellence.

On my 1997 youth national team, Cindy Parlow and Tiff Roberts really emerged as field leaders. It's contagious to be on a team with players like these because other players can't help but try to step up their game as well. All of the greatest leaders in our sport have one tangible quality in common — work ethic. Never underestimate the impact working hard can have on others. Be the example — let it start with you.

TIRELESS COMMITMENT TO WORK HARD

On the national team, Kristine Lilly is touted by her teammates as someone who leads through her work ethic. She never stops working, especially for her teammates. Christie Pearce, new to the national team in 1996, noted, "Kristine gives 120 percent in everything she does. There is never a moment in practice when she gives up." Kristine certainly has the respect and admiration of her coaches, teammates and opponents. "She's not the most vocal player on the team, but she is very vocal on the field through the way she plays," says Julie Foudy. "If I had to choose to rest all the responsibility on one player's shoulders, Lilly would be one of the first I'd choose. She's always there in the clutch and she's so consistent."

Tiffeny Milbrett, adds, "Lil quite possibly has a huge case to argue that she is the most underrated player in the world. But she doesn't worry about that stuff ... and she has a right to. To be honest, I don't think she worries about anything outside of trying to do her best day-in and

"If I had to choose to rest all the responsibility on one player's shoulders, Lilly would be one of the first I'd choose. She's always there in the clutch and she's so consistent."

— JULIE FOUDY

day-out. She is that consistent. We all go through days where we're trying 100 percent, but we're just awful. Whether or not Lil is the greatest or worst player on that field that day, you know she gave it her all. She just wants to play soccer. That means she loves what she does and she tries to do what she can everyday. That is why I admire her."

Leading by example goes well beyond just what happens in a match. "That's the easy part," says Kristine. "A game is when you are motivated to play. It's the fun part. Practice shows your true leadership."

THE EXAMPLE

"Leading by example is mainly about taking responsibility," says Kristine Lilly. "Little do you know, but people are watching how you train and what you are doing. In any kind of practice, if certain players that you look up to are doing things half-way and not fully, it affects the rest of the team. You have to take responsibility so everyone is giving everything they have. When you see another person stepping it up and pushing hard, you think, 'Okay, now I've got to step up.' The good thing about leading by example is that if you have the mentality and nature to always give 100 percent, you aren't doing anything differently than you would normally do. So you are an example no matter what. Players that naturally give 100 percent, don't really have any extra responsibility other than the fact that people are watching them."

Leaders take charge of the direction and success of their teams, and the levels of responsibility are numerous. Potentially, every action is evaluated. You must be sensitive to how you act in all situations. The most prevalent place, as Kristine alluded to, is during practice. If you want to be a leader for your team, you must train in a way that influences your teammates. If just a few players slack off in practice, the whole practice can be affected. On the other hand, when a few key personalities take responsibility for the tone of practice, the outcome is very different. For us, players like Lilly, Overbeck, Fawcett and Akers are always holding themselves accountable for the tone and standard of our training.

TRANSLATING LEADERSHIP OFF THE FIELD

Being a leader is often not easy. You can be resented by teammates who are not willing to live up to the standards you are setting. Some team members simply might dislike you. But it's not about being popular. Leading is about respect and effect. "I learned quickly that if I was going to do anything, I was going to do it right," says April. "That's the way I have always been. With that attitude, I was not going to lower my standards just to be accepted, liked or socially ingratiated. I would not call myself a perfectionist. I would never confuse those two things. I believe you have to constantly raise the bar on yourself."

People who are seen as leaders by example are often some of the more quiet players on the team. A perfect example of this type of leadership is Joy Fawcett. Joy comes to national team camps with two young children and all the paraphernalia that goes along with them. Julie Foudy describes the scene. "We see Joy walking through the airport with Carli in her arms, a diaper bag on one shoulder, Katey holding her hand, a stroller balanced on her head, and we just marvel at her. We call her Super Woman."

What you do speaks so loudly, no one can hear what you say.

Joy and Katey

Joy has the utmost respect from every player on the team because she is one of the most consistent players in the world on the field and off. "Joy does everything necessary to make sure she is prepared," says Brandi Chastain. "She doesn't have to be outspoken about the things she does. The neat thing about Joy is when we get into team activities, things that are not involved with soccer, people look to Joy. Before the Olympics, Colleen would give us a team-building exercise and everyone would say, 'Joy, how do we do it?' That's her time to give her input, and she feels very comfortable doing it. She is very calm. She doesn't panic. It will get done. And you can see it on the field."

When Christie Pearce joined the national team, she found a great way to learn was to watch Joy. "She is a great leader," Christie says. "She isn't necessarily a vocal leader, but she does it on the field in so many different ways, just her presence and her consistent play. She doesn't have to say much, but you know she's there, and it gives you confidence knowing she's there. As a newcomer, it was great to have her there. She knows what she is doing, and I know she is there to help out."

In addition, Carla Overbeck, the captain of the women's national team is unfailing in her leadership. She leads by example every day, on and off the field. No comment, action or statement goes without a desired outcome. She is a consummate professional. Her work ethic is constant. She has everyone's respect. Yet, she leads in different ways from Joy, Julie and Kristine. For example, Julie, our co-captain, leads through her work ethic and her gregarious personality. Finding your own leadership style is important.

VERBAL LEADERSHIP: CHOOSING THE MOMENTS

I recall when we went to Australia in the spring of 1997, there was a silence on the field. Something was missing. Then, it struck me. It was Carla's voice. Carla, who was not on the trip with us because she was pregnant, had always provided a verbal leadership and presence for this team. Her voice was noticeably absent. Verbal leadership, however, is not merely running chatter or being a cheerleader for your team. It's calculated instruction, encouragement, or whatever the team may need at precisely the right time and in the right tone of voice. The tone and timing of verbal leadership is an art. Carla is masterful at it.

"Vocal leadership, in itself, is so powerful," says Julie Foudy. "The prime example is Carla. She's so positive, and that helps us out a lot. Remaining positive is the hardest part. It's easy to take on a negative tone. When I get frustrated, my tone changes and sometimes instead of encouraging people, it can break down. I am conscious of it, and I work at it because I am also one of the more vocal players. It's my responsibility."

Carla has evolved into an incredible leader. There are many elements to her leadership style. Her work ethic and standard for excellence is vital to our day-to-day rhythm. Her on-field leadership is found both in large obvious moments and small, yet instrumental moments. She has worked hard on perfecting vocal leadership. "You just have to keep talking to them and encouraging them," she explains. "I think you really have to know each player and how to get to them, how to get them fired up. During the course of a game, if someone does something well, you encourage them by letting them know what they just did is what is going to help the team win. The other side of that, and I think this is where some people in leadership roles run into problems, is that they are too negative too often. It's okay to get after someone for doing something wrong, but when they do something right, you have to let them know, too.

"People know your personality off the field as well," adds Carla. "Maybe if you say something to them that isn't nice, they know you are just trying to make them better. They can take the bad things easier if there is something good in there, too. I'm a pretty compassionate person, and when people make mistakes, it's not my job as a player to jump all over them. That's what the coach is there to do. Obviously, the players know when they've made a mistake. They know they messed up, and they don't want someone jumping all over them. So I'm the first to say, 'It's okay. Do better next time.' Everyone is human, and certainly everyone is going to make mistakes. I'm much harder on myself than I am on anyone else."

Like all great players, leaders must be consistent, predictable and always hold themselves accountable for outcomes, their own and those of their team or organization. For example, Joy has standards for her performance that are nearly unreachable. She's very critical of her play, and her teammates often look at her as if she's lost her mind when she says she's had a bad game. "On the field she is so solid," says Lorrie Fair. "The games she thinks she played badly ... it's like, 'I didn't see that.' She's a great player. I think she is one of the greatest players in the world. It has been an honor for me to play with her. She is such a good person as well as a great player."

LEADING AS A CAPTAIN

Captains have an even more specialized leadership role. As a captain, you have either been elected by your teammates or appointed by your coaching staff to represent your team. It's an incredible honor and vital to your team. Yet it's important to understand that the title or the appointment in and of itself is not the critical thing. It's what you can do from this position that will make — or not make — you an effective leader. Like aspects of training, your leadership must constantly be evaluated, worked on and improved.

My '97 youth national team was captained, by an almost unanimous vote of her teammates, by Michelle French. She was a talented, starting member of our team, and we needed to have her on the field to win. But what she gave us went well beyond her ability to play soccer. She earned everyone's respect because she was the same person to everyone on the team. She was honest and conducted herself in a manner that everyone admired. They all wanted her to represent us and our country. For me as the coach, she was also invaluable. I could always go to her to find out how the team was holding up physically and psychologically. She was connected to everyone and treated everyone equally. She served as liaison between the me and the team.

"You have to be able to recognize what's going on with the team and convey that to the coaches and the players," says Michelle. "Paying attention to the small details and reading the pulse of the team is helpful. I enjoy people and that helped me tremendously. That's why it was easy for me to get along with everyone."

Another member of my team that summer, and a current member of the women's national team, Lorrie Fair, puts it well when she describes what qualities our captains embody. "Captains take the weight of the team on their shoulders," Lorrie says. "A lot of players have either one quality or the other, leaders either on or off the field, but only a few have both. And those are the players who really strike you as great people. They are great role models and the kind of people you want your children to look up to." Lorrie was referring to the national team's current captains, Carla Overbeck and Julie Foudy.

Leaders, our captains Carla and Julie, appreciate the need to get the most out of each player. Part of that means inspiring others to embody leadership qualities themselves. This does not mean that we have eleven leaders at all times but that each person's contributions are maximized, and that when put in places of leadership, they conduct themselves with effective leadership qualities. Like mentality, leadership is exemplified in the smallest of moments, as well as at game-breaking times. Leaders need to recognize times when their leadership is needed. Carla, Julie, Kristine, Joy and other veteran players are always the first to help unload the bus. They are the ones jogging on and off the field for a water break, they are on time and the tone of practice is always set by them. Through their behavior, they are passing on crucial information to our next generation of leaders, essential for excellence. Leaders develop leaders. If we need the tone of practice to change, we can always go to our leadership — not just our captains — and say we need more. And it happens. They carry a responsibility to get the most out of their teammates. Excellence requires constant striving. It's not an end point but a process much like all of the self-coaching tenets addressed throughout this book. Leaders help keep their team focused on this objective.

Carla is the consummate leader. She embodies the critical elements and fundamentals of a great leader. She is the example on the field. She sets the standard for our performance and high expectations for our team beginning with what she demands from herself. She has the necessary balance of encouragement, command, and hardness. She takes responsibility for her own success as well as the team's success. Everyday, she commits to excellence.

TAKING RESPONSIBILITY FOR YOUR ATTITUDE

In addition to taking responsibility for how you train, you can lead by taking responsibility for your attitude. The way you handle difficult situations, relate to your teammates and deal with staff and other people is very important. Do you respect and uphold team rules? Are you on time? Are you courteous? It gets down to the core of who you are as a person and how you conduct yourself in all situations.

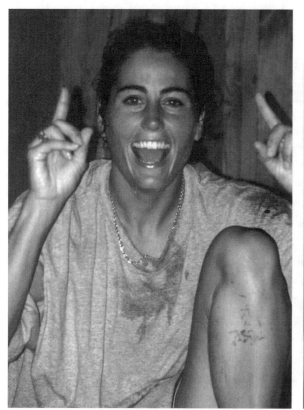

Julie Foudy (L) and Tiffany Roberts are two of the more dynamic personalities on the national team. They make you smile!

As Tracey Leone says, "A lot of it is about having qualities that other people would like to have themselves." Let's face it, things are not always going to go smoothly. The bus is late. The food is bad. You're tired from travel. The referee is horrible. Your coach gets on you. You had a bad day in school. Your teammate is having a nightmare. You are having a nightmare.

Your attitude can influence your team either positively or negatively. You choose. If you really want to lead, you need to appreciate that people are looking to you. They will respond based on signals you give them. Remember, good leaders are followed, so don't lead your teammates off a cliff. "To lead in the right way you have to be positive," says Tracey. "And that doesn't mean just with your coach, but with everyone involved — teammates, staff, parents of teammates. You want to always be respectful and courteous. It's almost like there is a microscope on you all the time."

LEADERSHIP QUALITIES

1. Listening is an important part of a leader's ability to understand, make decisions and act.
2. Utilize communication ability, verbal skills and body language.
3. Seek opportunity to learn from successful people.
4. Know your strengths. Lead from that place of strength.
5. Know your teammates.
6. Provide alternative ways of looking at a situation or information.
7. Be consistent.
8. Facilitate the creation of a team strategy or vision.
9. Provide alternatives, solutions and direction.
10. Take responsibility.
11. Believe in themselves.
12. Provide an example to others.
13. Make a difference.
14. Strive for excellence.

WAYS TO LEAD

BY EXAMPLE	How you train, prepare and conduct yourself
VOCAL	Encouragement and instruction
ATTITUDE	Choosing a positive response to situations
FIND SOLUTIONS	Providing solutions; being adaptable
ON AND OFF THE FIELD	How you conduct yourself; being professional; energetic
RESPONSIBILITY	Taking responsibility in training, matches and off the field
FLEXIBLE APPROACH	Recognizing different people's needs and what they respond to
RESPECTFUL	How you treat your teammates, coaches and others
SERVE AS A LIAISON	Between players, as well as between players and coaches
HIGH EXPECTATIONS	The vision and expectations begin with you

CHAPTER V
ROLE OF THE RESERVE

by Tracey Bates Leone

Dream Big

If there ever were a time to dare,
To make a difference, to embark on something
Worth doing, it is now. Not for any grand cause, necessarily, but for something that tugs at your heart, something that's your aspiration.
Something that's your dream.
You owe it to yourself to make your days here count.
Have fun … dig deep … stretch … Dream big
Know though that things worth doing seldom come easy
There will be good days and there will be bad days.
There will be times when you want to turn around, pack it up and call it quits.
Those times tell yourself that you are pushing yourself.
That you are not afraid to learn by trying and working.
Persist …
Believe in the incredible power of the human mind.
Of doing something that makes a difference.
Of working hard.
Of laughing and hoping.
Of lasting friends.
The start of something new brings the hope of something great.
Anything is possible.
There is only one you.
And you will pass this way only once.
Do it right.

— From A 1991 Teammate

This poem was passed around before the 1991 World Cup in China. It stays with me wherever I go. It's a constant reminder of the accomplishments of being part of a team … of the team that won the inaugural World Cup. And of everything that went into that dream coming true.

I think there were several reasons why we won, and one of them was the seriousness of the approach by the players who did not start, which was the role I served for four-and-a-half years. It's hard for me to know where to begin because I think the role of a reserve is a multi-faceted situation. But a good starting point when discussing anything in life is attitude and mentality. Attitude is one of the few things over which we have complete control in our lives. Attitude and hard work. I think it's crucial for a reserve player to understand her role, be positive about it and accept it. However, she must never be satisfied with it. You are on the team because you belong there. You are there because you want to be. You are there because you are good enough. You are there because you want to be the very best player on the very

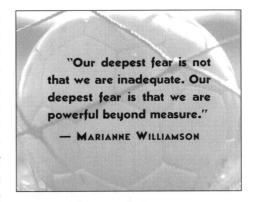

"Our deepest fear is not that we are inadequate. Our deepest fear is that we are powerful beyond measure."
— MARIANNE WILLIAMSON

best team. And this must be every player's attitude regardless of playing time. You are there to do everything in your power to be the best.

It's a commitment which must be made by all, especially you. You owe it to yourself and teammates to do everything you can and give everything you have toward your goal of being the best. I talk to my college team at Clemson all the time about having "No Regrets." We talk to our freshman after their first year about only having four chances to be the best in college and one of those chances is already gone. You have the opportunity of a lifetime — the opportunity to make a dream a reality. It's the ultimate opportunity, and you have to make the most of it in everything you do everyday. You don't want to look back after it's all over and wish you had done something differently or something more because you're not going to get the chance. So don't waste a minute. Don't waste a touch. Don't waste an opportunity by not laying it all on the line. When you look back, be able to say you did all you possibly could. I feel I can look back and truthfully say that. And it makes me very proud.

Different roles — starters and reserves — should not and cannot take away from anyone's dreams. Every player on the team has the same dreams: to be the best team in the world. The only difference between your role as a reserve is that you have a gap to close. You have an obligation to yourself to do all you can to close the gap, and you have an obligation to your teammates to do all you can every day to make them, along with you, better. Never take those responsibilities for granted.

You, the reserves, are a team within a team. We were on the 1991 Championship team. We all had the common goal of being the best player we could be, while making our teammates the best they could be. We tried our best to push them and ourselves to the absolute limit. Your attitude must be to out-work everyone, to do more than everyone on the team and everyone in the world. When you play against the starters, you give everything you have to win. If you do this day-in and day-out, you will be doing more than accepting the responsibilities. You will be moving closer to being the best — as a player and as a team. You must be ready for your shot when you get it. You must be ready "to play like a starter" when you get in the game. Think of an Olympic sprinter. How much work they put in for maybe ten seconds of their life. They must be prepared when the time comes, and so must you. The only way to be ready is by doing in training what I have mentioned above. Remember, there is only one you. And you will pass this way only once. Do It Right ... No Regrets.

Your attitude towards your role could be the difference in a positive way or a negative way. You can challenge yourself, your teammates to be the best every day and to be supportive and always strive for more. Or you can just go through the motions.

"The team I most dislike playing is our reserves.
They are always prepared to give us a battle."
— Julie Foudy

Chapter VI
The Reserve Mentality

By Wendy Gebauer

Wendy Gebauer's role with the 1991 World Cup team was important. She was instrumental in keeping a positive team-wide attitude. And in our third match of the Cup, Wendy scored a goal in a 3-0 win over Japan. This is part of a letter Wendy wrote for us to use to help our 1996 Olympic reserves frame their unique role and challenges.

In my opinion the biggest challenge for a player who is always on the edge of the envelope is two-fold. First of all, the reserve has to establish a realistic frame of mind as to exactly what their role is on the team. I think this can be a very hard thing to do, in most cases, because we all come from competitive environments where we were all the best players.

In so many cases, if the reserve has unrealistic expectations, then this is where many tensions enter into the picture. I'm not saying by any means that the reserve should be content with not starting. That's not the case at all. It's not the mentality which got them on the team in the first place. Once their role has been defined, then the reserve has to create goals which are both attainable and realistic, so as to continue to be motivated and confident.

Most of the time, because of the nature of the reserve's role, she has to create goals which keep them motivated from practice to practice because, for the most part, that's our competitive arena. The practice arena was as close to playing in a game as it gets a lot of time. I constantly reminded myself that I loved the game all my life, and that just because I was not getting a lot of match time, I was still doing what I loved. Even as a reserve I could still extract the same elements which I loved so much about the game from those practice arenas. The level of competition in practice was intense, we always played to win, and every element existed which you get in a game itself. The only thing lacking was the thrill of hearing 70,000 fans cheer from a great play. That's okay, however, because I could share the same thrill just by looking over at Tracey and acknowledging a brilliant assist in practice.

My role on the national team was that of reserve front-runner. In each game that I dressed out there was a possibility that I would be needed. In that situation, my focus had to be tremendous. I really believe that the focus is different for the starter. A starter can go into a match knowing exactly what their job is, as well as the strength and weaknesses of their match up. For the reserves it is really quite different. Not only are there pressures of trying to stay focused on the bench, but once they get their chance, they may only have five chances to touch the ball. Those five touches are very valuable for a front-runner. They will

Photo by Colleen Hacker

A great team. Left to right captain Carla Overbeck and Olympic alternates Saskia Webber, Amanda Cromwell, Thori Staples and Jen Streiffer.

very likely be the difference between scoring or not. For me, I had to figure out a way to be as confident as possible.

This is where I had to set my own confidence-building goals. I believe there were two things that made the difference for me: fitness and hard work. In practice, I was always able to remain confident by not just getting by in fitness but by continually setting new standards for myself. I knew that being fit would make the chances I got a whole lot better. This was a much easier goal for me to attain, but it was so important for my ability to remain motivated. It was one of those realistic goals from which I got a great deal of satisfaction. How hard I worked always directly translated into how I felt after a practice. I could not live with going to a training session and not giving 100 percent. I know there would be days when I could not hit the broad side of a barn, but I always believed that if I worked hard, and played to win things would go my way. Giving 100 percent in practice was also a very satisfying and attainable goal. I enjoyed leaving a practice thoroughly exhausted even if it was at the expense of getting trounced by a starter.

It was always very hard to just practice, practice, practice but not get much match time. I think there is a transition period which can be very different for each player. It's a true test of character and motivation. After all, where we came from we were all the best players, and the true test for the reserve comes in dealing with that. The quicker they can deal with it, the better off they will be and probably will become a more important piece of the puzzle. Writing that was obviously a lot easier than the reality of the situation.

Yes, I wanted to be in every game, getting as much playing time as possible. I know if I became complacent with my role as a reserve, I would not have lasted. You would be amazed at how my practice goals kept me incredibly motivated. In reality, the question I had to ask myself once my role was clearly defined was, "Do I want to be part of a great team, a chance few people get, or do I want to consume my life with feelings that tend to be so destructive not only for my confidence but also for the entire team?" I knew if I wore my feelings of frustration on my outer self, I would not be a positive player for team chemistry.

One of the most impressive elements of the '91 U.S. team was the leadership we received from a variety of different sources. Here is part of a letter I wrote to April Heinrichs after we won:

April, I have not always mentioned to you that your leadership was absolutely vital. I know there was no better person to do the job. The bonds between the starters and the reserves were just as strong as the bonds between starters. We were all family, and as you and I have talked about, some of the best friendships were between the starters and the reserves. That alone may have been the biggest reason for the lack of fire at times in the reserves. Because we were all so close you guys genuinely wanted to see us get our chances, and we were not at all (or at least I think) worried that we were a possible threat. We were all one big family on the same mission to win the first-ever World Championship!

My respect for you as a player and a leader when I was a reserve was indefinable — in my eyes a compliment from you as our captain went a long way. A huge part of the feeling and motivation I got was out of the fact that I knew we had a close friendship, and it was that closeness that made me want to do everything possible not to let you guys down.

I never questioned a compliment from you or the other starters, or wondered if it was from the heart. As tough as it got sometimes, in not getting playing time, I always knew that when we stepped off the practice field we were all such good friends. It was a group that I wanted to be with, and that was worth the sacrifice to me. Chemistry is such a huge part of the equation. We knew that, and I guess we've had enough time to figure it out, define our roles, and accept those roles, so that there was as little tension as possible for the team as a whole as we had to become more and more focused on the job ahead.

Photo by Mike Stahlschmidt

Tiffeny Milbrett was called upon to come off the bench to replace the injured Michelle Akers five minutes into the opening match of 1995 Women's World Cup, highlighting the importance of being prepared. She went on to score the first goal and celebrates with Tisha Venturini.

"Nobody can reach the top without
the unrelenting efforts of all."
— Michael Useem

CHAPTER VII
TEAM BUILDING EXERCISES

Team building is an active process by which you work on the inter-dynamics of your team. There are many ways you can help influence the shape and direction of your team. Most activities are fun. At the same time, they carry applicable lessons for you and your teammates. Both are important. Here are two you can bring to your coach or team. First, "team profiles," and then "team: 'I am ...' statements."

Establishing Your Team Profiles

Developing team profiles is a recognized model in psychological skills training. *(1)(2)* There are two ways this can be done. The first is as a team. The objective is to establish the qualities your team embodies and desires to uphold. The process of discovering these qualities will be enlightening to your team and serve as platforms that can be re-visited and as markers for measurement throughout your season. To develop team profiles do the following steps:

1. Form groups of players. You can split the groups any way you want, randomly or to get different players together by position, by who plays together, or whichever way you want.
2. Each player in each group comes up with a list of qualities that they feel describe the team. For example, with the U-20 National Team, we came up with qualities they felt were important to a world class team.
3. It should take several minutes. Once everyone has come up with their list, the small group discusses each other's qualities. Some you will find right away are common to the group.

Following team-building activities with the U-21 Women's National Team, Colleen Hacker reviews the lessons learned — "the obvious versus the essence."

Add those over to your next list. Then, discuss the remaining ideas each player has. The discussion is as important as the ultimate list. Players need to explain why they believe some qualities are important. Over time, you will add and abandon various qualities until your group has their list to present to the rest of the team. The list should be between twelve and sixteen qualities.

4. Next, the three or four groups get together and begin the same process as an entire team. Here is where your team defines what they want to be, and they are willing to measure themselves and the team as either upholding, or not, throughout the season or competition.

5. After you have the final list, spend time determining what proportion of the circle each quality takes.

6. As I mentioned, the process of creating your team's profile will in itself be fun. At the same time, you will come to an understanding about what is important to your teammates and commit together to what your common goal as a team is.

7. The profiles should be then used a few times during the season to determine how well you are working toward or are accomplishing the standards set forth.

In preparation for the 1996 Olympics, team-building skills were honed through a variety of exercises. At left, the "Jamaican Bobsled" team (group skits).

Below, a day rappelling that helped solidify our commitment to, and trust in, ourselves and each other. We came to know that we could accomplish anything together.

Performance Profiling can be done on a team or individual level. A Team Profile helps the team arrive at what characteristics they feel are important or should be exemplified by a successful team. Then, the team would use these profiles to rate their team on each characteristic. Periodically throughout the season, you can ask your team to rate themselves in the areas deemed important. After combining each player's ratings to create a mean score, you can determine your team's rating in each area. The information can then be used to help your team set goals.

The following were the characteristics our U.S. U-20 Women's National Team felt were necessary for our team to succeed internationally.

Group 1: Winners, leaders, hard workers, committed, tough, united, positive attitude, mental strength, confident, dominant, competitive, smart, proud, dreamers.

Group 2: Disciplined, cohesive, leadership, hard, passionate, technical, intelligent/organized, competitive, relentless, courage, professional, chemistry, motivated, patriotic/pride, winners.

Group 3: Committed, professional, smart, focused, fun, rhythmic, driven, unbelievable, motivated, sacrifice.

Group 4: Proud, fun, tough, relentless, energetic, unified/friends, role models, driven, feared, respected, classy, sexy.

Group 5: Mentality, striving/achievers, team players, hard work/relentless, encouraging, complete players, sacrifice/dedication, passion, smart, fit, strong, professionalism, unified.

Group 6: Mentality, physically fit, committed, confident, chemistry/friendship, intensity, heart/emotion, stylish, passionate, strong, focused, rhythmic, supportive, unselfish.

U-20 National Team Final List of Qualities:

Unified, proud, confident, dreamers, passionate, strong, winners, courage, respected, fit, skillful, leadership, feared, creative, relentless, committed, professional.

Positional Profiles

These profiles can be done by position as well as by team. For example, if your groups are formed by position, the forwards come up with their list, as do the midfield, the defenders and the goalkeepers. The result is a list of qualities that each position group feels describes them and by what they want to measure themselves. After each position has worked together to establish the objectives for their position, they must then assign percentages to every quality, assigning importance to each.

Our women's national team went through this exercise with Colleen Hacker during our preparation for the Olympics. It's a very powerful exercise and provides insight into what our players seek to embody as world class soccer players. It is important not to replicate what you learn about another team or how a team describes themselves by position. You want to learn what your team can be and desires to accomplish together.

Position profiles can be used individually and as a unit. Each player can rate themselves on their achievement of these determined characteristics of a successful player at this level. Or in our case, a world class athlete in this position. Then, the scores can be combined to determine the mean for each position. From this information you can set new goals and reinforce those you are accomplishing together. The Positional Profiles we established prior to the Olympic Games are included here.

KEEPERS

1996 United States Olympic Team

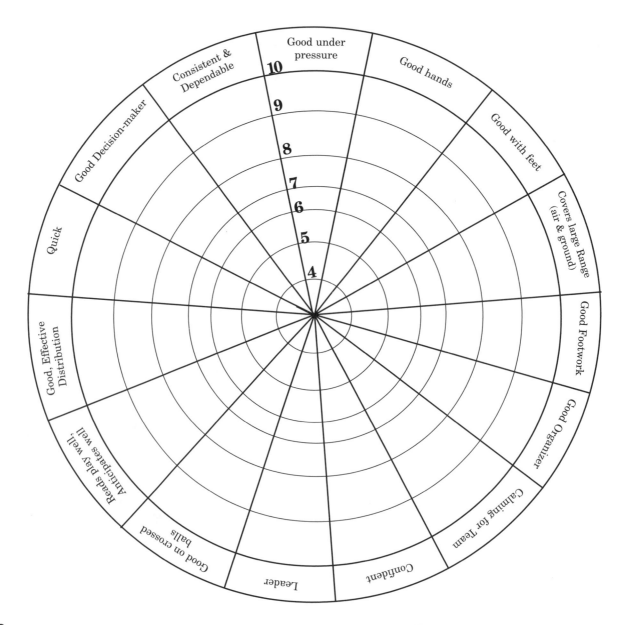

MIDFIELDERS

1996 United States Olympic Team

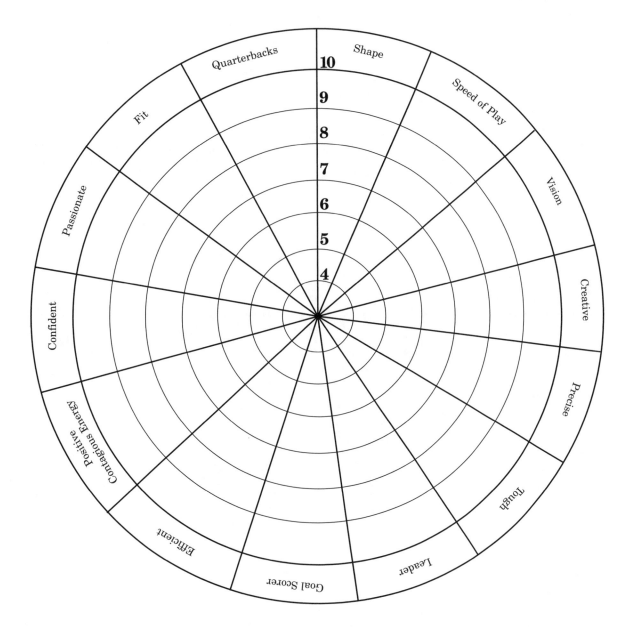

STRIKERS

1996 United States Olympic Team

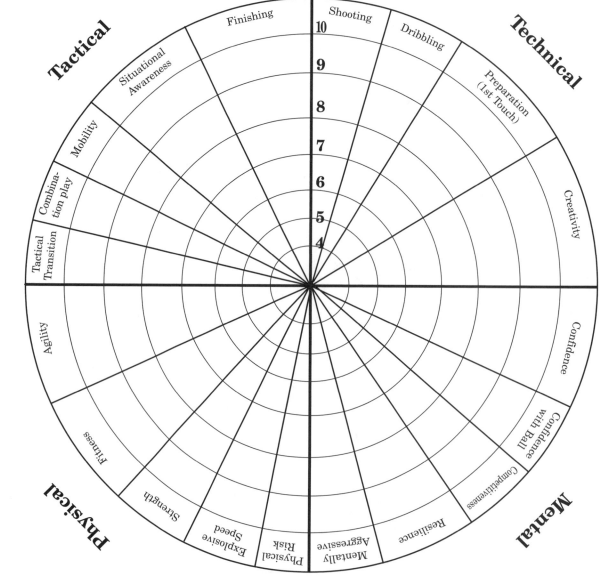

DEFENDERS

1996 United States Olympic Team

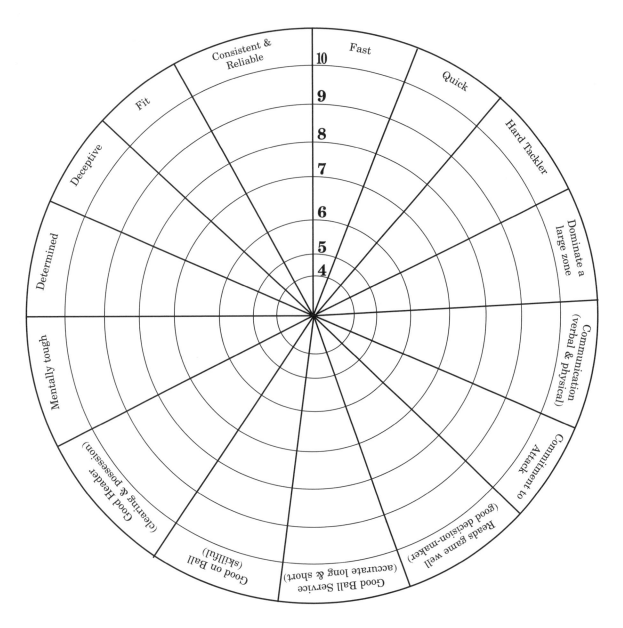

"I Am ... We Are"

In April 1996, Colleen Hacker, our sport psychologist, did an exercise with our Olympic team called "I Am Statements." It required each person to describe the contribution they make to the team by completing the phrase, "I am ..." three times. They did not have to sign their names to their statements. After each player came up with their three statements, we compiled them to come up with a collective list. When all the players' lists were put together, we had a very powerful statement, not only about each player, but about our team. This list, in essence, became a "We Are" statement. In addition, I did the same exercise with my U-20 National Team prior to the 1997 Nordic Cup championship run.

This is an easy activity you can do with your own team. The timing of it is also important. You can use it prior to going into a major tournament, and you can use it to remind yourself and your teammates about all the great qualities you have.

NATIONAL TEAM
"I Am ..." Statements

✔ strong mentally
✔ free on the field
✔ a fighter
✔ excited and anxious
✔ a team player
✔ a very fortunate person
✔ willing to do anything to help this team win
✔ trying to be emotionally and psychologically consistent
✔ aggressive on the field
✔ proud to be a part of this team
✔ strong
✔ improving
✔ a big gamer
✔ determined to make a difference in the lives of others off the field
✔ excited about participating in the greatest sporting environment
✔ lucky to be surrounded by such special people
✔ tough
✔ ambitious
✔ determined
✔ very competitive
✔ straightforward
✔ a person who operates from the heart
✔ wanting to learn and try new things from anyone and from life
✔ dedicated
✔ willing to learn
✔ a team player
✔ patient
✔ always looking for ways to improve my game

U-20 NATIONAL TEAM
"I Am ..." Statements

✔ a hard worker (3)
✔ ready to win
✔ driven
✔ hungry
✔ grateful
✔ a team player
✔ excited about this event
✔ willing to put the team before myself
✔ willing to give 100%
✔ fast
✔ ready to go into every 50-50 ball as hard as possible
✔ technical
✔ a fighter (2)
✔ a leader (2)
✔ a motivator
✔ good with the ball
✔ a smart player
✔ willing to do anything to win
✔ willing to sacrifice for my team
✔ courageous enough to never quit
✔ strong enough to deal with adversity
✔ relentless (2)
✔ fearless
✔ exciting
✔ willing to bust my butt for teammates
✔ willing to encourage others and keep others up
✔ a hard player and fit
✔ willing to do whatever we need
✔ going to win
✔ not going to make any mistakes
✔ excited to be a part of this group
✔ a good header
✔ willing to work for the championship
✔ tenacious
✔ mentally tough
✔ athletic
✔ reliable
✔ a team player
✔ focused
✔ aggressive
✔ confident

Epilogue

"True success is not apparent to the crowd."
— George Bernard Shaw

Epilogue

Our defining moments are not standing on the podium with gold medals around our necks and seventy-seven thousand people cheering for us. That's the easy part. Defining moments are found when no one is looking. They are found in how you conduct yourself as a person each minute of every day.

Remarkable moments can be found here in the stories of the greatest players and professionals in the world of women's soccer. Each story highlights the secrets of becoming a champion. The elements are all interwoven, comprising the process through which excellence is realized. The psychological dimension is rooted in all aspects of your training, and training mentality is a day-in, day-out, practice-to-practice, year-after-year commitment. Each story shows that no component of your training is devoid of these essential lessons. Your technical training is tied to your training mentality and to the constant ache that permeates your desire to achieve all that you can be.

Reading the stories and understanding the advice from some of the best in the world can be exciting, motivating and inspirational. But now, it's your turn to get started. Your challenge is to translate these lessons into your life and make your dreams a reality. The difference is about finding solutions, enjoying the process and seeing that your power is limitless. That is the hope of this book, that your thoughts and dreams become daily actions towards that end, that you embrace excellence as a process — the perpetual pursuit of a champion.

SUMMARY THOUGHTS: TRAINING FOR EXCELLENCE

1. TAKE RESPONSIBILITY FOR YOUR DEVELOPMENT; PREPARATION IS EVERYTHING

You are the important person in this equation. Realize that it is you, only you that can make anything happen for yourself. It begins with a choice. A decision to take responsibility for your development. Your coach, your family and friends are all only facilitators to this end.

"Self-coaching is mostly discipline and motivation. It's almost like if a coach isn't around, the kids sometimes feel like they can't play. And it shouldn't be that way. The coach can give you everything in the world you need to be a great player, but if you don't go out and work on them on your own, you won't get better."

— Lorrie Fair, U.S. National Team

"You need a team environment to play. However, that is not the time you develop. You develop when you do things on your own."

— Shannon Higgins Cirovski, 1991 World Champion

2. TAKE THE FIRST STEP — ORGANIZE YOUR LIFE

An important first step is to take a calendar and fill in all of your scheduled activities: From travel, training, games, family or school related events, and so on. This gives you an idea of when you can build in training time. If you don't schedule it in, time will slip away. You will always feel as if there isn't enough time. The best way is to make time for it, like you do for other aspects of your life. This time management skill will serve you in all facets of your life.

"It's hard. You definitely need to plan ahead, or the days just get away from you, especially if you have a job. I plan for the next day, 'When am I going to get my workout in tomorrow?' If I do it first thing in the morning, maybe I can get a second one later in the day."

— Julie Foudy, 1991 World Champion, 1996 Olympic Gold Medalist

"It definitely helps to be on a schedule because it makes you realize that you have time, and it might help you get out more."

— Joy Fawcett, 1991 World Champion, 1996 Olympic Gold Medalist

"Organizing your environment isn't easy. It isn't easy to stay and train instead of going to the beach or going to the mall or movies. It all depends what your objectives are and how much you are committed to those objectives. But if you don't write them down, I guarantee they will kind of flash in and flash out. You are not going to be 100 percent on target with all these things, no one is. But you will start to make strides in your game that will separate you from someone else."

— Tony DiCicco, Head Coach, U.S. Women's National Team

3. FIND A TIME THAT WORKS FOR YOU

Learn what works for you. This applies to much more than soccer. If you are an early morning person, then maybe that's when you get extra time in for studying, so you can train that afternoon, or vice-versa. Not all of you will enjoy training at the same time of day.

"As soon as I wake up, I have to go out and do my workouts. If I wait, I am not going to be very motivated by the end of the day. I like to get up and get it over with. It makes me feel better, because then I know I have the rest of the day to do whatever I want."

— Tiffany Roberts, 1996 Olympic Gold Medalist

4. KEEP A TRAINING JOURNAL OR LOG

Keeping a log is invaluable to your training for excellence. It serves to balance your training, provide you with information on over-training, and give you markers. These markers are important in realizing where you are, where you've come from and where you want to go. You can use the journal to set objectives for each day or week, and so on. Looking back at it will help you realize how hard you've worked. Sharing it with your coach may also allow you to get feedback and new ideas.

"It's good for someone to keep a log, just so they can make sure they are not just training one part of their game."

— Carla Overbeck, 1996 Olympic Gold Medalist, 1991 World Champion

"Having a training journal is a wonderful thing. Write it down, look at everything, and then make a plan to get to that point. You have to have a plan for every one of those objectives you've written down. Then you have to start working at taking care of every one of those plans. There is nothing easy about it. But once you have your plan in place, the source of confidence your plan will generate will take you to the next level as a player because you'll know you are getting it done. You'll know you are doing some things that no one else is doing."

— *Tony DiCicco, Head Coach, U.S. Women's National Team*

5. BALANCE YOUR TRAINING

Balance in your training is important. It will help prevent injury, allow you to systematically attend to all aspects of your training, and keep you excited and enjoying the journey and process of becoming a champion.

"I did a lot on my own. I had to be creative with my environments. I was more avid about playing soccer than most people. I loved doing it. I can recall all the fitness workouts because I did them on my own quite a bit. I always used the racquetball courts. I worked on first touch, one-v-one, two-v-two. You name it, I was doing it. Weightlifting was another aspect we had to get done."

— *Shannon Higgins Cirovski, 1991 World Champion*

6. PLAYING SHOULD ALWAYS BE YOUR TOP PRIORITY

Never lose sight of the importance of playing the game. It should be the top of your list, whether it is eleven versus eleven or two versus two. Playing should come first. That may require a little more work on your part--but the ability to organize your environment is a critical element in self-coaching.

"If I can play any kind of game I will."

— *Tisha Venturini, 1996 Olympic Gold Medalist*

7. FIND WAYS TO GET IT DONE

It will be a lot easier to find excuses about why you couldn't get it done than finding solutions. There will always be barriers between you and your dreams. Do not carry the misconception that those at the top have always walked an easy road. It just doesn't happen that way. These obstacles will be both internal and external. Recognize what you can control — fighting complacency, for example, and that which you may need to figure out ways to deal with, or overcome.

"You can always find ways."

— *Kate Sobrero, U.S. National Team*

8. CULTIVATE RESOURCES

One way to work around the challenges of self-coaching is to develop resources — other people, places to train or role models to watch. There are resources in front of us when we look for them. It's about training someone to help train you. Or developing training partners. Sometimes that might mean not one but two people. You might get one friend who is fitter than you to run with. You may need someone else to play one-v-one with you.

"When you go from an environment where they know what they are doing to an environment where you have to show somebody how to train you, it can be frustrating. You have to communicate what you want to them."

— *Mary Harvey, 1991 World Champion, 1996 Olympic Gold Medalist*

"If I want to train with someone, I ask. I call them up. Ninety-nine percent of the people don't ask. They just sit home and say 'I have no one to train with.' I just call. And, I've never been turned down. Call them! I know what I am training for and I know what I need. I organize my training around those needs. I find the people who can fill those needs for me."

— *Michelle Akers, 1991 World Champion, 1996 Olympic Gold Medalist*

9. BELIEVE IN YOURSELF

We all want validation. But the bottom line is you must believe in yourself. No one should be able to take away your dreams, nor should you rely on someone to be your source of confidence. Although it isn't always easy, and in some respects being a tough self-critic is a requisite to ultimate accomplishment, you must work to believe in yourself. This stretches far beyond soccer, to school, relationships, career and more.

"Things come full circle. It's hard when you don't achieve a small goal. But when you stay motivated and keep working, it will all come back and pay off. Start with believing in yourself."

— *Jen Grubb, U.S. National Team*

"You have to make a decision about what you really want to do. It's great to talk with your coach or your parents, but you are the one that really has to establish for yourself what is important and where you want to be."

— *Thori Staples, U.S. National Team*

10. KNOW YOUR STRENGTHS

You have special qualities as a person and as a player. Nurture them and let them grow. Your uniqueness is vital in getting to the next level. Know what you bring to your team on and off the field and to the lives of others. It's from this place of confidence that you will make a difference.

"As a player, you have to evaluate your strengths. For me it was my dribbling. You have to work on that one area because that's what makes you special."

— *Carin Gabarra, 1991 World Champion, 1996 Olympic Gold Medalist*

"One of your pillars must be outstanding. There has to be something about you that gets you to the next level. You have to make your strengths your strengths."

— *Shannon Higgins Cirovski, 1991 World Champion*

11. WORK HARD AT YOUR DREAMS

Having a dream is one thing, doing whatever it takes to make it a reality is another. Never underestimate the hard work that goes into accomplishing something great. It has often been said, 'If it were easy, everybody would be doing it.' The key is to appreciate and enjoy the process. You are on the success road. Don't sail on the hope of finding the "Someday Isle," a Hackerism, as we call it, a clever play on words makes the point simple. While it is important to have goals and distant dreams, be careful not to ignore all of the good things that are happening around you along the way.

"Keep working hard because you never know. I never thought I would be where I am."

— Kate Sobrero, U.S. Women's National Team

12. CHOICES ALONG THE WAY

You have to realize there are going to be difficult choices to make. But they are just that — choices! The inability to make hard decisions is an intangible factor that often eliminates many players from achieving their goals. Learn to prioritize your life in a way that you are a good student, you get your training done and are a good person.

"It was my belief that I didn't make any sacrifices. They were choices that I actively made, decisions that I didn't waiver over. Over and over, you will come face to face with opportunities that require you to prioritize your life."

— April Heinrichs, 1991 World Champion

13. BALANCE YOUR LIFE

Balance is a critical element to a successful life. We all know when things get out of balance, because we don't feel as good about things, or we feel as though we are on a treadmill, or that something is missing. Keeping winning and losing in perspective is important.

TIPS TO BALANCING YOUR LIFE:

1. Develop and work at the relationships in your life.
2. Work hard at school.
3. Have outside hobbies or activities that you enjoy.
4. Read.
5. Take time away from soccer.
6. Give back to the sport.
7. Give back to your community.
8. Take care of your mind, body and spirit.
9. Don't ever let soccer, sport or others define who you are or how you feel about yourself.
10. Be a good person.

"I am pretty even-keeled, whether we win the gold medal or I am on my lowest day. I enjoy a lot of things besides just winning, the things that come to me from soccer. I enjoy life, and soccer is only one part of my life. I don't depend on it to keep me fed."

— *Tiffeny Milbrett, 1996 Olympic Gold Medalist*

14. SUPPORT SYSTEMS

We all need people in our lives. Identify people who are supportive of your endeavors and let them know you appreciate it.

"The only time I can remember feeling burned out was after the Olympics. That was such an emotional experience and such a high point for me, that I was tired. But it wasn't so much from soccer. Part of it was being away from my family so much."

— *Tiffany Roberts, 1996 Olympic Gold Medalist*

15. HAVE A PASSIONATE REASON TO PLAY

Never lose sight of the game. That is an essential ingredient. Playing should be fun, full of life and your play must be passionate.

" A champion is passionate."

— *Tiffeny Milbrett, 1996 Olympic Gold Medalist*

16. TRY TO ESTABLISH A TRAINING MENTALITY FOR YOUR TEAM. BE THE STANDARD

Remember the fifth pillar is the entity of the team. Your challenge is to bring what you have learned, your passion and commitment to your team. You can, through your example, set the tone for your team. It may, at times, be unpopular. You may not succeed immediately. But neither can prevent you from trying and persisting. Your standard of excellence must remain your standard. Work to get all of your team's energy flowing in one direction.

"We are very competitive as a group. I don't think we are that much different talent-wise than a lot of other countries, but we put in that extra effort."

— *Lorrie Fair, U.S. National Team*

"You have to take responsibility so that everybody is giving everything they have. When teammates see another person stepping it up and pushing hard, they think, 'okay, now I've got to step it up.'"

— *Kristine Lilly, 1996 Olympic Gold Medalist*

17. RAISE THE BAR

This is the on-going challenge of training for excellence. There is little room for rest. Often, you will wonder if you have more inside you, is there yet another level you can climb? There will be times of doubt and uncertainty, even fear. Those are givens. It's what you do with the doubt, the fear, or the uncertainty. Enjoy the struggle as well as the prize. These times can still be some of the most rewarding of all, because you have overcome them and reached new heights you hadn't even been able to see.

"It's the art of never being satisfied."

— *Anson Dorrance, former head coach U.S. National Soccer Team*

18. Worry only about what you can control

You can control how well you play, how prepared you are, how hard you train, how good you are for team chemistry.

"A very strong focus needs to be understanding what you can control in a competitive environment and focusing on those things."

— *Colleen Hacker, Sport Psychologist, 1996 U.S. Olympic Team*

19. Be the kind of person everyone would like to be

Contribute to your team's chemistry and positive energy. Tracey Bates Leone always refers to one of her favorite lines that says,'What would the team be like if everyone on the team was like me?' Your team's chemistry begins with you. Never underestimate the importance of your attitude in life.

"We spend so much time together, you want to know about everyone's lives, enjoy them and have fun with them. And to me that translates onto the field. If you don't care about your team-mates, you aren't going to work as hard. I don't care what anybody says. You might work hard, but you are going to work harder if you care about the people you are playing with. If players get caught up in themselves, it affects team chemistry."

— *Kristine Lilly, 1991 World Champion, 1996 Olympic Gold Medalist*

20. Making a difference

Make a difference. Be active in your community. We have participated in the Smoke Free Kids Campaign, sponsored by the U.S. Department of Health and Human Services. It's something we feel very strongly about, and hope to discourage the use of tobacco among kids. We feel soccer and sports offer a great alternative to smoking. We spend time going into schools and speaking with young people. Soccer is our vehicle for community service. If you are interested in making your team a smoke free team or sponsoring a "Kick Butts Day," contact Ripley Forbes at http://www.smokefree.gov.

"A champion is all they can be in all facets of their lives. Someone who works every single day on being a better person."

— *Shannon Higgins Cirovski, 1991 World Champion*

21. Leadership

Decide to embody leadership qualities. Live in a way that makes a difference. Whether the sphere which you influence is small or large, you can become a leader and make a difference in the lives of others.

" When I think about a leader by example, I think about everyday stuff. What is she doing every single day. A leader by example is not someone who just performs well in games, they are going to perform well everyday in practice. They are going to work hard at it."

— *Julie Foudy, 1991 World Champion, 1996 Olympic Gold Medalist*

22. Live life Passionately!

Appendix A

Psychological Training Summary

1. Recognize the importance of your **psychological state in your performance**.

2. Appreciate that **you have control** over your psychological state.

3. **Choose your response** to situations. You have a choice.

4. **Confidence** is a critical factor in performance. Develop ways to work on your confidence.
   - Preparation and hard work.
   - Being fit.
   - Know your strengths and acknowledge them to yourself.
   - Overcoming obstacles.
   - Worry only about what you can control.
   - Act as if.

5. Your strengths will set you apart. **Be willing to standout.**

6. Understand that your psychological dimension is tied to **how you train**, what you demand of yourself and your willingness to push yourself everyday.

7. **Train on your edge** — Develop a training mentality that will develop you and your teammates, and prepare you for competition.

8. Embrace the **competitive mentality** on the field. Thrive in the most competitive and demanding of environments.

9. One-v-one and fitness are great ways to **train your psychological dimension**.

10. Practice **psychological skills**: imagery, goal setting, etc... like you would dribbling or shooting. What works for you may be different than what works for your teammate.
    - Imagery
    - Goal setting
    - Self talk
    - Controlling the "jitters"
    - Performance preparation

11. Develop your **pre-game preparation**. Have a consistent approach to matches. What works for you? This preparation should be the same whether you face the best or worst opponent. It should be consistent and independent of whether you start or come in off the bench.

12. Have good **support systems**. Not only friends and family who tell you what you want to hear, but find someone with an objective ear — someone who can help you look at things in different ways, and not just support what you already believe.

Physical Training Summary

1. **First make the choice to be fit.** Then be willing to do whatever it takes to be fit.

2. Have a **pre-participation evaluation by a physician.**

3. Remember, if you experience any pain or discomfort while trying any of the exercises outlined in this book, stop immediately and consult with a

4. Know the **physical demands of being a soccer player**.
   - **Aerobic** conditioning — **endurance** or distance, **longer, more steady state** periods of work.
   - **Anaerobic** conditioning — **shorter**, more explosive, **higher intensity** periods of work.
   - **Fartlek** training — periods of work-rest intervals.
   - **Speed** training — form running and speed endurance.
   - **Change of direction** as well as straight-ahead running.
   - Work on **balance, agility** and soccer-related movements.
   - **Strength** training — have a **qualified** strength and conditioning coach recommend and **oversee** your program.

5. With this understanding, train yourself for these demands.

6. Develop **creative solutions** if you have no access to a weight room.

7. Appreciate the **psychological dimension of fitness**. Conquer it. Develop confidence from it.

8. **Keep a training log** or record. Write down all of your training every day. (In Appendix B there is a blank training log and a sample log completed by our captain, Carla Overbeck.)

9. **Learn to eat well.** Nutrition matters. Becoming the best athlete you can requires good, sound nutrition.

10. **Recovery** is as important as training. Active recovery methods include *rest, cross-training, massage, stretching, the two-hour window, periodization.*

11. Periodization is a **systematic approach** to your training within a week, your season and over the course of the year that provides the necessary **balance** of training, competition, recovery and rest periods.

12. **Take care of your injuries**, through prevention, treatment and rehabilitation. Being injured is not an excuse to get out of shape.

13. Develop **habits** that will last a lifetime.

Technical Summary

1. **Spend time with the ball.** There is no mystery to developing a comfort level on the ball.

2. Always warmup and stretch

3. Racquetball courts or **wall work:** 20 minutes is worth a thousand touches!
   - **Dribbling** — play with the ball, develop a new move, be creative.
   - **1st touch** — knock the ball off the wall and receive it, emphasis on quality first touch
   - **Passing** — all surfaces
   - **Shooting** — driven, bent balls, volleying, one touch or two, placement finishing
   - **Turning** — taking looks, facing up, man-on turn, cut against grain, dummy
   - **Heading** — volley back and forth with the wall, power head, placement, jump and head

4. **Small-sided games:** You can put your technical skills on the spot in small-sided games. If you make the area small enough it will require better technique, because there will be **less time and space.**

5. **One-v-one:** Trains every dimension: psychological, physical, technical, tactical

6. **Two-v-two:** Good for combination play, first touch, technical solutions to tight spaces

7. **Soccer squash:** This is a great game for working on your **first touch** out of the air, as well as, **shooting** and **volleying.**

8. Don't forget **long-ball service** and **heading.**

9. **Train on your edge:** Remember it is **how you train** that will make the difference in your game. Many players can go out and hit the ball against the wall. Stay out of the "comfort zone." Do things quicker, more efficiently, and cleaner!

10. **Be creative** and find new ways to train technically.

11. **Find a training partner** or a friend or a family member who might be willing to help you.

12. **Technique will determine** the level at which you will be able to play the game.

13. **Make your technical strengths exceptional,** improve your deficiencies.

Tactical Summary

1. **Play the game** at the highest level possible.

2. **Be a student of the game.**

3. Watch the game
   - Evaluate your play
   - Learn from watching your teammates
   - Good club, high school or college teams
   - The women's national team, the men's national team
   - Professional matches

4. **How to watch a game**
   - **System of Play** or formation: Note the number of defenders, midfielders and forwards in that order.

4-3-3	Four defenders, three midfielders and three forwards
4-4-2	Four defenders, four midfielders and two forwards
3-4-3	Three defenders, four midfielders and three forwards

   - **Defensive Style:** How does the team defend? What are the team's defensive tendencies. Do they defend differently in different parts of the field?
   - **Offensive Style:** How does the team attack? What are the team's attacking tendencies. Who orchestrates their attack?
   - **Identify Personalities:** Who impacts the game? How? What do you like about how they play?
   - What are a team's strengths? Weaknesses?
   - How does the player in your **position play**?
   - What do they do on **restarts** offensively? Defensively?

5. Defense
   - **Man-to-man versus zone defense:** Man-to-man involves tracking players all over the field. Zone requires defenders to play areas of the field and players that enter their zone. Many teams play a combination of zone and man to man.
   - Understanding **principles of defense:** first defender's role, etc.
   - Positional play: **defensive responsibilities** of defenders, midfielders and forwards.
   - Role of the goalkeeper: positioning, shot handling, crosses, organizing the defense.

6. **Offense**
   - Possession.
   - **Direct and indirect attack.**
   - Positional play: **attacking responsibilities** of forwards, midfielders, defenders, goalkeeper.
   - **Box organization:** Runs — where (near, far, slot, trailing runs), timing and responsibilities.
   - **Flank service** — making choices of service into the box.
   - **Framing the goal.** Make the goal bigger by sealing off each post and the area in front of the goalkeeper. These are the areas that most rebounds or missed shots end up. By actively working to be in these areas, you will find yourself scoring more goals.

7. Tactical **evolution** of the women's international game.

8. **Learn and grow** from victory as well as defeat.

Team Summary

1. **"Team before I."**

2. Understand the **importance of being a good teammate**. Ask yourself, "What kind of team would we have if everyone were just like me?"

3. Be a **positive life force**.

4. **Choose your response to**
   - Winning.
   - Losing
   - Being cut.
   - Not starting.
   - Not playing as much as you would like.
   - Playing a new position.
   - Things going well for you or your team.
   - Things not going well for you or for your team.

5. **Team chemistry:** An essential ingredient to success. It's not a mystery; it's something that needs to be worked on every day by everybody.

6. **Leadership** is vital to any successful team. Find your own leadership style.
   - Lead by example.
   - Not all leaders are captains.
   - Work ethic.
   - Set high expectations for your team.
   - Know your teammates.
   - Create a cohesive unit.

7. **Role of the reserve:** If you are a reserve, find a way to help your team from whatever role you play. Don't have your situation affect the team negatively. Take responsibility for your development regardless of your playing time.

8. **Flexibility:** Are you willing to play a new position if your team needs you to? Remember, figure out how to bring your strengths into play from whatever position you are playing.

9. **Team building.** Be creative and come up with some activities for your team.

10. Learn how to travel well — Prepare for anything with a **"deal with it" attitude**.

11. **It matters** who you are and how you conduct yourself.

12. Give back to your community. **Make a difference** in the lives of others.

Appendix B

Listen to your body. If you experience any unusual discomfort while training, stop immediately and consult with your coach, parents and physician. Be sure to have a pre-participation medical evaluation before beginning any fitness training.

Fitness Self-Test 1

Date _____

Be sure to always warm up and stretch before performing these tests, and to cool down and stretch afterwards.

Test 1 — Cone Test

Set six cones down five yards apart. Run out and back to each cone, starting with the five-yard cone. Record time on each shuttle. Rest thirty seconds in between each. Run six to 10 times.

0— —-5— —-10— —-15— —-20— —-25

Shuttle 1 _____ Shuttle 2 _____ Shuttle 3 _____ Shuttle 4 _____
Shuttle 5 _____ Shuttle 6 _____ Shuttle 7 _____ Shuttle 8 _____
Shuttle 9 _____ Shuttle 10 _____

Heart rate immediately following: _____ beats/min
Heart rate one minute following: _____ beats/min

Push-up/Sit-up Test

Perform as many push-ups as you can in thirty seconds. Repeat performing as many sit-ups as you can. As you get stronger you can try to do these tests for a minute.

Push-ups

Place a shoe underneath your chest and use this as a marker. You must go down and touch the shoe with your chest on each push-up.

Sit-ups

Cross your arms on your chest and hold. Keep knees bent, feet on ground. When you come up on the sit-up, touch your elbows to your thigh. Go down so at least the small of your back touches.

Push-ups: _____ / 30 seconds
Sit-ups: _____ / 30 seconds

Illinois Agility Test

See description in Physical Testing chapter.

Trial 1 _____ seconds
Trial 2 _____ seconds

Double-leg Jump

Do three consecutive double-leg jumps. Do not rest in between each jump. Record distance. Use either a tape measure, the lines on the soccer field or a football field. Repeat two times.

1) Three-jump distance: _____ ft-in
2) Three-jump distance: _____ ft-in

Warm down. Good job!

Note: This can be used by goalkeepers as well. The cone test involves movements related to your position.

Fitness Self-Test 2

Date _____

Be sure to always warm up and stretch before performing these tests and to cool down and stretch afterwards.

Test 2 — 120's

Run the length of the soccer field. Time your first run. You have one minute before you must be back and ready to go again. Work to get back to the other end of the field as quickly as possible, so you have a longer rest interval. Try to keep each run the same as your first run. Repeat six to 10 times.

Run 1 _____ Run 2 _____ Run 3 _____ Run 4 _____ Run 5 _____
Run 6 _____ Run 7 _____ Run 8 _____ Run 9 _____ Run 10 _____

Heart rate immediately following: _____ beats/min
Heart rate one minute following: _____ beats/min

Push-up/Sit-up Test

Perform as many push-ups as you can in thirty seconds. Repeat performing as many sit-ups as you can. As you get stronger you can try to do these tests for a minute.

Push-ups

Place a shoe underneath your chest and use this as a marker. You must go down and touch the shoe with your chest on each push-up.

Sit-ups

Cross your arms on your chest and hold. Keep knees bent, feet on ground. When you come up on the sit-up, touch your elbow to your thigh. Go down so at least the small of your back touches.

Push-ups: _____ / 30 seconds
Sit-ups: _____ / 30 seconds

T-Agility Test

See description in Physical Testing chapter.

Trial 1 _____ seconds
Trial 2 _____ seconds

Double-leg Jump

Do three consecutive double-leg jumps. Do not rest in between each jump. Record distance. Use either a tape measure, the lines on the soccer field or a football field. Repeat two times.

1) Three-jump distance: _____ ft-in
2) Three-jump distance: _____ ft-in

Warm down. Good job!

Goalkeeper-Specific Fitness Self-Test 1

Date_____

Be sure to always warm up and stretch before performing these tests, and to cool down and stretch afterwards.

Pressure-training exercises   30 seconds work, 30 seconds of rest: 1:1 ratio is best. Number of exercises 6-8. It will be easier if you have a server or a training partner.

Record number of exercises performed _____
Rest interval _____ seconds

Push-up/Sit-up Test   Perform as many push-ups as you can in thirty seconds. Repeat performing as many sit-ups as you can. As you get stronger you can try to do these tests for a minute.

Push-ups   Place a shoe underneath your chest and use this as a marker. You must go down and touch the shoe with your chest on each push-up.

Sit-ups   Cross your arms on your chest and hold. Keep knees bent, feet on ground. When you come up on the sit-up, touch your elbow to your thigh. Go down so at least the small of your back touches.

Push-ups: _____ / 30 seconds
Sit-ups: _____ / 30 seconds

T-Agility Test   See description in Physical Testing chapter.

Trial 1 _____ seconds
Trial 2 _____ seconds

Double-leg Jump   Do three consecutive double-leg jumps. Do not rest in between each jump. Record distance. Use either a tape measure, the lines on the soccer field or a football field. Repeat two times.

1) Three-jump distance: _____ ft-in
2) Three-jump distance: _____ ft-in

Warm down. Good job!

Goalkeeper-Specific Fitness Self-Test 2

Date_____

Be sure to always warm up and stretch before performing these tests, and to cool down and stretch afterwards.

Agility-saving Fitness

Work with a partner or a timer (can be a friend). The partner or timer should keep balls saved at the exact point on the six-yard line in front of the post. Two balls are placed at the six-yard line, directly in front of each post. Start at one post and make a breakaway save diagonally to the ball in front of the other post. Get up quickly and side-on foot work back to the goal line (1 yd from corner) and jump to touch cross bar. Now save diagonally to the other ball and back to cross bar. Repeat whole sequence up to eight times. Rest 30 seconds between each. Do this at full speed and game intensity. Record your time.

#1 ____ #2 ____ #3 ____ #4 ____ #5 ____ #6 ____ #7 ____ #8 ____

Heart rate immediately following: ____ beats/min
Heart rate one minute following: ____ beats/min

Push-up/Sit-up Test

Perform as many push-ups as you can in thirty seconds. Repeat performing as many sit-ups as you can. As you get stronger you can try to do these tests for a minute.

Push-ups

Place a shoe underneath your chest and use this as a marker. You must go down and touch the shoe with your chest on each push-up.

Sit-ups

Cross your arms on your chest and hold. Keep knees bent, feet on ground. When you come up on the sit-up, touch your elbows to your thigh. Go down so at least the small of your back touches.

Push-ups: _____ / 30 seconds
Sit-ups: _____ / 30 seconds

Illinois Agility Test

See description in Physical Testing chapter.

Trial 1 _____ seconds
Trial 2 _____ seconds

Double-leg Jump

Do three consecutive double-leg jumps. Do not rest in between each jump. Record distance. Use either a tape measure, the lines on the soccer field or a football field. Repeat two times.

1) Three-jump distance: _____ ft-in
2) Three-jump distance: _____ ft-in

Warm down. Good job!

Sample Training Log

NOTE: The following is a sample from Carla Overbeck's training log. We are not including it so you can duplicate everything Carla does, but rather to use as a guideline to see the balance and variety in Carla's training. Adapt it to your own training. Remember, Carla is a world-class athlete who has developed a fitness base over many years.

CARLA OVERBECK

Sun. Nov. 2
off

Mon. Nov. 3
- coerver warm-up
- 3 120's, 3 sets of 40's, 3 120's, 3 sets of 40's
- long ball service
- lift weights (increase on bench & quads)
  10 x 100 lbs   (80 lbs.)
  8 x 105 "
  6 x 110 "

Tues. Nov. 4
- 3 vs 3
- 11 vs 11
- possession warm-up
- shooting

Wed. Nov. 5
- 4 - 100's ; 8 - 80's ; 12 - 60's ; 16 - 40's ; 20 - 20's

Thurs. Nov. 6
- 25 min. run

Fri. Nov. 7
- 25 min. run
- lift weights (hotel weight room stunk!)

Sat. Nov. 8
- 25 min run

Sun. Nov. 9
- 15 x hill sprints (sprint uphill) 20 sec.)

Mon. Nov. 10
off

Tues. Nov. 11
possession warm up
- 5 vs 5 (3 games) 8 min.)
- 7 sets of 50's
- 4 vs 4
- lift weights

Wed. Nov. 12
- possession warm-up
- 3 vs 3 w/ flank services
- box service (flighted balls)
- shooting drill
- 2 - 120's, 2 - cones, 2 - 120's, 2 - cones, 1 - 120, 1 - cone

Thurs. Nov. 13
- lift weights   (coerver's, long balls)
- 20 min run   - 30 min. in squash courts (heading

Individual Training Program Record

Name _____

Describe your training in the following areas daily.

Sunday _____

Matches _____

Small-sided _____

1-v-1 _____

Ball Skills _____

Functional Training* _____

Fitness _____

Wt Training _____

Other _____

Monday _____

Matches _____

Small-sided _____

1-v-1 _____

Ball Skills _____

Functional Training _____

Fitness _____

Wt Training _____

Other _____

Tuesday _____

Matches _____

Small-sided _____

1-v-1 _____

Ball Skills _____

Functional Training _____

Fitness _____

Wt Training _____

Other _____

Functional Training includes specific training in an area you may want to work; long ball, heading, individual defending, etc.

Wednesday _____

Matches _____

Small-sided _____

1-v-1 _____

Ball Skills _____

Functional Training _____

Fitness _____

Wt Training _____

Other _____

Thursday _____

Matches _____

Small-sided _____

1-v-1 _____

Ball Skills _____

Functional Training _____

Fitness _____

Wt Training _____

Other _____

Friday _____

Matches _____

Small-sided _____

1-v-1 _____

Ball Skills _____

Functional Training _____

Fitness _____

Wt Training _____

Other _____

Saturday _____

Matches _____

Small-sided _____

1-v-1 _____

Ball Skills _____

Functional Training _____

Fitness _____

Wt Training _____

Other _____

Self-Coaching Evaluation

Please evaluate yourself in the following areas. What are you doing well? What would you like to improve? How will you work on these aspects of your game?

Overall what do you think are your exceptional qualities? What do you bring to this team?

_____
_____
_____
_____

Overall what are the main areas you would like to focus on in your game?

_____
_____
_____
_____

Rate your overall performance this week/month/season (circle one).

Fair _____   Average _____   Good _____   Excellent _____

Rate your fitness level.

Fair _____   Average _____   Good _____   Excellent _____

Rate your technical proficiency.

Fair _____   Average _____   Good _____   Excellent _____

Rate your tactical play.

Fair _____   Average _____   Good _____   Excellent _____

Rate your psychological dimension — competitive mentality.

Fair _____   Average _____   Good _____   Excellent _____

Rate your contributions to team chemistry.

Fair _____   Average _____   Good _____   Excellent _____

Goal-setting reminders
1. Goals should be specific.
2. Measurable, i.e., to improve long-balls — 10 long-balls each day
3. Write them down.
4. Time frame — when (short-term and long-term)
5. Be accountable — assess.

With strengths and weaknesses in mind, please describe your goals and how you will accomplish them. (implementation and timeframe)

Self-Coaching Evaluation

Technical goals and implementation

Goal: _____

_____

Plan: _____

_____

Goal: _____

_____

Plan: _____

_____

Goal: _____

_____

Plan: _____

_____

Tactical goals and implementation

Goal: _____

_____

Plan: _____

_____

Goal: _____

_____

Plan: _____

_____

Goal: _____

_____

Plan: _____

_____

Psychological Goals and Implementation

Goal: _____

_____

Plan: _____

_____

Goal: _____

_____

Plan: _____

_____

Goal: _____

_____

Plan: _____

_____

Self-Coaching Evaluation

Physical goals and implementation

Goal: _____

_____

Plan: _____

_____

Goal: _____

_____

Plan: _____

_____

Goal: _____

_____

Plan: _____

_____

Team goals and implementation (A goal you set for yourself to positively affect your team or team chemistry. For example, say something positive to a teammate each day or help out with equipment, etc.)

Goal: _____

_____

Plan: _____

_____

Goal: _____

_____

Plan: _____

_____

Goal: _____

_____

Plan: _____

_____

Appendix C

Supplemental Conditioning Options

NOTE: Be sure to adequately warm-up and warm-down. Women's National Team standards are provided as target goals only.

Cones or Shuttles
❏ Put a marker down to indicate your starting point.
❏ Place a cone or marker at five, ten, fifteen, twenty and twenty-five yards.
❏ Starting at the first cone, run out to the five and back, the ten and back, and so on.
❏ Perform as fast as you can.
❏ Rest thirty seconds. Repeat six to ten times based upon fitness level. *If you are up to ten, add an extra 15 seconds of rest on 3, 6 and 8.*

WNT STANDARD — 8-10 IN UNDER 35 SECONDS

0 —— 5 —— 10 —— 15 —— 20 —— 25

Stinkettes
❏ Set a marker 25 yards out.
❏ Run out and back six times (300 yards total).
❏ Rest 45 seconds.
❏ Repeat three to five times.

WNT STANDARD — 60-70 SECONDS ON EACH

Stinkers
❏ Set a marker 40 yards out.
❏ Run out and back three times (240 yards total).
❏ Go for your best time on each one.
❏ Rest 45 seconds.
❏ Repeat three to six times.

WNT STANDARD — UNDER 55 SECONDS ON EACH

120's
❏ Run hard from one end of soccer field to the other. (100-120 yards)
❏ Work to jog back to starting point in 30 seconds or less.
❏ Rest an additional 30 seconds.
❏ Repeat eight to ten times based on fitness.

WNT STANDARD — 10 IN 17 OR 18 SECONDS

Combos
❏ Create a combination of the above. *For example, run two cones, followed by two stinkettes, followed by a 120-yard run.*
❏ Repeat the sequence. Total number of yards should be around 1500.
❏ Adjust rest intervals appropriately.

Fartlek

❏ Determine the length of runs and sprints you tend to make in a match.
❏ Over a period of twenty minutes perform intervals of work (hard runs or sprints) and rest or recovery (jog). *This trains recovery. Be sure to not recover so long that your heart rate is down to a baseline.*
❏ You can perform a 1:1 work to rest ratio, a 1:2 and so on. *For example, run hard from one telephone poll to the next.*
❏ Jog two telephone polls. *Try to keep your work as intense as possible and your recovery at as high a level as possible.*

Speed Endurance

❏ Be warmed up and stretched.
❏ Place markers 20, 40 and 60 yards out.
❏ Perform a series of "sprints" or hard cruise runs.
❏ Run past marker, decelerate slowly not to pull a muscle.
❏ Walk back to that marker. *You are trying to train your muscles to run hard repeatedly at, or near, your maximum.speed.*
❏ Rest sufficient time to be able to go at or near the same intensity. *If you have set a rest interval and find yourself ready to go before the rest period has expired, adjust the time. If you have set a time and are not ready to go, wait, to ensure the quality of your runs. If you do not take enough time to recover, this will become more like an interval or fartlek run, rather than training your speed endurance.*

Sample might look like this:
4 x 60s; rest 40 secs
6 x 40s; rest 30 secs
8 x 20s; rest 20 secs

Speed Movement Drills

High knees no arms	2 x 20 yards
High knees with arms	2 x 20 yards
Heel kicks	2 x 20 yards
Shuffle	2 x 20 yards
Carioca (fast feet)	2 x 20 yards
Backward run (fast feet)	2 x 20 yards
High skipping	2 x 20 yards
Skipping (fast)	2 x 20 yards

All-In-One Program

Warmup, stretch and perform program according to your own fitness level. This program should be done on a self-limiting basis.

Ball Control and Agility

6 minutes — Jog while dribbling ball with quick touches, changing direction and speed. Do this in a confined space where many changes and touches are necessary. Stretch intermittently.

1 minute — Head juggling

1 minute — Throw ball up, jump and while you are in the air, stop the ball with your head, settle the ball to your feet and move off quickly. Repeat.

1 minute — Thigh juggling

1 minute — Throw ball up, jump and while you are in the air stop the ball with your chest, settle the ball to your feet and move off quickly. Repeat.

1 minute — Foot juggling with no spin on the ball.

2 minutes — Starting in a sitting position, throw ball up, get up and stop the ball before it hits the ground, settle it to your feet, and move off quickly. Repeat using head, chest, thighs, both feet in that order to trap the ball.

2 minutes — Combined juggling using 14 parts of the body, head, both shoulders, chest, both thighs, outside, inside, instep and heels of both feet.

Technical Speed, Pure Speed and Endurance

1. Dribble in a figure "8." Use just the inside of both feet for six figure "8's," then use the outside of both feet for six more.

2. Rest by walking for 30 seconds.

3. Set a marker out about 25 yards from a starting point:

    a) Sprint dribble to marker.

    b) Sprint backwards to starting point.

    c) Sprint to ball.

    d) Collect ball and sprint dribble back to starting point.

4. Rest by walking for 30 seconds.

5. Set ball on the ground to your left and set a marker out to your right about 10 yards. Move 10 times from side to side, using the slide method of moving, without crossing legs.

6. Rest by walking 30 seconds.

7. To 10-yard marker and back; two-leg explosive jumps.

    To marker and back; single-leg explosive hopping — left foot first, then right, out and back.

8. Rest by walking for 30 seconds.

9. Carioca (lateral running criss-crossing legs) to 10-yard marker and back. Move 10 times from side to side as quickly as possible.

10. Rest by walking for 30 seconds.

11. From the starting points:

    a) Pass the ball to the 25-yard marker.

    b) Sprint to the ball.

    c) Collect the ball and accelerate to starting line.

    d) Make three passes.

Strength and Flexibility

30 seconds	Two-foot jumping forward and backward over the ball or cone.
15 figure "8's"	Standing position with legs spread and knees straight, roll the ball with your hands in a figure "8" pattern around your legs.
30 seconds	Two-foot jumping side to side over the ball or cone.
15 roll-arounds	Sitting position with legs extended, roll the ball with your hands around the soles of your feet and then back around your back.
30 seconds	Throw the ball up in the air, jump and catch the ball, and throw it back up before you hit the ground. Remember to "hang" in the air.
30 sit-ups	Touch the ball on the ground over your head, come back up and touch your toes.
15 to 30 touch and jumps	Start in a standing position with the ball in your hands. Touch ball on the ground by bending at the knees so thighs are parallel to the ground and then vigorously extend, jumping high with the ball over your head.
10-30 push-ups	

Shooting and Heading

For this section or the exercise, a soccer kick-wall (racquetball court, the side of a gymnasium, a tennis wall, etc.) will be necessary.

1. Technique work: Get 5 to 7 yards from the wall and shoot the ball. Shoot the ball first-time at the wall, making sure the foot is pointed, knee is over the ball, center of your foot is striking the center of the ball, and that all the power is derived from a quick snapping motion of the lower leg. Follow through. (2 minutes)

2. First-time shooting with power: Back off 20 yards and first-time the ball at the wall. Strike the ball hard and cleanly, regardless of the bounce, height, speed, etc., that the ball comes at you. Pick a spot on the wall to shoot at each time and keep the ball low. Follow through and land on your kicking leg. (6 minutes)

3. Receiving and shooting: Again, at 20 yards, strike the ball with power. As it comes off the wall, prepare it cleanly, and quickly fire another shot at the wall. The point of the drill is to develop a sound first-touch and a quick, hard shot. Follow through. (6 minutes)

4. From one to two yards away, first-time head juggling against the wall. (1 minute)

5. Back off between 5 and 7 yards, throw the ball up against the wall. As it comes off, head with power, getting your entire body into the heading motion. (2 minutes)

6. Get within 5 yards of the wall. Toss the ball against the wall to force yourself to jump to head it back at the wall. Catch the ball after you have headed it each time. Make sure your toss forces you to the peak of your jump. Remember your technique and head with power. (3 minutes)

This entire fitness program should take 50 minutes to an hour. It is important that you go through the entire program without pause, other than planned rest intervals.

If possible, a small-sided game would be an ideal way to finish off your training. If you are alone, do functional training of some aspect of your game.

Adapted from NCSCP

APPENDIX D

References

Psychology Section

(*1*) In 1989, two researchers, McCaffrey and Orlick (1989) described the key psychological elements for the success of elite athletes. The list includes the following ten qualities:

1. Total commitment
2. Quality rather than quantity of practice
3. Imagery practice on a daily basis
4. Clearly defined goals
5. Focusing totally on one play at a time
6. Recognizing, expecting and preparing to cope with pressure situations
7. Practice and tournament plans
8. Distraction control strategies
9. Post-tournament evaluations
10. A clear understanding of what helps you play well versus poorly

It should make sense, then, to focus on the development and refinement of these essential psychological skills in designing your own performance enhancement mental game plan.

(*2*) Research has shown that there are significant differences between elite and pre-elite athletes in terms of their psychological characteristics (Gabriel, Mahoney & Perkins, 1987). In their study of elite athletes (National, Olympic or World class competitors) and pre-elite performers (major University athletes), researchers found that pre-elite athletes tended to report that:

1) Anxiety interfered with performance
2) The impact of anxiety increased with intensity
3) Their concentration was less consistently focused on their performance
4) And that their coaches were a more important factor in their success than elite athletes

(*3*) Feltz & Landers, 1983

(*4*) Hall, Rodgers and Barr, 1990

(*5*) Moritz, Hall, Martin & Vodocz, 1996

(*6*) Research by Barr, Hall and Rodgers (1990) reveals that national and international athletes use imagery more than recreational and regional level performers. They are also more likely to use kinesthetic (feeling) imagery, more structured sessions, more likely to see themselves winning and successfully performing the entire skill. These top-level performers typically use imagery in bed at night and also before a contest.

(*7*) Gould, 1993; Orlick, 1986; Weinberg, Burton, Yukelson & Weigand, 1993

(*8*) The Association for the Advancement of Applied Sport Psychology provides a directory of sport psychologists who have been certified under their prescribed standards of education and professional training. This certification directory is available by contacting Dr. Bonnie Berger at the University of Wyoming. The USOC *Sport Psychology Registry* (719-578-4722) is another national resource that provides a list of approximately 100 sport psychologists who have met their certification process.

Beyond the two certification directories, individuals who want to work with qualified sport psychologists should seek referrals from coaches, organizations and national governing bodies who have worked directly with a particular professional. Because comfort, credibility and good communication skills are so essential to a consultant's effectiveness, athletes and coaches should spend the time necessary to select the person that most fulfills their unique needs, personality, competitive issues and value structure. There are also many books, journals and articles available for personal reading and reference. A few are listed below:

The Sport Psychologist

The Journal of Exercise and Sport Psychology

The Journal of Applied Sport Psychology

Foundations of Sport and Exercise Psychology (1995) by R. Weinberg and D. Gould

Advances in Sport Psychology (1992) by T. Horn

Applied Sport Psychology (1993) by J. Williams

In Pursuit of Excellence (1980) by T. Orlick

Physical Section

(1) Five Speeds of a Soccer Player, by Vern Gambetta

(2) Nutritional Guidance to Soccer Players for Training and Competition, by Kris Clark

(3) Data courtesy of Don Kirkendall (UNC) and Patty Marchak (Duke), Steve Slain, Dave Oliver (Sports Specific Training, Orlando, Fla). Data collection was made possible by Grants from Nike, INC and USOC Sports Science and Technology and the Women's National Team Staff. Thanks also to the support of Carolina Utd.SC for their participation in the youth aspects of this project.

(4) To order the Yo-Yo Intermittent Recovery Beep Test, write:

Performance Conditioning Press	Perform Better
P.O. Box 6819	11 Amflex Drive
Lincoln, NE 68506	Cranston, RI 02920-0090
(402) 489-9984	(800) 556-7464

Technical Section

(1) Weil Coerver Soccer, Weil Coerver

Goalkeeping

(1) Training Manual for Goalkeepers, Tony DiCicco and Paul Cacolice.

Team

(1) The Leadership Moment, by Michael Useem

(2) Butler, R.J., Hardy, L. *The Performance Profile: Theory and Application, Professional Practice, The Sport Psychologist,* 1992:6:253-264

(2) Dale, G.A., Wrisberg, C.A., *The Use of a Performance Profiling Technique in a Team Setting: Getting the Athletes and the Coach on the Same Page, The Sport Psychologist,* 1996, 10:261-277

About The Author

Lauren Gregg is the assistant coach for the United States Women's National Team and head coach for the U.S. Women's U-21 National Team. She is the first woman to serve as an assistant coach or head coach for any of U.S. Soccer's national teams. During her tenure, since 1989, the national team won the first FIFA Women's World Cup in China in 1991, took third in the 1995 FIFA Women's World Cup in Sweden, and won the gold medal at the 1996 Olympic Games. She also led the U-21 WNT to the Nordic Cup in 1997 — her first year as head coach.

Gregg was born in Rochester, Minn. At the age of nine she moved to Wellesley, Mass. It wasn't until her junior year in high school that Wellesley had a varsity girls' soccer team. But her passion for the game was evident from the beginning.

After playing for two seasons on the men's junior varsity team at Lehigh University where there was no varsity women's program, Gregg transferred to the University of North Carolina. At UNC, she helped the Tar Heels to the first AIAW Women's Soccer National Championship. In 1982, she co-captained the team that won its second consecutive national championship — the first NCAA National Championship. She earned All-America honors two straight years. Finding a year-round approach to soccer at UNC, Gregg let go — formally at least — of her other sports. (She had earned varsity letters in three sports — soccer, basketball, lacrosse.) Gregg trained with, and competed for, the U.S. Women's National Team following her collegiate career. Her international experience includes playing with the national team in the North America Cup in 1986.

She earned her undergraduate degree at UNC in psychology with honors, and received the Marie James post-graduate scholarship as the Atlantic Coast Conference's top graduating female student-athlete. She went on to earn her Master's in Education, in Counseling and Consulting Psychology, from Harvard, while serving as assistant women's soccer coach.

In the fall of 1986, at the University of Virginia, she began building one of the most successful women's soccer programs of the decade. After only four years, her team received a number one national ranking. She earned a trip to the NCAA Final Four in 1991 and a total of seven consecutive NCAA tournament bids (1988-94). She was named the NSCAA Coach of the Year in 1990, the first woman to receive the honor. Gregg was the first woman to lead a women's soccer team to the NCAA Division I Final Four. She resigned after the 1995 season to devote full attention her position as assistant coach of the U.S. Olympic team and the quest to win the Gold. She is the only coach in the U.S. to have helped coach a team to a national championship, a world championship and an Olympic Gold Medal.

Referred to as a "renaissance woman" by one of her professors, she took her responsibility to make a difference very seriously. Lauren's involvement in the community has been ongoing. She has been a long-time spokesperson for the U.S. Department of Health and Human Services Smoke Free Campaign. She speaks frequently on leadership, motivation, coaching and player development related topics. She serves on the Soccer for the Challenged Committee, the Project Gold Committee, and works with the outreach program Soccer in the Streets. In addition, Gregg has been instrumental in the Olympic Development Program at all levels. She is a contributing writer for such publications as the NSCAA Journal, Soccer News and Women's Soccer World.

Lauren currently resides in Charlottesville, Va.

For additional copies of **The Champion Within**, check with your local bookstore, or order directly from JTC Sports, Inc. with your check or money order — $27.95 (includes s&h)

JTC Sports, Inc., PO Box 3293, Burlington, NC 27215

For credit card orders, call:

800-551-9721

Other titles by JTC Sports, Inc.

Standing Fast, *Battles of a Champion*
by Michelle Akers

This is the story of how Michelle went from being the best women's soccer player in the world, to being perhaps the bravest. Suffering from Chronic Fatigue Immune Dysfunction Syndrome, she set her sights on becoming a world champion, fought through five Olympic matches and left Athens, Georgia with a Gold Medal. Includes over 40 pictures, personal diaries and quotes from coaches and teammates. Michelle also shares how her faith helped her turn an illness into a blessing and a miracle.

Training Soccer Champions
by Anson Dorrance

Dorrance is one of the most successful coaches in the world, and a sought-after motivational speaker. In this book, he shares his methods and philosophies in coaching, and his insights into training female athletes. Includes an actual "Manager's Stat Pack" used by the University of North Carolina women's team, complete with drills, data sheets and several actual practice rankings; stories, letters and quotes from former players.

$15.45
(includes s&h)

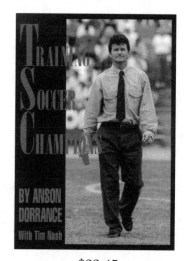

$22.45
(includes s&h)